THE
ORIGINS
OF
CONSCIOUSNESS

A STUDY OF THE
TEN LUMINOUS EMANATIONS

By Rav Yehuda Ashlag
Commentary by Rav Michael Berg

VOLUME 2

For further information:
The Kabbalah Centre
155 E. 48th St., New York, NY 10017
1062 S. Robertson Blvd., Los Angeles, CA 90035

1.800.Kabbalah
www.kabbalah.com

Printed In China, April 2025

ISBN: 978-1-952895-33-3
The Origins of Consciousness Volume 2

The Study of the Ten Luminous Emanations (Talmud Eser Sefirot) by Rav Yehuda Leib haLevi Ashlag is a commentary on the principles of the Wisdom of Kabbalah from the Writings of the Ari (Kitvei ha'Ari) by Rav Isaac Luria (the Ari z"l): Tree of Life (Etz Chaim), Entrance to the Gates (Mavo She'arim), and the Eight Gates: Gate of Introductions (Sha'ar haHakdamot), Gate of Teachings of Rav Shimon bar Yochai (Sha'ar Ma'amrei Rashbi), Gate of Meditations (Sha'ar haKavanot), and so on. The Study of the Ten Luminous Emanations is divided into 16 volumes, in true order from easier to more difficult subjects, with two commentaries—Ohr Pnimi and Histaklut Pnimit—as well as a Table of Questions and Answers that help the beginner.

1. Ohr Pnimi (Inner Light) Commentary (inside the blue box) – A pinpointed commentary on the difficult and concealed words and concepts of the Ari that are brought up on every page with true clarity of the concepts in their spiritual character, divested of space, time, and corporeality. This commentary brings these concepts close to the mind of anyone who studies it.

2. Histaklut Pnimit (Inner Observation) Commentary (inside the blue box) – This is a general commentary that expounds upon each and every idea, guiding and bringing close these ideas to be understood in the mind of every average student who desires this wisdom. It is located in each volume following the words of the Ari and the Inner Light Commentary.

3. Table of Questions and Table of Answers – This is an explanation of the main words and concepts brought up in each and every volume of the Talmud Eser Sefirot. It is very good and necessary to review and remember the concepts. These tables follow the Inner Observation commentary.

4. Insights of Rav Michael Berg (outside the blue box) – Inspiring explanation on the teachings of both the Ari and Rav Ashlag that bring these concepts down to earth, focusing on how we can practically apply them in our daily life and what this means for our spiritual growth. These insights are adapted from Rav Michael Berg's Ten Luminous Emanations classes.

VOLUME 2

CIRCLES (IGULIM) AND STRAIGHTNESS (YOSHER)

עִיגּוּלִים וְיוֹשֶׁר

TABLE OF CONTENTS

INTRODUCTION BY
RAV MICHAEL BERG

As we begin Volume 2 of the Study of the Ten Luminous Emanations (Talmud Eser Sefirot) it becomes more complex. At times, it may be a struggle to ensure that we are constantly pushing ourselves to have a true understanding of what is being discussed. Rav Ashlag says that at this point in the Study of the Ten Luminous Emanations we must have a strong grasp of all the previous sections in Volume 1 of this series because, as we continue, our ability to be clear about the true meaning of the words becomes more challenging.

In Volume 2, we begin to learn about the concepts of Circles and Lines, which Rav Ashlag reminds us are not to be understood in their literal sense because it is much deeper than that; we are not discussing physical Lines and Circles but rather levels of consciousness. It is important that we are continually stretching our minds to understand what is being said and to not see physicality but rather the depth behind it instead.

An example that comes to mind are those optical illusion images popular several years ago. When quickly glancing at these images all you would see is an unrecognizable compilation of geometric patterns. Yet when you concentrate on the two dots in the center of the image, as instructed, suddenly a complete picture appears. The same is true with the Study of the Ten Luminous Emanations. For most people, at first glance, this study may seem like jumbled geometric patterns. Yet when we truly strain and focus our mind to really grasp what is being spoken about, suddenly a whole new image appears.

Below, the Zohar, Mishpatim 97-102 tells us that the Light of the Creator and the Light of the Torah are revealed and concealed.

> The old man said, "How confused are the people in the world, who do not regard the Torah in the true way. The Torah calls to them daily with love, but they do not care to turn their heads to listen to it."

1

This is likened to a beautiful woman who is beloved, and hides in the secret of her chamber. She has a lover unknown to men, who is in hiding. Because of the love he bears for her, he always walks around the gate to her house and looks everywhere. She knows that her lover always goes around her house's gate, so she opens a small aperture in that hidden chamber where she stays, and reveals her face to him. Then immediately she is concealed again. None of those who were with the lover see or observe, save the lover alone, whose entrails, heart, and soul go out to her. And he knows that because of the love she has for him, she is revealed to him for a moment to arouse the love of him.

It is so with the Torah that is revealed only to its lover. The Torah knows that the wise-hearted paces around its gate every day, so it reveals its face to him from within the chamber and immediately returns to its place to be hidden again. None of those with him know or behold it but he himself, and his entrails, heart and soul yearn for it. Hence the Torah is revealed and concealed and lovingly goes to its lover to arouse love with him... That man approaches, and it begins by speaking to him from behind the veil that it spreads before him, of matters according to his understanding, until little by little he will pay attention... Afterwards it speaks with him in riddles from behind a thin sheet... When he frequents it, it is revealed to him face-to-face, and tells him all the obscure secrets and obscure ways that were hidden in its heart since primordial days.

Then that man is a ruler, a man of the Torah, the master of the house, since it revealed to him all its secrets and has not kept or concealed from him anything. The Torah said to him, 'Have you seen the allusion I gave you in the beginning. It contained such and such secrets, this is the way it is." He then sees that one must not add or diminish from the words in the Torah. Then the literal meaning is as it is, so that not even one letter must be added or taken away. Therefore the people in the world must take heed to chase after the Torah and love it, as we learned."

The Zohar reveals that the Light of the Creator, and certainly the Wisdom of Kabbalah and the Light of the Torah never come completely revealed. Even after the Light is revealed It conceals Itself again, and only someone who is always pushing themselves to hold on to the revelation will merit to truly understand it.

The Rav told me that many years ago he had spoken to one of Rav Ashlag's students who had informed him that no one could understand the fifth volume of Talmud Eser Sefirot, which is about *Mati velo Mati*. When the Rav mentioned this conversation to Rav Brandwein, Rav Brandwein told the Rav that unfortunately many of Rav Ashlag's students did not comprehend this study. He reassured the Rav that he is meant to understand the section of *Mati velo Mati*, as well as all the other sections of the Talmud Eser Sefirot.

In Volume 1 of the Study of the Ten Luminous Emanations it is easier to maintain clarity about what is being spoken; however, as we continue with Volume 2, a whole new reality appears; one that takes time and effort to delve into and fully grasp. And when we do, we will see this other world open up for us.

We have become trained to look at our world through a physical lens—we see walls, we see structures. As most of you know, sometimes we use something physical, such as wine on Purim, to open up Spiritual Gates and begin breaking down the barriers between what we think we understand about our world and what truly is. And when we sincerely take the time to study the Ten Luminous Emanations and wrap our heads around its true meaning, we begin to sense this true reality.

After personally reviewing Volume 2 before we delve into it together, it became clear to me that we should always question whether anything in our understanding of this wisdom is still physical. And if there is, then we are not comprehending what is being conveyed. This is a process of breaking down the barriers where our mind will easily go. For instance, when Rav Isaac Luria (the Ari) speaks of Circles and Lines, it is much easier for our mind to attach itself to that literal understanding of physical Circles and Lines, when in reality that is so far from the truth.

We now begin a section that takes constant effort, and the beauty of this, and certainly the gift that Rav Ashlag gave us here, is that it opens up our minds. I cannot stress this enough: when we truly take the time to ponder this wisdom, our effort opens up tremendous Spiritual Gates.

INNER LIGHT
(OHR PNIMI)

CHAPTER 1

Chapter 1 explains the Ten Circular Sefirot that were revealed after the Contraction (Tzimtzum). They are encircled by the Endless Light (Ohr Ein Sof), and all the Light of the Circular Sefirot is bestowed to them by the Line. It contains 11 subjects:

1. The Line is like a thin channel.
2. The extension of the Endless Light into the space.
3. The extension took place very slowly.
4. The Circle is not attached to the Endless but is connected to it by means of the Line.
5. The Endless Light (Ohr Ein Sof) surrounds and bestows upon the Circle from afar.
6. The Line is called Adam Kadmon.
7. The sequence of the emergence of the Ten Circular Sefirot.
8. The Line connects all the Circles together.
9. Each World and each Sefirah is composed of Ten particular Sefirot, each of which include Ten particular Sefirot, *ad infinitum*.
10. Circular Sefirot encircle each other like layers of an onion.
11. Each Circle that is closer to the Ein Sof than the other is considered superior and better than it. Thus, this World, being in the Middle Point that is the farthest from the Endless, is of the utmost physicality.

א) וְקַו זֶה כְּעֵין צִנּוֹר דַּק אֶחָד, אֲשֶׁר בּוֹ מִתְפַּשֵּׁט וְנִמְשָׁךְ מֵימֵי אוֹר הָעֶלְיוֹן שֶׁל אֵין סוֹף, אֶל הָעוֹלָמוֹת אֲשֶׁר בִּמְקוֹם הָאֲוִיר וְהֶחָלָל הַהוּא.

1. This Line[1] is like one[3] thin channel,[2] through which the Waters of the Supernal Endless Light (Ohr Ein Sof)[4] extend and flow into the Worlds that are situated in the place of that air and space.

ב) וְהִנֵּה בִּהְיוֹת אוֹר הָאֵין סוֹף נִמְשָׁךְ בִּבְחִינַת קַו יָשָׁר תּוֹךְ הֶחָלָל הַנַּ"ל, לֹא נִמְשָׁךְ וְנִתְפַּשֵּׁט תֵּכֶף עַד לְמַטָּה, אָמְנָם הָיָה מִתְפַּשֵּׁט לְאַט לְאַט, רְצוֹנִי לוֹמַר, כִּי בַּתְּחִלָּה הִתְחִיל קַו הָאוֹר לְהִתְפַּשֵּׁט, וְעָם תֵּכֶף בִּתְחִלַּת הִתְפַּשְׁטוּתוֹ בְּסוֹד קַו, נִתְפַּשֵּׁט וְנִמְשָׁךְ וְנַעֲשָׂה כְּעֵין גַּלְגַּל אֶחָד עָגֹל מִסָּבִיב.

2. As the Endless Light was drawn as a Straight Line[5] into the aforementioned space, it was not drawn and extended all the way down instantly but rather it extended very slowly.[6] What I mean to say is that at first the Line of Light began to extend, and right then and there when it started to extend[7] in the secret of a Line, it extended and was drawn, and it became like one Wheel,[8] circular all around.

ג) וְהָעִגּוּל הַזֶּה, הָיָה בִּלְתִּי דָּבוּק עִם אוֹר הָאֵין סוֹף הַסּוֹבֵב עָלָיו מִכָּל צְדָדָיו, שֶׁאִם יִתְדַּבֵּק בּוֹ, יַחֲזוֹר הַדָּבָר לִכְמוֹת שֶׁהָיָה, וְיִהְיֶה מִתְבַּטֵּל בְּאוֹר אֵין סוֹף, וְלֹא יֵרָאֶה כֹּחוֹ כְּלָל, וְיִהְיֶה הַכֹּל אוֹר אֵין סוֹף לְבַד כְּבָרִאשׁוֹנָה. לָכֵן הָעִגּוּל הַזֶּה סָמוּךְ אֶל עִגּוּל אֵין סוֹף, וּבִלְתִּי מִתְדַּבֵּק בּוֹ. וְכָל עִקַּר הַתְקַשְׁרוּת וּדְבֵקוּת הָעִגּוּל הַנֶּאֱצָל הַהוּא עִם אֵין סוֹף הַמַּאֲצִיל, הוּא עַל יְדֵי הַקַּו הַהוּא הַנַּ"ל, אֲשֶׁר דֶּרֶךְ בּוֹ יוֹרֵד וְנִמְשָׁךְ אוֹר מִן אֵין סוֹף וּמַשְׁפִּיעַ בָּעִגּוּל הַהוּא.

3. This Circle was not attached to the Endless Light that surrounded it from all its sides,[9] for had it been attached to It, it would have returned to the way it used to be and become void in the Endless Light.[10] Its power would not have been apparent at all, and all would just be the Endless Light, as it had been in the beginning. Therefore, this Circle was close to the Circle of the Endless, yet not attached to It. And the main connection and attachment of that emanated Circle with the emanating Endless[11] is via that aforementioned Line[12] through which Light descends and flows from the Endless and bestows to that Circle.

ד) וְהָאֵין סוֹף סוֹבֵב וּמַקִּיף עָלָיו מִכָּל צְדָדָיו, כִּי גַם הוּא בִּבְחִינַת עִגּוּל סָבִיב עָלָיו, וְרָחוֹק מִמֶּנּוּ, כַּנַּ"ל. כִּי הוּא מֻכְרָח שֶׁהֶאָרַת אֵין סוֹף בַּנֶּאֱצָלִים תִּהְיֶה דֶּרֶךְ קַו הַהוּא לְבַד, כִּי אִם הָיָה הָאוֹר נִמְשָׁךְ לָהֶם דֶּרֶךְ גַם כָּל סְבִיבוֹתֵיהֶם, הָיוּ הַנֶּאֱצָלִים בִּבְחִינַת הַמַּאֲצִיל עַצְמוֹ, בִּלְתִּי גְּבוּל וְקִצְבָה.

4. The Ein Sof encircles and surrounds it from all its sides,[13] since it too is in the aspect of a Circle[14] all around it and far from it, as previously mentioned. It is stipulated that the Illumination of the Endless upon Emanated Beings would be via that Line alone because if the Light had been drawn to them from all around them as well,[15] then the Emanated would have been in the aspect of the Emanator Himself, without limit or ration.[16]

ה) וְהִנֵּה הָעִגּוּל הַזֶּה הָרִאשׁוֹן הַיּוֹתֵר דָּבוּק עִם הָאֵין סוֹף, הוּא הַנִּקְרָא כֶּתֶר דְּאָדָם קַדְמוֹן, וְאַחַר כָּךְ נִתְפַּשֵּׁט עוֹד הַקַּו הַזֶּה וְנִמְשָׁךְ מְעַט וְחוֹזֵר לְהִתְעַגֵּל וְנַעֲשָׂה עִגּוּל ב' תּוֹךְ עִגּוּל הָא', וְזֶה נִקְרָא עִגּוּל הַחָכְמָה דְּאָדָם קַדְמוֹן. עוֹד מִתְפַּשֵּׁט יוֹתֵר לְמַטָּה, וְחוֹזֵר לְהִתְעַגֵּל, וְנַעֲשָׂה עִגּוּל ג' תּוֹךְ הָעִגּוּל הַב', וְנִקְרָא עִגּוּל בִּינָה דְּאָדָם קַדְמוֹן. וְעַל דֶּרֶךְ זֶה הָיָה הוֹלֵךְ וּמִתְפַּשֵּׁט וּמִתְעַגֵּל, עַד עִגּוּל יוֹד, הַנִּקְרָא עִגּוּל מַלְכוּת דְּאָדָם קַדְמוֹן. הֲרֵי נִתְבָּאֵר עִנְיַן הַיּוֹד הַיּוֹד סְפִירוֹת, שֶׁנֶּאֶצְלוּ בְּסוֹד יוֹד עִגּוּלִים זֶה תּוֹךְ זֶה.

5. And so, this first Circle that is the most attached to the Ein Sof is called Keter of Adam Kadmon.[17] Then this Line extended further, was drawn a little[18] and again curled and formed a second Circle within the first Circle.[19] This is called the Circle of Chochmah of Adam Kadmon.[20] It then extended further down, curled again and formed a third Circle within the second Circle and was called the Circle of Binah of Adam Kadmon.[21] And so in that manner it continued to extend and curl, all the way until the tenth Circle that is called the Circle of Malchut[22] of Adam Kadmon. Thus we explained the subject of the Ten Sefirot,[23] that were emanated according to the secret of Ten Circles, one within the other.[24]

ו) וְהִנֵּה הַבְּחִינָה הַמְחַבֶּרֶת כָּל הָעֲגוּלִים יַחַד, הִיא עִנְיַן קַו הַדַּק הַזֶּה הַמִּתְפַּשֵּׁט מִן הָאֵין סוֹף, וְעוֹבֵר וְיוֹרֵד וְנִמְשָׁךְ מֵעָגוּל אֶל עָגוּל, עַד סִיּוּם תַּכְלִית כֻּלָּם. וְדֶרֶךְ הַקַּו הַזֶּה נִמְשָׁךְ הָאוֹר וְהַשֶּׁפַע, הַצָּרִיךְ לְכָל אֶחָד וְאֶחָד מֵהֶם.

6. And so the aspect that connects all the Circles together[25] is this thin Line that extends from the Ein Sof, passing through,[26] descending[27] and extending[28] from Circle to Circle to the final objective of them all.[29] Through this Line flows the Light and the abundance that is needed to each and every one of them.

ז) וְהִנֵּה כָּל עוֹלָם וְעוֹלָם יֵשׁ בּוֹ יוּד סְפִירוֹת פְּרָטִיּוֹת, וְכָל סְפִירָה וּסְפִירָה פְּרָטִית שֶׁבְּכָל עוֹלָם וְעוֹלָם, כָּלוּל מִיּוּד סְפִירוֹת פְּרָטֵי פְּרָטִיּוֹת, וְכֻלָּם כַּגְלָדֵי בְצָלִים זֶה תּוֹךְ זֶה, עַל דֶּרֶךְ תְּמוּנַת הַגַּלְגַּלִּים כַּנִּזְכָּר בְּסִפְרֵי תְּכוּנָּיִם.

7. Each and every World has Ten individual Sefirot, and each and every individual Sefirah in each and every World comprises Ten individual Sefirot.[30] And they are all as layers of an onion, one within the other, like the image of the spheres mentioned in astronomy books.[31]

וֹ) כָּל עָגוּל וְעָגוּל מִכָּל הָעוֹלָמוֹת כֻּלָּם, אֲשֶׁר בְּתוֹךְ הֶחָלָל,
כָּל הַקָּרוֹב אֶל אוֹר אֵין סוֹף יוֹתֵר מֵחֲבֵרוֹ, הוּא עֶלְיוֹן מְאֹד
וּמְשֻׁבָּח מֵחֲבֵרוֹ, עַד שֶׁנִּמְצָא כִּי הָעוֹלָם הַזֶּה הָאַרְצִי הַוְּחָמְרִי,
הוּא נְקֻדָּה הָאֶמְצָעִי תִּיכוֹנָה, תּוֹךְ כָּל הָעֲגוּלִים כֻּלָּם, בְּתוֹךְ
כָּל הַמָּקוֹם הֶחָלָל וַאֲוִיר הַפָּנוּי הַנַּ"ל. וְגַם הוּא מְרֻחָק מִן הָאֵין
סוֹף הָרִחוּקָה גְּמוּרָה, יוֹתֵר מִכָּל הָעוֹלָמוֹת כֻּלָּם. וְעַל כֵּן הוּא
כָּל כָּךְ גַּשְׁמִי וְחָמְרִי בְּתַכְלִית הַגַּשְׁמִיּוּת, עִם הֱיוֹתוֹ נְקֻדָּה
אֶמְצָעִית בְּתוֹךְ כָּל הָעֲגוּלִים, וְהָבֵן זֶה הֵיטֵב.

8. Every single Circle from all the entire Worlds that are in the space—
the one closer to the Endless Light (Ohr Ein Sof)[32] than its neighbor
is superior and finer than it, until you find that this Earthly and
material World is the Middle Point within all the Circles, inside
all this place of empty space and vacant air, mentioned earlier. It is
also the farthest from the Ein Sof, more so than any of the Worlds.
It is therefore utterly material and physical because of it being the
Middle Point inside all the Circles, and understand this well.

1. This Line[1] is like one[3] thin channel,[2] through which the Waters of the Supernal Endless Light (Ohr Ein Sof)[4] extend and flow into the Worlds that are situated in the place of that air and space.

1. **This Line:** Namely, the Line drawn from the Ohr Ein Sof, blessed be He, into the space after the Tzimtzum. [See Volume 1, Chapter 2, Section 2].

In Volume 1, the Ari and Rav Ashlag explain the concept of the Tzimtzum. The Vessel, the Desire to Receive for the Self Alone, wanted to become more perfected, and asked the Light of the Creator to leave. This created a vacuum, an empty space. The Ari explains that after the removal of the Creator's Light from the Endless Vessel, a much-more diminished amount of Light called the Line was revealed. Rav Ashlag reminds us that when the Ari uses the word "Line" he is not speaking about a physical line—there is no line and no Light flowing—it is simply a representation of a much more diminished Light. Even the highest World, Adam Kadmon, which is way beyond our comprehension, is only a sliver of Light, compared to the Endless Light.

In the Histaklut Pnimit (Inner Observation) Rav Ashlag begins delving deeper into this section of the Ari. He says that what we are discussing here is something we should not even be talking about, because it refers to the Higher Worlds, the Upper Three Sefirot—of which we almost never speak.

The kabbalists tell us that throughout human existence, most people have felt certain levels of love, and all of this love has been accumulated into a reservoir. On Shabbat, we sing a song with words that originate from the Musaf Prayer of Rosh Chodesh: *Ahavat olam tavi lahem* (Give them eternal love), which can also be translated to mean, "Give them the love of the world." With this song, we ask the Creator to reveal to us and to the world the completeness of this reservoir of love that has existed throughout the history of the world. Imagine that all of this love, felt throughout human history, does not even come close to being a sliver of Light, compared to the Endless World. Knowing this we can begin to, at least, have some appreciation for how diminished and far away we are from the complete revelation of the Creator's Light, as well as what it means for us as we get closer and closer to the Endless World. Even this Line (Kav), this tiny sliver of Light, is something that is way beyond our comprehension.

---

2. **One thin Channel:** The Vessels of the Ten Sefirot of Straightness are called Conduits or Channels (*Tzinorot*), since they limit the paths of the Light that flows through them with great control and precision so that It does not extend in the Vessels except in specific ways. This resembles a channel that very precisely limits the water passing through it so the water flows and emerges out of it in the same shape of the channel—whether narrow or wide—without any change whatsoever.

Now we are entering a whole new World—the World of the Line—a World within which Light is not given freely nor completely, and the Vessels are incomplete and do not receive everything, and to some degree do not even desire everything. In this World, the Light revealed is constructed and changed. In the Endless World, Light was pure and simple. In the World of the Line, Light is no longer simple and is greatly affected by the Vessel. Rav Ashlag makes clear that nothing concerning the Light ever changes. The Light is always simple, and will remain simple forever. This discussion concerning what is happing from the moment of the Tzimtzum onward, is simply from the perspective of the Vessel; how the Vessel perceives the Light, which is why the Ari uses the word Tzinor to speak of the Vessels of this new World. Just as a water hose or pipe diminishes, constricts, and forms the type and shape of the water that flows through it, so too in this new World of the Line, the Light that is revealed is diminished, changed, and exact.

For this reason, the Lights that pass through those Channels are called Ten Sefirot of Straightness, since they are drawn according to the laws of these Channels with straightness and justice, meaning that within the purest Vessel, the most important Light is clothed and so on, without any change, due to the powerful control of the Channels that reside on them.

In the Endless World, Light was given to Vessels that simply wanted to receive regardless of how pure their desires were or how connected or disconnected they may or may not be. The Light simply flowed everywhere. In the Ein Sof, the World of Truth, there is no justice or exactness; there is no concept of purer or more connected. But in this new World of the Line, the laws of exactness comes into effect; one either deserves the Light or does not deserve the Light. If one is purer one gets more Light, and if one is less pure one gets less Light.

> And this power to control in the mentioned Channels is due to the fact that whatever is a Desire in a higher level is a compelling force in a lower level that emanated due to it.

Why is it that in this new World the Light is restricted? What happened in the Endless World? Rav Ashlag explains that in the Endless World, there was an Endless Vessel and the Creator gave to it endlessly. The Vessel said: "I want to perfect myself; I want to ultimately achieve a Desire to Receive for the Sake of Sharing; I want to achieve complete Similarity of Form with the Creator." So the Creator, in response, said: "To allow you to work on yourself I have to create a reality where you at least perceive it as if the Light has been removed." Thus the Creator contracted the Light.

In this new World, the law is that the Desire to Receive for the Self Alone cannot receive Light because the Vessel asked for the Light to be removed. The Vessel cannot now wake up in this new World of the Line and say, "This was not a very good idea. I should not have asked the Creator to bring a reality with thousands of years of work, pain, suffering, and death. I want all the Light back." Now there is justice: if you deserve you receive, if you do not deserve you do not receive. What changed?

Rav Ashlag answers, "Whatever is a Desire in a higher level," meaning a previous spiritual phase, which is the cause, "is a compelling force in a lower level." Whatever is an effect of that cause is now governed completely by the cause, which is the Desire of the Upper Worlds. In the First World, the World of the Endless, the Vessel could choose whether to receive or not receive, and said, "I no longer want to receive Your Light; I no longer want to receive with a Vessel that desires to Receive for the Self Alone." Rav Ashlag explains that any decision, any desire in the Upper World, in the World of

Cause, becomes an unbreakable law in the Lower Worlds. The beauty of Rav Ashlag's revelation is that he not only gives us an understanding of how our world came to be, he also teaches us many important spiritual laws, and this very striking spiritual law has many ramifications.

A simple example to illustrate this concept is of a teacher and a student. The teacher is the Upper World, the cause, and the student is the Lower World, the effect. If a teacher has certain blind spots—things that for whatever reason they have not corrected or are not correcting, these blind spots have an effect in the Lower World, on the student. For instance, even if a teacher has taught their student many other great things, it will nonetheless be impossible for the teacher who, at this moment in their own life, cannot control their anger, to impart to their student how to control anger, no matter how hard they try. What is more, if the teacher attempts to impart this, their own personal barrier to change, which they have now imbued in their student, is stronger in the student than their own barrier because "what is changeable in the cause is unbreakable in the effect." Even if, a year later, the teacher has an epiphany and is now able to control their anger, the teacher has still left their student slightly damaged because, to whatever degree it was difficult for the teacher to transform, it is going to be that much harder for the student to change. This is true of teacher to student, parent to child, and is true of any cause-and-effect relationships we experience.

Here we learn the tremendous significance of being a teacher. The gravity and danger in being a cause lies in the fact that whatever is a desire is a barrier built by the cause, and can be changed only on the level of cause. Once it comes into the effect—into the student or the child—it will be much more difficult for them to change because we are creating laws for our students and our children that will be much harder to break for them than it is for us. All of us, whether we are aware of it or not, are constantly becoming a cause to someone else's effect—and in doing so, we are not only giving over the good things, we are also giving of ourselves and are creating a soul. It says of Abraham, "…the souls they created in Charan…." (Genesis 12:5) When you are a teacher, when you are a parent, you are creating a soul. Whatever is a desire in the cause, in the teacher or the parent, whether good or bad, is now an unbreakable law in the Lower Worlds. This gives us an appreciation for the tremendous danger and seriousness of being a teacher because we are creating laws that will be much harder to break in our students and children, than it is for us.

Therefore, Rav Ashlag tells us that beginning in this new affected World of the Line there is no more choice. The Desire to Receive for the Self Alone, the Fourth Phase, cannot receive Light, cannot be fulfilled, no matter what the Vessel says because "whatever is a desire in the Upper Worlds becomes an unbreakable law in the Lower Worlds."

Therefore, the Contraction (Tzimtzum) upon the Fourth Phase that in the Circular Vessels is found as free will, becomes in the Linear Vessels that are caused by them [the Circular Vessels] an aspect of force and control that obligates them so. This force is called Curtain (Masach), as shall be discussed.

In the Endless World, the Vessel could say, "I want to receive" or "I don't want to receive." Now in this new World of the Line (Kav) there are no decisions. This Curtain (Masach), this new creation of a barrier between the Vessel and the Light, between desire and its fulfillment, in this World of the Line means that Light can no longer, ever, come into a Desire to Receive for the Self Alone—the Fourth Phase. It is that simple. Obviously, there is no physical curtain or barrier but until something else happens, at this point in the World of the Line, there is nothing the Vessel can do to Receive for the Self Alone.

Now we have quite the conundrum: There cannot be Light without a Vessel, and if the only Vessel until now has been a Vessel that Desires to Receive for the Self Alone, how is Light going to be revealed? Rav Ashlag will explain, further on, that there has to be a new type of Vessel created.

This is the secret of what it says in the Tikunim: "rearrange (lit. reverse) *ratzon* (רצון; desire) and you will find *tzinor* (צנור; channel)." This is as we said that the Channel functions as a Curtain, which signifies forceful Contraction, meaning that it prevents its Desire from receiving with the Fourth Phase due to the Supernal Force that compels it. Thus, it is contrary to the substance of the Vessel itself, namely the Desire to Receive, since it holds itself from fulfilling its Desire. Therefore, they said, "reverse *ratzon* (desire) and you will find *tzinor* (channel)." In other words, the matter of the Channel is the opposite of Desire, as it subjugates its Desire and does the opposite of what it wants.

Therefore, throughout all the writings and the commentaries we find that when we want to name and emphasize the matter of the departure of the Light from the Fourth Phase, we call it Contraction (Tzimtzum), and when we want to emphasize the additional force of Tzimtzum from the side of the Light of the Line that did not extend to the Fourth Phase, we define it as Curtain (Masach). The Masach is the force that prevents the Light from spreading into the Fourth Phase. And when we discuss the entirety of the Vessel, namely the Vessel and the Masach together, we define it as a Conduit or Channel. And when we discuss the Light, the Vessel, and the Masach together, namely the Light that has entered according to the size of the Channel, it is defined as a Line. And when we discuss a Vessel that has no Masach, we define it as a Circle.

As we enter this new, scary, diminished, and darkened World of the Line, we still have memory of these empty Circular Vessels of the Ein Sof that do not have a problem with Receiving for the Self Alone. In this new World where only a slight amount of Light is revealed, and a Masach, a barrier prevents any Light from being revealed to the Fourth Phase, the Desire to Receive for the Self Alone, the beautiful aspect of the Circular Vessels still remains.

All that occurred at the Tzimtzum, when the Vessel asked the Creator to remove the Creator's Light, is that the Light departed from the Vessels. Nevertheless, these pure and simple Circular Vessels that existed in the Endless World still remain. They are still around and they do not disappear. There is still the Circular Vessel that knows what it is like to be completely filled; that does not think that there is any reason why Light cannot flow everywhere or why Light cannot go into a Desire to Receive for the Self Alone.

It is very necessary to have this terminology extremely clear in our mind as we begin this process. In the Introduction to the Study of the Ten Luminous Emanations ("And You Shall Choose Life"), Rav Ashlag explains that every time we think about these concepts of the Line or discuss the Circular Vessels, as we understand them, we are awakening these Lights in the Upper Worlds, and then this Light shines a little bit and comes down into our world. And when we have gratitude for how amazing this Light is, we also gain an appreciation for the gift that we have been given of being allowed to study this wisdom and reveal this Light.

I personally find this to be both an exciting, but also a very necessary, spiritual process. Therefore, the deeper we delve and the harder we push ourselves to comprehend and have clarity and think through what we are discussing, the more this Light is revealed. If our brain does not begin to hurt a little when contemplating these concepts, then we are not working hard enough.

---

3. **One:** The Ari specifies the word "one" to exclude the Correction of the Three Columns [Right, Left, and Central] that was made in the World of Atzilut. He teaches us that in the World of Adam Kadmon there is not yet this Correction of the Three Columns, rather there is only One Column alone. The reason is that the whole Correction of the Three Columns was made later in the World of Atzilut and is the result of the conjoining of the attribute of Compassion with Judgment, as we will explain in its place. Here we are dealing with the World of Adam Kadmon where this conjoining has not yet taken place and thus there is but One Column alone.

Those who are familiar with Rav Ashlag's commentary on the Zohar, the Sulam, know that he often discusses the concept of the coming together of Mercy and Judgment, and the creation of the Three-Column System. He frequently quotes the Midrash, which says that initially the Creator wanted to create our world using the attribute of Judgment, but upon seeing that the world would not survive He brought Judgment together with Mercy, creating this new Three-Column System. It is also clear from Rav Ashlag that our connection really begins with the Worlds of Briyah, Yetzirah, and Asiyah, even though it is within the World of Atzilut, which corresponds to the Sefirah of Chochmah that the Correction of the Three Columns occurred.

We know that the entire purpose of the Tzimtzum was to enable a place of Correction for the Vessel (the Desire to Receive of the Self Alone). However, after the Tzimtzum there is an important realization. It becomes clear that the Vessel, Malchut, the Desire to Receive for the Self Alone, cannot connect to the Light because they are complete opposites. The Light is all sharing. The Vessel is all receiving.

Rav Ashlag explains in the Introduction to the Zohar ("Thought of Creation") that immediately at this point there is the creation of two Systems: the System of Holiness and the System of Impurity—and that the System of Impurity is completely disconnected from the Light of the Creator. Anything that has to do with the Desire to Receive for the Self Alone is completely disconnected from the Light of the Creator.

Yet if the Desire to Receive for the Self Alone, the Vessel, is now relegated to the System of Impurity, which is disconnected from the Light of the Creator, how do we correct it? We cannot even touch it. As Rav Ashlag will make clear, a new system—the concept of Returning Light (Ohr Chozer)—comes into effect, where the only way to receive now is if our thoughts are: *I want to Receive for the Sake of Sharing*. Receiving for the Sake of Receiving—because I want it—is no longer part of the System of Holiness.

The entire purpose of the Tzimtzum is because the true Vessel—the Desire to Receive for the Self Alone—wants to be corrected. In the World of Adam Kadmon there are two Systems: one Holy and connected and the other Impure and completely disconnected, and the entire purpose of Creation is for the one that is disconnected—for the Vessel.

Thus we are left in a peculiar situation. If the purpose of the Tzimtzum is to allow the Desire to Receive for the Self Alone to be corrected and consequently this new reality in the World of Adam Kadmon is one within which the Desire to Receive for the Self Alone is relegated to completely disconnect from the Light of the Creator, what do we do? If we cannot touch it, we cannot correct it. And if we cannot correct it, the whole purpose of the Tzimtzum is almost lost.

Therefore, there is going to have to be a Second Contraction (Tzimtzum Bet), which is precipitated by the fact that we will create a new reality where the System of Impurity and the System of Holiness are somehow intertwined; where Desire to Receive and Desire to Share are somehow brought together. This is really who we are. We are a creation after the Second Contraction (Tzimtzum Bet), after Judgment and Mercy intertwine. Judgment represents the Desire to Receive being completely pushed out, and Mercy represents the Desire to Receive for the Self Alone being brought into and mixed in with the System of Holiness. Once we have brought little sparks of the Desire to Receive for the Self Alone into the System of Purity, then we can begin working with it, begin to fix it.

Just to clarify, the importance of the correction of the Tzimtzum Bet is that prior to this, the Desire to Receive for the Self Alone in the World of Adam Kadmon is on the side. It cannot be touched because obviously we cannot correct something with which we are not in alignment. This is who we are; we are body and soul. The body represents the Malchut, the Vessel, the Desire to Receive for the Self Alone that is completely disconnected from the Light of the Creator. Our soul represents the part of us that is connected to the Light of the Creator. Now, after the Tzimtzum Bet, it is mixed together. The Zohar says that it is a miracle that these two elements can coexist. Yet this miracle had to occur so as to allow us to have within us that disgusting, at least for now, Desire to Receive for the Self Alone so we can work on it and fix it.

This could not be achieved in the World of Adam Kadmon because in that World there is no Right and Left together. In the World of Adam Kadmon, there is only the Right (Desire to Share); the Left (Desire to Receive for the Self Alone) is not part of that system anymore. We will get into the details of this as we go further, but for now it is important to understand that here, in this World of Adam Kadmon, there is no Correction of the Three Columns, there is only the System of Holiness and the System of Impurity—Light and darkness. Light being represented by the Desire to Share. Only afterwards, in the Realm of Atzilut, will there be the Correction of the Three Columns. This is why the Ari says that in this first revelation of the World of the Line there is only One Line, meaning there is no mixture of Right, Left, and Central.

The entering of the Light into the receiving Vessel of the emanated is termed "Extension" (See Volume 1, Table of Terminology Answers, entry 14), and it has already been explained [in the previous paragraph] that the receiving Vessel in this emanated is termed by the word Channel (Tzinor) (see there as to the reason).

When the Ari says that in this new reality of the Line, the Light flows into the Vessel, one could mistakenly assume that the Light now comes in. Yet as Rav Ashlag makes very clear, the Light does not move; Light does not come in nor come out—Light does not flow. The Light is here always: The Light was here from the beginning; the Light is here at the end; the Light is here in the middle. It never went away. It is important to remind ourselves that when we mention Light flowing into this Vessel of the Line, we are not discussing the Light being affected—Light being there and not being there—we are talking about the Vessel's perception of the Light. Now the Vessel perceives the revealed Light as coming into it.

It is important to realize that this entire interaction of us feeling the Light at times in our spiritual work—Light not being there before and now coming in—is an illusion of the Vessel; an illusion we have created. The Light is always here; we simply happen to have been blind to it. The reason Rav Ashlag wants to make this clear is, when we read, "the Waters of the Supernal Light of the Ein Sof extend and flow," it literally sounds like the Light is flowing, the Light is being affected. Yet we now know the Light is never affected. All we are discussing here is the way the Vessel perceives the Light.

And the way the Light is revealed is dependent on our consciousness. If our consciousness is that the Light is not here and now we are revealing it, then the Light is not here. An essential teaching of the Baal Shem Tov is that even when we do not feel the Light, we have to know that it is here. By knowing that the Light is here, we are allowing it to be revealed.

When someone goes through a stage of darkness and thinks that the Light is not there, not only is the Light not there for them, they also make it even more difficult for the Light that is there to be revealed to them. Yet when someone knows with certainty beyond logic that, even when they do not see the Light, the Light is there and it is their illusion that they currently do not see this Light, this makes it that much easier for this Light to eventually be revealed to them. It is essential to have this constant consciousness.

> 4. **The Waters of the Supernal Endless Light:** There is a known value in distinguishing between the steps in the birth of a Partzuf (Spiritual Structure), where there the Four Phases of Desire are called: Light, Water, Firmament, and a Hundred Gates or a Hundred Blessings. This is due to the transposing of the Lights not in their place, where, due to this exchange, the Light takes on the form of Water, as will be explained in its place.

This is a remarkable revelation once we comprehend it. As the Light becomes revealed through any Partzuf (Spiritual Structure), the Light itself (and we are not talking about the Light but the way the Vessel perceives the Light) is in a diluted form, meaning that a lower level of Vessel does not perceive the same Light as the Higher Vessel. Thus it is not only a diminishment of quantity of Light that one has when one goes to a lower level of connection, there is also a difference in quality of Light that one receives, that the Vessel receives, when it is at a lower level.

In other words, there is less Light revealed in Binah than in Chochmah; there is less Light revealed in Zeir Anpin than in Binah; there is less Light revealed in Malchut than in Zeir Anpin. And apart from the diminishment of Light revealed in Malchut, from the Vessel's perspective, the quality of the Light, meaning the type of Light is also different. Rav Ashlag explains that Light, Water, Firmament, and One Hundred Blessings each represent different qualities of Light that are perceived by the Vessel as it goes from one stage to a lower stage. Why does this happen? Why is Light, when perceived by the Vessel, not the same quality at a lower level than at a higher level? "This is due to the transposing of the Lights not in their place," because when Light is revealed not in its right place, it cannot have the same quality.

For instance, there is a difference to experiencing Lag B'Omer at Meron or the Idra Raba, and Tisha B'Av in Jerusalem, or Rosh Hashanah or Yom Kippur in Israel, where the Light is truly revealed, and participating in these connections in Los Angeles or other cities around the world. When we experience these connections outside of Israel it is "the transposing of the Lights not in their place;" it is not where this revealed Light is directly, and certainly one will feel that there is a difference. Light not revealed in its place becomes diminished in both quantity and quality. When we discuss the first diminishment of the Vessel's perception of the quality of the Light, it is no longer Light, it is now referred to by the term Water. Of course, this does not mean water in a literal sense, but it refers to a diminishment of the quality and quantity of Light.

The Rav [the Ari] is teaching us that the source for this matter takes place here with the emergence of the Line. The Light that extends in the form of a Line, in relation to the Supernal Light, is considered as Water (Mayim). Therefore, he specifies, **"the Waters of the Supernal Endless Light,"** for with the extension of the Light into the narrow Channel, the Light is greatly diminished from its value in the Endless (Ein Sof), and it is considered like Water in relation to its previous value.

In this section, where we discuss the World of Adam Kadmon—a World that is beyond our comprehension—it is important to realize that most of us have almost never tasted the true Light of the Creator. Unfortunately, we often do not even taste from the Worlds of Atzilut, Briyah, Yetzirah, or Asiyah. We mostly taste from the lower Worlds of our world, which is like a drop in the ocean.

The only way to partake of, to taste, true Light is in the Endless World. In the Endless World all the Light was revealed in its proper place, completely. When we taste of an Upper World, the World of Adam Kadmon or of the Worlds of Atzilut, Briyah, Yetzirah, and Asiyah, we do not taste the true Light of the Ein Sof. We taste a diminished form of Light as perceived by the Vessel, which is not of the same quality or purity as in the Endless World. Even in the World of Adam Kadmon, the first World revealed after the Tzimtzum, it is a diminished quality of Light, termed Water.

As we think about and hopefully grasp this concept, we begin to realize the tremendous pain of the Light of the Creator spoken about in both the Zohar and the Midrash. In addition to the fact that the Creator cannot reveal the totality of His Light in our world since the Tzimtzum, which caused tremendous pain, suffering, and darkness in our world, the Creator cannot even reveal the quality of that Light in our world, which causes tremendous pain in the Supernal Worlds.

There are two parts to this teaching: first, to realize the pain of the Light of the Creator and second, to be conscious of the pain of our soul. The kabbalists say that if we could hear the yelling of our soul we would not be able to stand it, because it knows how little we allow it to taste of the true essence of Light of the Creator. Feeling this pain should drive us to really desire to do whatever we can to perfect the Vessel to be able to truly taste, not only the quantity of the Light of the Creator but a purer quality. Every time we elevate ourselves, we are not simply revealing more Light, we are also revealing a better quality, a purer form of Light for ourselves. This is a very important understanding.

The positive side, of course, is that by recognizing the small amounts of joy we experience in our lives from partaking of a small quantity and diminished quality of the Light of the Creator, we can begin to grasp the type of fulfillment and joy that can be ours and for the world once we begin to truly partake of a greater quantity and quality of the Light of the Creator.

2. As the Endless Light was drawn as a Straight Line[5] into the aforementioned space, it was not drawn and extended all the way down instantly but rather it extended very slowly.[6] What I mean to say is that at first the Line of Light began to extend, and right then and there when it started to extend[7] in the secret of a Line, it extended and was drawn, and it became like one Wheel,[8] circular all around.

Although the World of the Line is diminished in quality and quantity in relation to the Ein Sof, Rav Ashlag makes very clear that one of the saving graces is that in the World of Adam Kadmon there are still the Vessels of the Endless World, the Circular Vessels. And Circular Vessels does not mean that they have a form of a circle but rather that they originate from the Ein Sof, where the Vessel of Desire to Receive for the Self Alone, Malchut, is not deemed to be lower.

It is important that they are there because if not for the reality of these Circular Vessels that once partook of the complete revelation of the Light of the Creator in the Endless World, we would all give up, since we can never draw something we do not have a connection to. These Circular Vessels are the doorway to the Final Correction (Gemar haTikkun). It is the consciousness of: *I know that we once had and will again have complete revelation.*

The Ari explains here it is true that the pure Circular Vessels exist in the World of Adam Kadmon, but they are also going to receive some of the diminished Light that is going to be revealed in that World. Therefore, it is not as it would seem from the literal translation, that a new Circle is being created. Rather, this Light that is revealed through the Line goes into that Circular Vessel of the Endless World, thus keeping a connection with the Ein Sof.

The fact that we have the Circular Vessels is our hope and is the pathway by which we will achieve Correction. Therefore, we should be reflecting on the Circular Vessels all the time. The consciousness of the Circular Vessels is perfection, completeness, the Endless World. The Baal Shem Tov says, "Where our mind is, is where we are." The more time we spend thinking about the Circular Vessels, the more time we are connected to that perfection, and the more time we are actually revealing this perfection in our world.

Hopefully we will all find ourselves constantly contemplating the Circular Vessels because this is what brings that Light into our world, and there is nothing this world needs more than the consciousness of this perfection of the Circular Vessels. By awakening our mind to it, we reveal it and by revealing it, we bring the world and us a step closer to the Final Correction.

---

5. **A Straight Line:** A Light that extends according to the rules of the Four Phases, gradually, that is, from purest to coarsest and stops at the Fourth Phase, is called a Straight Line.

Rav Ashlag makes it clear that in this new World, when the Ari speaks of a Straight Line (Kav Yashar) he is referring to a much more diminished form of Light that is revealed in descending order from the purest to the least pure, from the Vessel that is deserving to a Vessel that is less deserving. The amazing revelation of the Ari and Rav Ashlag is that before the Tzimtzum, before the Vessel asked the Light of the Creator to be removed, the Light of the Creator did not differentiate between better or worse, more pure or less pure, more righteous or less righteous. The Light simply flowed. We should never forget that the Essence of the Light of the Creator goes everywhere regardless of whether one deserves it or not. The true Essence of the Light of the Creator shines everywhere. It is only in this new Illusory World created by the Vessel—a world within which we still live—that the concept of being more deserving, less deserving, closer, further, purer, less pure, exists.

After the Tzimtzum there is a revelation called a Straight Line, which, as Rav Ashlag says, indicates Light revealed through justice, through what is right. Meaning, if you are more deserving you get more Light, if you are less deserving you get less Light.

6. **Instantly… very slowly:** Do not misinterpret the words "instantly" and "very slowly" mentioned here as applying to a timetable because spirituality is above time, as is known.

Rav Ashlag makes clear that the concept of time is an illusion of the Negative Side. Light is neither revealed in any direction nor at any speed because there is neither time nor space in the spiritual World. This concept of time being an illusion is something we need to remind ourselves of constantly because it can diminish and remove a lot of the pain we experience in our lives. The Negative Side wants us to be stuck in the moment and believe that a situation we are in right now will be long suffered.

In the truest sense, in the reality of our world there is no time. And if there is no time, then anything that is difficult at this moment but will not be difficult in a year or two from now, is really not a difficulty at all. The Rav always spoke about the fact that through this consciousness we can diminish time; we can take away the time between cause and effect. Obviously, the ultimate level to reach is where there is no time—where the bonds of time do not hold us back and certainly do not cause us pain. Therefore, the next time we find ourselves in a situation where the Negative Side wants us to think that not only is there difficulty now, but this pain is going to be here for an overwhelming amount of time, we have to remind ourselves that in a true sense, there is no time, in the real world.

Rather, "all the way down instantly," means without change of stages, whereas "very slowly" means according to the development of the stages. What he refers to is the development of the order of the well-known Four Phases, as he will explain presently.

It is essential that we learn this language. When we read that something is happening quickly in the writings of a true kabbalist, the Zohar, or in the Writings of the Ari, it means that there is no differentiation between a higher level and a lower level, more deserving or less deserving, more connected or less connected. A process that is dependent on levels, where this Light is revealed to someone slowly, because today he or she is at a certain level and tomorrow they will be on a higher level and therefore receives more, is not the ultimate true process. This is a process that is within in this Illusory

World. Therefore, when we discuss the Light of the Creator being revealed "quickly," we are talking about Light being revealed without paying attention to the different levels, to who is more deserving or who is less deserving.

Concerning the revelation of Mashiach, Isaiah 60:22 says that it can come "in its time (be'itah)" or "I will hasten it (achishena)." What does this mean? Rav Ashlag explains that "in its time (be'itah)" means that we unfortunately stay in the world where there are levels: where there are people who deserve more and those who deserve less; where there will be those who will go through pain and those who will not experience pain. Then there is the ultimate of "I will hasten it (achishena)" or as the kabbalists say, Yeshu'at HaShem keheref ayin "the Creator's salvation is as the blink of an eye." And the way we connect to the level of achishena, where the Redemption or the assistance from the Creator comes in an instant, is by consciously going beyond the realm of time, beyond the realm of deserving or less deserving.

Therefore, when the Ari discusses Light that is revealed slowly, the term slowly does not mean the time it takes to go from beginning to end, but rather it means paying attention to levels of deserving and levels of purification. Meaning the Light goes to the more deserving, more than it does to the less deserving. And then to the even less deserving, it takes its time. It takes its measure. The Light is breaking down and being revealed to everyone only to the degree that they are deserving.

Rav Moshe Chaim Luzzatto (the Ramchal; 1707–1746) in his book *Mesilat Yesharim* ("Path of the Just") speaks about the importance of *zerizut* (alacrity; quickness of spirit). When a person acts without *zerizut*, when a person acts lethargically, slowly, they are not allowing the Light of the Creator to be revealed completely, everywhere. They are forcing the Light of the Creator to be revealed only to the degree that their Vessel is deserving. When a person acts with *zerizut*, with quickness, they are closing the gaps of time, allowing the Light of the Creator to be revealed even when a person is undeserving. The Ramchal explains that these two qualities in a person—either doing things quickly or doing things slowly and lethargically—determines whether this individual is truly connected or not connected to the Light of the Creator.

Now we can understand this on a deeper level. When a person is acting slowly, when a person is acting with laziness, they are connecting to the Realm of the Line, they are connecting to the reality where the Light is revealed only to the degree that they are deserving and in the time that they are deserving. When a person acts with quickness (*zerizut*), when a person does the spiritual work quickly and with vigor, it is an indication that they are connecting to the Realm before the Contraction (Tzimtzum), the Realm where the Light of the Creator is revealed everywhere all the time. This Realm is the Realm we want to connect to. We want to draw the Light completely, all the time, to everyone, everywhere.

Therefore, the way for us to connect to the reality the Ari calls "instantly," where the Light of the Creator is revealed everywhere instantly all the time without paying attention to the different levels, is with quickness. If one is connecting to the consciousness of the reality of slowly, slowly (le'at, le'at), then they are connecting to the Realm where levels matter, where Light can only be revealed more in some places and less in others because those are the levels they deserve.

I hope that this inspires us to understand the importance of doing our spiritual work with alacrity so that we can connect to the Realm of Instantly (Techef), the Reality before the Contraction (Tzimtzum). In the new reality that the Ari calls the Line, the Light is revealed in a greatly diminished form and is not revealed into the great Vessel of the Fourth Phase.

---

7. **When it started to extend:** Namely, the root of the novel Extension called the Line, for since it is a new emanation there is a unique root distinguished in it that shines to it from the aspect of its newness, which is called the Sefirah of Keter of the Line. From this Keter, the Light of Ein Sof extends into the Line, following the Four well-known Phases. The First Phase is called Chochmah; the Second Phase is called Binah; the Third Phase is called Zeir Anpin, and the Fourth Phase is called Malchut. The Ari comments on this sequence saying, "it extended very slowly;" so at first Keter extended, followed by Chochmah, Binah, Zeir Anpin, and so on. (See Volume 1, Table of Terminology Answers, the word "After").

As mentioned previously, in the World of Adam Kadmon there is a diminished revelation of the Light of the Creator. It is important to understand that this new Reality of the Line cannot receive its Light from the same Source as the Vessel once did in the Endless before the Tzimtzum. Since it is a different and new reality, its source of Light has to be different.

We may think that the Light of the Creator is revealed to everyone in the same way, with the same quality and from the same source. Meaning, that the source of Light of the Vessel in the Ein Sof, which we call 'the Creator,' is also the source of Light of the Line, and also our source of Light. This is not true. When a new reality is formed—and here we are discussing the Reality of the Line—a new source of Light is created.

We know that the Light Itself does not change, and that the only change is the way the Vessels (we) perceive the Light. The unfortunate reality is that we are now in a World of not only diminished Vessels, we are also in a World where we receive from narrow sources and not from the totality of the Light of the Creator. For example, if someone is in need of healing, or someone who we are praying for is going through a difficult health issue, we meditate in the prayers on *Rofe Cholim* (Healer of the Sick; the Amidah). When a person is going through a different problem, he prays not to a different Creator, but to a different source within the Creator. *Ozer Dalim Matir Asurim* (helps the poor, unbinds the imprisoned; ibid.).

The reason we meditate using different prayers for different situations is because unfortunately we cannot take in the totality of the Light of the Creator. And when we cannot take in the totality of the Light of the Creator, we force the Creator to diminish even the source from where we receive our Light. I hope this very important concept awakens in us an understanding of the pain we cause the Creator. The Creator wants to give us all the Light, completely, in its total form, all the time. Yet because we live in a world where we do not see and cannot appreciate nor take in the totality of the Creator's Light, when we experience a problem, we say to the Creator, "Help me with this specific problem." And when we experience a different problem, we ask the Creator to help us with that problem. This is our unfortunate reality, and as long as we are within this realm, this is the way we have to pray, that is the way we have to connect.

However, this is not where we want to be. We want to enable the Light of the Creator to give us everything; where we ask and are able to receive the totality of the Light of the Creator. As Rav Ashlag mentions, the Kabbalists say: more than the calf wants to suckle, the cow wants to give to its calf; thus more than we desire to receive from the Light of the Creator, the Creator wants to give to us.

When someone is experiencing a health challenge and prays that the Light of Healing from the Creator should come to them, what they are in fact saying is: "The Light of sustenance, the Light of fulfillment, all the other Lights, do not come to me. I want only this minute form of Light to come to me." Meaning that the totality of the Light of the Creator cannot be the source of that Light. The source has to be different. They are asking the Creator to create for them a tiny, minute funnel and constrict His great Light. Asking the Creator to constrict the totality of His great Light is only from the person's perspective. And since we now know that the Light of the Creator does not change, what we are in fact doing is putting a veil upon the totality of this Light.

To help us understand this concept, imagine the sun is shining through a window. We place a window curtain with four tiny holes on it, over the window. Obviously, the light of the sun is shining onto that window covering in its totality, but by placing the covering over the window we only allow four beams of the totality of this sunlight to reflect on the wall. This is what we do all the time.

When we ask for healing, we ask the Creator to create a source of Light that only funnels Light of healing, while removing and diminishing all the rest of the totality of the Light that can be revealed. Thus, as well as this diminishment of Light that the Vessel draws, the Vessel also forces a different, new source for that Light to be created. Here the Ari and Rav Ashlag explain that when a new creation is created, it makes it so that a new source has to be created that is specific in revealing Light to this new creation.

Therefore Rav Ashlag says that when we discuss the Keter, the first Sefirah, of Adam Kadmon, we are not talking about the first Vessel of Adam Kadmon, we are discussing this new source of Light that has to be created for this new Vessel, which receives diminished Light. Thus, the World of Adam Kadmon no longer receives from the totality of the Creator, the Endless Light, but rather receives from Keter of Adam Kadmon, from this new source of Light that has to be diminished.

Just to use another example, in schools there are different grades, and obviously the wisest teacher teaches the highest class. If a child has less of an understanding he goes to the teacher of first grade; if he has more of an understanding he goes to the teacher of second grade. The Creator is the highest-grade teacher, and He sees that you are only ready for first grade. He says, "You know what? I would like to be your teacher but I cannot. You are only ready to learn the ABC's. So I will create for you a first grade teacher. You will learn from him. If you awaken your Vessel a little bit more, then you are ready now for the second grade teacher. You are still not ready for Me, you are still not ready for the greatest teacher."

This is our relationship with the Creator. Whenever our Vessel, our desire, is diminished, the Endless Light of Creator says, "You are not ready for Me to be your Source. I have to create a little tiny source, a little tiny world for you to be able to work within." Unfortunately this is what we are forcing the Creator to do all the time. Through our consciousness and our actions, we are letting the Creator know that we are not ready for the totality of Creator's Light. We want this little thing, we want this little world. And the Creator replies, "If that is all you desire, if this is all you are ready for, because I want to give and this is the only way you are allowing Me to share, I will have to create this little fake illusory reality for you." But know that your source is no longer the purity of the Light of the Creator. You now have a different source. You have a Keter of whatever World you are in.

---

8. **One Wheel, circular all around:** When the Light of the Line is clothed within the Circle it is called a "Wheel." For the meaning for the word "Circle," see Volume 1, Terminology Answers, entry 41. Also see Volume 1, Chapter 1, Section 20.

Previously the Ari mentioned that this Light is revealed slowly, depending on how much each Vessel deserves and on how pure they are. Now as this Light is beginning to be revealed, there is this revelation of a Circle.

It is important for us to know how this world came into being because then, on a deep level, we can understand what the world as a whole is meant to do and what our purpose is in this world. Thus, we are reminded that although a tremendously diminished amount of the Light is being revealed in this the new reality of the World of the Line, the saving grace is that these Circular Vessels (Kelim D'Igulim) of the Endless World are still in this new World. And these Circular Vessels know what it is like to have the totality of the Light of the Creator revealed to them.

The Creator did not simply throw us out here with nothing with which to work on ourselves. The Creator left us the Circular Vessels that know what it is to truly receive the Light. This consciousness of the Circular Vessels—to desire and thus have the totality of the Light of the Creator completely—did not disappear after the Tzimtzum. The Ari informs us that although the revealed

Light of the Line is now in a diminished form, this Light also shines to the Circular Vessels.

How do we know if we are truly connected to these Circular Vessels of the Endless World? It is by how satisfied we feel. When we awaken the consciousness of the Kelim D'Igulim within, we can never be satisfied. We feel that no matter how much Light we reveal, our spiritual work—both for humanity as a whole and each of us personally—is to keep filling up the Circular Vessels. Until ultimately we have brought enough Light back into the Circular Vessels of the Ein Sof that we now allow the total revelation of the Light—which is Mashiach.

When the Ari says, "it extended and was drawn, and it became like one Wheel, circular all around" it is not that a new Circle becomes revealed but rather that the Light goes back into the original consciousness of the Circular Vessels, the Vessels of the Endless World. Thankfully this consciousness of the Circular Vessel that receives everything completely, always remains. We know if we are truly in this consciousness because it never allows us to be satisfied. We are constantly being reminded: "It is great that you did all this but remember what it was like to have everything?" Therefore, if someone is truly doing the spiritual work, every Line they reveal, every diminished amount of Light they reveal, goes back into the Circular Vessels and reminds them: "There is so much more for you to do."

3. This Circle was not attached to the Endless Light that surrounded it from all its sides,[9] for had it been attached to It, it would have returned to the way it used to be and become void in the Endless Light.[10] Its power would not have been apparent at all, and all would be the Endless Light, alone as had been in the beginning. Therefore, this Circle was close to the Circle of the Endless, yet not attached to It. And the main connection and attachment of that emanated Circle with the emanating Endless[11] is via that aforementioned Line[12] through which Light descends and flows from the Endless and bestows to that Circle.

Here, a question can be raised. Earlier Rav Ashlag explained that after the Tzimtzum there is the Curtain (Masach) in the Lower Worlds. The Vessel in the Endless World requested that the Light of the Creator be removed; and Rav Ashlag explained that anything that is a desire, a decision in the Upper Realms becomes an unchangeable law in the Lower Worlds. This reality after the Tzimtzum is why the Light of the Endless World cannot go into the Circular Vessels and into the Fourth Phase, and why the Circular Vessels receive the Light only through the Line. Yet here, Rav Isaac Luria (the Ari) seems to give us a secondary reason why the Light does not go into the Circular Vessel. What is the need for this secondary reason if the main reason was already explained?

One of the things we learn as we study the Writings of Rav Isaac Luria and Rav Ashlag is that for any true reality there are many reasons. There could be more than one reason, one cause, for every occurrence, which can create confusion if we are not aware of it. In one instance, the Ari or Rav Ashlag would give one reason for a reality, and then in another place they will give a secondary reason for the reality. Of course, all of these are not contradictory, but different reasons for the same reality.

This is why here again Rav Isaac Luria (the Ari) is telling us that the reason the Vessel, the Circular Vessels, do not receive from the Endless World, is because if they did they would recede back into and be enveloped and swallowed up into the Endless World, and not be able to give a space to do our work; that is one reason. But there is another reason, which Rav Ashlag spoke at length earlier, which is that after the World of Tzimtzum, after the Vessel decided that it wanted the Light of the Creator to be removed so that it will have a place to do its work, Light cannot come into these Vessels anymore; there is now a Masach, there is now a spiritual law that does not allow the Light to come into these Vessels.

---

9. **Not attached to the Endless Light:** In other words, all the Light that exists in the Circles is only from what they receive from the Line, whose illumination is considered a new illumination since it contains only the Three Phases, as said. It is, therefore, different from the Ohr Ein Sof that encircles as Circular Light (see Volume 1, Inner Light Chapter 2, Section 3).

This is what the Ari meant in saying it is "not attached to the Endless Light," meaning that the form of the Circular Light of Keter of the Circles is not equal to the Light in Endless, since Similarity of Form is the cleaving among spiritual entities (see Volume 1, Terminology Answers, entry 12; and Volume 1, Inner Light Chapter 2, Section 2). And "encircles" (*sovev*), alludes to a causing factor.

When we read Rav Ashlag's explanation of the Writings of the Ari, one may question from where Rav Ashlag received his wisdom. If you read the Writings of the Ari and then you read Rav Ashlag's explanation of it, most of us would not come to the understandings that Rav Ashlag came to, no matter how many hundreds of years we would spend studying it. So there are a few answers you could give. First is that it really is in the Writings of the Ari, as Rav Ashlag said, he did not add anything to the Ari, he only explained what is already written. Another answer could be that it makes sense and it fits perfectly with the Ari. But these are not sufficient answers.

Aside from the fact that we know Rav Ashlag received all his knowledge from his teacher, Rav Ashlag also reveals that he got assistance from the soul of the Ari, who came to him and taught him all the secrets that the Ari did not have the ability to reveal when he was physically in this world. This gives us a real appreciation for the revelations of Rav Ashlag, which he received not only because his soul merited it but also because our generation merited it, and because we need this wisdom in this time.

For example, the Ari uses a simple word: sovev (surrounds it). But Rav Ashlag reveals to us that it does not mean one Light surrounding another Light, rather it "alludes to a causing factor," since the root of the word is *sibah* (cause). The Endless Light does not physically surround these Vessels but is instead the cause of these Vessels. This is important.

When Rav Ashlag arrived in Israel from Poland, he attended what was then a great school of kabbalists in the Old City of Jerusalem, and he was hoping to find wisdom. As he sat there with the scholars, he realized that, although they had been studying the Writings of the Ari for many years, they had no idea what the Ari was discussing. When they came across the words in the Writings of the Ari, they understood them to reflect physical structures. He asked them, "Is there not more? Do you think there really is a Light, a Line, and a Circle, and that the Endless World literally physically surrounds these

Circular Vessels?" They answered, "Yes." And of course, Rav Ashlag told them we cannot understand these concepts to be literal.

In *Beit Sha'ar Hakavanot* ("The House of the Gate of Meditations"), Rav Ashlag explains that one of the reasons we cannot fully depend on what we have today from even the true kabbalists, is that their writings were often written down by someone else, or they were taken and disorganized. He uses the example of the Rashash (Rav Shalom Sharabi, 1720–1777) that people took some of the things the Rashash wrote earlier in his life, which he then later came to understand on a deeper level, and printed it all together, creating a mixture of concepts.

We need to really appreciate that without this revelation from Rav Ashlag there would simply be no way in a thousand years for anyone to have a true grasp of the Writings of the Ari, and yet here we are simply studying from the Writings of Rav Ashlag and we have an understanding of the words of the Ari that nobody in history could have ever had.

---

10. **Had it been attached to It, it would have returned to the way it used to be:** In other words, had its illumination been present in all Four Phases like the Light of the Endless, its form would have been the same as the Endless and attached to it. In that case, it would have been completely annulled within the Endless and indistinguishable.

11. **The main connection and attachment:** The Light that extends from the Ein Sof toward the emanated is called Direct Light (Ohr Yashar). This Light connects with the emanated through a clothing of Returning Light (Ohr Chozer) that rises up from the Curtain (Masach) by means of Binding by Striking (*Zivug deHaka'ah*), which shall be explained later.

This is one of Rav Ashlag's great revelations. Although this is something the Ari mentions, it is Rav Ashlag's revelation behind what this means that forms the basis of this entire teaching of Rav Ashlag. Rav Ashlag explains that in the World after the Tzimtzum, the Vessel (we) cannot receive if we are taking pleasure for ourselves from it, and therefore a new type of receiving was created. This new type of receiving is called Returning Light. In this parable from *P'ticha leChochmat haKabbalah* ("The Introduction to the Wisdom of Kabbalah"), Rav Ashlag gives an analogy to expand on this concept of Returning Light, this new way of receiving.

> "We need to understand how this Returning Light became a Vessel of Receiving. At first, it was just Light pushed away so as not to be received, yet now it serves an opposite function to its own nature. I shall explain it to you by means of a parable from the realities of this world. It is human nature to like and appreciate the attribute of giving, while finding the attribute of receiving from another disgusting and lowly. Thus when someone comes to a neighbor's house and the neighbor asks him to stay for dinner, even if he is very hungry he will refuse to eat because it is contemptible and lowly in his eyes to receive a gift from a neighbor. Yet when the neighbor entreats him sufficiently, that is, until it is apparent to him that he will do him a great favor by eating, he agrees and eats with him. He no longer feels himself as receiving a gift and his neighbor as the benefactor."

Since we are of the Creator, we innately enjoy sharing, and we innately do not like to receive free gifts all the time. We certainly enjoy free gifts every once and a while, and some even more than that, but over time no person would enjoy only receiving unearned free gifts.

Let us say you come to your friend's house, and the friend asks you to eat. You might be starving and have a real desire to receive that food, but you would be embarrassed, since you do not want to inconvenience your friend. Yet you are still starving. So you say, "No, I am not going to receive," because you do not want to receive that gift from your friend. But if the friend insists and says, "Please, I really want to feed you," and you see that by allowing him to give you a meal it is actually fulfilling his desire. So you say "Okay." But what are you saying okay to? You are saying, "I realize that this is going to give you so much pleasure, so I am willing to allow you to prepare a meal for me."

In Rav Ashlag's parable, the man went to his neighbor's house, and his consciousness is, "I want to receive for myself alone. I am starving. I wish I had a great meal in front of me now." But he resists and stops himself. So when his friend says, "I can prepare for you a great meal," he says, "No." The neighbor still keeps on begging until the man says, "Okay, I will allow you to feed me." It is a real transformation that he goes through. He makes a decision: *I am not going to eat, unless it is going to give him pleasure. I no longer want to receive because I am hungry. The only reason why I want to receive is because it is going to give my friend pleasure.*

The crucial distinction here is that it is not enough that my friend also experiences pleasure in hosting, while I also enjoy and satiate my hunger. Two things must happen. First, a total rejection of my Desire to Receive for the Self Alone. A rejection of satiation. Only then can I develop a new way of receiving, which is to give the other person pleasure. The food is still coming to that hungry stomach. My hunger is going to be satiated through the food, but my consciousness has completely changed. Whereas, in the first moments the reason why I wanted to eat was to fulfill my selfish desire, I now have come to a complete transformation of my desire.

I think many of us had experienced this either from the one side or the other, where, you still want to Receive for the Self Alone, but you do not want the person to know that you are receiving for yourself alone. Therefore you let him beg, so that he now thinks that he is doing you a favor, and you know that he thinks he is doing you a favor, but you are still only doing yourself a favor. You are still only fulfilling your selfish desire. This is not what we are talking about.

What we are talking about is going through a transformation. You begin with a selfish desire, you want to fulfill what Rav Ashlag calls the Fourth Phase. You want to have the meal, and your friend is asking you to have the meal, so the Light is there and the Vessel is there. But you say, "No. I am not going to eat as long as my eating is for the purpose of fulfilling my selfish desire to Receive for the Self Alone." Then you wait. You wait until, on the one hand, you see that your friend is really going to have pleasure from your eating. And this second part, which is much more difficult, you come to the point where although you are starving, you are not eating to fulfill that desire. You are only eating to give pleasure to your friend. This is what the Vessel goes through when we talk about Returning Light and Binding by Striking. It is a very deep and important transformation of consciousness.

The true concept of Returning Light (Ohr Chozer) is when we have actually transformed. *When I eat that steak, I do not have any sense of pleasure for myself. The only sense of pleasure that I have is that my friend is now enjoying giving me. It is true that my stomach is being filled, it is true that my hunger is being satiated, but my selfish desire is not being satiated.*

When we grasp what this means, we realize how tremendously difficult it is to achieve this consciousness because although we are satisfying our hunger, we are not satiating a selfish desire to eat, and the only sensation we experience is the pleasure our friend is experiencing in giving us this meal. This is a very important distinction to make because the Fourth Phase, the Desire to Receive for the Self Alone, cannot be a Vessel; selfish desires cannot be filled. The challenge is that the Vessel into which the Light is going is still the same—the stomach is the same stomach. However, what is the consciousness, what is the desire behind it? Rav Ashlag continues:

> "Although hunger and appetite is a Vessel of Receiving specific to eating and the man was sufficiently hungry and had enough appetite to accept his neighbor's meal, he could not taste anything due to shame. But when the neighbor began to entreat him and he kept refusing, new Vessels of Receiving for eating began to be fashioned in him, since the neighbor's power of entreaty and his own power of refusal, while increasing, will eventually join into the sufficient amount to turn his attribute of Receiving to the attribute of Giving. Eventually he can imagine himself doing a favor and giving satisfaction to his neighbor by eating."

Rav Ashlag stresses here that this is true Returning Light. It is the battle of forces between my friend's Desire to Share, and my pushing back of my Desire to Receive that creates a new consciousness, a new type of receiving—a Receiving only for the Sake of Giving Pleasure.

I recommend reading this parable again and again, because when we understand this process, we realize that this constant battle against our Desire to Receive for the Self Alone and the pushing of Desire to Share encapsulates our entire purpose in life. The Creator's Desire to Share will be the process by which we transform our selfish Desire to Receive into what it is meant to be. In this step of the process that is receiving through Returning Light—receiving only when it gives pleasure to the Light of the Creator or to someone else—you come to a place where you really know and feel that by eating it, *I am doing him a favor.* Your consciousness is: *When I eat that piece of steak, I am not enjoying it in a selfish way.* When we truly grasp what this means, we realize how far we are from this reality.

The reason this is confusing is that the steak is still going into our mouth. In addition, we have used these taste buds for so many years to take in and enjoy selfishly, so it is difficult to now come to a place where we can eat that piece of steak, be doing our friend a favor, and not enjoy it in a selfish way. Obviously this cannot happen through one meal or one situation. Rav Ashlag makes it very clear, this pushing of two forces is a lifetime of work.

> "Then Vessels of Receiving are formed concerning his neighbor's meal. It is now considered that his power of rejection turned into the main Vessel of Receiving for the meal, rather than the hunger and the appetite, even though they are actually the usual Vessels of Receiving."

I want you to think about this teaching until you are sure that this distinction is clear. The Ari and Rav Ashlag are talking about a reality where not only is the other person transformed but we have also transformed, which is more important. *I have transformed through the process—I no longer taste selfishly, I only taste the pleasure that I am giving my friend as he enjoys me eating the steak that he has prepared.*

Rav Ashlag continues in the *P'ticha LeChochmat HaKabbalah* ("The Introduction to the Wisdom of Kabbalah"), Section 16:

> From likening it to two neighbors, we can understand the said subject of Binding through Striking (*Zivug deHaka'ah*) and the Returning Light (Ohr Chozer) rising due to it, which become new Vessels of Receiving for the Supernal Light instead of the Fourth Phase. The issue of the Striking of the Supernal Light hitting the Curtain (Masach), trying to flow to the Fourth Phase can be likened to the neighbor's entreaty to eat with him. Just as he desperately wants his neighbor to accept his food, so too the Supernal Light wants to flow to the recipient. The matter of the Masach striking the Light and pushing it backward can be likened to the rejection and refusal of the neighbor to accept the dinner—rejecting the favor. Just as you find that it is the refusal and rejection that turned into the proper Vessel of Receiving to receive the neighbor's dinner, so too can you imagine that it is the Returning Light rising due to the Striking of the Masach and its rejecting the Supernal Light that turned into a new Vessel of Receiving for the Supernal Light—instead of the Fourth Phase that served as a Vessel of Receiving before the First Contraction (Tzimtzum Alef). This was only established in the Partzufim of Holiness of Atzilut, Briyah, Yetzirah, and Asiyah. In the Partzufim of the Klipot, however, the Fourth Phase serves as a Vessel of Receiving. The reason they are separate from the Supernal Light is that the change of form of

the Fourth Phase separates them. Thus the Klipot and the Wicked are considered dead. They are separate from the Life of Life by their Desire to Receive. Understand this because it cannot be explained further.

It is important to understand that whenever Rav Ashlag says, "it cannot be explained further" this is one of those concepts that you have to allow the brain to absorb and mull over repeatedly because the true depth of comprehending comes through the constant pondering of it.

The only way to receive after the Tzimtzum, and remain connected to the Light of the Creator, is through Returning Light. Meaning receiving without partaking any pleasure in the receiving, and only taking pleasure in whatever pleasure the giver is experiencing. This is the only way to receive Light and still be connected to the Light of the Creator. For those of us who take our study seriously, this concept is something we need to truly take days, if not weeks, to really internalize because unfortunately this new way of receiving is still contrary to the way most of us receive, and may be contrary to some of the ways we even understand our spiritual work.

Therefore, when we look at our spiritual work and assess our spiritual progress, what becomes clear is that only to the degree that we have elevated and perfected ourselves—where we partake greater and greater pleasure from someone else's joy—is the degree we can receive the Light of the Creator. When we really look at ourselves, we will, unfortunately, see how much greater is our partaking of pleasure for ourselves in the Fourth Phase through selfishness than the pleasure we partake of when others give to us or in the pleasure that others receive.

What has to be clear is that after the Tzimtzum, the only way truly to receive Light, the only way to connect to the Light of the Creator is to grow our Vessels of Returning Light (Ohr Chozer). This is the basis of all of our spiritual work; it is the basis of the teachings of Kabbalah, and this is certainly the basis of Rav Ashlag's revelations. To grow our ability to partake of pleasure when others are having pleasure in sharing with others is the only type of Vessel connected to Holiness, to the Light of the Creator.

Each of us has to take a stock of our spiritual lives and determine how much of our Vessel is of the Fourth Phase—meaning that the pleasure we are feeling is because we are receiving. How much of the joy and the fulfillment we have in our lives is from the Vessel of Returning Light, where we are partaking pleasure in someone else's pleasure in sharing with others? To be clear, to whatever degree our Vessel is of Returning Light is the degree we are connected to the Light of the Creator. To whatever degree our Vessel is of the Fourth Phase, of taking internally and enjoying it just in ourselves, is the degree we are disconnected from the Light of the Creator.

If we really internalize this, we begin to realize how far we are from where we are meant to get to because the ultimate purpose of our lives, and of our spiritual work, is to come to the point where the only pleasure we feel is in sharing with others or in another's pleasure in giving to us. This is the only Vessel within the realm of our work that can keep us connected to the Light of the Creator. And of course the beauty of this is that there is no way that we will ever receive as much fulfillment as when we truly begin living with this type of Vessel because only a sliver of Light (*nehiru dakik*) can come into the Vessel of the Fourth Phase—into the Klipot or the Vessels of the Desire to Receive.

Light that comes into the Vessels of Returning Light is endless. Pleasure experienced in sharing with others, or pleasure felt in someone else's pleasure in giving, is the only connection one can make to the Endless Light. This is something that Rav Ashlag says cannot be explained further. Again, my sincere hope is that we take the time to both clarify and internalize this, and look at our lives based on this understanding.

The next step then is to define what we have to begin doing differently to really develop these Vessels of Returning Light within us because this is the ultimate. Everything else that we are doing should only be to awaken true Vessels of Returning Light within ourselves.

This is called "connection," since this Returning Light that rises from the Masach of the Fourth Phase, from the Straight Line grips and holds the Supernal Light in the Circle. This is done in such a way that wherever the Returning Light does not clothe the Supernal Light, that Light is considered, from the standpoint of the emanated, as if it did not exist, since the Emanated Being cannot attain it without the clothing called Returning Light. This shall be explained later.

The Light that comes from the Light of the Creator is called Direct Light (Ohr Yashar), and can only be bound into the Vessel, to us, through Returning Light (Ohr Chozer). This Returning Light is the only way to make Light shine in the Circular Vessels of the Endless World. Light that does not have a Vessel of Returning Light is considered as if it is not there. Of course, it is an illusion; the Light is always everywhere. Yet as far as the Vessel is concerned, whatever it does not bind through the Vessel of Returning Light, is not there.

Let us assume one person is able to take pleasure in giving 20% of his time in a day, and 80% of his time in receiving. This means that the only amount of Light he can receive that day is 20%. If the next day, this person is able to perfect himself more and take pleasure 30% of his day in sharing with others, the Creator could then give him 30% of His Light, and so on, and so forth.

The only way the Light of the Creator is attached to the Vessels, to us, is to the degree that there is a Vessel of Returning Light. Eventually, of course, the purpose of our lives is to come to the point where all the pleasure we receive day in and day out is only in sharing with others or in the pleasure that others are receiving when they are giving to us. Remember that the Light of the Creator is always around. However, as far as the Vessel, we, are concerned, the only revealed Light that we can receive is to the degree that we have a Vessel of Returning Light. To whatever degree our pleasure is taken in receiving for ourselves alone, the Light of the Creator is concealed from us. There is no way around this.

> This resembles, in spite of the great difference, a wax candle. So even though the main ability to shine comes from the amount of wax in it, the Light is not connected to the wax but to the wick. When the wick is consumed, the candle is extinguished, even though much wax still remains.

Rav Ashlag compares the Light of the Creator to the wax of a candle. A candle containing enough wax to shine for 100 days, with a wick that can only shine for ten seconds, will only shine for ten seconds. Similarly the Light of the Creator is Endless, it is always here for us but can only shine to the degree that we partake pleasure in sharing.

To be clear, this is not about how much we share, it is about our essence. Let us not fall into the trap of simply thinking that because we spent 80% of our day sharing that we are now going to necessarily receive 80% of our

Light, because the actions we do are only a tool to change who we are in our essence. Through sharing 80% of our time, we will come to the point one day where we partake pleasure in sharing in 80% of our being. The determining factor of how much Light of the Creator is revealed to us is our essence, who we are, what gives us pleasure. It is not about the actions—how much sharing we do—it is about how much we have transformed our essence. Therefore, actions of sharing are simply ways to enable a transformation of our essence.

The degree that my essence feels pleasure in giving is the wick, and the Light of the Creator is the wax. When the wick is done, the light goes out no matter how much wax the candle has. The Light of the Creator is endless and is with us endlessly, but it can only shine to us depending on size of our wick—how much of our essence partakes of pleasure in giving. To whatever degree our being, our essence has transformed, is how much of the Light of the Creator will be revealed to us. This is everything. It encompasses all the Wisdom of Kabbalah. We need to keep integrating this concept, making it part of our being, because this is the entire work we came to this world to do.

Before we go further there is a beautiful teaching from the Ohev Yisrael (Rav Avraham Yehoshua Heshel of Apt) that I would like to share with you. He says that one of the ten tests for Abraham was given to achieve his ultimate level of perfection was when the Creator came to him and said, "Leave your house where you were born, the house of your father, and go to the land that I will show you." (Genesis 12:1) And immediately after that, the Creator said, "From you, I will make a great nation, and I will give you endless blessings." (Genesis 12:2) The Creator gave Abraham an entire list of amazing blessings that are going to come to him when he listens to what the Creator asks of him. The Ohev Yisrael asks, "What kind of test is this? Why is 'leave your house' considered one of the tests of Abraham?" If God said to us, "I want you to take a long trip, and afterwards you will be the wealthiest person in the world. You will be the leader of the world, everyone will know that all the blessings of the world flow from you," I do not think there is one person who would not take that trip.

The Ohev Yisrael explains that the test of Abraham concerned his motivation. Was Abraham going to go because this is what the Creator wanted him to do? This is the way the Creator wanted him to reveal Light in the world? Or was it because of all the blessings that Abraham knew he was going to receive? The test was how pure could Abraham be. Could Abraham hear that he will have endless blessings, endless wealth, and still only go because this is what the Creator wanted him to do?

If God came to us and said: "Do the spiritual work and I promise that you will be the wealthiest person in the world. All the blessings that people want will come through you," could you imagine any of us being able to now do the spiritual work only because it reveals Light in the world and will help other people? This was the test of Abraham, and is the test we have in our world. Either we have the choice every day to partake of pleasure selfishly, which seems like the shortcut, the easy route, or we can do the difficult work of transformation.

---

12. **...is via that aforementioned Line:** The reason is that there is no Masach among the Circles to raise Returning Light, without which the emanated has no connection to the Supernal Light, as said before (in Section 5). It has been explained there that the Vessel of the Line is termed by the word "Channel," and it is greatly inferior to the Circular Vessels that were revealed with the First Contraction (Tzimtzum Alef) before the emergence of the Line, look there for the reason. Therefore, the Rav [the Ari] teaches us that even though the Circular Vessels are significantly higher than [those of] the Line, they nevertheless receive no Light through their own initiative. All the Light in them, they are obliged to receive through this much inferior Line, for the said reason.

This concept is beautiful just in simple understanding, but it also holds a tremendous life lesson. There are the perfect Vessels that once felt and partook of the Endless Light. Now there is the Line (Kav) or the Channel (*Tzinor*), which is a much more diminished, much darker way of receiving Light—Returning Light. Now the only way for the Circular Vessels to receive Light is through these darkened Lower Vessels, which is an inferior way of receiving.

There is a concept in the Talmud that states, "One should never disregard the blessing of an ordinary person." (Tractate Megillah 15a) There is something about our world that came into effect here that makes it so that Lower Realities reveal Light for Higher Realities. We have a beautiful new reality here, where the Lower Reality of the Line can shed Light to the Higher Reality, which is the Circular Vessels. The Baal Shem Tov, and certainly the students of the Baal Shem Tov, talk about the holy thieves—this concept that in our world, even though the Lower Realities are obviously much less perfect, much less pure than the Higher Realities, the only way for the Higher Realities to receive Light is through the less pure ones.

This revelation has many ramifications. Whenever we feel ourselves on the lower end of the spectrum spiritually, we should remind ourselves that although there are two realities—the pure Circular Vessels of the Endless World and the lower reality of the Line—the only way for the perfect Vessels to receive Light now is through these imperfect Vessels.

4. The Ein Sof encircles and surrounds it from all its sides,[13] since it too is in the aspect of a Circle[14] all around it and far from it, as previously mentioned. It is stipulated that the Illumination of the Endless upon Emanated Beings would be via that Line alone because if the Light had been drawn to them from all around them as well,[15] then the Emanated would have been in the aspect of the Emanator Himself, without limit or ration.[16]

13. **The Ein Sof encircles and surrounds it from all its sides:** Within each Sefirah we distinguish two kinds of Light that are called: Inner Light (Ohr Pnimi) and Surrounding Light (Ohr Makif). The Light that is clothed within the inside of the Sefirah is called Inner Light, whereas the Light that cannot be clothed inside its interior, due to the boundary there, is considered as remaining in its root, and [the Sefira] receives from it an illumination from afar that is called Surrounding Light. The Rav [the Ari] teaches us that even though the Circles are far from the Ein Sof, meaning that the Difference of Form between them is very great, they nevertheless receive a kind of illumination from the Ein Sof from afar called Surrounding Light. It shines in two ways: generally and particularly. "Encircling" indicates the general Surrounding Lights, while "surrounding" indicates the particular Surrounding Lights.

This is the first time in the Study of Ten Luminous Emanations where there is a clarifying discussion of the Surrounding Light. The Ari explains that the totality of the Light of the Endless World cannot shine into this new reality of the Line because there has to be only receiving through the Vessel of Returning Light. Yet now there is a new concept called Surrounding Light where Light encircles and shines to a Vessel that does not deserve that this Light shines to it.

As mentioned previously, if the Light of the Endless World shined into the Vessel, even into the Fourth Phase—a Vessel that Desires to Receive for the Self Alone—the Vessel would be swallowed up within the Light of the Endless World, and not achieve the purpose for which the Tzimtzum occurred. This would cancel out the desire of the Vessel for the removal of the Light to allow it to transform itself and achieve a higher level of Unification (*Dvekut*) with the Creator.

Rav Ashlag explains that there are two types of revelation of Light; there is Internal Light and Surrounding Light. Light that is manifest within the Vessel is Internal Light. Surrounding Light cannot become manifest within the Vessel because of a barrier that is an exact measurement of how much Light a Vessel can receive and still only receive for the Sake of Giving Pleasure. Therefore the Vessel, we, at every point have to make a very important decision: How much fulfillment can we receive and still take no pleasure in the receiving, but only take pleasure in the pleasure that this gives the Creator to give me? Meaning, the only sense of pleasure that we get out of this receiving is that we know that the Creator wants to give this to us. This is called Inner Light. The barrier exists when the Vessel is unable to receive only for the Sake of Sharing. Of course we know that this is only from the Vessel's perception because the Light of the Creator shines everywhere, all the time.

We should clarify the following concerning this section of Rav Ashlag: firstly—and this is true in our lives—there is now a barrier between us and the Light of the Creator, and this barrier is the basis of any lack of fulfillment that we have in our lives. Something that many of us, unfortunately, still have not realized yet is that in the world in which we live the Light cannot come into a Vessel that wants to solely receive and enjoy from that receiving. This has to be clear to us.

How much of what we have in our lives can we honestly say we receive pleasure from only because we know that the Creator enjoys giving it to us? It is not that we enjoy receiving it and the Creator enjoys giving it to us. If we are still taking pleasure in this Light, there is a barrier, this Light cannot come in. I think for many of us this important thought process is foreign—it is something we do not often think about, if ever.

How much are we trying to develop an ability to diminish our selfish Fourth Phase Desire to Receive the Self Alone, and awaken a Returning Light within ourselves? And if we are honest with ourselves, we are very far from this consciousness. This is something that is beyond most of our awareness. However, the reality is that this is where we need to get to.

In The Wisdom of Truth, Rav Ashlag quotes the Rambam as saying that there are certain concepts that you do not teach to someone right away. And this specific concept we are discussing here is one that you do not teach people right away because, as he says, you have to know if that person is ready to hear it. I hope we are all ready to hear it, and understand that this is where we need to get to.

I think people sometimes get confused with the concept of Receiving for the Sake of Sharing, which is probably an intermediary step, meaning I can enjoy it also, and give pleasure while I am selfishly receiving it. We have to get to a higher level than this. We have to get to a level where the only joy we partake of in the receiving is the pleasure that it gives the Creator to give to us. When we look at our lives and wonder why we only have a small amount of fulfillment, it is because inherently we, the Vessel, know that if the Creator gave us the other 95 percent we would be enjoying it selfishly.

In the Vessel of the Fourth Phase, Light cannot be revealed because there is an unbreakable barrier between fulfillment and the Vessel. And this barrier is: How much of that will you enjoy selfishly in your Fourth Phase Vessel, and how much of that will you enjoy only for the Sake of Sharing? And whatever that number is, is where the barrier is. This is the first concept.

The second concept is the Surrounding Light, which I am very excited to discuss in a deeper way. In the Endless World, the pure shining Light of the Creator shined without looking at whether the Vessel deserves or does not deserve this Light. After the Tzimtzum there was the revelation of the Straight Line, meaning if you deserve you receive Light and if you do not deserve you do not receive Light. There is an exact barrier so that to whatever degree we can bring ourselves to partake of the Light of the Creator only for the sake of giving pleasure, this is how much we receive; anything more than that we cannot receive. Much of what Rav Ashlag is revealing to us concerning this new reality of the Line is the exactness of this Light.

Now suddenly there is this new concept of Surrounding Light (Ohr Makif), where even though we do not deserve this Light, it shines to us "from afar." What does "afar" mean? In this World of Straightness (Yosher) after the Tzimtzum, Light only shines if we earn it, if we deserve it, if we transform ourselves to the point where we remove the barrier so that you can receive more Light. It is an exact World, it is a World of Judgement (Din). So how does this concept of Surrounding Light suddenly fit in? The fact that the Surrounding Light still shines to us, to the Vessel, seems like one of those concepts we cannot fully comprehend.

The Creator says to the Vessel, "You said you need the Contraction (Tzimtzum), you need to perfect yourself even further, so we will create this whole Illusory World of the Line where the Light only comes in if you earn it, if you transform yourself enough." The Inner Light is this new illusion that the Vessel wanted and needed to create. But the Creator cannot help Himself. The Creator loves us so much, so He says, "For your game, you, the Vessel can only receive Inner Light if you make this transformation. Nonetheless I have got to shine. I know this Light is for you and I cannot give you all of it right now, but I have got to shine to you something from the perfection, something from the totality." This is the Surrounding Light. The Surrounding Light is the expression of the Creator's love to us. The Creator says, "I cannot help myself. I love you too much. I know you have not earned it, and you do not deserve it, but as far as I am concerned, in the Endless World, the Light shines forever."

I hope everyone is as excited as I am about this new understanding of the Surrounding Light. The Creator cannot help but shine the Light of the Endless World. In this Illusory World we still live in, no matter how much the Vessel tries to create barriers and realities where this Light does not shine, "the Ein Sof encircles and surrounds it from all its sides." Although the Light cannot become complete Inner Light, nevertheless the Light of the Endless World still has to shine.

This concept of Surrounding Light manifests in many ways in our lives. I am sure we have all had these moments, where we have a realization or feeling, which we are aware is not something we have earned and not something that is part of us, but is from beyond—this is the Surrounding Light. Hopefully, we taste it every once in a while.

Very often when people begin their spiritual work there is excitement and they are gung-ho, and it is great for a little while but then the real work starts, and this is when people start dropping off, when people stop growing. The Baal Shem Tov explains that when a person begins their spiritual work, the Creator shines to them Light from this Surrounding Light that they do not deserve. However, as this is not their Inner Light, it cannot last. This shining of the Surrounding Light is necessary because without the Surrounding Light, forget it, we have no hope. This is why, very often in the beginning of one's spiritual work there is much excitement and desire to push ourselves to grow and comprehend more. However this is not earned excitement, this is something that is not ours. It is not our Inner Light, it is the Surrounding Light. And as the Baal Shem Tov teaches, eventually we want it to be taken away, and it is taken away; this is where the work begins.

As we continue in our spiritual work, it is important to know that whenever we receive these gifts of Surrounding Light, it is not something that was earned but is something that shines from the Endless World. All of us should be striving to keep getting these gifts from the Surrounding Light.

Another significant lesson this teaches us—which is something the Rav always did with almost everyone, and that was to talk to them about something that was beyond their comprehension or understanding. Why? In these instances, the Rav was shining Light to them from their Surrounding Light. The idea being that if we keep a person within their Inner Light, they are never going to grow.

The task of a teacher is not to simply assist a student to manifest their Inner Light, more importantly, it is to awaken to them their Surrounding Light by teaching them things that are beyond them. Not everything of course—you do not want to completely blow someone out of the water—but you do want to make sure that you always teach something that is a bit beyond them because only with this connection to their Surrounding Light is there hope that they will really grow.

As we continue with this study, the Ari shows us that the Surrounding Light is the driver of our change. The Vessel, we, had this great idea that we are going to earn the Light but the reality is that if everything had gone as we had planned, it would have been over. The Vessel, we, would never have come back to Cleaving (*Dvekut*) with the Light of the Creator. As we will learn and the Ari and Rav Ashlag make very clear, without the Surrounding Light pushing on us, the Vessel, to receive more and more, the Vessel would never awaken itself enough to receive the Light of the Endless World. We need to understand that the Vessel's plan was so flawed; that if not for the Creator's abundance of kindness and caring, this transformation would have never occurred. Now we understand even deeper that the Endless World surrounds and shines to the entirety of the Vessel in this new reality of the Line.

This is one of these concepts that you can only speak about so much but it is something to really grasp because based on our understanding is how much of that Light we receive. It is important to really deepen both our knowledge and also our appreciation for the Surrounding Light. Every time we comprehend something, every time that we have a connection that is beyond us, it is important to thank the Creator for this shining of the Light of the Surrounding Light because we do not deserve this Light. The shining of the Light of the Endless World to us is a gift that the Creator sort of slipped in that does not make sense within this whole process. Not only is it awesome to have, but certainly without it is impossible for this process to end with the Final Correction (Gemar haTikkun).

---

14. **Since it too is in the aspect of a Circle:** He teaches us that this Surrounding Light (Ohr Makif) that the Circles receive from the Ein Sof shines on and encircles them from all their sides, that is, in all Four Phases. Even the Fourth Phase where the Inner Light (Ohr Pnimi) does not shine receives an illumination from afar by means of Surrounding Light from the Endless. The reason he gives is that the Ein Sof "too is in the aspect of a Circle," which means that the Light of the Endless is called Circular Light since it does not differentiate between the stages but shines and fills the Fourth Phase as well (as said in Volume 1, Inner Light Chapter 2, Section 3, look there). Therefore, its illumination even reaches the Fourth Phase of the Circles, albeit from afar, as explained.

This teaching has many important, positive ramifications. Even in this place that—based upon what the Vessel had created—was going to be completely dark, the Light of the Endless World still shines. Thus, in its simplest form, Surrounding Light is the Light of the Endless. And although we receive some of this Light, for it to shine even in the Fourth Phase—the Vessel of the Desire to Receive for the Self Alone—is a tremendous reality. Although this is the one place where, from the moment of Tzimtzum until the Final Correction, the Light no longer shines—yet this Surrounding Light does shine.

So there are two types of Surrounding Light. The first type concerns the transformation of the Vessel. As mentioned previously, if we can enjoy only 10% of the Creator's gifts to us for the Sake of Giving Him pleasure in this giving, we only receive 10% percent of this Light. The other 90% of fulfillment does not come internally but shines as Surrounding Light. The second, even deeper type, shows the true love of the Light of the Creator to the Vessel of the Fourth Phase that only Receives for Itself Alone. Even though this Vessel is meant to remain dark from the time of the Tzimtzum until the Final Correction, it still receives Surrounding Light.

Thus, there are two completely different levels of Surrounding Light. One is the potential of our Vessel within this process of Correction. The second is beyond comprehension; it is that the Light still shines into complete darkness. No matter where a person is at in their life, whether he is "unmet potential," which is the first level of Surrounding Light or whether he is in complete darkness, the Surrounding Light shines there. I hope this is clear, and that we take the time to go over and really grasp and understand the beauty of Surrounding Light (Ohr Makif).

---

15. **The emanated would have been in the aspect of the Emanator Himself:** See above, Section 10.

16. **Without limit or ration:** The Tzimtzum and the Masach formed over the Fourth Phase so it would not receive Light within it is what creates a "limit" on the Light, for it limits how far it can extend, as [this Light] stops at the border of the Fourth Phase. The entirety of the reception of the emanated, which was diminished due to the Tzimtzum, is called "ration."

---

5. And so, this first Circle that is the most attached to the Ein Sof is called Keter of Adam Kadmon.[17] Then this Line extended further, was drawn a little[18] and again curled and formed a second Circle within the first Circle.[19] This is called the Circle of Chochmah of Adam Kadmon.[20] It then extended further down, curled again and formed a third Circle within the second Circle and was called the Circle of Binah of Adam Kadmon.[21] And so in that manner it continued to extend and curl, all the way until the tenth Circle that is called the Circle of Malchut[22] of Adam Kadmon. Thus we explained the subject of the Ten Sefirot,[23] that were emanated according to the secret of Ten Circles, one within the other.[24]

Rav Ashlag and the Ari explain that there is this strange reality where the Light cannot come directly into the Circular Vessels that existed in the Endless World because the Tzimtzum necessitated a world where the totality of the Light of the Creator is not revealed. "Circular" meaning that they have no barriers, no upper and lower, they are perfect Vessels that can receive all the Light. Therefore, the Light that is revealed in this First World of Adam Kadmon (Primordial Man) has to be revealed through the Line, through a diminishment of the Light, and can no longer be received internally, selfishly, in the Desire to Receive. The only way to receive in this new reality is in sharing; by giving to others is the only way we can receive.

With this description of the Ari and Rav Ashlag, we have to be very careful not to imagine physical circles within circles. The words "it is within," inform us that this is a lower level of consciousness, a lower level of connection, meaning it is the effect of the one before it. We have to be very clear—these Vessels exist always.

This teaching helps us truly appreciate the revelations of Rav Ashlag. Although one can read this literally and mistakenly think that these Circles are forming around the Line that is expanding, it is not true. As the Ari and Rav

Ashlag explain, these Circles are the original Circular Vessels of the Endless World. And as was explained earlier, we need to remember and retain all these concepts in our mind all the time.

These Circles always exist, but what is happening now in this new Reality called Adam Kadmon is that Light is being revealed to them through the Lower Vessels called the Line. It is the Line that is changing, not these Superior Circular Vessels that are being created.

The Ari says this new reality called Adam Kadmon has Ten Circular Vessels that each receive their Light through the Line; through a different diminished form of receiving. Here the Light revealed is dependent on how much is the Vessel's Desire to Receive Light only for the Sake of Sharing, only for the Sake of Giving Pleasure to the Creator. Whatever that amount is, is how much Light is received. Obviously in Keter, which is the purer of the Vessels, there is a larger Desire to Share more and therefore Keter can receive more. In Malchut, which is the lowest, there is the least Desire to Share, therefore less Light is revealed in Malchut.

The difference between the Light that is revealed in Keter, Chochmah, or Binah of Adam Kadmon and so on, is dependent on how much Light the Vessel desires to receive and not enjoy selfishly, but only enjoy it for the Sake of Giving Pleasure to the Creator. For instance, in Keter, the Vessel Desires to Receive 100% of the Light only for the Sake of Sharing. In Chochmah, the Vessel Desires to Receive only 90% of the Light for the Sake of Sharing, and therefore only 90% of the Light is revealed, until Malchut. The further down we go, the further we are from the Endless World in Similarity of Form, the less Light that is going to be revealed. This is the way Light is revealed in this new World of Adam Kadmon.

There is a beautiful teaching in the Portion of Bamidbar concerning the counting of the Israelites. The kabbalists explain that the purpose of the counting in the portions of the Bible is to create an attachment between the lower Terrestrial Man, us, and the Upper Man, the Adam Kadmon (Primordial Man) because unfortunately what happens is that throughout our incarnations all our negative actions sever this attachment between Terrestrial Man and Adam Kadmon, the Original Man. And Rav Ashlag explains in the Table of Questions and Answers at the end of this Volume that although Adam Kadmon is way beyond where we are now, it is our source and is eventually where we need to arrive at.

It says in the Midrash regarding the verse, "which I command you this day" (Deuteronomy 11:13) that every day the words of the Torah should be new to us. So it is important—especially for those of us who have been around the Centre for a while and are familiar with the terms like the Five Worlds of Adam Kadmon, Atzilut, Briyah, Yetzirah, and Asiyah—that we always look at the teachings anew, as if it is our first time. Therefore, each of us can and should take at least a good twenty minutes or more to try to figure out what each term we learn means.

For instance, why, after the Tzimtzum, did the Creator call this almost untouchable First World, Adam Kadmon (Primordial Man), when the Names of the Worlds of Atzilut, Briyah, Yetzirah, and Asiyah do not refer to human beings? In fact, as the Ari explains, most of our work has to do mainly with the Worlds of Briyah, Yetzirah, and Asiyah; we hardly even deal with the World of Atzilut. Yet the First World, Adam Kadmon, is the one where humanity is mentioned. I am sure that there are many secrets here.

What I am saying is that we not just simply take a term that we have heard many times and accept it as such, accept that this is what it is called. We should delve deeper. For instance, if the First World of Adam Kadmon, there must be tremendous layers of significance to it. It is important to take the time—like Rav Ashlag is going to do here—to talk about the Names of the Sefirot, and the Names of the Lights. There is a lot that we can uncover besides having a profound intellectual understanding but also in feeling these Names and Lights, sensing them, and connecting more deeply to them.

---

17. **This first Circle that is the most attached to the Ein Sof is called Keter of Adam Kadmon:** We need to understand the distinction in the naming of the Ten Sefirot. Sometimes we call them Four Phases, as mentioned before, and sometimes by the Names Yechidah, Chayah, Neshamah, Ruach, Nefesh. And sometimes we call them Keter, Chochmah, Binah, Zeir Anpin (which itself comprises six Sefirot) and Malchut.

It is important to note that Rav Ashlag's revelation is twofold: to give us an explanation and to awaken in us a desire to delve deeper into these teachings and not just accept them as is. Although here he does not explain the why and what each of the Names of the Sefirot represents, he does awaken us to the fact that we should not just accept it, and know that there is a reason for each

Name, and there is a reason why at different times we use different Names. There is a system here, and the only way to connect deeper to the system is to constantly question: "Why is Keter called Keter? Why is Chochmah called Chochmah? Why do we sometimes speak of the Four Phases and sometimes talk about the Sefirot?"

Whenever we come to the terms Nefesh, Ruach, or Neshamah, we are not discussing the totality of the Vessel, we are simply talking about the Light that goes into the Vessel. It is also interesting to note, as we said earlier, that usually when we mention our soul, we are speaking about the Neshamah. We do not even discuss Chayah and Yechidah, which represent the Upper Worlds—Adam Kadmon and even Atzilut—because most of our connection is to the last three Worlds of Briyah, Yetzirah, and Asiyah. But, as Rav Ashlag says, never to forget that our original connection, the source of our reality is Adam Kadmon, the First Man.

The idea is that when we discuss the aspect of the Vessels specifically, meaning the material aspect of the emanated alone, we define the Names of the Ten Sefirot as the Four Phases in the Desire to Receive, as mentioned before.

But when we discuss specifically the aspect of the Light that is clothed within these Vessels, we then call them Nefesh, Ruach, Neshamah, Chayah, and Yechidah. And when we discuss the Vessels alone, but we need to emphasize the Impressions of the Lights they have within them when they are emptied of the Light associated with them, we then call them: Keter, Chochmah, Binah, Zeir Anpin, and Malchut.

The origin of the Ten mentioned Vessels, named Keter, Chochmah and so on, are immediately distinct in the World of Tzimtzum before the emergence of the Line, after the departure of the Light of the Endless from the Ten Sefirot, when the Vessels remained empty of Light. These are called the Ten Circles, as mentioned earlier.

Here Rav Ashlag explains that whenever Light that was once in a Vessel is removed, it leaves a Residue, an Impression that never goes away. This is a tremendous revelation. Whenever we hear or read the terms Keter, Chochmah, Binah, Zeir Anpin, and Malchut, in the Zohar and other writings of the kabbalists, this is discussing the lack that is in the Vessel, and the Impression that is left.

In the Endless World, where all Vessels are filled, there is no Keter, Chochmah, Binah, Zeir Anpin, and Malchut. There is Nefesh, Ruach, Neshamah, Chayah, and Yechidah, there is the Four Phases. We cannot refer to them as Keter, Chochmah, Binah, Zeir Anpin, and Malchut because those terms for these Vessels only represent when these Vessels are lacking, and they have this Residue left in them.

I hope we all appreciate how huge this revelation is because one of the dangers with studying from a young age is that even when we get older we still look at what we have studied with the eyes of our youth. For instance, some of us began studying the Torah when we were three years old, which is obviously a very shallow level of comprehension, and the hope is that as we get older, we come brand new to it and our understanding is deeper.

But unfortunately what the Negative Side wants us to do is just add on to what we know and not completely throw out what we think we understand and come to it fresh and brand new. This is true certainly of all of us, and even for someone who has been studying for five years. If a person comes to the study after five years and in his mind he thinks, *Now I will add to what I know*, what he is building upon is lack because what he understood when he was in his first week of study is very little. If the knowledge that he then gains in the years after is based on what he gained in the first few years, then he is basing it on a tremendous amount of lack.

In the Prologue of the Zohar it says that before a person prays, they have to connect to Abraham, Isaac, and Jacob, and certainly also to the great kabbalists like Rav Shimon bar Yochai because if our work begins from where we are now, we can accomplish very little. However if we take the work of Abraham, Isaac, and Jacob, and we consciously think: *I am working on top of their work*, then whatever we do can bring the Final Correction (Gemar haTikkun).

If a person views their work as their own, it will take them a million years to get up to what Abraham, Isaac, and Jacob achieved; maybe after a hundred and twenty years they will be at the lowest levels of the work of Abraham, Isaac, and Jacob. Yet there is this gift. There is this trick. We are able to attach our consciousness and ourselves to Abraham, Isaac, and Jacob, as well as to Rav Shimon bar Yochai. And when we do this, whatever we are doing can accomplish tremendous things, can bring the Final Correction (Gemar haTikkun).

It is important that when we come to something that we have learned or to concepts that are already somewhere in our mind, we consciously think: *I want to push all that aside, I want to learn this brand new because hopefully now I am smarter. I have more information. I am in a higher place spiritually and am able to receive more.* If this is not the way we come to this wisdom then we build on lack and that will not get us anywhere. When we study with someone from the Zohar or any of the writings of the kabbalists, even if we know a concept, it is better not to simply repeat it but to go back to the book and read it and explain it to them from there, because if we are explaining it to someone from our memory we are giving over to them whatever we have. We are not giving over to them from the kabbalist. This has many ramifications to it, but the most important one is to make sure, as much as we can, that every time we come to study, whether it is Zohar or the Talmud Eser Sefirot that we have studied from already, to always try to push aside all the earlier knowledge that we have and come brand new to it.

To summarize what we have learned: Rav Ashlag explains that whenever we refer to Keter, Chochmah, Binah, Zeir Anpin, and Malchut, we are referring specifically to the Vessels that once had Light that has left and only a Residue of this Light remains in them. The first time this ever occurred with the Circular Vessels, the Vessels that once had the complete Light in the Endless World, was before the World of Adam Kadmon. After the Tzimtzum, where the Vessel requested the Light be removed, these Circular Vessels are now left lacking and only have a Residue or Impression of the Light. This is the only reality where the terms Keter, Chochmah, Binah, Zeir Anpin, and Malchut are referred to.

It is known that even though the Light left them, nevertheless what remained in each and every circle was an aspect of an Impression from the Light that was in them. In other words, a very small illumination from the entirety of the previous Light remained in each Vessel. This illumination causes the Vessel to yearn, so that it does not rest nor will be tranquil until it will again draw all the Light it had before in Its quantity and Its quality. This Illumination is called "an Impression." Know that the content of the Names of the Ten Sefirot—Keter, Chochmah, and so on—mainly defines the Impressions of the Light that remained in the Ten Vessels.

This concept of Reshimu (Impression or Residue) is both beautiful and remarkable. As an aside, I was re-listening to the tapes from when Yehuda and I first began studying the Talmud Eser Sefirot (Study of the Ten Luminous Emanations) with the Rav over twenty years ago. The first tape I listened to was all the way at the beginning. The Rav said that to understand the beauty of having this tiny spark of Light that holds within it every aspect of the Light that was once there and is left in the Vessel, is almost impossible. One of us on the cassette spoke about the concept of DNA as being the only way to connect to this concept.

Obviously, we are not talking about physical space or size, but rather in spiritual terms where a small aspect can contain everything else. This is a concept that is true throughout existence. For instance, the Midrash says that every letter of the Torah has the power to resurrect the dead, because if the totality of the Light of the Torah, which is the Tree of Life (Etz haChaim), has the power to resurrect the dead, then every aspect of the Torah has the power to resurrect the dead.

The Residue (Reshimu) of the totality of the Light that once was revealed in this Vessel holds within it, in its DNA, all of the Light that was revealed. This minute aspect has within it everything that was in the Ein Sof, and this is what awakens the desire in the Vessel. This is what pushes the Vessel to say, "I cannot rest. I cannot stop growing. I cannot stop changing. I cannot stop revealing Light because I remember that once I had more Light than this." Thus with every spark of Light we receive, our Reshimu is reminding us there was more.

Rav Ashlag gives us the foundational understanding of this concept. The words Keter, Chochmah, Binah, Zeir Anpin, and Malchut, do not represent Light, they represent the Impression or Residue (Reshimu). And if we truly want to understand what each of these words mean, we have to know that these Names represent an aspect of lack. Rav Ashlag explains that this concept of Impression or Residue (Reshimu) is basically the driver for all of our spiritual work. Thus, if we are lacking drive in our spiritual work this is because we are lacking a connection to the Reshimu. On a deeper level we are lacking a connection to Keter, Chochmah, Binah, Zeir Anpin, and Malchut.

As we are reading and studying this now—and hopefully all of us will be mulling over this concept of the Reshimu—we are not simply grasping its meaning, we are also awakening that feeling, that connection to the Reshimu. The only hope that humanity has, and each of us personally have, to truly accomplish what we came to this world to accomplish is for the Reshimu to drive us. When a person has a strong connection to this Residue of the Circular Vessels, the Residue of the Light that was in the Endless World, then they have a strong desire to do spiritual work. If they lack this connection to that Reshimu, they lack drive to do the spiritual work.

The way I view this section in the Study of the Ten Luminous Emanations is not so much as a study as it is a prayer from us to the Creator: "Please allow us to connect to the Reshimu." To the degree we are truly connected to the Reshimu, the Residue that each of us has within us of the totality of the Light of the Endless World that we once experienced, is how much spiritual drive we have. To the degree we are disconnected from the Reshimu, we are disconnected from our spiritual drive.

As the kabbalists teach, when someone experiences a certain difficulty, it is good to go to the particular section in the Torah and in the Zohar that deals with it and repeat this section repeatedly. These are the verses from Rav Ashlag to repeat repeatedly to awaken the Reshimu within us because this is our hope and the source of our hope. The reason all of us can slack off in our spiritual work is simply that we have not connected to the Reshimu. This study is not only to awaken the Reshimu within us but also to let us take this a step further; we want to awaken this Reshimu in the world. Once a person has this connection to the Reshimu, "this illumination causes the Vessel to yearn, so that it does not rest nor will be tranquil until it will again draw all the Light it had before in Its quantity and Its quality."

From here you can know that no desire can be fathomed throughout the Worlds, not even a slightest awakening of Desire—whether in the Upper or Lower Beings, and even among the physical Inanimate, Plant, Animal, and Human—that does not have its origin in the Ten Circular Sefirot.

All desires that are ever awakened in anything, in any aspect of Creation, stem from those Circular Vessels—from that Residue of remembered Light. For instance, when you are thirsty and have a desire for water—an aspect of this desire stems from the Residue. A tree has a desire to be watered; this desire comes from the Residue of the Circular Vessels. Rav Ashlag makes very clear that every single awakening of desire in our world, on all levels—whether in the Upper Worlds, Lower Worlds, Inanimate objects, Plant, Animals, or Humans—only stems from the Reshimu of the Circular Vessels, the Residue of the Light that we once had in the Endless World. This amazing concept by and of itself opens up so many gates of understanding and is one that we really have to constantly contemplate.

Along with this, we also understand that no Desire can be awakened at all in an entity, unless a sufficient fulfillment for that Desire appeared previously.

The idea is that it was already well explained in the first part of the Book (Volume 1) that the Desire to Receive is not the first cause of the Light or of its fulfillment, as people think, but the exact opposite. The Light and the fulfillment are the reason for the Desire, since the Desire to Share that is necessarily included in the Supernal Light brought forth from its quality, the Desire to Receive, within the emanated because what is a Desire in the Higher becomes an obliging force and stipulation for the Lower. Study there well. Thus, the Supernal Light became a cause for the revelation of the Four Phases in the Desire of the emanated, and these are the roots for all the Desires that appear in the Worlds.

Therefore, how can a Desire appear without a cause; that is, without the Supernal Light that produces it? This is like saying that there is a creature in the World without a mother and father that gave birth to it.

This amazing revelation of Rav Ashlag explains that our desires in this world are the opposite of what most people think. Why are we motivated to do things like eat? Is it because we are hungry? Rav Ashlag makes very clear in The Wisdom of Truth that the only reason anyone lifts up a finger is to fulfill one of his selfish desires, and we think that this desire is the cause, and the effect is the action that we take—which is backwards. The only way all levels of desire are awakened in our world is if there was a previous fulfillment of this desire.

The reason we have desires, experience needs and lacks, is that there is Light waiting to fill these desires, needs and lacks. And as we think about these two beautiful revelations, it becomes clear that they are obviously interrelated. First, Rav Ashlag says that all the desires that have and will ever be awakened in our world—great and small, good and bad, in the Upper Worlds, in the Lower Worlds, for physicality, for spirituality—all stem from the Impression of the Circular Vessels, that Residue of Light that once fulfilled the Vessels of the Endless World. The second revelation is that any awakened or felt desire, need, or lack is not the cause. It is an effect of existing Light to fulfill that desire. The reason we repeatedly read these concepts from Rav Ashlag is that these words awaken both an understanding in our mind and an awakening in our soul.

In the first moments of Creation, it was not the Vessel that drew the Light, it was not the Vessel that was the cause but rather the other way around. First came the Desire to Share. The Light of the Creator, the Desire to Share, created the Vessel, created a necessity, a desire for that Light to come into being. The First Cause in Creation and therefore the First Cause forever is the fulfillment, the Light. The Light is the cause of the desire, and the desire is the effect.

Rav Ashlag does not differentiate between good or bad desires, holy or impure desires. All desires come from the Reshimu of the Circular Vessels, from that Residue of the Light we once had. This means that in our lives, we each are given a specific quota of desire. The question is how we will use this desire—because desire once used is used. A person can awaken selfish desires and fulfill them. Selfish desires also stem from the Residue (Reshimu), and by awakening and acting upon a desire for negativity or for things that are of a selfish nature, we use up our reservoir of Reshimu and now unfortunately we have less Reshimu to complete our Tikkun (Correction). To complete our Tikkun, we need all of this desire—the full quota.

It is the Reshimu that pushes us to change, to grow. This reservoir of Reshimu that we have in our soul is what will push us from where we are now to where we have to get to, to fulfill our Tikkun. If a person has a hundred measures of transformation that he has to achieve in his life, and is therefore born with a hundred measures of Reshimu, then for every one degree of transformation and growth he has to go through, there is one degree of push of Reshimu. If a person takes this amazing reservoir of power (Reshimu) from the Circular Vessels, and uses up 50 measures for selfish things, unfortunately at that point, one could say the furthest he can get to in his Tikkun this lifetime is 50 percent of the way. He will not have the motivation, the drive to complete the final 50 percent because he has used up that reservoir on selfish desires.

We have to be careful in our comprehension of this because sometimes people can go to the extreme. Although this is not directly connected to what we are discussing, Rav Ashlag explains that every time we eat and drink, there are sparks of Light that we need for our correction in that food. One of the things we forget for all sorts of reasons, but mostly because our ego blinds us, is that we think things are not exact. Let us assume a person has to elevate a hundred sparks of Light to complete their soul in this incarnation. They are given a cup of water a day, containing a quarter of a spark of Light or however you want to quantify it. To elevate this spark of Light within this water, they can either say a blessing, meditate or once they have drunk the water, they can use the strength they receive from the water to reveal Light. In all these situations they have now brought their soul one-quarter of a spark of Light closer to their goal. Yet if they use food in random ways and do not elevate those sparks within the food, they have still used up this Reshimu. A person is not given an unlimited amount of sparks to elevate; we are given an exact amount.

Rav Ashlag reminds us that every spark of Light is given exactly and is necessary for our Tikkun. Although the realization that all of us have wasted some of these sparks may be scary, there are other ways of Correction. Certainly moving forward, I hope this awakens a tremendous amount of appreciation for everything that we are given and that we continue to ponder over these amazing revelations of Rav Ashlag because there is no way we can truly grasp what is being revealed by simply reading it once or even a hundred times. Every time we think about these concepts, we comprehend them on a deeper level. These are concepts that are not only necessary for our study, they are necessary for our true spiritual work.

First, Rav Ashlag says that our every desire stems from the Reshimu, the Residue of the once fulfilled Light that has come to us from the Circular Vessels. Second, no desire is ever awakened as a cause. Awakened desire is an effect of Light ready to be revealed. To take this further, this means that when a person has a great desire for something negative to accomplish their goal, they have awakened this desire all the way from the Vessels of the Ein Sof, from the Circular Vessels. They are grabbing this desire that can propel them to accomplish incredible revelations of Light, and by using it in this negative way, are literally sticking it in the ground. We need to know that when we use our Reshimu to accomplish some selfish goal, we are taking from our reservoir of connection to the Vessels in the Ein Sof, and now there is going to be less of it for us to complete our task in this world, Heaven forbid.

Therefore, every time we have a desire, we should know that this desire is not a cause of anything, it is an effect. It is Light ready to come to us, and now we have a choice as to how we are going to manifest this desire. Are we going to manifest it in a positive way, in a way to propel us forward or are we going to manifest it in a negative way? There are famous stories of the great Tzadik, Rav Levi Yitzchak of Berditchev (1740–1809), who would get very excited when he met people who were terribly negative. He would tell them, "If you take that desire and change it around you can reach the highest heights."

Even if a person becomes awakened with a great desire to do something negative, this desire is the Light telling them: "I am here to fulfill your Vessel." Yet, unfortunately, what usually happens is that we disregard this awakening and use it for the negative. It is important we know that every single awakening of desire, whether it manifests in our mind for something terribly negative or something extremely positive, is the Light of the Creator saying: "I want to fulfill you." This is the cause of that desire.

> You also already know that in the Ein Sof the entire existence and all the creatures worthy of appearing in the Worlds exist and are set, in all their magnitude and their utmost glory and perfection that is destined to be revealed in the Worlds for them (as is explained in Volume 1, Inner Observation Section 11. Study the whole section).

As a reminder, every time we read about the perfection that exists in the Ein Sof, we draw this perfection to our world. We take a step closer toward the Final Correction when we discuss this. Rav Ashlag is saying that in the Endless World all the Vessels were completely fulfilled, and every Vessel, everything in the world achieved its perfection.

> Evidently, all the Desires that are destined to be revealed already emerged and appeared in the Endless (Ein Sof), and they were also filled to their utmost completion and fulfillment. This completion and fulfillment, which is the aspect of the Supernal Light, is what produced and revealed those Desires. In such a way that the fulfillment of the Desire precedes and causes the revelation of that Desire associated with that fulfillment, as explained.

Now you shall understand well the matter of the Impressions (Reshimot) that remained in the Ten Circular Sefirot, after the Tzimtzum and [after] the disappearance of all the completion and fulfilments that were in these Four Phases, called Ten Circles. The meaning of these Impressions is that all kinds of Desires, which were filled while in the Ein Sof but were now lost from them, were well impressed and engraved in them. Therefore, of necessity, they remained craving and yearning for all those fulfillments and perfection they had—and this is what is called Impressions.

This is what we said before that no revelation of a Desire of any entity can be imagined, both in the Upper Worlds and in the Material World that does not have its root in those Ten Circular Sefirot, in such a manner that there are two roots that precede the existence of all post-Tzimtzum Worlds. One is where every Desire already exists complete in all its glory and fulfillment, and this is the reality that exists in the blessed Endless.

The second is where all Desires stand totally empty of the fulfillment associated with them from before, that is, from the Endless. This is called the World of Tzimtzum. All the Vessels and material of the Created Beings are drawn from the World of Tzimtzum. This certainly refers only to empty Vessels, and Desires that have lost their fulfillment, since the entire fulfillment for these Desires extend from the blessed Ein Sof. Remember these two facts well. They are among the most essential to remember throughout the study of this wisdom.

Rav Ashlag says these two facts are most fundamental and necessary, not just for our mind but for our soul. He explains that there are two sources for everything. There is the perfection, the fulfillment of all desires of all beings that exist in the Endless World, and then there is the complete lack of fulfillment with Residue that exists in the World of Tzimtzum. Since we are the creations, our matter, our essence is from those Reshimu, those Vessels of the World of Tzimtzum. And the fulfillment of our desires, the fulfillment of our Light and the bringing of the Final Correction is to connect the World of Tzimtzum, which has the Vessels with the Reshimu—complete lack but with a Residue of Light—and the Endless World, where the perfection exist. The melding together of these two Worlds is our spiritual work.

The root of everything that ever comes in the future comes from these two concepts: the perfection of the Ein Sof, and the complete lack in the World of Tzimtzum where the Light was removed. These two are the sources for everything that follows. And Rav Ashlag says we have to make sure we remember this throughout the study.

In *Resheet Chochmah* ("The Beginning of Wisdom"), Rav Eliyahu de Vidash, a student of Rav Moshe Kordovero, writes that you cannot be living your life with two types of desire. To the degree that one has a desire for selfishness, a desire to fulfill his Desire to Receive for the Self Alone, he diminishes his amount of desire for the Light of the Creator. He says that these two desires are like fire and water that cancel each other out.

If we want to be able to fulfill our Tikkun, we have to make sure that we are pushing ourselves to awaken the desire that is rooted in the Circular Vessels of the Endless World and not abuse it nor push it down to the Klipot but instead use it for its purpose. Therefore, every desire that is ever awakened within us has only one purpose—to reconnect us back to the Circular Vessels so that we can have the one and only true desire in the world, which is to connect once again to the Endless Light of perfection.

---

18. **Was drawn a little:** Do not mistakenly interpret that it was drawn to a place and area, Heaven forbid. Rather, the process of anything becoming denser is called "drawing from above downward" because the pure is considered to be above and the coarse is considered to be below. This is gauged by the Similarity of Form to the Fourth Phase, because whatever is closer to the Fourth Phase is considered denser, and whatever is farther from it is considered purer. "Drawn a little" means that it became a little denser. The words "was drawn" refers to the Light of the Line.

Here Rav Ashlag is revealing to us another very important spiritual concept. Whenever we come across the concept of drawing of Light, it means that the Light is becoming less pure and more coarse. Anything that is becoming less spiritual, less pure, more of the Desire to Receive for the Self Alone, is called the process of being drawn down. When we come across this concept of "drawing Light" *lehamshich*, what we are actually discussing is Light being diminished, Light being adulterated in some way, Light being drawn closer toward the Desire to Receive for the Self Alone. When we say something is more pure, this means more removed, farther away in consciousness from the Desire to Receive for the Self Alone.

We each experience the Light of Shabbat, the Light of the Holidays, even the study of the Zohar, in a different way. Why? Let us assume it is Shabbat and two individuals are each on a different spiritual level, so the pure Light of Shabbat comes down and becomes increasingly less pure to the person who is on the lower level. This distance between spiritual levels is not distance in space or time but distance in spiritual purity. They are both drawing the Light of Shabbat from the same Source, but as the Light has to be drawn down lower and lower, it is, of necessity, becoming coarser and coarser, less and less pure. Therefore, their experience of a connection has to be different because their connection depends on where they are in their purification process. Where we are spiritually tells the Light what kind of Light we can experience. If someone is on a lower level, more selfish, more disconnected, more in Difference of Form with the Light of the Creator, and receives the Light from a higher level, they would not be able handle it, they probably could not even appreciate or feel it. Therefore, in this process, the Creator has to reduce the Light even more.

To help us understand this concept, Rav Ashlag brings a parable about two individuals who performed the same great favor for a king. One of them was relatively smart and appreciated the good things in life so the king paid him back in gold coins. The other person was not very bright, and the king knew there was no point in giving him gold coins because he would not know what to do with them; he would not appreciate them, so the king brought him a meal, a good steak because he could enjoy and appreciate that. The goodness flowing from the king to both of them was the same; the king wanted to do good for both of them.

This is the process each of us goes through, and the Light goes through too, in dealing with us. The Light observes our level of Difference of Form and determines how coarse and how diminished the Light has to be for us to experience it. The lower, more selfish a person is, the coarser, less pure is the Light. Every time we make a connection, depending on where we are in our purification process, is the experience of the Light that we will have. Therefore everyone's experience in the same connection will always be different.

The second idea, related to this, is that in our World, Light that is drawn will always go from the purer to the less pure. This is a spiritual law. Just like water, Light can only go from higher to lower. Rav Ashlag, in the Wisdom of Truth, in describing the love that needs to exist between friends, says that every friend has to look at the other friend as if he is the greatest person in the world, regardless of whether it is true or not. This is the only way a person can develop spiritually. Why? Because every person that we interact with has something that they can share with us, regardless of whether we are smarter than them or more spiritual than them. Every person has something that they can give us and that we need to receive from them.

But if we perceive that we are higher than another individual, they will never be able to share with us because the Light cannot flow in this way. In our world, the Light flows from the higher, purer level to the lower, coarser level. The only way we can receive from others is if we put ourselves below them. Even if it is not true, we still have to create this illusion in our mind because then we can receive from them. This is a very important concept.

The explanation of this "drawing" is that in every single Sefirah there exists Ten Sefirot, which is the case both in a Sefirah of the Ten Sefirot of the Circles and a Sefirah of the Ten Sefirot of Straightness. When the Ten Sefirot of the Sefirah of Keter came forth, the Line first emerged in the aspect of its Upper Three Sefirot [Keter, Chochmah, Binah], which is called the Head of Keter of Straightness. Its illumination extended to the Sefirah of Keter of the Circles, which also comprises Ten Sefirot, as mentioned earlier. These Ten Sefirot of Keter of the Circles encircle only the Upper Three Sefirot of the Ten Sefirot of Keter of the Line.

Afterwards, when the Ten Sefirot of Keter of the Circles were totally completed, then "this Line extended further" and "was drawn a little," which means it produced its Lower Seven Sefirot to complete the Keter with Ten Sefirot of Straightness. In such a way that these Lower Seven Sefirot of Keter of the Line were drawn downward, that is, they became coarser than all the Ten Sefirot of Keter of the Circles. Therefore no aspects of Circles encircle upon these Lower Seven Sefirot, since the Circles are higher than them, meaning purer. And as you already know, whatever is higher than its neighbor is purer than its neighbor.

This can be a little confusing, so please read it as many times as needed because it is important that we first understand the basic technology before we delve into its spiritual ramifications.

Why is this so? Why is there an affinity between the First Three Sefirot of the Keter of the Line and all Ten Sefirot of the Circles? And what does it mean? We are not discussing physical concepts here of the First Three and the Lower Seven Sefirot. The Ari and Rav Ashlag refer to the First Three Sefirot as the Head (*Rosh*), and the Lower Seven as the Body (*Guf*). The difference between the Head and the Body is that the Head is where decisions are made while the Body is where those decisions are carried out.

We know that in this new reality after the Tzimtzum, the Vessel said, "I will receive Light only if I can receive it for the Sake of Giving Pleasure to the Creator. Whatever amount of Light I do not feel I am ready to experience only for the Sake of Giving Pleasure to the Creator, I do not want and cannot receive." But it is a two-step process. For instance, say there is someone who realizes that they are gaining weight—that they want to lose—because they eat too much bread and meat. First, before every meal, they have to make a decision not to eat the slice of bread or the huge steak but I rather have a little chicken with vegetables. Then their arms and hands can cut the chicken and vegetables and they can eat this food. The decision is in the Head where nothing becomes manifest. Manifestation occurs with the Body.

The thought process of the Vessel, after the Tzimtzum, deciding that it will only receive Light to the degree that it can Receive it for the Sake of Giving Pleasure to the Creator, occurs in the First Three Sefirot. When we discuss the First Three Sefirot of Keter of the Line, we are talking about the consciousness within which the decision is made. There is no actual receiving or manifestation of Light in the First Three Sefirot. The Lower Seven Sefirot is where the Light is received and manifestation occurs.

From the spiritual standpoint, the Head (First Three Sefirot), does not even want to manifest the Light; it is not in a rush to manifest the Light—which is a more elevated, purer level of being. Clearly there are two realities. There is the place that makes the spiritual decisions: "How much can I Receive for the Sake of Sharing," which is a higher, more elevated, purer state of being. And there is the Lower Seven Sefirot, which is the reality where, after that decision is made, the Vessel says, "Okay, let me receive that Light, but make sure that I am Receiving only for the Sake of Sharing." The actual receiving and making sure is in the Body.

This is true throughout the study of Kabbalah. Whenever we discuss the First Three Sefirot and the Lower Seven Sefirot, or the Head and the Body, we are talking about levels of consciousness. It is almost as if the Head is the gatekeeper and the Body is the person who receives it. I hope it is clear because it a tremendously fundamental and important understanding.

The First Three Sefirot is a much more elevated state because it is a place where no Light is drawn or revealed into a Vessel; it is where the decisions and the discernment of how much Light can be received only for the Sake of Giving Pleasure in the Lower Seven Sefirot are being made. Rav Ashlag and the Ari tell us that it concerns the affinity. The Similarity of Form between the First Three Sefirot is greater with the Creator than the Lower Seven Sefirot because the Lower Seven Sefirot are the places where Light already comes into the Vessels. There is more of a taking in the Lower Seven Sefirot; it is of a lower spiritual purity.

Therefore, all Ten Sefirot of the Keter of the Circular Vessels, which are pure since they have come completely and directly from the Endless World, have affinity with the First Three Sefirot because both are in a much more elevated state. Whereas the Lower Seven Sefirot called the Body, is a coarser, less pure spiritual state of being. It is where the Light becomes manifest. Therefore, the Circular Vessels do not have as much affinity with the Lower Seven Sefirot.

There is a famous adage in the Talmud that states, "Rav Yehuda said that Rav said, 'Each and every day a Divine Voice emerges [from Mount Horeb] and says, "The entire world is sustained by [the merit of] My son Chanina [ben Dosa], and [yet for] Chanina, my son, a kav of carobs is sufficient from Shabbat eve to Shabbat eve."'" (Tractate Ta'anit 24b) This is the same idea here. Rabbi Chanina ben Dosa lived in the Level of the First Three Sefirot. He said, "This is what the world needs to eat, this is what I can give to the world. For me, I want just a little bit of carob." The Head is the purer place that does not want to receive, it just wants to see how much it needs to give the Body; how much the Body can handle.

Rav Ashlag said the Ten Sefirot include Ten Sefirot within them. I have to say, this was a concept that I could not grasp the first few times I learned it with the Rav. I did not understand its importance. It seemed relatively arbitrary to me that each Ten Sefirot has Ten Sefirot within it. Knowing there are billions and billions of Sefirot within every Sefirah almost loses its meaning and one's grasp on reality. It is like standing in the Hall of Mirrors at the amusement park. Suddenly there are hundreds of images of you in mirrors upon mirrors all around you, and you are not even sure where the exit door is or where to go because everything is so confusing in this almost infinite reality.

But there are tremendous lessons to learn from this. For instance, before we do any Mitzvah (Precept), we recite a prayer called *LeShem Yichud* (For the Sake of Unifying) that says, "I am performing this particular Mitzvah or prayer, with all the Mitzvot included with it." The kabbalists explain that every single spiritual action has at least an element of all 613 other spiritual actions within it, giving us an understanding of the limitless potential of every action. From this idea, I realized that even atoms, the lowest level of physical matter, as well as the lowest level of spiritual matter, the lowest spiritual action, has within it an aspect of everything else in the world. Nachmanides (the Ramban) says that through one spiritual action a person can complete all 613 Precepts.

Let us assume I would like to drink some water and before I do, I make the blessing on the water, thus revealing a tiny speck of Malchut of Malchut. But this Malchut of Malchut has Ten Sefirot within it. What are these Ten Sefirot that are within Ten Sefirot? These are aspects of everything else that exists in the world. These are aspects of every other reality in the physical and spiritual worlds. Thus when I make this blessing, I realize that with this one blessing over the water, I am touching every aspect in our universe. Every action that I do connects a millionth of a millionth of Malchut of Malchut because every Ten Sefirot has Ten Sefirot within it, has Ten Sefirot within it, and so on. A single action connects all these billions of Sefirot within everything, which is why it is necessary for there to be an endless amount of Ten Sefirot within even the minutest of essences of reality because everything has to touch everything. Since every action I do, every infinitesimal spiritual Light I reveal, encapsulates an endless amount within it —endless to the extent it includes everything. It touches upon everything, it touches upon everyone, it touches upon every aspect of Light in our world.

We may think that to make a blessing on water is not such a big deal. Yet do you know how many billions of Sefirot you are touching? Do you know that those billions of Sefirot are not just arbitrary Sefirot out there; they have attachments to all the other billions of Sefirot everywhere else in the world? They have attachments in everyone else in this world and in the spiritual Worlds as well. We are influencing not only billions of Sefirot but more directly we are connecting to everything and everyone else in the world.

This is something that always excited the Rav. When science began discovering the unbelievable depth of reality that exists in the smallest amount of matter, it became apparent how much more so it is in the spiritual realm. We can use this revelation of science of the physical matter and apply it to the spiritual matter. To know that everything has an endless reality within, and that this endless reality touches upon everything else is incredible.

The reason for this is understood by what was explained earlier (Section 12) that the Circular Sefirot precede and are more valuable than the Linear Sefirot, since there is no aspect of Masach whatsoever in the Circles.

Now we are going deeper into the explanation of why this is so and what it means. After the Tzimtzum, the Vessel wants to draw the Light back, yet in this new reality it will receive Light that it knows it can only Receive for the Sake of Giving Pleasure to the Creator. This is represented by the Ten Sefirot of the Line. The Circular Vessels that existed in the Endless World had no Masach, as they were fine to receive Light for themselves alone, and thus they can only receive from the First Three Sefirot of the Line, and they do not receive from the Lower Seven Sefirot of the Line.

Rav Ashlag explains that Ten Sefirot of the Circular Vessels are much more elevated, purer, more connected to the Light of the Creator than the Sefirot of the Line, because the Circular Vessels are the perfect, untouched Vessels of the Ein Sof. The Line is a new way of receiving that restricts the Light to the degree that the Vessel can Receive It only for the Sake of Sharing. The Circular Vessels do not care about any of this; they are the Vessels of the Ein Sof. The Creator wants to share, they want to receive and can receive.

The World of the Line within which we live is a lower level of receiving because the Masach, this whole calculation of the barrier for Receiving for the Self Alone, comes in. We can only receive in this watered-down version of receiving, which is Receiving only for the Sake of Giving Pleasure. However the higher, purer, stronger, better way of receiving, in real terms, is the Desire to Receive for the Self Alone—the Circular Vessel's way of receiving in the Ein Sof, before there were calculations and the whole concept of a Masach.

This changes our whole perspective on receiving. We usually think selfish receiving is much lower and more coarse than Receiving for the Sake of

Sharing. And although that is true, it is only true in our limited World of the Line. In the True Reality of the Ein Sof it is the higher way of receiving.

This Curtain (Masach) that is present in the Sefirot of Straightness is situated in the center of the Sefirah, namely in the last aspect of the Head of the Sefirah, meaning in the last aspect of the Upper Three Sefirot of the Ten Sefirot of Straightness that exist in each and every Sefirah of Straightness, as mentioned earlier, which are also called the Head of that Sefirah.

We understand that each one of these Ten Sefirot is divided really into two parts. There is the Head (*Rosh*) and there is the Body (*Guf*). The Head is still pure and does not have the Masach. In the Head's understanding the Vessel can receive endlessly, so there is no need for a Masach. The need for a Masach is in the Body, where it begins calculating how much it can Receive only for the Sake of Sharing. Here Rav Ashlag explains that the Line, the Masach, the barrier for the Light begins after the Head, the First Three Sefirot: Keter, Chochmah, and Binah. What this means in essence is that Keter, Chochmah, and Binah are not restricted by how much they can Receive for the Sake of Sharing.

When we said that the Curtain (Masach) is included in the Linear Sefirot, this relates to the Lower Seven Sefirot of each Sefirah, which are situated below the Masach. This is not the case with the Upper Three Sefirot, which is called the Head, as they have no aspect of Masach, since they are situated above the Masach.

Consequently, these Upper Three Sefirot are completely similar to all the Ten Sefirot of the Circles since they both have no aspect of Masach yet, and therefore they are of the same category. So it is considered that the Ten Sefirot in each Sefirah of the Circles encircle the Upper Three of each Sefirah of the Line. However, the Lower Seven Sefirot of each Sefirah of the Line, which are already below the Masach, and the Masach is already included in them, are more inferior to the aspect of the Circles. And we know that whatever is inferior to its neighbor is considered to be lower than its neighbor. They are therefore considered to be below all the Ten

Sefirot of the Circles, and no aspect of the Circles can be found in the place of these Seven Sefirot, since the Circles are more important and superior to them, as explained.

Thus, it has been well explained that there is a vacant space between each and every Sefirah of the Circles, as the measurement of the Seven Sefirot of the Sefirah of Straightness located there. All Ten Circular Sefirot of the Sefirah of Keter encircle only the Upper Three Sefirot of the Keter of the Line, but the Lower Seven Sefirot of Keter of the Line are drawn below all the Ten Sefirot of Keter of the Circles. After these Seven Sefirot of Keter of the Line finish, the Upper Three Sefirot of the Sefirah of Chochmah of the Line begin to emerge, encircled by all Ten Sefirot of the Sefirah of Chochmah of the Circles. Thus between the last aspect of the Keter of Circles until the first aspect of the Chochmah of Circles there is a vacant space, within which exists the Lower Seven Sefirot of the Keter of the Line, around which no aspect of Circles encircle. It is the same way between Chochmah and Binah, and the rest of the Sefirot.

I hope this is clear, if not, please reread this section as many times as necessary until you have clarity. The Ari and Rav Ashlag make a distinction between the Head and the Body. The Head is the place where we make decisions. However, nothing manifests in the Head; manifestation occurs through the Body. Therefore, even though after the Tzimtzum the Vessel can now receive when it receives only for the Sake of Sharing, in its Head it has to decide how much pleasure it can receive only for the Sake of Giving Pleasure to the giver. When the mind decides that it can Receive only one degree of pleasure for the Sake of Sharing, it is now the gatekeeper for the Body and allows the Body to experience only one degree of pleasure because the Head (brain) has decided this is how much pleasure the Body can Receive only for the Sake of Sharing. This is why there is a difference between the Head and the Body.

This new reality that exists in the Keter of the Line, also exists in our world. A student of Rav Ashlag once asked Rav Ashlag what kind of job he should look for. Rav Ashlag told him to take a job where he would use his body and not his mind, because it is better use up the body for something mundane and not the mind because the mind is of a higher consciousness. Thought (*Machshava*) is a very powerful tool because our mind is connected to the perfect Circular Vessels (Kelim D'Igulim). Therefore, it is possible for a person to become connected in his mind in one second. Now for the body to come along it might take a much longer time; but in our mind we can be connected to perfection in a second.

In these Worlds that are now emerging after the Tzimtzum, the Head, or the First Three Sefirot—Keter, Chochmah, Binah—can correspond to the Circular Vessels. They can be one. This is also true for us. Our mind, even before our body, can be unified with the Circular Vessels. When we realize what this means, we also understand the danger of using our mind in a negative way. Every morning, when we recite the Sacrifices (Korbanot), there are sacrifices that are brought specifically for negative thoughts. Negative thoughts are very dangerous because they damage on a higher plane, and if these thoughts lead to actions, it is even worse because they have manifested. Since our Head corresponds to the Circular Vessels, this means that when we damage our thoughts, Heaven forbid, we are damaging some of our connection to the Circular Vessels.

When a person does negative actions with his body—although it damages, this damage is in the lower reality of World of the Line, in the World after the Tzimtzum. But when we damage our mind, we are damaging Circles, we are damaging on a much higher level. Hopefully, this awakens within us an appreciation for what we focus on. Unfortunately, throughout our lifetimes, we have managed with our thoughts and actions to maybe put coverings on our mind. But in its true essence, our mind is connected to the Circular Vessels.

A famous teaching from the Baal Shem Tov states: "Where a person's mind is, he is completely." With our mind we can be completely connected to the Light of the Creator, more so than with our body. There are stories of the Tzadikim who actually decided to leave their body because they realized that where their mind could take them in that moment, their body would still drag them down. The reason Nadav and Avihu, the two children of Aaron, left this world is because they realized that with their mind they would achieve so much more than they could with their body holding down their mind. Nevertheless this is not the level where we are at.

Hopefully this awakens in us is a greater appreciation for our mind and also the damage, God forbid, that negative, selfish thoughts can do. These negative thoughts damage on a higher plane than even actions because our mind is connected to the Circular Vessels. When we awaken thoughts of negativity, selfishness, Desire to Receive for the Self Alone, we damage our connection to the Circular Vessels. This may be a dangerous thing to say, but actions that we do without our mind damage much less than when we damage our mind. This is a very important understanding.

---

19. And again curled and formed a second Circle within the first Circle: You need to be very careful here not to get confused by imaginary descriptions of straight or circular areas and space, which befall our imagination due to the language style. Remember throughout this [discourse] that Straight Illumination means that the Light enters Vessels in which there is a Curtain (Masach) over the Fourth Phase, and a Circling Illumination means that the Light enters Vessels in which there is no Masach over the Fourth Phase.

The words *He'ara Yeshara* (Straight or Direct Illumination) represent a lower type of receiving that is within a Vessel that has a Curtain (Masach), meaning there is a barrier as to the amount of Light that can be received. Light can be received only to the degree that the Vessel can Receive it solely for the Sake of Sharing. When we discuss a Circular type of receiving, this type of receiving comes into a purer, more elevated Vessel that does not have the barrier, the Masach in it.

Rav Ashlag is revealing to us here the misunderstanding we have concerning the way the spiritual world works. We usually prefer things to manifest in a direct way, not in a roundabout way. We want to get the money, the understanding, right away. In reality, however, receiving directly is the lower way of receiving, and receiving in a roundabout way is a higher level of receiving.

Rav Ashlag discusses repeatedly the concept of certainty beyond logic (*lemala min hada'at*), which hopefully strengthens our understanding that our perception of how to receive is wrong. We want things to come directly, we do not want there to be an entire roundabout process. But in truth, the higher level of receiving is Circular Illumination (*He'ara Mitagelet*), a Circular type of receiving. There are many ramifications to this teaching.

Whoever has read from Rav Ashlag soon notices how he never goes from a question to an answer. For instance, in the Introduction to the Ten Luminous

Emanations, Rav Ashlag beings with a whole slew of questions. He goes from one topic to another and then comes all the way around to an answer. This is also true of the Rav, both in his lectures and in his writings. It is always Circular, never direct from one point to another.

Although most of us think direct lines bring clarity, the true connection to the Circular Vessels, the true connection to the Endless World, is Circular. This concept has a lot of manifestations in the way we view our work, how we want things to be presented to us, and the way we want our spiritual work to be. The more Circular it is, the more connected it is to its true essence.

In discussing Korach's mistake, the Pri Tzadik (Rav Tzadok Hacohen of Lublin) says:

> "The Ari explains that there are levels that are called the aspect of Circles (Igulim), and there are those that are called the aspect of Straightness (Yosher). The Circular Vessels existed before the Creation of our world. The Aspect of Straightness began in the world of Correction (after the Tzimtzum). In future times (Mashiach), the Circular Vessels will be completely revealed. This is the secret of what it says in Tractate Ta'anit 31a, 'in the future the Holy One, blessed be He, will make a dance (*machol*) for the Righteous.' Machol can also mean circular. And Korach's mistake was that he thought that after the Giving of the Torah, the revelation of the Circular Vessels had already occurred. Therefore he said, 'Everyone is holy…' (Numbers 16:3) since all the Israelites were on Mt. Sinai."

Unfortunately, Korach was wrong; Mashiach had not occurred yet. The Circular Vessels were not revealed yet. But we know that nothing written in the Torah is mentioned in vain. This is so beautiful. When Korach says, 'Everyone is holy and the Creator is within them,' (Ibid.) it means that the Creator is the central point and we are all back to the Circular Vessels. Through the words of Korach, no less, Korach reveals to us again the Circular Vessels. What Korach really said was, "Do you not know Mashiach has come already? Do you not know that the Circular Vessels are revealed again, and we can connect to them again?"

Rav Ashlag explains that two realities exist: First, the Reality of the Line, which is a diminished receiving of Light—the Vessel can only receive whatever amount of Light is solely for the Sake of Sharing. Second, a simultaneous Circular Reality where although in their essence the Circular Vessels can receive endlessly, after the Restriction of the Light, they can only receive whatever diminished Light this new reality reveals.

However, remember that even though there is no Masach over the Fourth Phase in the Circular Vessels, the Fourth Phase there still cannot receive any illumination after the First Contraction (Tzimtzum Alef), since all the Light that exists in the Circles must be received through the illumination of the Line, which is a Straight Illumination (as mentioned in Section 12), and the Light of the Line does not shine at all upon the Fourth Phase since it is drawn from the force of the Masach, as explained.

Rav Ashlag explains that we have two competing natures here—the essence of the Circular Vessels, which have no problem to Receive for Themselves Alone, and the essence of the Line, which is to only Receive when it is solely for the Sake of Sharing. In this new reality the Circular Vessels only partake of whatever Light the Line reveals, meaning at whatever stage this Vessel is it will receive a certain amount of Light only for the Sake of Sharing, and will give some of this Light to the Circular Vessels.

Thus, the lack of Light in the Fourth Phase of the Circles is not due to the Vessels, as they have no Masach, but rather due to the Tzimtzum Alef that resides on them. And since the Tzimtzum Alef is not considered a lack (see Volume 1, Inner Observation, Chapter 3) therefore all the Four Phases of the Circular Vessels are equal in rank without any difference between great and small (as said in Volume 1, Inner Light, Chapter 1, Section 19). All the darkness in the Fourth Phase is because of the Light that is received from the Line, as it does not shine there, as explained.

Rav Ashlag always makes clear that the reason things occur is as important as what is occurring. Therefore, when a lack occurs for a reason that is not negative, it does not cause any darkness, it does not cause any change. In the Fourth Phase, the lack of Light that is coming to the Great Circular Vessel is not because the Vessels do not have the ability to receive. They are the same Vessels that existed in the Endless World (Ein Sof); there is no barrier for them to Receive for Themselves Alone. The only reason they are not receiving is because of the original removal of Light, which as we have discussed previously did not occur because of any lack but rather because the Vessel wanted to elevate and perfect Itself. Here these perfect Circular Vessels that can receive endlessly are now receiving Light that cannot shine perfectly, cannot shine completely.

Now that these Circular Vessels are receiving diminished Light, has something changed within them? The answer is no. There is no change that occurs in these Vessels. The essence of the Circular Vessels is perfect, even if at this moment they are receiving less Light. The reason they are receiving this diminished Light is because something else is occurring—which in this case is the fact that the Line can only shine a diminished amount of Light. This very important concept teaches us that where our consciousness is, regardless of what is being manifested right now, is more important than what is happening. As long as the reason Light is not being revealed is because of a situation beyond the realm of our influence, that darkness or that lack of Light does not influence us.

The deeper we immerse ourselves in this Study of the Ten Luminous Emanations the more it stretches our mind. At this point, we realize that although the Circular Vessels are receiving less Light, so much so that their real Vessel, their real Desire is not being fulfilled, this does not influence their consciousness. The reason why it is not receiving great Light is not because of a change or a deformity in its own essence, but only from where it receives the Light.

For instance, when the sun shines into a room with enormous windows, it lights up the entire room. However if there is an eclipse and the sun is blocked, no light shines into the room. Most of us can clearly envision two different realities: one where the light is shining into the room and another where light is not shining into the room. The room itself does not change; the room's essence is not influenced by whether the light is shining now or not shining now because the cause for the light not shining is not its own defect, it is not its own spiritual disconnect.

I know this is complicated, nevertheless one of the practical lessons we can gain from this is that where our consciousness is, is what affects our connection, not what we do and what is happening. In the book And You Shall Choose Life, Rav Ashlag reveals something revolutionary. What makes someone a Tzadik (Righteous Person) who is connected to the Light of the Creator? And what makes someone Rasha (Wicked Person) who is disconnected from the Light of the Creator? Most of us will think that a Tzadik is someone who acts in the right way, shares, does all the right things, makes all the connections, and Rasha is someone who harms other people, who does negative things. Yet Rav Ashlag says this is the wrong way to view it.

We cannot discern a Tzadik and a Rasha by observing what they do. Rav Ashlag explains that what determines whether a person is a Tzadik or a Rasha, is how this person views the world. If a person sees perfection, sees only Light, they are perfect. If a person sees darkness, lack, and bad people, they are dark and negative. It is not the things we do, it is our conscious perception of the world around us that determines whether we are completely connected or completely disconnected. A person can be in complete lack, as the Fourth Phase is in this reality, but if their consciousness is of perfection, they are perfect. It is important to think about this fundamentally necessary concept until we grasp its meaning.

Rav Ashlag says, "there is no human being to whom the following three degrees do not apply: the degree of the wicked, the degree of the middling, and the degree of the righteous. They are called degrees because they are derived from the degrees of understanding His Providence." ("And You Shall Choose Life," Section 129)

I really hope that this revolutionary idea is clear because it is not the actions that we do nor the connections that we make, but our perception of the world around us, our perception of the manifestation of the Light of the Creator in the world that determines how connected we are. When a person's perception of the world around him is one of negativity, where he sees darkness and negative people, this is an indication that he is disconnected. This is who is given the name of a Rasha. Whatever other thoughts they have, whatever games they play, even things that they say, makes no difference.

What do we see when we look at the world? Do we see perfection? Do we see only good people? Do we see only the Light of the Creator? Unfortunately, most of us do not. Nonetheless if you want to know what the ultimate level of connection is—what is a Tzadik—it is someone who sees only righteousness.

With this you will understand that after the Circles received the Light through the Line, it caused a differentiation of great and small to be formed in them even in the Ten Sefirot of the Circles, where Zeir Anpin is superior and greater than the Fourth Phase, Malchut, since there is no

Light in Malchut whereas in Zeir Anpin there is Light, since He is the Third Phase. In the Sefirah of Binah of the Circles, the Light is greater than in Zeir Anpin, since She is farther from the Fourth Phase than He is; She being the Second Phase, and so on. However, all these grades are not due to the Vessels but due to the Light of the Line they receive. And remember this!

The point Rav Ashlag is making is that even though we have two realities—the reality of the Line, which receives a diminished amount of Light and the reality of the perfect Vessels, which can receive Light endlessly—when the Light shines in different degrees from the Line to the Circles, giving more Light to Keter, less Light to Chochmah, even less Light to Binah, and even lesser Light to Zeir Anpin, and no Light to Malchut, it does not affect change in the Circular Vessels.

The reason there are different levels of Light shining into the Circular Vessels is not because these Circular Vessels are different or lacking but rather it is because where these Vessels are receiving the Light from is different. Why is this important to know?

Many times in the Study of the Ten Luminous Emanations we are given two pieces of information that do not make sense together. And this is one such occasion. On the one hand there is a difference in Light being manifested on the Circular Vessels, but on the other hand it makes no difference, because the reason it is occurring is not because of something wrong in the essence of the Circular Vessels, but because of where they are receiving their Light.

For those of us who have been blessed to be around true spiritual teachers, this is a reality that we begin to sense. When a person truly is connected to the Light of the Creator, they are able to see two opposites coexisting. What's more, they can see that at the root level the differences do not make a difference to them.

This teaching also helps us understand the mistake of Korach. When Korach came to argue with Moses and Aaron, it sounded like Korach was a jealous, egomaniac who wanted the position of High Priest. In reality, as the kabbalists teach, Korach was a very elevated soul and had very strong, correct arguments. As a matter of fact, as Rav Ashlag says, there is no logical answer to Korach's argument; he was absolutely 100 percent correct. The problem with Korach is that these arguments caused separation. One of the lessons is that to cause damage, to cause pain to another person, even if you are 100 percent right and your reasons are right, can only be wrong. But on a deeper level what this shows us is that what Korach was lacking and what Moshe had, is the ability to see opposites; to see things that seemed to be wrong, that seemed to cause a difference, that seemed to cause a higher and a lower, that seemed to cause lack and Light, and still be able to see that it makes no difference.

This is a delicate spiritual level to arrive at. Certainly, those of us who had the merit to be around the Rav and Karen got the sense of what it means to connect to this level. All of Rav Ashlag's teachings are really based on this concept. We cannot begin to understand the Study of the Ten Luminous Emanations until we gain this consciousness.

Rav Ashlag explains that whatever is true in the Supernal Worlds is also true in our world. If we are not yet capable of seeing opposites, seeing someone who we can judge as lacking, as being diminished and realize that it makes no difference, then we cannot connect to the teachings of Kabbalah. This is what Rav Ashlag is teaching us here. Being able to see something that objectively seems dark, seems diminished, seems imperfect, irrespective of the reasons behind why, and still finding an ability within our consciousness and heart to say, "It makes no difference because the cause if it is not their own essence," this is true Kabbalah.

20-21. The Circle of Chochmah of Adam Kadmon... the Circle of Binah of Adam Kadmon: It has already been explained that this is how we call the Four Phases. Their root, namely, the Desire to Share included in the Supernal Light, is called Keter. The beginning of the extension toward the emanated being is the First Phase called Chochmah; the Second Phase is called Binah; the Third Phase is called Zeir Anpin or the six Sefirot: Chesed, Gevurah, Tiferet, Netzach, Hod, and Yesod; and the Fourth Phase is called Malchut.

There are only a few times Rav Ashlag mentions that one must make an effort to publicize a teaching, and one of them is when he discusses why it is so important to study Kabbalah. He says that when we say the actual Names of the Sefirot—Keter, Chochmah, Binah, Zeir Anpin, and Malchut—out loud, especially now in this section of the Study of the Ten Luminous Emanations where he explains each of these Names, we awaken these Lights from Above to shine to our soul. More important than any understanding we may gain, is the fact that we are saying these words: Keter, Chochmah, Binah, Zeir Anpin, and Malchut. This is the singular purpose of the study of Kabbalah and certainly of the Study of the Ten Luminous Emanations.

Rav Ashlag explains that each of us has a tremendous reservoir of untapped, unmanifested Light, and every time we say one of these words, one of those codes, a Light shines from our personal unmanifested potential reservoir of Light to our soul. Moreover, as we say these words repeatedly, this Light gets stronger and stronger, and we are able to manifest it. It is important to remember—especially here when we are now discussing the Names of the Sefirot and why they are named in this way—to know that the purpose of the study is not solely to understand but more importantly, it is to have a reason to use these words so that we can awaken this Light to our soul.

> It has also been explained that only when we discuss the primordial material in them, we name them the Four Phases and their root. However, when these Four Phases already include their Impressions as they were in the World of Tzimtzum, they are called Keter, Chochmah, and so on, as was well explained earlier.

We have discussed the concept of Reshimot (Impressions) previously, where although, after the Tzimtzum, all the Light and perfection of the Endless World was taken away, this Light left an Impression of Light. That Impression is our driving force. What drives us? Those of us who have a drive to grow, to connect to The Light of The Creator, to connect to the study, what pushes us? From where do we receive that drive? It is from the Reshimot, from the Residue, from the Impressions of that great Light that is in the Vessel.

When we use the terms Keter, Chochmah, Binah, Zeir Anpin, and Malchut, we are specifically referring to the Vessels with the leftover Impressions of Light. Therefore, on a deeper level, whenever we say the words Keter, Chochmah, Binah, Zeir Anpin, and Malchut, we are awakening within our own Vessel the memory of the perfection, the memory of the complete fulfillment we had in the Endless World. And in awakening these Reshimot (Impressions), we give ourselves the drive to connect to the Light of the Creator, to truly do our spiritual work. These Reshimot are our driving force.

It is important that we constantly remind ourselves of what Rav Ashlag said that the reason we learn the Study of the Ten Luminous Emanations is because we need to awaken this reservoir of unmanifested Light. It is said that without the spread of the study of Kabbalah, humanity does not have the tools to be able to reveal this reservoir of unmanifested Light and then, Heaven forbid, Mashiach and the Final Correction (Gemar haTikkun) cannot come. By studying and saying these words, and repeating them, we awaken these Reshimot (Impressions), and in awakening these Impressions time after time, we make ourselves able to manifest this Light and therefore bring about the Gemar haTikkun.

We shall now explain the reason for these particular Names. The root is called Keter (Crown) since it is not clothed in the Vessels of the emanated, but circles around and crowns it from outside its Vessels, and [the word] Keter כתר (or *katar*) is from the expression of encircling.

One of the understandings that this gives us is that the more elevated Light is Light that is not yet manifest. As Rav Ashlag points out, our perception of reality is very often the opposite of what is true. For most people, the greatest Light is Light that is manifested in our lives in the form of blessings. Yet in truth the ultimate Light, the highest level—Keter—is Light that is not manifest in a Vessel. Light that becomes manifest is further down the Line.

All too often, we are invested in the results. Even in our spiritual work, in our spiritual connections, we want the results right away. We want our Malchut right away. We do not want a connection to Keter—we do not want a connection to Light that is surrounding and crowns the Vessel—we want Light that is manifest. Yet to the degree that we have this type of a desire, we are pushing away the Light of Keter because manifested Light is the Light of Malchut, which is a much lower, reduced quality and quantity of Light.

Rav Ashlag explains that Keter is not really part of the Vessel, it is the seed or the Light that surrounds the Vessel before it becomes manifest. To connect to the ultimate Light, to connect to the Light of Keter, we have to come to the point where we desire Light that is not yet manifest. When you speak to successful people, it becomes evident that even on a physical level, when we are doing the work and are stressed and want the results to become manifest right away—even the results on the lowest level will not become manifest. On the spiritual level, of course, we know this also means that we will never connect to that Light of Keter. The desire to manifest the results right away in our world removes us and pushes us away from the ultimate Light of Keter.

Sometimes people would come to Rav Ashlag when they wanted a quick miracle in a certain situation and he would tell them, "This is not what I deal with." It is true that there is an aspect of the Light of the Creator that one can manifest quickly in the physical world, but that was not the work of Rav Ashlag, and hopefully, for those of us who are serious about our spiritual work, this is also not our goal. Our goal is Keter. Our goal is unmanifested Light. We must train ourselves to not be stressed about the results because if we are stressed about the results all the time or if we are focused only on the manifestations all the time—not even leaving an opening for the Keter (Crown), for the Surrounding Light, for the Light that is not yet manifest on the Vessel—we push away the greatest Light.

> The First Phase is called Chochmah (Wisdom) since from it comes the Wisdom of the Torah, as well as all forms of wisdom in the World in their final version.

The level of Chochmah holds within it and encompasses all of the wisdom of the world, not just all the wisdom of the Torah, all the spiritual wisdoms, but even the physical wisdom: sciences, physics, math, etc. Rav Ashlag also specifies that it holds the wisdoms "in their final version." Forget about the spiritual sciences, but even the physical sciences—most study is at a certain mid-point, not at the ultimate; physics are looking for a grand unified theory, they are still searching for the ultimate.

What is wisdom? Most people misunderstand wisdom to mean attaining a certain level of knowledge. However, Rav Ashlag makes very clear that if you are not connected to the ultimate complete state of wisdom, you have not attained Chochmah. You might have some knowledge, you might have gained some Da'at, but Chochmah, true wisdom, is the only wisdom in its ultimate form.

> Our sages, of blessed memory, have already defined this word very well by saying: "Who is wise? He who foresees that which is about to come."

> (Tractate Tamid 32a) Meaning, as soon as he looks at something he can see that which will come out of it, that is, he sees all the future outcomes from it until the ultimate result.

True Chochmah, true wisdom, is a level each of us needs to aspire to achieve. Knowing what has happened until now or even having a certain amount of information about depths of what is happening now, is not wisdom. True wisdom is being able to see what will come forth, what will be in the future. Wisdom means that you see everything that will become manifest from a situation or an object. You see in an atom everything that will happen to it forever. Wisdom is when you come to truly understand things at their source. You not only understand all that has happened until now, and all that is happening now, but you also have the ability to see into the future.

Therefore, it says, "A wise person is greater than a prophet" (Tractate Bava Batra 12a) because a prophet is given prophecy in a narrow view—to see the future in a certain instance. A *chacham*, a person who has truly achieved wisdom, who is able to see the ultimate result in every situation and in every object. There are certainly great righteous souls like the Seer of Lublin (Rav Yaakov Yitzchak haLevi Horowitz, 1745–1815), who have had this ability. Just by seeing a person's name, he was able to see everything that they have done, and everything that they will do.

One of the purposes of the study of Kabbalah is to come to Chochmah, to True Wisdom. Kabbalah is referred to as *Chochmat haEmet*, the Wisdom of Truth, the truth of everything. When we truly attain an understanding, a connection to the Wisdom of Truth, the Wisdom of Kabbalah, we gain the ability to see. Because of the Rav's connection to and mastery of the Wisdom of Kabbalah, he was gifted with the ability to see what will happen, not just what is going to happen tomorrow or the next day, but to see all that will manifest. As Rav Ashlag says, "he sees all the future outcomes from it until the ultimate result."

After Rav Ashlag passed away many people came to Rav Ashlag's house and grabbed all kinds of things that they felt they deserved, and the same thing happened when Rav Brandwein passed away. And the Rav said that there is only one thing that he was in pain that he did not take, because the Rav did not take anything; there was a letter that Rav Ashlag wrote about a lengthy vision he had experienced. At one point in his vision he had asked the Creator, "Give me the level of prophecy," and the Creator replied, "Do you not understand that I have given you way beyond that. Do you want me to put you lower than where you are now?" Rav Ashlag had achieved the level of Chochmah, he had achieved the level of seeing to the end of everything. Seeing to the end of everything is greater than prophecy because prophecy is simply the ability to receive a vision in a specific situation for a specific outcome. It does not give a wide view of everything. Chochmah (True Wisdom) is the ability to see the end in every situation.

And what is the ultimate true end? There is a beautiful commentary by Rav Yonatan ben Uziel in the Portion of Pinchas on the verse where the Creator gave Pinchas a gift: "My covenant of peace." (Numbers 25:12) In his Aramaic translation of the Torah he writes that at this point, Pinchas was changed into an angel with both the ability to see the future and be around for that future.

Before Rav Ashlag passed away, the last verse that he said was, *Orech yamim asbiehu ve'arehu bishu'ati* (Length of days I will satiate him, and I will show him My salvation.) (Psalms 91:16) This idea of being able to see the end, to see the Final Redemption (Gemar haTikkun) comes from the source of Chochmah (Wisdom). When an individual achieves True Wisdom through the study of Kabbalah, through the study of the Zohar, they are able to see the Redemption (Ge'ula) because if one can see the end of all processes, they see the end of the global process as well. Hopefully this awakens within us a true desire to achieve Wisdom (Chochmah). And we achieve Wisdom through the study of the Kabbalah, through the Study of the Ten Luminous Emanations, through the study of the Zohar.

In discussing the verse: "He gives wisdom to the wise." (Daniel 2:21), Rav Brandwein asked the Rav "If someone is wise, why give him wisdom? Wisdom should be given to the unwise. The wise already have the wisdom, so why give them wisdom?" Rav Brandwein then explained that this verse means that the Creator gives wisdom to someone who has the desire for wisdom. A person has to truly yearn for Chochmah (Wisdom), and this yearning combined with the study will bring him wisdom. Study without yearning, and yearning without study will not bring it. But if a person has a yearning, a true desire and prays for wisdom, and they study, they will achieve this level of Chochmah. Hopefully this awakens within all of us a true desire for achieving this level of Chochmah.

For example, saying a physician is very wise means that in every disease he examines, he clearly sees all the possible outcomes that can emerge from that disease, to the last result. So too when he examines a certain medicine, he fully grasps all the effects that the medicine can have in the body of the sick person, and similar to it.

Today, when new therapies or drugs are brought out to market, although the medical professionals who came up with them saw many of the side effects—which are confirmed in the commercials of these new therapies or drugs—unfortunately other side effects often only become apparent after the drug has been consumed. These medical professionals are not able to see all of the effects and, as we know, sometimes therapies and drugs have to be taken off the market.

When it comes to a cure, a true great doctor is able to see all of the ultimate results and all of the ultimate effects of this cure. Unfortunately there probably are not many doctors on this level. Rav Ashlag says that if we want to truly know if a doctor is wise, he would need to have this level of Chochmah. At least in his field of medicine, he would be able to see a disease and know all the ultimate outcomes of what will happen at the end, as well as know all the possible effects and side effect of the cure that can and will occur at the end.

The same applies to a wise biologist, for when he looks at some entity in nature he clearly sees all the outcomes that that entity produces when it is joined with the entire reality. This applies to all kinds of wisdoms, in such a way that the parameters of the name of the wise individual or the complete wisdom is only the "seeing of the outcome" from every detail in reality, until the end result.

What we should be asking for through our study and the work that we do is to awaken a desire for True Wisdom, because each of us to one degree or another is meant to achieve this level of Chochmah, this level of Wisdom.

From this you will also understand the sure definition of the Name Binah (Understanding). The entire ability to contemplate (*hitbonenut*) in order to foresee outcomes from any part of reality, both in the Holy Torah and in external [wisdoms], comes from the Sefirah of Binah, and therefore it is called Understanding. From the Sefirah of Malchut (Kingdom) comes the aspect of absolute dominion through force and coercion, such as the fear of government, and therefore it is called Kingdom. The rest of the Sefirot will be explained later in their place.

Keter is the Encircling Light. Chochmah is the ultimate achievement of Wisdom—the ability to see all the end results. Binah is the process of contemplation until true wisdom is achieved.

Rav Ashlag explains that Malchut literally means Kingdom—the power to "rule over" certainly the spiritual world as well as physical matter. If I were to ask people whether they would rather have great wisdom or the ability to control both the physical world and the spiritual world, I think most people would probably want to have the ability to control the physical and the spiritual worlds. What this indicates is just how backwards our mind is.

Both Rav Ashlag and the Rav often remind us that the things that are less important to people are indications for us of a source of great Light. For instance, the Third Meal of Shabbat is of great importance because most people do not pay any attention into it. Many people participate in the Friday Night connection, and for others the Shabbat Morning connection is important, but Third Meal is unimportant to most people. An indication of how warped and backward our desires really are is that for most of us the desire for Malchut, the desire to be able to rule is more important than going after the attainment of Chochmah. Unfortunately, some individuals even derive joy from ruling or controlling other people.

When we discuss Malchut (Kingdom), it says, "I [God] rule over man, but who rules over Me? The righteous person. As I issue a decree and [the righteous person] nullifies it." (Tractate Mo'ed Katan 16b) Although the term "righteous" might be lofty, we are all meant to achieve this ultimate level of righteousness and true connection, because when a person achieves their ultimate level they are literally able to control both the physical and the spiritual worlds, and even control the Creator. The Creator wants us to get to the level where we actually have control—Malchut—over the Supernal Worlds.

We find in the Torah instances where, for example, Abraham argues with the Creator, Moses argues with the Creator. How did they achieve this level? They achieved it by taking responsibility. To the degree that a person acts and truly takes responsibility for the world, is the degree they have control. This is not something we can lie about to ourselves. How much of our focus in life is directed at taking responsibility to change the world, to bring Light to the world? To the degree that we take upon ourselves responsibility for the world, is how much of this gift of Malchut—being able to rule over the physical and the spiritual worlds—we receive.

There is no [place] to ask about this: if it is so, then the Sefirah of Binah should have preceded Chochmah, since the contemplation and the yearning to see the outcome precedes and causes the eventual perfection, namely the foresight of the outcome, which is called Chochmah (Wisdom). I have indeed already explained to you that the sequence of the emanation of the Worlds is contrary to our understanding. The fulfillment of the Desire precedes and causes the revelation of the Desire (see earlier, Section 17), and the perfection precedes and causes the revelation of imperfection, since the stages so develop and descend from the blessed Endless (Ein Sof), Contraction after Contraction, down to this most flawed World.

Rav Ashlag asks a question that answers so many questions: "if it is so, then the Sefirah of Binah should have preceded Chochmah, since the contemplation and the yearning to see the outcome precedes and causes the eventual perfection, namely the foresight of the outcome, which is called Wisdom."

In truth, the fulfillment of any desire precedes the desire for it. Light precedes lack. This concept is one that should be often repeated as it is so beyond our understanding. Our normal perception is, I am hungry and then I eat, I have some lack in my life and therefore the Creator fulfills it in one way or the other. Yet in the spiritual Worlds, the fulfillment comes first and only then is the desire awakened.

In the Ashrei Prayer we recite: "The will of those who fear Him will He do." (Psalms 145:19) It can also translate as "He creates desire for those who fear Him." How does He create desire? By creating the Light for that fulfillment first. Whenever we have a lack, whenever we have a desire, it is not that we are desiring something new. The Creator first creates the fulfillment of the desire and then we start feeling a lack. We should know that anytime we feel lack, anytime we feel a desire it is simply the Creator telling us, "I have something for you and I cannot just give it to you. I have to first awaken within you a desire."

Imagine wanting to feed a loved one the most amazing food, but they are not hungry for it. Now imagine you had the power to create a ravenous hunger within that person, how great would that be? You prepare the meal first and then when they come home you are able to create within them a tremendous hunger for great food. We do not have that ability, but the Creator does. He creates first the fulfillment of the desire, and then we start feeling a lack. What an amazing concept.

Now we understand that Binah, the process of achieving Chochmah, comes after, because the way we view the world is wrong. We view the world as coming from darkness into Light, from imperfection to perfection, from lack to fulfillment, which is exactly the opposite of the truth. The truth is that perfection precedes imperfection, completion precedes lack, Light precedes darkness. We experience these lacks and darkness to awaken us for growth so as to receive that Light that is already there. Therefore, as Rav Ashlag says, Binah follows Chochmah because the complete totality and revelation of Wisdom precedes the process to achieve this Wisdom.

This concept has tremendous ramifications. Often the Negative Side tells us there is so much work for us to do, so how are we going to achieve it all in one lifetime. Yet in reality, if we know that in the true order of things we were in completion before we were in lack, we can climb that mountain in a second because we were actually at the top of the mountain before we were at the bottom.

When we truly grasp that the completion always comes first, that the revelation comes before the lack, before the darkness, then we realize that we can be transformed in a second. When Joseph the Righteous was to be released from the jail, the words Pharaoh says in the Torah are: "Bring him quickly." There is a kabbalistic saying that says, "The Salvation of the Creator is as the blink of an eye;" that the assistance from the Light of the Creator can come like the snap of a finger. We should not get lulled into the opposite because we see our world as a world of processes. The true reality is that fulfillment comes first, perfection comes first. When we truly understand this and that our view of the world is absolutely backward, we begin to grasp how in one second we can achieve perfection because the perfection is here, it came first. I hope that this awakens in us excitement for our ability to achieve this perfection quickly.

---

22. The Circle of Malchut of Adam Kadmon: The First World that was emanated after the Contraction (Tzimtzum) is called the World of Adam Kadmon, and it is also called the World of Keter. The Four Worlds— Atzilut, Briyah, Yetzirah and Asiyah–clothe this Adam Kadmon.

Before we continue, I would like to repeat the process we have been learning up until now. The First Three Sefirot—Keter, Chochmah, Binah—of Keter of the Line are revealed and Light is drawn. Then all the Ten Sefirot of Keter of the Circular Vessels, the Endless Vessels, receive their Light only from these First Three Sefirot. Following this, the Lower Seven Sefirot of the Line are revealed. The Circular Vessels do not receive any of their Light from these Lower Seven Sefirot because these Sefirot have within them the concept of the Curtain (Masach)—the limiting of the Light—where Light can only be received when the Vessel has a Desire to Receive Only for the Sake of Sharing.

Rav Ashlag makes very clear that the original Primordial Man, the World of Adam Kadmon has everything within it—all the Light, the fulfillment of the descending Worlds, which are: Atzilut corresponding to Chochmah; Briyah corresponding to Binah; Yetzirah corresponding to Zeir Anpin; and Asiyah (our physical world), which corresponds to Malchut.

We should not think of the Five Worlds as Adam Kadmon at the top and below that are the other four Worlds in descending order with our physical world at the end of the last World called Asiyah. This is not the way it is. Rather there is a Great World called the World of Adam Kadmon, the First World that came into existence after the removal of the Light, and the other four Worlds that come afterwards—Atzilut, Briyah, Yetzirah, and Asiyah—simply surround the original First World. No new Light is going to be revealed by these four Worlds. As a matter of fact, they are simply forms of diminishment of that original Light. They are lesser Lights than the original Light of the First World called Adam Kadmon. When Rav Ashlag says that they "clothe" the original Light, this means they are veils upon the Original Light.

For instance, there is a much more diminished Light in the World of Asiyah, the World in which we live, than in the World of Adam Kadmon. When speaking of the wisdom of the Torah, the Kabbalists explain that there is the Wisdom of the Torah that is in the World of Adam Kadmon, which is endless wisdom, endless information, and then as this Light—the Wisdom of the Torah—descends into the World of Atzilut, it becomes the Wisdom of Atzilut, which is the same Wisdom as in the World of Adam Kadmon but it is more concealed. And this process of the Wisdom being more and more concealed continues as it descends into each of the Worlds of Briyah, Yetzirah, all the way down into the World of Asiyah. Therefore the Wisdom of the Torah that is revealed to us—the physical Torah we read with its stories and peculiar things that do not make a lot of sense—is simply the diminishment of understanding as that same original Light comes down into our world.

In his Introduction to the Study of the Ten Luminous Emanations, Rav Ashlag explains that the reason the Wisdom of Kabbalah is so important is because it is the deeper, less concealed, original Wisdom of the Torah. Thus, when we read strange things in the Torah, which is almost in every reading to one degree or another, this is simply the clothing of the Wisdom of Torah that is revealed in the World of Asiyah. The Wisdom of Kabbalah is more elevated and therefore it is a more revealed, clearer understanding; it is the same Light. When we read about murder in the Torah or about all kinds of negative things, this is not the essence of the Light, it is a clothing, a concealment, a veil, that was put on the original Light of the Torah of Adam Kadmon, the Torah of the First World, as it comes down into our world.

To illustrate this, the kabbalists give an example of a man who is wearing masks. Clearly, under all these masks it is the same person. Regardless of the masks he is wearing, when you really get to know him, you will see that he is the same person with or without the masks. However if you do not get to know him, if you only see the surface—as, unfortunately, many people do when they look at the Torah and only see the physical stories—you are being fooled by the masks.

The importance of the Wisdom of Kabbalah is that it is a considerably unmasked Light of the Torah. Even what we read and study the Zohar, the Writings of the Ari, the revelations of Rav Ashlag, it is still not the ultimate unmasking and revealing of the secrets. Unmasking is the work we have to do to continue our comprehension of the original Wisdom. The reason the Wisdom of Kabbalah is so important is because although it is not completely revealed, it is a less concealed form of that original Light.

Thus when we discuss that the World of Adam Kadmon is the original First World and it is complete, and that the other four Worlds—Atzilut, Briyah, Yetzirah, and Asiyah—are clothing, veils, upon this First World, it means that it is the same Light in all the Worlds, except that in our world this Light has many more veils around it. As the Ari said, the first Ten Sefirot include within them the totality of all revelation. This is a very important point in the history of our world before human beings came into existence. In the spiritual formation of our world, the first Ten Sefirot that came about after the Contraction (Tzimtzum), after the Vessel desired and the Creator agreed to conceal the Light completely, are revealed in this World of Adam Kadmon.

> 23. **Thus we explained the subject of the Ten Sefirot:** Even though there are but four levels, that is, the well-known Four Phases, they still include Ten Sefirot. The reason is that the Third Phase, called Zeir Anpin or Tiferet, has in it six Sefirot called Chesed, Gevurah, Tiferet, Netzach, Hod, and Yesod. The reason for it will be explained in its place.

This revelation of the Ari and Rav Ashlag is the source of all of the Wisdom of Kabbalah; it is the root of everything. Although throughout Kabbalah we discuss the Ten Sefirot, in essence there are really only Four Phases of the Vessel becoming a Vessel.

Therefore, concerning the Ten Sefirot, in essence there is Keter, which is not really revealed Light but rather the Source, and then there are the Four Phases: Chochmah, Binah, Zeir Anpin, and Malchut, where Zeir Anpin or the Third Phase of the Vessel has six Sefirot within it—Chesed, Gevurah, Tiferet, Netzach, Hod, and Yesod—and together with Keter, it amounts to ten. It is important to remember that at its core throughout the entire study it is about the Four Phases—the stages that any essence, us included, goes through to become a true Vessel, to have a true desire.

Here you need to know the specification found in the Book of Formation (*Sefer Yetzirah* 1:44), "ten and not nine," for this indicates a great matter. It has already been explained that all of the illuminations of the Sefirot from the Supernal Light, even the Circular ones that are in equality, do not shine upon the Fourth Phase called Malchut. The term "Sefirah" exclusively indicates Light and Vessel together, that is, when the Supernal Light is clothed in a Vessel. But a Vessel without Light does not bear that name, since Sefirah is derived from transparency (*sapiriyut*) and clarity.

For this reason, one might think that Malchut is not a Sefirah, Heaven forbid, since the Supernal Light does not shine within it, as explained. This is why the author of the Book of Formation specifies that there are Ten Sefirot, not nine, Heaven forbid, for Malchut is also considered a Sefirah.

The reason is that the entire connection of the Supernal Light to the Ten Sefirot is affected specifically by the Returning Light (Ohr Chozer) that Malchut raises upward by means of the Masach in Her (as mentioned in Section 11).

Of course, the question is, why would we think there are nine? This is not some arbitrary choice of options where we have an endless range of numbers to choose from. There is obviously a very logical reason we would think that there are only nine Sefirot, yet Abraham the Patriarch in the Book of Formation (*Sefer Yetzirah*) makes it clear to us that there are Ten Sefirot.

After the Tzimtzum, the Desire to Receive for the Self Alone, the Fourth Phase, Malchut, the tenth Sefirah, can no longer be a way to receive any fulfillment, any Light because the Vessel is no longer able to receive in a direct way. In Kabbalah, the language that is used is very exact and precise. Rav Ashlag explains that the term Sefirah literally refers to "Light and Vessel together." There are other terms for Vessels without Light. However, whenever we use the term Sefirah, which literally translated means "shining/illumination" it indicates that there is a Vessel and there is a Light filling that Vessel.

Therefore, Ten Sefirot, Ten Illuminations means that even Malchut, the Fourth Phase, the Desire to Receive for the Self Alone, receives Light in some way. Yet this is not true because we know that after the Tzimtzum, the Desire to Receive for the Self Alone, the Fourth Phase, Malchut cannot receive any more Light. In fact, Malchut is completely dark because the rule is that the Desire to Receive for the Self Alone cannot receive Light. Malchut is a Vessel without Light and should not be referred to as a Sefirah (Shining) or as a stage that shines, because it does not shine. Instead, a completely new process has to occur, called Returning Light (Ohr Chozer).

For clarity's sake, we will review this concept of Returning Light again. The simple example Rav Ashlag uses is of a person who is hungry and comes to visit his friend. He has a Desire to Receive food for Himself Alone but at the same time is embarrassed and does not want to feel uncomfortable. So when offered food, he says, "No." He has created the Masach, he has stopped the Light from coming in; he has stopped the fulfillment of his Desire to Receive for the Self Alone. An argument ensues, where the host is begging him to eat, and he keeps refusing. This is not a game. When we discuss the Vessel, this has to be in truth. Eventually it reaches the point where the host has made it so clear to his friend how much joy it will give him to give his friend food, and the friend has also come to the point where he does not really want to satiate his hunger anymore. He has truly removed that desire. At this point, when both things have occurred, he accepts the food from his friend.

This is a step I think many people do not really comprehend. It is not that we are still hungry and only eating to satiate our hunger, while at the same time to alleviate our embarrassment we need him to play his game to make him feel like he is giving us. That is only one half of what has to occur. The other half, which is a very difficult process for most of us to go through, is to come to the point where we really do not want to eat anymore to satiate our hunger. We are still hungry but our Desire to Receive for the Self Alone, our desire to satiate our hunger has been completely removed, and then we eat purely to give pleasure to the person giving us the food. Of course, the food goes into our stomach and satiates our hunger but we do not enjoy the food selfishly. The only way we can give pleasure to the person trying to force us to eat is by satiating our hunger, but we have come to such a point where we no longer eat this food to fill our selfish desire in any way.

The Desire to fill that hunger for the Self Alone is what no longer can exist and this basic hunger is called the Fourth Phase, Malchut, the tenth Sefirah. In the Endless World before the Tzimtzum, the Vessel could be selfish. In our world that hunger cannot be satiated in this direct way. This hunger can be satiated only when we have come to the point where we do not eat the food at all for the purpose of fulfilling our own selfish desire, and really only eat to give pleasure to the person giving us the food.

The engine that drives this entire process is the Desire. If we never had a Desire to Receive food, if we did not have any hunger, we could not develop ourselves to come to the point where we only eat to give our friend pleasure and satisfy our hunger. Thus, the driver, the cause for this entire process is the Fourth Phase, the Desire to Receive for the Self Alone, the Malchut.

> Therefore, on the contrary, She is the most valuable among the Ten Sefirot, for without Her the Light would not connect with the Upper nine Sefirot, as explained there. For this reason, it is considered as if She were all Light. Understand this, and it shall further be explained in its place.

Rav Ashlag reveals something very important point here. Although the Fourth Phase, Malchut, the Desire to Receive for the Self Alone is never satiated, never filled with Light in this new existence of the World of Tzimtzum, nevertheless She shines. Malchut is called a Sefirah because She is the cause of the abundance of Light that is revealed. In fact, Rav Ashlag says that no Light could be revealed if not for the process that entails this Desire to Receive for the Self Alone.

There is a famous section of the Zohar (Terumah 673) that speaks about the Evil Inclination. The Zohar brings the story of a king who wanted to see if his son was ready for leadership, so he tells him: "Please be careful of the women that you go with, I want you to be an elevated person." Then the king hires a prostitute to try entice his son in all kinds of ways. The son, of course, does not fall prey to the prostitute, and the king sees that his son is ready for the next level of leadership. The Zohar asks who has enabled all this Light, who has enabled all this love and giving from the king to prince, from father to son? It is the prostitute. So is the prostitute good or bad? Of course the prostitute is good; she is the cause of all that is now going to happen.

Although Malchut does not receive Light in a direct way, She causes this Light to be revealed and is considered not only one of the Ten Sefirot but the most important of the Ten Sefirot, because if not for the Desire to Receive for the Self Alone then the Light cannot have been revealed in any of the Sefirot.

These beautiful words of Rav Ashlag are important for us to understand because they have great ramifications for our spiritual work—not the least of which is the idea that whenever we assist someone to reveal Light in any way, we receive that Light. Even if someone is a most terrible person, if they have enabled others to reveal Light, all of that Light comes back to them. Even if they are completely dark, the fact that in one way or another they have enabled others to reveal Light, they receive that Light.

Rav Brandwein explained to the Rav that there are those who are capable of doing the spiritual work, and then there are others who, for whatever reason, unfortunately, at this point in their Tikkun process are not yet open to make their own correction. Rav Brandwein said that for these people there is another route called Supporters of the Torah (*Tomchei de'oraytah*).

Rav Ashlag taught Rav Brandwein, and Rav Brandwein taught the Rav, this whole concept of enabling those who are not yet ready to do the correction in their Tikkun process, to assist others in one way or another to reveal this Light, so that they can receive that Light in return. Hopefully enough of that Light will then spark their ability to make their own correction. The Zohar speaks about these people who do not reveal the Light themselves but support the revelation of Light. These Supporters of the Work are referred to as Netzach and Hod. Meaning, there are some people that will do the work, and there is hope for those people who for whatever reason, are not yet ready, capable, or inspired to do the work to be Supporters of the Work. Like the Malchut here, although completely dark, because She enables a revelation of Light, She shines greater than all of the other Sefirot.

The importance of helping those of us who are trying to complete our own Tikkun is key. We need to know that when we have enabled others to reveal more Light in their own lives than we can possibly reveal in ours, this gives us a much greater ability to receive Light. The Rav would often talk about the idea that there are people who simply want to study Kabbalah and then there is those who try to disseminate the Wisdom of Kabbalah. He warned those who are studying the Wisdom of Kabbalah only for themselves and doing their own Tikkun to be careful and hopeful that they can do it all by themselves. But if not, we have to also make sure that a large part of our spiritual work is dedicated to disseminating this Wisdom outward because then, even if for whatever reason, we cannot receive a tremendous amount of Light internally, like Malchut, but are facilitating others to receive this Light, we shine greater than all the Light revealed.

These beautiful words of Rav Ashlag bear repeating: "Therefore, on the contrary, She is the most valuable among the Ten Sefirot, for without Her the Light would not connect with the upper nine Sefirot, as explained there. For this reason, it is considered as if She were all Light. Understand this."

> 24. **Ten Circles, one within the other:** See Volume 1, Inner Light, Chapter 1, Section 19.

It is imperative we know that no geometric terms of intersecting Lines and Circles mentioned in this study are about physical shapes but rather levels of consciousness. These are "ten Circles, one within the other" on a level of consciousness.

When Baal Shem Tov would see something that was made by a craftsman, he was able to tell his students all the thoughts this craftsman had while he was making that object, because we imbue all that is of us into everything we create. Therefore, the purpose of the Study of the Ten Luminous Emanations is not simply the study itself but to really shape and transform our mind to start thinking like the Creator.

I want to bring in the words of Rav Ashlag, because clearly they are worth reviewing:

> "This is why the Rav [the Ari] is particular when he says: 'The place of that space was Circle-like all around,' meaning, not an actual end, but like the end in a round image, which its end is in its center. This way, you can imagine those Four Phases as four Circles within each other like onion layers. The central Circle is the Fourth Phase, surrounded by the Third Phase, which in turn is surrounded by the Second Phase, which is surrounded by the First. In this way, there is no discerning up or down, right or left, among them. For the first phase, for example, encircles all of them with its first half from above, while with the second, it encircles them all from below. It is thus with the other phases, and therefore, there is no up and down, right and left, in such a way that among them there is none greater above the other, but they are all the same, as one [entity] equally even."

Here we learn that there is a dichotomy concerning the concept of Circles within Circles. On one hand, having one Circle on the outside and other Circles on the inside could indicate one Circle has more or less importance than the other; that the outermost Circle is higher than the inside Circles. Yet Rav Ashlag says that even if the outermost Circle, on some level is more important, when the outermost Circle reaches the bottom of both Circles, the innermost Circle at this point is higher than the outer Circle. It is obviously not about Circles; it is not about geometrical forms, but rather it is to be on a level of having both—some difference but also not some difference.

Obviously the ultimate level is to come to the point where we do not see any negativity around us at all. As mentioned previously, a true Tzadik (Righteous Person) sees no negativity around him. But there is a level in between a Rasha (Wicked Person) who sees negativity around him all the time and a Tzadik who sees no negativity, and this middle level is to see someone who, for instance, is a thief, and not allowing that to create judgment. The concept of the Circle is to be able to have some information but for that information not to make a change. To be able to live without judging is what a lot of spirituality concerns. It is not about being blind but rather being able to have two concepts living together; where we can see someone as a thief but this does not make us think any less of them, we do judge them as a bad person. It is about being able to have both good and bad together in our consciousness, when we look outside of ourselves.

This is why the Ari describes the Ten Sefirot of the Circle of Adam Kadmon as Circular. On the one hand there is still a higher and a lower and yet there is not. It is an interesting concept. We really need to take the time to make sure this concept is clear because it is not about Circles, but being able to entertain the idea that there is a difference and yet no difference. Whenever the Ari, the Zohar, and the kabbalists speak about the term Circle, they are implying that there is a situation that has two sides that are not the same but somehow there is unity.

6. **And so the aspect that connects all the Circles together[25] is this thin Line that extends from the Ein Sof, passing through,[26] descending[27] and extending[28] from Circle to Circle to the final objective of them all.[29] Through this Line flows the Light and the abundance that is needed to each and every one of them.**

25. The aspect that connects all the Circles together is this thin Line:
Explanation: You already know that in the Ten Circular Sefirot there is a break and vacant space between each Sefirah, namely as the size of the [Lower] Seven Sefirot of the straight illumination in that Sefirah (as said in Section 18). However, among the Ten Sefirot of the Line there is no break between them whatsoever. They start from the Light of Ein Sof and extend up to the Middle Point, which is the Fourth Phase called Malchut, as there is no more aspect below it, as explained. Thus among the first Ten Sefirot that extended from the Ein Sof in the secret of a Straight Line, which are also called the Ten Sefirot of Adam Kadmon, there is no space at all between them.

The Ari says that in the Endless World the Ten Circles are all one. The Light flowed from Keter of the Circles to Chochmah of Circles. It was a direct flow. It was unencumbered—a complete unified whole. The Ten Circular Vessels received all of their Light in order from the Endless Light. Now it is not like that anymore. After the Tzimtzum, the Circular Vessels are now broken up; there is a lack of unity. But as we will see, this lack of unity is taken care of by the Line.

I know this process is difficult to grasp the first few times we learn it but hopefully the more we review it, the clearer will be our comprehension. In the World of Adam Kadmon, there are the Ten Sefirot of Keter of the Line, Ten Sefirot of Chochmah of the Line, Ten Sefirot of Binah of the Line and so on, which are Straight—Keter, Chochmah, Binah, Chesed, Gevurah, Tiferet, Netzach, Hod, Yesod, and Malchut. And we also have the Ten Sefirot of Keter of the Circles. As we learned previously, because there is a Similarity of Form between the First Three Sefirot of Keter of the Line and the Ten Sefirot of Keter of the Circles, the Ten Sefirot of the Circles only receive their Light from the First Three Sefirot of Keter of the Line. And although the Lower Seven Sefirot of Keter of the Line receive Light, they do not shine any of their Light to the Ten Sefirot of Circles, which creates a separation, a space between the Ten Sefirot of Keter of the Circles and the Ten Sefirot of Chochmah of the Circles, and so on. I hope we all take the time to really have complete clarity about this process.

In the Endless World, the Light came to the Circles; it was one unified whole. In this new World called Adam Kadmon, the First World that emerges after the

Tzimtzum, there is the Line, indicating a new way of receiving that includes Restriction, Binding by Striking, and Returning Light. This represents a new way of receiving where the Fourth Phase, the Desire to Receive for the Self Alone, cannot be fulfilled. The Circular Vessels do not live in this World of Tzimtzum and cannot relate to this type of receiving. It is a different reality.

The Circular Vessels can relate to the First Three Sefirot of Keter of the Line because there is still no manifestation—no Light being given into a Desire to Receive for the Self Alone since it is only in thought. Now the Circular Vessels cannot draw any Light, they can only receive their Light through the First Three Sefirot of the Line because the Lower Seven Sefirot of the Line are already where the Returning Light—the concept of Receiving Only for the Sake of Giving Pleasure—is manifest.

Assuming we now have clarity, what this means is that there is a disconnect that occurs between Keter of the Circles and Chochmah of the Circles. And Rav Ashlag reminds us that the space created between Keter of the Circle and Chochmah of the Circle is not a physical space but a Difference of Form between the Lower Seven Sefirot of Keter of the Line and the Ten Sefirot of Keter of the Circles. Normally this is seen as something negative, because we cannot have separation. If there is separation, there is no Light. But here—and this is a beautiful thing—somehow a separation (*perud*) is created that still allows for revelation of Light.

Therefore, the Ari says that the Ten Sefirot of the Line connect the Ten Sefirot of the Circles as well, since the Lower Seven Sefirot in each Sefirah of Straightness connect the Ten Sefirot in the higher Sefirah of the Circles with the Ten Sefirot that are in the Lower Sefirah of the Circles.

These Lower Seven Sefirot act as the connective tissue, as a unifier between the Ten Sefirot of Keter of the Circles and the Ten Sefirot of Chochmah of the Circles. This is amazing because on the one hand the Circular Vessels of Keter say to these Lower Seven Sefirot of Keter of the Line: "I do not want your Light. You are of a different lower quality than I am. I cannot receive your Light." And on the other hand, if Keter of the Circle wants to become a complete Vessel and be unified with Chochmah of the Circle and then with Binah of the Circle, and so on, it needs the unity that comes through the Lower Seven Sefirot. It is a paradox. The beauty we keep witnessing throughout the

Study of the Ten Luminous Emanations is that there are always two opposing elements, which at the same time create unity.

The reason is that the illumination of the Ten Sefirot of Chochmah of the Circles that receive from the Upper Three of Chochmah of Straightness necessarily passes through the Lower Seven Sefirot of Keter of Straightness. After all, the Upper Three of Chochmah of Straightness must receive from the Lower Seven of Keter of Straightness and bestow it upon the Ten Sefirot of Chochmah of the Circles. Thus the Lower Seven Sefirot of Keter of Straightness connect the Ten Sefirot of Keter of the Circles with the Ten Sefirot of Chochmah of the Circles. And so on from Chochmah to Binah, and so on in this manner.

There is a dichotomy here. It seems as though the Ten Sefirot of the Circular Vessels look down upon the Lower Seven Sefirot of Keter of the Line. And yet, Rav Ashlag says that the beauty is that the only way that there will ever be a unification and connection between Keter of the Circle and Chochmah of the Circle, and so on, is through these Lower Seven Sefirot. Thus something that creates a lack of unity, creates unity.

This is the same idea in the Portion of Pinchas. The splitting of the Hebrew letter Vav (ו) in the word shalom (שׁלֹום) represents the distance between the Lower Seven Sefirot of Keter of the Line and the Ten Sefirot of Keter of the Circles. And even with this separation in this letter Vav, this is one time where the Sefer Torah is still considered Kosher because this separation is actually the source of the unity between Keter of the Circles and Chochmah of the Circles.

This teaches us many lessons. All too often we are quick to judge an action as creating separation when, in reality, on a deeper level, it is the one singular way to create unity. This is a concept that has many ramifications, and certainly as we discuss the World of Adam Kadmon, the one thing that brings together all of the Ten Sefirot of the Circles is the Lower Seven Sefirot of the Line—the aspect that seems to be the most diminished.

In the Halel Prayer we recite: "The stone that the builders rejected has become the chief cornerstone." (Psalms 118:22) The Midrash says that when they were building the Holy Temple (Beit haMikdash), they wanted to use only the best stones. There was one stone that really wanted to be a part of the Holy Temple but as they were looking at it the builders felt it was not good enough. Yet when the builders came to construction of the Holy of Holies, the holiest place in the Holy Temple, they realized that they were missing a stone to complete this structure. They remembered this one stone that they had previously rejected and went to look for it. It fit perfectly. The stone the builders had pushed aside became the cornerstone for the Holy of Holies.

This is the same idea. The Ten Sefirot of the Circles say to the Lower Seven Sefirot of the Keter of the Line: "We do not want you, you are too far away." Yet these Lower Seven Sefirot of the Keter of the Line are what support the entire unity of the Ten Sefirot of the Circles because without the Lower Seven Sefirot of Keter of the Line there would be no connection, no unity between Keter of the Circles and Chochmah of the Circles.

The lesson here is that many times we put aside this as unimportant, not right, and yet in the end, we discover that the only way to achieve unity is by taking what we put aside as unimportant and making it the highest most significant of all. This is the paradox the Ari is talking about here: "The aspect that connects all the Circles together is this thin Line." I hope you really internalize this beautiful concept.

---

26. **Passes through:** The Line, which is a Straight Illumination, penetrates, so to speak, the roofs of the Circles, passes through the Circles, descends and is drawn all the way to the end, namely to the Middle Point. But surely this is not referring to a space or area. To understand this, we need to know that no Light is revealed throughout the Worlds, both in the Upper and in the Lower, that does not extend from the blessed Endless (Ein Sof) before (lit. above) the Contraction (Tzimtzum). It must evolve and pass through all those levels and Worlds that exist between that World, where the receiver of the revelation of the said Light is located in, and the Ein Sof that is before the Tzimtzum.

Rav Ashlag explains that each Light we reveal, even the smallest amount of Light, has to originate from the Ein Sof. Sometimes I think that we perceive the Ein Sof as literally a million miles away from where we are—not in physical terms but in spiritual dimensions. It is important to know that every single time we do an action that reveals Light, this Light does not originate from the

Worlds of Atzilut or Briyah or even come from the World of Adam Kadmon. Each Light we reveal, even the minutest amount, originates from the Ein Sof, the Perfect World before the Tzimtzum, and has to flow through all the Worlds and all the levels that exist between us and the Endless World—which is a long trip.

Although here we are mostly learning about the World of Adam Kadmon, we learn that no spark of Light that we reveal, that we connect to, flows directly to us. Instead this Light has to flow from the Ein Sof before the Tzimtzum through all the Worlds and all the levels and all the people that precede us— our parents, our grandparents, our great grandparents, and so on. This Light flows throughout the chain of humanity, as Rav Ashlag calls it, all the way down to us.

You already know that there is no lack in spirituality. Therefore, it cannot be said at all that this revelation—namely, the new Light that evolves through the levels—is missing from the first level when arriving at the second, or that it is missing from the second when arriving at the third like a material object that passes from place to place. This cannot be at all in spirituality, where no lack exists. Rather, it necessarily remains in every single level while passing to the other. The matter of it coming into another level is likened to lighting a candle from another candle, where the first does not lack at all. It is in a manner that the revelation of Light that comes to a certain level in the World of Asiyah was already attained by all the levels throughout the Worlds between the Ein Sof before the Tzimtzum and the receiver in the World of Asiyah.

Using the example of a candle, let us assume that there are 100,000 stages between the Endless World and us—even though there are much more than that. We have to know that by lighting a single candle, we have just lit a 100,000 other candles because light has to go through the Ten Sefirot of Adam Kadmon, which means Keter of Adam Kadmon got lit, Chochmah of Adam Kadmon got lit, and so on to every level until where we are. Therefore, even though we may have revealed a minute amount of Light in the World of Asiyah, when we multiply this Light by a million, this is the amount of Light that we reveal. When we truly grasp this concept we realize that, especially in our generation, even the smallest action we do reveals a tremendous amount of Light because so much takes place. So many Worlds have been created between us and the Upper Worlds, and every Light we reveal lights a candle in every single one of those stages until it comes down to where we are. Can you imagine how much Light we reveal? Obviously, the clearer our awareness is of this concept, the more powerful it is.

Hopefully this amazingly beautiful lesson gives us a true appreciation for even the smallest action that we do in our world. No action is too small.

Those of us who had the merit to be around the Rav, and its true for any true kabbalist or righteous person, saw the emphasis he put on even the small connections. They all have an appreciation for the fact that every spark of Light we reveal originates from the Endless World, and even more so, that whatever small Light we reveal here, or experience here, so much more is being revealed in the Upper Worlds.

According to this, it is found that the illumination of the Straight Line has to pass through the Circular Vessels, since the aspect of the Circular Vessels precedes the Line, since they emerged immediately with the Tzimtzum, but the Linear Vessels emerged afterwards with the Line. Therefore, this illumination that passes through never moves from there, as we said that there is no lack [or disappearance] in spirituality.

What we learned until now is that in the reality after the Tzimtzum, the Light first comes to the Line, and then from the Line to the Circular Vessels. Rav Ashlag is saying that there is actually a step before that. There is actually a back and forth that occurs here. Because the Circular Vessels precede the Line in spiritual time and are the cause, the Light from the Endless World has to first come into the Circular Vessels and then from the Circular Vessels to the Line. Then the First Three Sefirot of the Line shine into the Ten Sefirot of the Circular Vessels.

You also need to know that regarding the said development of Light from place to place there are two aspects of remnants in the places of passage. The first aspect is a Permanent Remnant, which means that it blends and connects with the Light already present in that level and they unify as one, as if they were always one thing. The second aspect is only a Passing

Remnant, that is, the illumination does not blend and unite with the Light of that place into one but remains there as a distinct aspect of its own.

This is what the Ari teaches us: that this Light of the Line that passes through the levels of the Circle is not considered as a Permanent Remnant but only as an aspect of a Passing Remnant. This teaches us that it does not mix with the Light of the Circles into one aspect but remains there distinct as an aspect of its own. This is why the Ari is specific in saying "and passes through." Understand this.

The reason for this is that the Light in the Line precedes the Light in the Circles, since the Circles receive their Lights only from the Light of the Line. This is why the Light of the Line is much more important than the Light of the Circles, and therefore it does not mix with the Light of the Circles, as mentioned earlier. The Light of the Line is called the Light of Ruach, and the Light of the Circles is called the Light of Nefesh.

There are five different levels of Light: Nefesh, Ruach, Neshamah, Chayah and Yechidah; Nefesh being the lowest, Ruach being above it. And here Rav Ashlag explains that the Light of the Line is called Ruach, and the Light of the Circle is called Nefesh. There are so many paradoxes that are occurring here.

It says in the Talmud, *yagata umatzata taamin*, "If you toiled and found, believe" (Tractate Megillah 6b). Rav Ashlag speaks about this a lot in the Introduction to the Talmud Eser Sefirot (And You Shall Choose Life), if you work for something and you gain it, then trust that you will keep it. Some people understand that phrase literally to mean, "If you worked hard, and you found it, then believe that you found it." However the deeper understanding is, "Only when you work for something and then you get it, can you trust that it will remain with you;" that it will be a Permanent Remnant that will stay forever.

Even when a person receives great Light, if they did not earn it, this Light will not stay with them. It is said that at the time of the Splitting of the Red Sea, even the lowest soul saw visions greater than those of the Prophet Ezekiel. Yet if they merited to have such great visions, what happened to them afterwards? The answer is that these great visions were not theirs, they were Passing Remnants. Since they did not earn them, even though they received these great revelations, they remained on the level of a Passing Remnant, as a non-stable type of Light that does not mix into their essence.

In this Study of Ten Luminous Emanations we learn that the underlining law of our world is that even as Light comes through us, which we somehow become connected to, if we do not work hard to earn it, this Light will not stay. It will not be a Permanent Remnant. We can have the greatest revelations, but if we are not working hard for them, these revelations will not stay. They will be a Passing Remnant.

Unfortunately, throughout history there have been many people who have merited revelations and great connections but because they did not do the work to earn it, it was a Passing Remnant. It can stay with them but it does not become part of their essence. Therefore, only if you have worked hard for something, and then you have achieved it, then can you trust that it will stay with you. Otherwise, like the Circular Vessels here who receive the Light first but did not work for it, this Light does not become part of their essence. Their Light is considered less—Nefesh. The Light of the Line is Ruach because the Line worked for it. Although, the Light that comes to the Line to become Ruach comes first through the Circular Vessels, because they did not work for it, it does not become part of their essence.

Although many of us have merited to receive Light and assistance of others, for all kinds of reasons, if we do not do the work to earn this Light and assistance, it will remain on the lowest level—the level of Nefesh. Only when we work for this Light can we merit for this Light to be of a higher degree, like of Ruach. This is a very important lesson.

---

27. **Descends:** Every extension of Supernal Light to the emanated is called a "descent," which implies that while it extends it becomes gradually denser. As you already know, the purest is called Up Above and the coarsest is called Down Below. And since the Light becomes gradually denser as it extends, it gradually descends from above downward.

The reason for this coarsening that the Light undergoes as it extends is because it extends following the sequence of the Four Phases, beginning with the First Phase until it reaches and hits upon the Curtain (Masach) in the Fourth Phase. Thus it becomes gradually denser, since the First

---

Phase is the purest, followed by the Second Phase, and so on until the Fourth, the coarsest of them all (see Volume 1, Inner Light, Chapter 1, Section 14).

Although we have already discussed this process of the Light, it is important to reawaken this again. Whenever we speak about the Light descending, this means that a lesser degree of the Light is being revealed. This helps us understand why, for example, everyone's Shabbat experience is different. The Light revealed is the same, but depending on where a person is at, is how much density (*aviyut*) has to be added to that Light of Shabbat so that each person can receive it.

The further away a person is from the Light of the Creator, meaning the more Desire to Receive for the Self Alone a person has, the more layers have to be added to any Light that is revealed to them. Thus when someone does not necessarily feel the Light, when it is hard from them to feel the Light when they make Shabbat Connections, this is an indication that by the time this Light goes through all the levels of density until it gets to them, it is a small amount. It is not that there is a lack of the Light of Shabbat but because they are so far away from this Light, it has to become darker until this Light can come into their Vessel. This is true of any spiritual connection that we make.

There is a famous story about Rav Zusha of Anipoli (1718–1800), who would go crazy, jump away from the table and run outside whenever he would hear the first word of a lesson his teacher, the Magid of Mezritch (1704–1772), would utter. He could not take the amount of Light. The other students would get upset because he would make such a ruckus every time the Magid would begin speaking. The Magid explained to his students that because Rav Zusha was so pure of the Desire to Receive for the Self Alone, he received all the Light right away from one word. The rest of the students who had more of a Desire to Receive for the Self Alone did not get the Light right away. It was not that they were bad. This Light had to go through a process of becoming darker and coarser, so that by the time this Light came to them, they were able to handle it.

Of course, what we should all hope for is that as we grow and diminish our Desire to Receive for the Self Alone, we are able to make it so that the Light coming down to us does not have to become so clothed in density until we can receive it.

28. **And is drawn:** The term "and is drawn" is used to express the Linear Illumination, while "curls" expresses the Circular Illumination (as above, Section 18).

29. **The final objective of them all:** This refers to the Fourth Phase of the Circles, which is called the Middle Point. It is what is called the material globe in this World. At first, the Atzilut aspect in the World of Adam Kadmon extended to this World but after the Second Contraction (Tzimtzum Bet) took place, which it is called the World of Nekudim (Dots), the conclusion of Atzilut of Adam Kadmon then rose to the aspect of the point of the World to Come (Olam Haba), whose place is considered above the World of Briyah, as shall be explained in its place with the help of God.

This made it so that the Light of Adam Kadmon does not shine to our world anymore. It stops in the level of the World to Come (Olam Haba). What we should understand is that if this Light was once revealed down to our world, it means we can connect it.

It is interesting though, because in the Inner Observation (Histaklut Pnimit) Rav Ashlag says that these Circular Vessels are something we do not even discuss. Yet here Rav Ashlag and the Ari spend many pages discussing them, and we are spending hours learning about them. We are being given permission here to talk about something that is even beyond our abilities, and what we are meant to discuss. But as we study this First World of Adam Kadmon that shined all the way down initially to our World, what we are doing is awakening this Light again.

The Ari says that the last Circle is called the Middle Point. We now know that this is not a physical central point because even before the Tzimtzum, the purpose of the entire process of Creation was to go to this Middle Point. This Middle Point, our physical World, is not so called because it is the innermost Circle but because it is the central purpose of Creation. The World of Atzilut is the first Light that emerged from the First World of Adam Kadmon that came about after the Tzimtzum. The first time it emerged, all the Light of Atzilut of Adam Kadmon shined all the way down to our world. Then a process called the Second Contraction/Restriction (Tzimtzum Bet) created a distance between the Light that came from Adam Kadmon, our World, and the World of Atzilut.

This Tzimtzum Bet is a second removal of Light. The Worlds as they are set up now, with the Light of Atzilut shining all the way down to our World does not allow for the correction we need to make and therefore the Vessel, a second time, said to the Light: "Hide higher, hide in a different place." This occurred in the World of Dots (Nekudim). Then the conclusion of Atzilut of the World of Adam Kadmon—which in its initial form previously shone all the way down to our physical World—was removed, pushed up, and elevated higher until the border, the limit known as the World of Briyah, called the World to Come (Olam Haba).

The term Olam Haba is very often misunderstood. People think that Olam Hazeh (This World) represents our physical World, and Olam Haba represents the World a person goes to after they die and leave this physical World. Yet Rav Ashlag makes very clear that the term Olam Haba does not refer to the World that only exists after a person dies but that it is a level that can be reached in our World as well. Olam Haba represents the World within which the flow of the Light is constant. Haba means "comes all the time"—that the shining of the Light of the World of Atzilut comes to this World all the time, and it is in the World of Briyah where our interactions really occur, which is below the World of Atzilut.

In this next stage of the World of Dots (Nekudim) where the Vessel says: "No, the Light needs to go up even higher," there is now a border. The Light of the Endless in this form of Returning Light shines until the World of Atzilut, and then from the World of Briyah (Olam Haba) and lower, this Light does not shine.

Rav Ashlag explains that a reason the Tzimtzum Bet had to occur is because there has to be an incorporation (hitkalelut), an element that everything is part of everything else. The way we understand it logically is that before the First Contraction (Tzimtzum Alef), every Sefirah, every part of Light is its own separate entity. They come together as a unified whole but they are each defined and separate. Through the process of the Second Contraction (Tzimtzum Bet)—and what will happen as we learn further as these Worlds are coming about—it becomes a mixture, where every element becomes a part of another element. Even the smallest element of the Spiritual World includes within it all the other aspects of the Spiritual Worlds. This is important because then it is possible for any part of Creation to fix the entire Creation.

The Zohar says, and the kabbalist teach, that every person is a Small World (Olam Katan). This means that there is something within each one of us that is attached to everything in this world, from the galaxies in the universe to the planets. Each of us has a connection to every part of the physical and spiritual realities. The overriding concept is that after the occurrences of these processes, everything becomes a part of everything else. This theme is going to be a constant throughout what we learn.

7. Each and every World has Ten individual Sefirot, and each and every individual Sefirah in each and every World comprises Ten individual Sefirot.[30] And they are all as layers of an onion, one within the other, like the image of the spheres mentioned in astronomy books.[31]

One of the basic teachings of Rav Ashlag is that when we discuss something being Circular, it represents the concept that neither one is higher than the other. When two Circles are one within the other, although on the top half of the Circle the outermost Circle is higher, when we go to the bottom part of the Circle, what was the higher part of the Circle above becomes the lower part of the Circle below. Thus concerning all these thousands upon thousands of Sefirot that exist within each Sefirah, there is no higher and lower.

30. **Comprises Ten individual Sefirot:** You will understand the reason for the comprising of the Sefirot mentioned according to the well-known rule that there is no disappearance in spirituality, and every Light that passes from place to place acquires an eternal position in all those aspects it passed through, as said above in Section 26. And since every lower Sefirah emanates from a higher Sefirah by way of cause and effect, consequently the lower is considered as passing through the higher.

Therefore, all the Sefirot must be comprised of each other. For example, when the two first Sefirot, Keter and Chochmah, emerge, the Light of Chochmah must emerge from Ein Sof, out of which everything emerges. And then the Light of Chochmah must pass through the Sefirah of Keter before reaching the Sefirah of Chochmah, since the Sefirah of Keter caused its emergence.

Since the Sefirah of Chochmah passed through there it acquired its position there, and now there are two Sefirot in Keter—Keter and Chochmah. In the same way, after all the Ten Sefirot of the Supernal Light emerged from above downward to Malchut, all nine Sefirot below Keter had to pass through Keter, since it was the first cause for all their emerging, and so they all acquired their place there since there is no disappearance in spirituality, as mentioned earlier. Therefore, all the lower nine Sefirot, of necessity, are in Keter itself since they passed through there, as explained.

All Light that comes down to our World has to flow from the Endless World. As the Vessel begins to form, Keter births Chochmah, Chochmah births Binah, Binah births Zeir Anpin, and Zeir Anpin births Malchut. Obviously, all the Light that comes from the Ein Sof to the other Ten Sefirot has to come through Keter and therefore Keter is no longer simply Keter it becomes Keter and Chochmah, then it becomes Keter, Chochmah, and Binah, and then it becomes Keter, Chochmah, Binah, and Zeir Anpin because all the Light that passes through to birth the next Sefirot becomes part of its essence as well. Each Sefirah becomes all the other Lights of the Sefirot that flow through it.

This gives us an appreciation for the amount of Light that we receive as we help others grow and reveal their own Light. Of course there are many teachers who have good teaching skills and can excite their students, which is great. But that is not the purpose. The purpose is for this student to be able to begin the process of drawing their own Light. Only if that is what I help my students do, then obviously all the Light that goes to them, goes through me, and I grow and grow. This indicates that if we do not feel energized after helping someone else, it is an indication that there is something wrong with what we are guiding them to do.

The Ari says that the highest, most elevated consciousness in everything that we do—in the spiritual work, in the study—is to reveal Light from the

Supernal Worlds. Similarly, when we assist others, our focus should be on how to help them reveal more Light. Through this process, whatever Light they receive we will have to receive more. This is a beautiful and important understanding.

Keter begins with a spiritual Light, and then as Keter gives Chochmah the ability to become Chochmah, all the Light that is coming to Chochmah, Keter receives, causing Keter to expand. Then as Keter assists the process of Binah, whatever Light has to go to Binah comes to Keter, expanding Keter even more, and so on. Thus in the end, Keter has not only helped nine Sefirot come about but more importantly Keter has now grown nine times because Keter retains all the Light that has gone through it to create the other Sefirot. Hopefully this is the process each of us experiences as we assist and guide others reveal their Light.

> In the same way, there are, of necessity, nine Sefirot in Chochmah, since the eighth Sefirot below it had to pass through it as they did through Keter. And so [there are] eight Sefirot in Binah for the said reason, and so seven Sefirot in Chesed, and so on, and one [Sefirah] in Malchut since it is the lowest. And it is known that Malchut elevates Ten Sefirot of Returning Light from Herself upward, which envelop the Ten Sefirot of the Supernal Light called the Ten Sefirot of Direct Light. This Returning Light is called the Light of Malchut, for She has no other Light.

We know that in this new reality called the Line, Light can only be received through the process of Returning Light, meaning that the Vessel can only receive whatever amount of Light, fulfillment, it Desires only for the Sake of Giving pleasure to the Creator. This process of Returning Light is what binds the Light of the Creator to the Vessel. Without the Returning Light, the Light cannot come into the Vessel, because in this new reality after the Tzimtzum the Vessel said: "I do not want to receive any Light in the Desire to Receive for the Self Alone, any Light that is selfish Light. The only Light I want to receive is Light that I can Receive for the Sake of Giving Pleasure to the Creator." That is Returning Light. So the Returning Light is the Vessel that holds, that attaches, the Light of the Creator to the Vessel after the Tzimtzum.

At this stage, in the World of Adam Kadmon, the Vessel says: "I know that I am strong enough and I am able to receive the totality of the Light of all

Ten Sefirot only for the Sake of Sharing." Once Malchut has gone through this consciousness process, then this Light becomes manifest in the Vessel. Malchut is the reason Keter has Light. Malchut is the reason Chochmah has Light. Malchut is the reason Binah has Light, and so on. The beauty of this necessary process is that only now does Malchut become the cause of all the other nine Sefirot.

In the Endless World, Malchut is simply an effect. She is the last, the end of the Revelation of Light of the Creator. Now, through the process of Returning Light, through this process of consciousness, Malchut becomes the only cause that allows and enables Light to become manifest. Therefore all the Light of Keter comes through Malchut. All the Light of Chochmah comes through Malchut, and so on. Malchut is the cause that enables the Endless Light, the Direct Light, to become bound and manifest in the Vessel. Malchut is what creates the consciousness of Returning Light.

This beautiful new concept now in effect in the World of Adam Kadmon after the Tzimtzum is that Light can shine from the Lower to the Upper. In the Endless World, Light only shines from the Upper to the Lower, from the Ein Sof to the Vessel. This is called the Awakening from Above (*itaruta dil'eila*). Now, there is a new reality where the Vessel, Malchut, we, can actually affect something. We can affect even the Supernal Worlds. This new concept called the Awakening from Below (*itaruta dil'tata*) only becomes possible because of the concept of Returning Light where this consciousness of Malchut is not only able but is the only way in which the Vessel receives Light.

This Returning Light is always called "Ten Sefirot that rise upward." See Volume 2, Inner Observation Chapter 6, Section 66, where it is explained that Malchut is called Keter for those Ten Sefirot since She is the cause for their emergence. The one next to Her is called Chochmah and the third grade from Her is called Binah, and so on. It is found here that the purer it is the smaller it gets, to the point that the real Keter receives merely the Malchut part from this Returning Light. Study there well.

Here we find that whatever is pure, meaning whatever has less of a Desire to Receive, is considered lesser because the greater Desire to Receive you have, the greater Returning Light you can create if you have the ability to restrict. Therefore concerning Returning Light, it becomes important to have a greater desire. It is astonishing how many paradoxes there are here. In this new reality, the more Desire to Receive for the Self Alone, the more important the Vessel is because of its potential to transform.

Thus in real terms, the highest Vessel, which is Keter of Direct Light, actually receives the lowest Light. In this new reality, Keter, the pure, less Desire to Receive for the Self Alone element of the Ten Sefirot of Direct Light receives and manifests only the smallest amount of Light. Even though all these Ten Sefirot have transformed, from where Keter began it was a small desire and thus was only able to manifest a small amount of Light.

For instance, if we seat ten individuals at a table, assuming they all are capable to really transform their consciousness and only eat for the sake of elevating the sparks of Light in the food, obviously the person who has the greatest desire to eat, and therefore also the greatest capacity, will manifest the most amount of Light. The individual who can only eat a little amount, will be able to transform it and elevate the spark, but the amount of Light that they reveal is much less. When we have a greater desire and are able to transform it, then we are able to reveal more Light. When we have a lesser desire and are able to transform it, we reveal Light but it is a lesser degree of Light.

This lesson also helps us understand the concept of Teshuvah as we come to the month of Elul (Virgo). The worse a person has behaved up until Rosh Chodesh Elul (New Moon of Virgo), the more capacity they have to reveal the Light of Teshuvah through Elul and Rosh Hashanah because they have built a greater Desire to Receive for the Self Alone. Now it is true that it will be more difficult for them to transform in Elul than it would be for someone with a lesser desire, with less darkness created, with less selfishness awakened. But it is also true that if they are able to transform, the purer person will reveal and manifest less Light in Elul than a person who has been impure throughout the year.

Rav Ashlag explains that in this new reality of the World of Adam Kadmon after the Tzimtzum, Keter, the purest, highest of all the Vessels receives only a minuscule amount of Light, and therefore is referred to as Malchut, the Lowest Vessel, of Returning Light. The initial desire of Keter that it began with and transformed was much less, and therefore the Light that it can reveal is much less.

Realize, therefore, that these Ten Sefirot from below upward are all found in Malchut, since they all pass through Malchut, as Malchut is their root. They all thus acquire a place in Malchut. It is therefore found that Malchut is also comprised of Ten Sefirot. Nine Sefirot of Returning Light (Ohr Chozer) pass through Yesod, and thus there are Ten Sefirot in Yesod— one Sefirah of Supernal Light, which is from above downward, and nine Sefirot of Returning Light (Ohr Chozer), which are from below upward that must pass through it.

In the same way, there are Ten Sefirot in Hod—two from above downward, namely the Light of Hod and the Light of Yesod that passes through Hod, and eight from below upward. In the same way there are Ten Sefirot in Netzach—three from above downward and seven from below upward, and so on. This way, after the emergence of the Ten Sefirot of the Supernal Light and the Ten Sefirot of Returning Light, each one of necessity becomes composed of the complete Ten Sefirot. This applies to the minutest details *ad infinitum,* where this system of inclusion surely applies. This is not the place to expound upon this. See Inner Observation (Chapter 9) where we expanded upon this at great length.

I hope this basic underlying necessary and important process becomes very clear to all of us. Each element of the Spiritual World becomes part of every other element. We, each person, who is called a Small World (Olam Katan) has an attachment, a part of everything else in this World. Hopefully this awareness makes us appreciate the power that we have because everything that we do affects everything else. However, the Negative Side does not want us to realize there are millions of attachments that go out from us to the World. Everything in this world is attached to us. When we do something negative, when we fall spiritually, we draw all of those attachments down with us as well. When we elevate, we elevate all of those attachments with us as well. And more importantly, everyone else is also attached to everything. If we lower someone else, if we hurt someone else, we not only hurt this person, we hurt all the attachments to them as well because they are attached to everything. Therefore, when we hurt another person, we have lowered everything. We have lowered the entire physical world and the entire spiritual world. Once we realize the attachments that become a part of everything through this process, we begin to appreciate both our own and everyone else's greatness and as well as the damage we do when we fall and the damage we cause to the world if we make another fall.

This is a very important concept. Rav Ashlag says regarding the whole process of Tzimtzum, and especially when we get to the Sin of Adam, that there was no other way that the world could have come into existence. Because there has to be this incorporation in order for humanity to have the ability to correct everything. And that is the process that we are learning about now. How everything became a part of everything so that we, humanity, can both control and influence everything.

In the Book of Formation (*Sefer Yetzirah*) it discusses the concept of Olam, Shana, Nefesh (World, Year, Soul), that everything in the world has three basic elements to it: the way it influences the world, the way it influences time or the year, and the way it influences the individual. There is an interaction, where everything really is of the same DNA.

Just as Keter has within it all aspects of all the other nine Sefirot, and so on, so too do each of us, to some degree, have an aspect of the entire world and every person in this World. Rav Ashlag's whole idea of Global Responsibility stems from this concept. Since we are intertwined and interconnected in this way, we have both a responsibility and more importantly, the ability to influence everything else. Every person is a Small World (Olam Katan) because everything is included within everything.

In the morning connections we count thirteen ways the Torah can be expounded upon, and one of them is: "Anything that was part of a general statement that was then singled out from the general statement to teach something. It was not to teach about itself that it was singled out, but to teach about the entire general statement." In other words, whatever happens to anything that was part of a group and then removed from the group, is not only happening to itself but is also happening to the rest of the group. The same idea applies here because all the Worlds, every Sefirah, every person—after the Tzimtzum all the way down until our World—has within them elements of everything else. Therefore we can influence everything else. Hopefully this gives us a great appreciation for the power that each of us possesses and how interconnected we are with everything else in existence.

I always like to discuss things that on the surface look contradictory in the words of Rav Ashlag. In explaining how each of the Ten Sefirot has within it of the other Ten Sefirot, Rav Ashlag tells us that Keter has its own Light and

Keter also has the Light of all the other nine Sefirot because all the other nine Sefirot flow through it. Rav Ashlag explains this all the way down to Yesod. And then it seems like he is saying that the Light of Malchut that flows through Yesod makes Yesod and then the Returning Light from Malchut completes all the Ten Sefirot. This indicates that whatever Light is missing in the Direct Light that comes from the Creator is made up in the Returning Light. The ultimate explanation is that Malchut does not have any of Her own Light, does not receive any of Her own Light because the only Light that She has is the Ten Sefirot of Returning Light. Therefore Malchut has Keter through Malchut of Returning Light. The contradiction, it would seem, in Rav Ashlag's explanation is that initially he seems to imply that Yesod has one of the Sefirot of Malchut of Direct Light. And then, in the later explanation he makes it clear that there is no Light in Malchut.

This bears repeating again. Rav Ashlag initially says: "Malchut has one Light of Direct Light," but we know that Malchut does not have any Light of Direct Light. Then Rav Ashlag explains that the concept of Returning Light completes all the Ten Sefirot, and says, "Malchut is the cause of the Ten Sefirot of Returning Light. So Malchut has Ten Sefirot of Returning Light."

The apparent contradiction is that on the one hand, Rav Ashlag seems to be saying that Malchut has one Sefirah of Direct Light, and on the other hand he makes it clear that Malchut has no Sefirot of Direct Light, only Ten Sefirot of Returning Light. This is the same with Yesod where on one side, Rav Ashlag seems to imply that Yesod has two Sefirot of Direct Light and eight Sefirot of Returning Light, and on another side he makes it clear that Yesod only has one Sefirah of Direct Light and nine Sefirot of Returning Light.

Nevertheless, the answer is simple, which also shows us something about the way Rav Ashlag teaches. When explaining a concept, Rav Ashlag initially gives over the big picture, and in the big picture he does not discuss the details that are necessary for the comprehension of the big picture. When Rav Ashlag talks about Yesod in one place as having two Sefirot of Direct Light, and Malchut having one Sefirah of Direct Light, this is not true. But in order to clarify the concept he explains it in this way. Then when he starts going into the details, Rav Ashlag explains the true essence of the depth of it, which is that Yesod has only one Sefirah of Direct Light and nine Sefirot of Returning Light. Malchut has no Sefirah of Direct Light and Ten Sefirot of Returning Light, and so on for all the other Sefirot.

The reason Rav Ashlag seems to originally be implying differently is only because, in explaining the general concept of interconnectedness, he had to be nonspecific. But later, he delves more into the details to get the clearer picture, and this is where the clarity comes from.

This important structure is true whenever we teach or assist someone. Sometimes we get stuck because we want someone to understand everything initially, but what Rav Ashlag is telling us is that we do not have to understand everything initially, he will explain it to us at our level. Even though this would imply something that is not necessarily correct, on our level he has to give it to us this way until we are able to go a little bit deeper, and then he can give us the complete truth. We should not be too invested in giving someone a complete picture if they are not ready for all of it. Rav Ashlag makes it clear that first we give the big picture, and then we can go into the details.

In talking about this idea of incorporation (*hitkalelut*) the Ari teaches us that everything in this World is intertwined. I want to awaken the fact that as we read this, as we study this, we are awakening this incorporation. As we always know, consciousness is so important. This morning we prayed, we studied Zohar, we will do more actions that reveal Light. How can we make it stronger? How can we make it really have a ripple effect to the entire world? The Ari is teaching us here that everything in this world is intertwined, and I am intertwined with the entire world. How do I strengthen the power then of my spiritual actions to really have that ripple effect which is innate within us? By studying this. When we read these words from Rav Ashlag we actually awaken that connection between ourselves and everything around us.

When we study these words from the Ari that speak about the intermingling, the interconnectedness of everything with everything else in this World, and therefore of ourselves with everything else, we actually awaken this energy, this consciousness, this power within us. After we study this, and understand it, our next prayer, our next spiritual action will literally be even more powerful because we have awakened this Light. We have awakened this interconnectedness within us, and therefore we create a more powerful ripple effect to the rest of the World. It is important to know that when we study, we are not simply learning, we are awakening this energy, and more importantly we awaken this energy within ourselves. Thus as we study this idea that we are connected to everything and therefore can influence everything, these words from the Ari and Rav Ashlag awaken that energy within us.

Unfortunately not everyone studies from the Writings of the Ari, certainly not enough people study from the writings of Rav Ashlag, and what this means is that over time, because of the lack of this study, there is a weakening of the links between everything. When there is diminishment of the study of Kabbalah that relates to and talks about the interconnectedness of everything, when this is not studied by enough people, this consciousness is not awakened enough in the world and it causes a weakening of that connection. Therefore, it is so important that we have this study because by learning this we reawaken the bonds between all of humanity. Through our consciousness, and through our work, we can reawaken bonds that exist but are weakened over time by them not being exposed or learned or spoken about.

This reminds me of a teaching from the portion of Ki Tetze that is related to what we are discussing. It says "If you see your fellow's ox or sheep gone astray, do not ignore it…." (Deuteronomy 22:1) The Tiferet Shlomo (Rav Shlomo haKohen of Radomsk, 1801—1866) says, "Very often we find in the Zohar where the students of Rav Shimon bar Yochai say: 'Woe to us when you will leave us, Rav Shimon,' or 'Woe when Rav Shimon bar Yochai leaves this world.'" He raises a very logical point. Can you imagine sitting in front of your teacher and he tells you something amazing, and you say, "Wow! You know, when you die it is going to be pretty bad!" They are sitting with Rav Shimon Bar Yochai while he is teaching them amazing wisdom, and all the time throughout the Zohar what do they say? "Woe, when you die!" What is that? Do you think Rav Shimon bar Yochai really wants to be reminded every time he teaches his students? Obviously Rav Shimon bar Yochai would not care, but what kind of thing is this to say to your teacher? It is a very perplexing comment for them to continuously be making in the Zohar.

The Tiferet Shlomo continues: "But the explanation of this is based on a verse in Psalms: 'Remember me, Lord, when You favor Your people.' (Psalms 106:4) Literally, it means that King David is asking the Creator to, 'Remind me of the needs of the people.' When King David began the process of writing and reciting the Psalms, this tremendously spiritual process elevated him from one World to the next World. And he began to forget because when in the spiritual Worlds, the mundane needs and worries of the people seemed so far removed from him it could not come into his consciousness. King David was afraid because he knew that when he elevates into the Upper Worlds and looks down on this World, all the things that people are concerned about becomes insignificant. Therefore, King David prayed to the Creator, "Please do not allow me to become detached. Even when I elevate to the Supernal

Worlds, please make sure that I can remain tethered, that I can remain connected to the needs of the World, although they may seem mundane from that high level." Therefore, in the Talmud in Berachot (3b), it says that every morning, the sages would come to King David and remind him that the people need food, sustenance, and have other things. Why? It was not simply to remind him because he is the king rather it was also to tether him back, to reawaken that connection between his soul as it becomes more and more elevated, to the needs of our world. Therefore it says, 'If you see your fellow's ox or sheep gone astray, do not ignore it...' (Deuteronomy 22:1) talking to the Righteous Souls, saying that even when they elevate, they should not become untethered, and lose their connection to even what would seem mundane worries."

There is a famous story that took place during of the time of the Inquisition and the expulsion from Spain. It concerns a Tzadik (Righteous Person) in this world who met the soul of the Ramban, Nachmanides (Rav Moshe ben Nachman, 1194–1270), after he had left this world, and said, "Do you not see all the trouble that is happening in the world?" And he replied, "You know, all the things that people worry about like life and death and disease, from up there none of this is important because there the whole picture is clear. So the details, a person dies today, is sick today, is so unimportant when one has the clarity of the big picture." And although that is true, there is a danger because what happens then is that they cannot help us since they are so removed. "You are afraid because you lost all your money? But do you not realize that in your next incarnation, in 150 years from now, everything is going to be great for you?"

Yet this is not where we are now. Therefore, we want to tell Rav Shimon, to tell the Ramban, "We are living here now, help us!" There is a disconnect, and there is important work to be done to bring this connection back again so that they can actually help us. Therefore what Rav Shimon's disciples were saying was: "Even while you are here, please Rav Shimon bar Yochai, as you are still in the physical world alive and also where your soul is going to elevate to, and all of our problems are going to seem meaningless, do not forget us. Reconnect!"

This is an important part of the work that we do. The Zohar tells us that after the Destruction of the Temple, Moses sees the destruction and he goes to Hebron, to where the Patriarchs and Matriarchs are buried, and he wakes them up. Why does he have to wake them up? The Patriarchs and Matriarchs are called, "Those who are sleeping in Hebron" because it was not that they did not see what was happening, but that from where they are it is so unimportant. "So it will take another 2,000 years until it all gets worked out." I mean when you can see the big picture 2,000 years is not a big deal. Yet Moses awakened Abraham—and Abraham, comes to the Temple and the Creator says, "What is my beloved, what is my friend doing in my house?" This is our work. The Zohar says that if not for the prayers of righteous people that have passed on, the world would be destroyed. In truth, if we had the assistance from Rav Shimon, from Abraham, Isaac, and Jacob, the Redemption (Ge'ula) will come. The problem is not that they do not care; they are so elevated that the problems of our world do not seem important to them, and our job is to bring them back and say, "No! It is important. Take care of this. Abraham, Isaac, and Jacob take care of this now!"

It is even deeper than this. The Zohar says very clearly that a person can never pray without first awakening Abraham, Isaac, and Jacob. Ninety percent of our work needs to be to tether back Abraham, Isaac, and Jacob, and Rabbi Shimon bar Yochai to this World. And in doing so we have the Redemption. As we learn from the Study of the Ten Luminous Emanations and the Zohar, our work is to reawaken those bonds between the righteous and our World, as well as the bonds between ourselves in the world. And also realize that through our study and through awakening our consciousness we strengthen those bonds, and by strengthening these bonds they have a greater influence on the World. This is a beautiful concept and also a very necessary one.

> 31. **They are all as onion layers one within the other:** Meaning that whatever is higher surrounds that which is lower than it equally on all sides, without a distinction of levels (see above Section 14).

This means that the shining from the Upper Worlds to the Lower Worlds is complete. Meaning, looking at the view from Above to Below, at every level the flow of Light, the sharing of Light is complete. The Higher Vessel never looks at the Lower Vessel and says, "You are only 60% perfect therefore I will only give you 60% of the Light." The Higher Vessel, the giver, is always a perfect giver; always giving 100%. We will see that it is the Vessel that has trouble in receiving this Light, and therefore something happens. But Rav Ashlag is making very clear that the shining from the Upper to the Lower is complete always. The Light shines completely—not just from the Endless World to our World, but from every previous level to the one below it. Unfortunately, as we will see, it is the Vessel, the lower level that puts upon itself these veils that limit the amount of Light that it feels, that it receives. But in the giving of every level to its next level it is in a Circular way, which means it is complete without differentiating higher or lower.

8. Every single Circle from all the entire Worlds that are in the space— the one closer to the Endless Light (Ohr Ein Sof)[32] than its neighbor is superior and finer than it, until you find that this Earthly and material World is the Middle Point within all the Circles, inside all this place of empty space and vacant air, mentioned earlier. It is also the farthest from the Ein Sof, more so than any of the Worlds. It is therefore utterly material and physical because of it being the Middle Point inside all the Circles, and understand this well.

This is actually the first time in our studies that the Ari discusses our World. Everything we have learned until now is of the spiritual realm. And it seems that the Ari is saying not such good things about our World—that because it is the most physical, it is the furthest away from the Endless World since physicality, form, is only of a nature that corresponds to the Desire to Receive for the Self Alone.

Yet one could question, "What is so bad about a table? Although it has a form, it is not selfish by its nature?" However it is important to be clear that there is the spiritual DNA of anything that has physical form, and anything that is material, by its very nature makes it the furthest away from the Ein Sof. The entire concept of materialism and physicality can only come about in the World furthest away from the Ein Sof. Therefore, anything that relates to, and is connected to materialism and physicality is of the Desire to Receive for the Self Alone, is as the Ari says: "It is also the farthest from Ein Sof, more so than any of the Worlds."

Based on the words of the Ari, Rav Ashlag, in Section 31 said that when we discuss the Circular Vessels—Circles, within Circles, within Circles—this means that the Upper Realms always give to the Lower Realms completely.

Yet we find out here that the further the Circle is from the Ein Sof, the worse off it is, the less Light it has, and the worst is our physical world in the middle.

How do we reconcile these two concepts? If the Upper Circles give completely to the Lower Circles, then the lowest of Circles should have everything because each Circle is giving everything to the next Circle, until you reach the Middle Circle. The Middle Circle should have everything because none of the Circles throughout this Tree have held anything back. And if this is true, then why does the Ari say here that the closest Circles are more connected, have more Light of the Endless World?

The answer is an important concept that Rav Ashlag speaks about a lot. We need to understand, that although it is true that every level gives to the next level completely, meaning that even in our World everything is here, it is also true that the physicality and materialism of our World is the veil upon the perfection of the sharing of the Endless World. Thus although from the perspective of the Ein Sof, every World—from Adam Kadmon to Atzilut, from Atzilut to Briyah, from Briyah to Yetzirah, from Yetzirah to Asiyah, to our physical world—has given everything, we, the receivers, have these veils upon us.

Knowing this awakens us to the fact that this is not a paradox, it is the truth. From the Endless World's perspective, every Circle to the next Circle and every World to the next World gave everything completely. It is we, the receivers, who put these veils upon us. Although it may seem as if the lowest Circle upon which we live, the physical World, is far away from the Ein Sof, we need to know that this is our false perception of our physical World. In truth, we received everything. The Ari says that this physical World has everything that the Endless World has but it is the veils of physicality that we have put upon ourselves that makes our World seem different and furthest away from the Ein Sof. This is from the perspective of the Vessel, not the perspective of the Light.

For instance, when the World of Yetzirah looks at the World of Asiyah, it sees perfection, yet when the World of Asiyah looks back toward the World of Yetzirah, it sees lack. It sees the World of Yetzirah, as having more than it. From the perspective of the Upper Worlds, the next level below it looks down and sees perfection, yet because of the veils we have put upon ourselves, when the lower level looks up, it sees how much less it has than the Worlds of Yetzirah, Briyah, Atzilut, and higher up. Hopefully this strengthens our clarity about the foolishness of the illusion within which we live, an illusion the Ari says is caused by the physicality and the materialism of our world.

---

32. **Whichever is closer:** You already know that the concept of "close" does not refer to place, Heaven forbid, but rather it refers to Closeness of Form. You also know that from the Ein Sof to the Middle Point there are Four Phases of the Difference of Form, which themselves are the Ten Circular Sefirot, where the Middle Point is the Fourth and coarsest Phase.

Based on the words of the Ari, Rav Ashlag, in talking about the big picture, said that the Circle that is closest to the Endless World (Ein Sof) has the most Similarity of Form to the Endless World and is external. The further inward the Circle is, meaning the more spiritual distance there is between the Circles of the Ein Sof, the more physicality there is, the more separation there is.

Whenever we discuss Circles being closer, this means that they are more alike in their essence to the Endless World; they have more of a Similarity of Form. Therefore, when we talk about the Circle of our World being furthest away from the Ein Sof it means that our world has the most Difference of Form; it has much more Desire to Receive for Itself Alone and thus less Light than all the other Circles. Our world is the most separated from the Ein Sof.

Yet Rav Ashlag keeps reminding us that the purpose of the Creation is this innermost Circle—our World—which is a paradox. We have to keep reminding ourselves that although there is the purity of the Worlds of Adam Kadmon, Atzilut, and Yetzirah, the purpose of the Creation of our physical World was for the transformation of the filth that is within this innermost Circle, the transformation of the dirt of our Desire to Receive for the Self Alone.

The first Circle called Keter serves as the root inspiring these Four Phases, as mentioned earlier. It is obvious that the Circle of Keter, which is the purest of all Circles, has a form in closest affinity to the Endless than them all. The First Phase, which is a little denser than it, is farther from the Ein Sof than Keter. The Second Phase, which is denser, is farther from the Ein Sof than the First Phase. The Middle Point, eventually, which is the coarsest, is considered farthest of all from the Ein Sof.

There should not be a question about this based on what was written earlier (Volume 1, Chapter 1, Section 19) that there is no aspect of above and below among the Circles, for what is meant here is that after the Circles received within them the Illumination of the Line, a distinction of above and below was made in them, as well as all the attributes applicable to the Line.

Earlier, in Section 32, Rav Ashlag made it clear that the Circles do not cause any difference, meaning the Circle of the First Phase shines all of its Light in totality and sees no difference from the Second Phase. Yet here, Rav Ashlag says that once the Light of the Line begins shining into the Circular Vessels, we now see a Difference of Form even within the Circular Vessels. From the Higher Vessel's perspective, there is no difference. It is the Lower Vessel that perceives these differences of higher and lower. It is important to never forget the overriding lesson from Rav Ashlag that all this Change of Form that we see is only from the perspective of the Vessel. "For I, the Lord, have not changed." (Malachi 3:6) The Creator, the Light, the Essence never changes. Everything we discuss now—that even within the Circles there is a Difference of Form that is produced because of the Light of the Line that is coming in—is only from the perspective of the Vessel. From the perspective of the Light, from the perspective of the higher to the lower, there is never a difference. It is important to always keep this in our mind.

When we discuss the innermost Circle being the most distant from the Endless World and the outermost Circle being most in Similarity of Form to the Endless World, never forget that it is the filth of our world, which is so far away from the Endless World, that is the purpose of our Creation.

During the Ten Days of Judgment, between Rosh Hashanah and Yom Kippur, many Tzadikim like the Baal Shem Tov, the Magid of Mezritch, Rabbi Elimelech of Lizhensk, would often talk to their students about their different prayers. They had Ruach HaKodesh, the ability to see what their students asked for during these ten very important days. In one instance, Rav Yechiel Michel of Zlotchov (1725–1781) spoke to one of his students who owned a little pub where he would sell food and drink and often rent out a few rooms in the back, and said, "I know what you prayed for. Starting from the evening prayer of Rosh Hashanah, you told the Creator, 'All I want to do in this world is be spiritual. All I want to do is to study and to pray. I do not want to have to waste my time doing this work because right now I have to worry about taking care of the people who come in. And rather than me having to worry about all that, please give me all the money that I need for the entire year, even if it is not a lot whatever it is going to be. Give it to me all at the beginning of the year and then I will dedicate to the work of the Creator for the rest of the year. I will study and I will pray without any worries.' Then in the morning prayer of Rosh Hashanah, you began thinking and said to the Creator, 'You know what? If I get all of that money in the beginning of the year, I might still invest time worrying about it. So, God, please give me half of the money in the beginning of the year and then six months later, give me the other half of the money so that it is not that large of an amount.' Then came Minchah of Rosh Hashanah, and again you thought about what you had requested and said to the Creator, "If You give me half-and-half it would still be too big of a quantity. Please give me a quarter in the beginning and every three months after that, give me another quarter. This way I will be free from the worries about money but also free from worrying about how to invest it and I will be able to do the work that You want me to do.' And do you know what the Creator answered to all four of your requests? The Creator said, 'What I want from you is to have the money worries and not spend all of your day in prayer and study. I want you to have all of that trouble of this world and still find those five minutes in the afternoon to pray Minchah and those ten minutes later at night to study a little bit.'"

This is what the Creator wants from our World: "It is not in the heavens." (Deuteronomy 30:12) The purpose of our World, the Purpose of Creation was not the outermost Circles: Adam Kadmon, Atzilut, Briyah, and Yetzirah, it is Asiyah, the innermost, filthiest Circle.

Rav Brandwein told a similar story to the Rav concerning Rav Elimelech of Lizhensk and one of his students. After the prayers, Rav Elimelech told his student, "I know what you asked for. You asked from the Creator to give you the ability to study and to do the prayers but not receive any pleasure from it, not receive anything in return. You said, 'This is the ultimate. I want to do the work and receive nothing in return.' And do you know what the Creator said to this request? The Creator said he does not want your prayers, and he does not want your study."

We know ultimately that the Purpose of Creation is "to do good unto His created beings;" for the Creator to be able to share His abundance with us. If a person has come to a point where he receives nothing from his prayers, he receives nothing from his study, this is not the Purpose of Creation because the Purpose of Creation is to transform our Desire to Receive for the Self

Alone into the ultimate pleasure, which is the Desire to Share, which is *devekut*, cleaving to the Creator.

At the Binding of Isaac, which we read about on Rosh Hashanah, the Creator says to Abraham: "Take your son, your only one, Isaac, whom you love…." (Genesis 22:2) Why did the Creator not just say to Abraham, "Take your son Isaac and slaughter him."? Instead the Creator tells Abraham three things: "Take your son" "your only one" and then He says "Isaac." The kabbalists explain that every time the Creator said one of these phrases, a tremendous amount of love for his son awakened in Abraham that never existed before. When the Creator said "whom you love," a new, tremendous amount of love was awakened within Abraham, making the test of the Binding of Isaac that much greater.

When we read that the Ari says this World within which we live "is the furthest away from the Endless World. It is therefore utterly physical and material," this can awaken within us a distaste for our world, but we also have to remember that the only Purpose of Creation is the filth of our World. To be in this filth, to be in this disgusting physical, material world and still be able to transform it, is our work in this World.

INNER LIGHT
(OHR PNIMI)

CHAPTER 2

Chapter 2 expounds upon the Ten Linear Sefirot—how they emerge and develop, and of what they comprise. It includes seven subjects:

1. The sequence of the emergence of the Ten Linear Sefirot.
2. The Five Parts of Soul in the Lower Man: Nefesh, Ruach, Neshamah, Chayah, and Yechidah.
3. Both in the Circles and in the Straightness there is Surrounding Light and Inner Light, an exterior Vessel and an interior Vessel.
4. The Light of the Circles is the Light of Nefesh, and the Light of Straightness is the Light of Ruach. First the Circles were emanated, then the Straightness.
5. Arich Anpin of the Circles shines to Aba and Ima of the Circles in the form of windows, through its Three Columns—Right, Left, and Central. From them, Light is drawn to all the Circles in such a way that all the details that are in the Straightness are also in the Circles.
6. Adam Kadmon extends from the Endless until the end of Atzilut, and all the Worlds are included in it. We have no permission to study it.
7. We do not deal with the Circles, but only the Straightness.

א) וְעַתָּה נְבָאֵר בְּחִינָה הַב' עֶיֵּשׂ בְּיוֹד סְפִירוֹת, הֲלֹא הוּא בְּחִינַת אוֹר הַיָּשָׁר, כְּדִמְיוֹן ג' קָוִין, כְּצוּרַת אָדָם הָעֶלְיוֹן. וְהִנֵּה דֶּרֶךְ הַקַּו הַנַּ"ל, הַמִּתְפַּשֵּׁט מִלְמַעְלָה לְמַטָּה, אֲשֶׁר מִמֶּנּוּ מִתְפַּשְּׁטִים הָעֲגוּלִים, גַּם הַקַּו הַהוּא מִתְפַּשֵּׁט בְּיָשָׁר מִלְמַעְלָה לְמַטָּה, מֵרֹאשׁ גַּג הָעֶלְיוֹן שֶׁל עֲגוּל הָעֶלְיוֹן מִכֻּלָּם, עַד לְמַטָּה מִתַּוְוחִית סִיּוּם כָּל הָעֲגוּלִים מַמָּשׁ, מִלְמַעְלָה לְמַטָּה, כָּלוּל מֵיוֹד סְפִירוֹת, בְּסוֹד צֶלֶם אָדָם יָשָׁר בַּעַל קוֹמָה זְקוּפָה, כָּלוּל מֵרְמַ"ח אֵבָרִים, מִצְטַיְּרִים בְּצִיּוּר ג' קַוִים יָמִין וּשְׂמֹאל וְאֶמְצַע, כָּלוּל מֵיוֹד סְפִירוֹת בִּכְלָלוּת, וְכָל סְפִירָה וּסְפִירָה מֵהֶם נִפְרֶטֶת לְיוֹד סְפִירוֹת, עַד אֵין קֵץ.

1. Now we will explain the second aspect in the Ten Sefirot. It is the aspect of the Straight Light, resembling the Three Columns in the form of the Supernal Man. Through this aforementioned Line that extends from above downward, and from which the Circles extend, this Line also extends directly from above downward; from the top of the upper roof[1] of the highest Circle of them all, down to the very bottom conclusion of all the Circles, from above downward, comprising Ten Sefirot, in the secret of an Image (Tzelem) of a Straight Man[2] with an erect posture,[3] having 248 organs[4] assuming the shape of Three Columns—Right, Left, and Central—including Ten general Sefirot, where each and every Sefirah is divided into Ten individual Sefirot, ad infinitum.

ב) הִנֵּה יֵשׁ בָּאָדָם הַתַּחְתּוֹן ה' בְּחִינוֹת אוֹרוֹת, שֶׁהֵם: הַנֶּפֶשׁ, רוּחַ, נְשָׁמָה, וְחַיָּה, יְחִידָה. וְהֵם ה' מַעֲלוֹת, זוֹ לְמַעְלָה מִזּוֹ, וְהוּא סוֹד ה' פְּעָמִים "בָּרְכִי נַפְשִׁי אֶת" וְכוּ', כַּנִּזְכָּר בְּמַסֶּכֶת בְּרָכוֹת (דַּף י עַמּוּד א'), שֶׁהֵם כְּנֶגֶד ה' בְּחִינוֹת עֶיֵּשׂ לַנְּשָׁמָה.

2. The Lower Man[5] has five kinds of Lights, which are: Nefesh, Ruach, Neshamah, Chayah, and Yechidah.[6] They are five ranks, one above the other,[7] and this is the secret of the five mentions of, "Bless the Lord, my Soul (Nefesh)" (Psalms 103 and 104), as illustrated in Tractate Berachot 10a, since they allude to the five aspects the soul has.

ג) וְהִנֵּה בְּחִינַת הַיּוּד סְפִירוֹת הָעֲגוּלִים כֻּלָּם, יֵשׁ בָּהֶם כָּל הַבְּחִינוֹת הַנַּ"ל, שֶׁהֵם: אוֹרוֹת וְכֵלִים, וְהָאוֹר נֶחֱלָק לְאוֹר פְּנִימִי וְאוֹר מַקִּיף, וְהַכְּלִי נֶחֱלָק לְחִיצוֹנִיּוּת וּפְנִימִיּוּת. וְכֵן בְּחִינַת יוּד סְפִירוֹת דְּיָשָׁר בְּצִיּוּר אָדָם, יֵשׁ בּוֹ כָּל הַבְּחִינוֹת הָאֵלּוּ בְּעַצְמָם גַּם כֵּן.

3. As for all the Ten Circular Sefirot, they have all the said aspects, which are Lights and Vessels.[8] The Light is divided into Inner Light and Surrounding Light.[9] The Vessel is divided into Exterior and Interior[10] Similarly, the Ten Sefirot of Straightness in the form of Man have all those aspects in themselves as well.

ד) אָמְנָם, הַחִלּוּק שֶׁיֵּשׁ בֵּין הָעֲגוּלִים לְהַיָּשָׁר, הוּא, כִּי י' סְפִירוֹת דַּעֲגוּלִים הֵם בְּחִינַת הָאוֹר הַנִּקְרָא נֶפֶשׁ, וְיֵשׁ בָּהֶם אוֹר פְּנִימִי וְאוֹר מַקִּיף, פְּנִימִי וְחִיצוֹן: שֶׁיֵּשׁ לָהּ בְּחִינַת יוּד סְפִירוֹת שֶׁל כֵּלִים, וּבְכָל כְּלִי מֵהֶם יֵשׁ פְּנִימִיּוּת וְחִיצוֹנִיּוּת, וְגַם יֵשׁ יוּד סְפִירוֹת שֶׁל אוֹרוֹת, לְכָל אוֹר יֵשׁ בּוֹ אוֹר פְּנִימִי וְאוֹר מַקִּיף. אֲבָל הַי' סְפִירוֹת דְּיָשָׁר, הֵם בְּחִינַת הָאוֹר הַנִּקְרָא רוּחַ, שֶׁהוּא מַדְרֵגָה גְּבוֹהַּ עַל מַדְרֵגַת הַנֶּפֶשׁ, כַּנּוֹדַע, גַּם הֵם כְּלוּלִים מֵאוֹר פְּנִימִי וְאוֹר מַקִּיף, גַּם יֵשׁ לָהֶם יוּד סְפִירוֹת דְּכֵלִים, וּבְכָל כְּלִי מֵהֶם יֵשׁ בּוֹ פְּנִימִיּוּת וְחִיצוֹנִיּוּת. וּפְשִׁיטָא הִיא שֶׁבְּחִינַת הַנֶּפֶשׁ נֶאֱצְלָה תְּחִלָּה, וְאַחַר כָּךְ נֶאֱצַל הָרוּחַ.

4. However, the difference between the Circular and the Straight [Sefirot] is that the Ten Circular Sefirot relate to the Light called Nefesh,[11] and they have Inner Light and Surrounding Light, Inner and Outer. [The Circular] has the aspect of the Ten Sefirot of Vessels, and in each Vessel there is Interior and Exterior, and it also

has Ten Sefirot of Lights, each Light containing Inner Light (Ohr Pnimi) and Surrounding Light (Ohr Makif). But the Ten Sefirot of Straightness relate to the Light called Ruach,[12] which is a level above the level of Nefesh, as is known. They too comprise Inner Light and Surrounding Light and contain the Ten Sefirot of Vessels, and in each Vessel there is Interior and Exterior. It is obvious that the Nefesh aspect emanated first, and then the Ruach was emanated.

WRITINGS OF THE ARI, SHA'AR HAHAKDAMOT, PAGE 11

ה) גַּם בִּהְיוֹת הַיּוּד סְפִירוֹת בִּבְחִינַת עֲגוּלִים, זֶה בְּתוֹךְ זֶה, יֵשׁ בָּהֶם כָּל הַבְּחִינוֹת עַל קַבָּלַת הַשֶּׁפַע עַל יְדֵי סְפִירוֹת שֶׁבְּקַו הַיָּשָׁר, וְהוּא, כִּי בַּעֲגוּל הַכֶּתֶר, הַנִּקְרָא אֲרִיךְ אַנְפִּין אוֹר הַתִּקּוּן, יֵשׁ נֶקֶב אֶחָד וְחַלּוֹן בְּצַד יָמִין הָעֲגוּל, וּמִשָּׁם יוֹרֵד אוֹר אֲרִיךְ אֶל עֲגוּל אַבָּא, וּמֵאִיר אֵלָיו. וְעוֹד יֵשׁ חַלּוֹן שֵׁנִי, בִּשְׂמֹאל הָעֲגוּל שֶׁל אֲרִיךְ, וְיוֹצֵא הָאוֹר עַד צַד שְׂמֹאל דְּעֲגוּל אַבָּא אֲשֶׁר בְּתוֹכוֹ, וְנוּקְבוּ וְנַעֲשָׂה בּוֹ חַלּוֹן, וּמִשָּׁם נִמְשָׁךְ הָאוֹר עַד עֲגוּל אִמָּא, שֶׁבְּתוֹךְ עֲגוּל אַבָּא, וּמֵאִיר בּוֹ. וְנִמְצָא כִּי בַּעֲבוּר הָאוֹר תּוֹךְ שְׂמֹאל עֲגוּל אַבָּא, אֵינוֹ לְאַבָּא עַצְמוֹ, וְאֵינוֹ עוֹבֵר שָׁם רַק דֶּרֶךְ מַעֲבָר בִּלְבַד, אֲבָל עִקַּר הָאָרָה הִיא לְאִמָּא. וְנִמְצָא כִּי אֲרִיךְ אַנְפִּין, מֵאִיר לְאַבָּא וְאִמָּא יַוֵּד, כְּמוֹ שֶׁהוּא בְּעִנְיַן הַיָּשָׁר שֶׁלָּהֶם מַמָּשׁ. וְאַף כִּי הֵם עֲגָלִים זוֹ בְּתוֹךְ זוֹ, יֵשׁ לָהֶם קַוִּים יְשָׁרִים: יָמִין, וּשְׂמֹאל, וְאֶמְצַע, בִּבְחִינַת הַחַלּוֹנוֹת הָאֵלּוּ שֶׁבָּהֶם. וּמִשָּׁם, נִמְשָׁךְ הָאוֹר בְּיוּד סְפִירוֹת דְּעֲגוּלִים, דֶּרֶךְ קַוִּים יְשָׁרִים מַמָּשׁ, בְּכָל הַפְּרָטִים עַצְמָם כֻּלָּם, אֲשֶׁר בְּיוּד סְפִירוֹת דְּקַו יָשָׁר דְּרוּחַ, מַמָּשׁ.

5. Even while the Ten Sefirot are in the aspect of Circles one within the other,[13] they contain all the aspects of the receiving of abundance that are in the Ten Sefirot of the Straight Line,[14] as follows: in the

Circle of Keter—called Arich Anpin after the Correction[15]—there is a hole and a window[16] on the right side of the Circle,[17] and from there the Light of Arich descends to the Circle of Aba,[18] shining to it. There is another window on the left side of the Circle of Arich; the Light emerges to the left side of the Circle of Aba, pierces it so that a window is made in it,[19] from which Light flows to the Circle of Ima within the Circle of Aba, shining to it. Thus when the Light passes through the left of the Circle of Aba it is not for Aba's own sake, as it only passes through there in passing.[20] Rather, the Illumination is mainly for Ima. Thus Arich Anpin shines upon Aba and Ima together, as is the case regarding Their Linear [Sefirot]. And even though They are Circular, one within another, They do have Straight Lines[21]—Right, Left and Central—via the aspect of these windows in them. And from there, the Light flows into the Ten Circular Sefirot through actual Straight Lines, in all the particular details themselves that are actually in the Ten Sefirot of the Straight Line of Ruach.

WRITINGS OF THE ARI, ETZ CHAIM, GATE 1, BRANCH 2

ו) וְהִנֵּה הָאָדָם קַדְמוֹן הַזֶּה, מַבְרִיחַ מִן הַקָּצֶה אֶל הַקָּצֶה, מִן קָצֶה הָעֶלְיוֹן עַד קָצֶה הַתַּחְתּוֹן, בְּכָל וְכָל הָאֲצִילוּת הַנַּ"ל. וּבְזֶה הָאָדָם נִכְלָלִין כָּל הָעוֹלָמוֹת כְּמוֹ שֶׁאֲבָאֵר בְּעֶזְרַת הַשֵּׁם. אֲבָל, בִּבְחִינַת פְּנִימִית וְעַצְמוּתוֹ שֶׁל אָדָם זֶה, אֵין לָנוּ רְשׁוּת לְדַבֵּר בּוֹ וּלְהִתְעַסֵּק כְּלָל.

6. This Primordial Man[22] (Adam Kadmon) "extends from end to end"[23] (Exodus 26:28); from the Upper end to the Lower end, throughout the entire aforementioned space of Atzilut. All the Worlds are included inside this [Primordial] Man, as I shall explain with the Creator's help. But of the Interior aspect and essence of this Man[24] we have no permission whatsoever to speak or discuss.

ז) אָמְנָם בַּתְּחִלָּה יָצְאוּ יוֹד סְפִירוֹת דֶּרֶךְ עָגֹל, אֵלּוּ תוֹךְ אֵלּוּ, וְאַחַר כָּךְ בְּתוֹךְ הָעֲגוּלִים, נִמְשַׁךְ דֶּרֶךְ יָשָׁר כְּצִיּוּר אָדָם אֶחָד, בְּאֹרֶךְ כָּל הָעֲגוּלִים הַנִּזְכָּרִים לְעֵיל, וְאֵין אָנוּ עוֹסְקִים כְּלָל בִּבְחִינַת עֲגוּלִים, רַק בִּבְחִינַת יָשָׁר לְבַד.

7. Indeed, at first, Ten Sefirot emerged in a Circular way, one within the other.[25] Then within the Circles the Likeness of a Man extended in a Linear way along all the aforementioned Circles.[26] We do not deal with the Circular aspect at all,[27] just the Linear aspect alone.

1. Now we will explain the second aspect in the Ten Sefirot. It is the aspect of the Straight Light, resembling the Three Columns in the form of the Supernal Man. Through this aforementioned Line that extends from above downward, and from which the Circles extend, this Line also extends directly from above downward; from the top of the upper roof[1] of the highest Circle of them all, down to the very bottom conclusion of all the Circles, from above downward, comprising Ten Sefirot, in the secret of an Image (Tzelem) of a Straight Man[2] with an erect posture,[3] having 248 organs[4] assuming the shape of Three Columns—Right, Left, and Central—including Ten general Sefirot, where each and every Sefirah is divided into Ten individual Sefirot, *ad infinitum.*

This is the first time in the Study of the Ten Luminous Emanations where the Ari mentions the concept of the Three Columns—Right, Left and Central; Chesed, Gevurah and Tiferet—and explains that it is only through the process of the Three Columns, these three types of Light, that Light can be revealed. It is interesting to note that Rav Ashlag makes clear that although the Ari mentions it here, this entire reality of the Three Columns does not actually occur at this point in our study. It follows after the Second Contraction (Tzimtzum Bet).

We have mentioned previously that even though this was obviously the way it was supposed to be, the Ari never personally wrote a book on Kabbalah from beginning to end. Instead, the Ari taught Rav Chaim Vital, and whatever Rav Chaim Vital learned he wrote down in whatever order he learned it. An important lesson and one of the beauties of Rav Ashlag is that in putting together the Study of the Ten Luminous Emanations, Rav Ashlag literally took sections apart from different pieces of the Writings of the Ari and put them in an order. But being as Rav Ashlag was not the one to compose the Writings of the Ari, even in the sections that he compiled, Rav Ashlag was not able to bring in only the sections that pertained to what he wanted to discuss. This is why here Rav Ashlag says that although the Ari mentions the Three Columns—Chesed, Gevurah, and Tiferet, this is not the time to discuss them because they have to do with a later section.

On a deeper level obviously it is important that when we go back to the words of the Ari, we not disassociate one from the other. Rav Ashlag could have written from his own teachings, as we know he did in the Introduction to the Wisdom of Kabbalah, and that by itself would be powerful, since we know Rav Ashlag got an Ibur of the Ari. But there is power to that higher revelation of the Writings of the Ari. Rav Ashlag would not have written the Study of the Ten Luminous Emanations simply with his own commentary because there are different levels of consciousness that one connects to in this study. Thus Rav Ashlag had to have the original Writings of the Ari and then create his commentary on them.

To know that we cannot disassociate the two is something we have to keep in our consciousness. Sometimes we go to the commentary of Rav Ashlag because it is clearer or it really talks to the point. Yet there is a higher level of consciousness that comes from the Writings of the Ari that could not be revealed simply by the explanations of Rav Ashlag.

Here the Ari begins by giving us a clear picture of what exists after the Tzimtzum. In this new reality, there are the Circular Vessels and also the Linear Vessels of the Line. And the Vessels of the Line can be viewed as a perfect Upright Standing Man consisting of 248 body parts that include Ten Sefirot that each have within them another Ten Sefirot. Yet what does this mean on a spiritual level? Rav Ashlag reminds us that these words are not referring to a physical man but rather to the Supernal Man, of whom we are manifestations. What we have in the physical is really a mirror of what exists in the spiritual Supernal World. Yet, as we will learn from Rav Ashlag, we are not considered as this perfect Supernal Man, who existed before coming down to this world.

---

1. **From the top of the upper roof:** The Keter in a World or a Sefirah is considered to be the roof of that World or Sefirah, whereas Malchut within any World or Sefirah is considered to be the ground of that World or Sefirah. The topmost Circle is the Sefirah of Keter, and the roof of that Keter is the Keter of the Ten Sefirot of this Keter.

It is interesting that every once in a while the Ari uses the word "roof" (*gag*), which Rav Ashlag tells us refers to the Keter. Besides revealing to us the process of the Creation of our world, both the Ari and Rav Ashlag are also opening our eyes to the meanings of everything else in our world. They are showing us that even in a house, or in a room, the roof represents the power of Keter. In the Torah it says, "If you build a new house, you shall make a railing for your roof, so that you do not bring bloodguilt on your house if anyone should fall from it." (Deuteronomy 22:8) Concerning this verse, the kabbalists explain that the roof represents Keter and the railing is a way for us to connect to that Light of Keter.

The Ari uses the word "roof" to indicate that the Light shines from Keter of the Circles all the way to the Malchut of the Circles because—although the word Keter is a purer, spiritual word, and the word roof is more physical—he is revealing to us the reality of our physical world. And on an even deeper level, since the purpose of the study is not to leave this wisdom in the Upper Worlds but rather to purify our world, we have to make it physical.

In The Wisdom of Truth, Rav Ashlag discusses the Language of the Branches. When a kabbalist sees a physical roof, their mind sees Keter. And since an important part of the Study of Ten Luminous Emanations is to purify our world and to bring this Supernal Reality into our world, the Ari does not always stick to the same words. Instead of using the word Keter, here the Ari says roof (*gag*), which represents the highest level of that World, of those Sefirot. Here the Ari is explaining that both the Light of the Circles and the Light of the Line shine from the roof of the outermost Circle, meaning from the Keter of Keter of Adam Kadmon all the way down to Malchut of Malchut of the lowest World.

> 2. **An Image (Tzelem) of a Straight Man:** The clothing of the Mochin are called Tzelem, derived from [the word] *tzel* (shadow). The Straight Illumination, which includes the Upper Three Sefirot, is called Man since it receives the Upper Three Sefirot with the clothing of Tzelem. This is a lengthy matter that does not belong here.

Mochin is a word that although it is not exact, it can be interchanged with the word "Light." Mo'ach is the word for "brain," and Mochin represents the higher types of Light.

We call someone a Man when the Light of the First Three Sefirot—Keter, Chochmah, Binah is enclothed in the proper Vessels called Tzelem. In other words, when the Light shines in the right places. And although Rav Ashlag says that "this is a lengthy matter that does not belong here," we will discuss this a little more because this concept has many ramifications.

The problem with most of us is that, yes, we reveal some Light but because we have not revealed all of the Light, whatever Light is revealed goes into the wrong Vessels. The only time perfection exists, the only time that all of the Light is revealed and therefore all the Light in the right Vessels, is when the totality of Light is revealed. The word Tzelem represents the Vessels for the Mochin, for the higher Light, for the Light of the Upper Three—Keter, Chochmah, Binah. When the Light of the Upper Three Sefirot is revealed in the Mochin, in the Vessels of Tzelem, meaning you have the perfect Light in the perfect Vessel, this is called an Upright Man.

We really cannot be considered a person until this happens. Unfortunately most of us exist where the Light that we reveal is not the ultimate Light, and then Lights get mixed up in different Vessels. It is interesting that the evolutionary theory of Creation has this whole concept of bent over pre-historic forms until one comes to the upright person. So whether the Creator actually put that into the process or whether this is a theory that they tapped into, there is truth to it. In the spiritual evolution of humanity most of us are still hunched over beings. The perfection, as it existed when the Line came about, will only exist at the End of the Correction. Where one has the highest Lights and the highest Vessels is the only time we could call someone a person.

Although here the Ari says that the initial revelation of the Line came in a form of an Upright Standing Man, which means that the Lights were in their perfect Vessels and completely aligned, this is not the reality within which we exist now. For instance, in the Amidah Prayer (Shemoneh Esrei), when we bend down, this signifies these different types of Light. When Light is not coming into the right Vessel, the body takes on different shapes as well because it connects to different Light.

Rav Ashlag explains that we are not capable of having the Mochin in the Vessel of Tzelem, in their perfect Vessels, in our world. Our world is still not the place for the Mochin of the Upper Three in the Vessels of the Tzelem. Hopefully in reading this, although as Rav Ashlag says that this is not the time to be discussing it in the Study of the Ten Luminous Emanations, we will merit a time when it is the place to have the Light of the Upper Three and the Vessels of the Upper Three.

---

3. **With an erect posture:** The Head of every Sefirah and Partzuf (Spiritual Structure) is the Upper Three Sefirot—Keter, Chochmah, Binah. The Lower Seven Sefirot—Chesed, Gevurah, Tiferet, Netzach, Hod, Yesod, and Malchut—in each Sefirah and Partzuf are considered as the Body of that Sefirah and Partzuf. When they are in order—meaning, when the Lights of the Upper Three are in the Vessels of the Upper Three, and the Lights of the Lower Seven are in the Vessels of the Lower Seven— the Partzuf is considered as having "an erect posture."

But if the Lights of the body are placed in the Vessels of the Upper Three rather than the Lights associated with them, then the Partzuf is considered as not having an erect posture, since the aspect of the Head is not more important than the aspect of the Body, as even in the Head only the Lights of the Body are used. This is called the "bowing of the head," when the Head and the Body are at the same level.

In the Amidah Prayer (Shemoneh Esreh) there are four instances when we bow down. In the portion of Ekev in the Zohar, Rav Ashlag explains that the physical process of bowing down our head is one of removing the Upper Three Lights because with our physical action we create a spiritual effect. This whole process of bowing down in the Amidah is based upon the concept that the physical hunching over represents the spiritual hunching over when the Upper Lights are not being revealed. By bowing down we are indicating that we are not ready for the Ultimate Light, even as we are connecting. We are saying, "Do not give us the Upper Three, only give us the Lower Seven." As I mentioned previously, this entire theory of evolution that states humanity came from the apes, which are hunched over, and then evolved into a man who stood upright clearly has a correlation to this spiritual concept of standing upright.

The Midrash says that the Generation of the Flood and the Generation of the Dispersion seemed like really bad people. "...the earth is filled with lawlessness because of them." (Genesis 6:13) The world obviously needed to be destroyed because of the Generation of the Flood who had created some great severance from the Light of the Creator. But the reality is, and the Midrash and the commentaries on the portion of Noah, confirm that these were very spiritually elevated Generations. These Generations were so close to achieving immortality (*techiat hamatim*) and the removal of death (*bila hamavet lanetzach*)—achieving the End of the Correction.

We know that whenever there is an opening for great revelation, there is also an opening for great darkness. Concerning the Generation of the Flood, yes we can look at how they fell, but we also have to appreciate how spiritually elevated they were—how close they were to correction. It says, "It was then that men began to invoke the Lord by Name" (Genesis 4:26), meaning connecting in some way to the Light of the Creator. Rashi (Rav Shlomo Yitzchaki, 1040–1105) says that at that time they were worshiping idols, and they called the idols, "God." Yet both the Sforno (1475–1549) and the Ibn Ezra (1093–1167) explained it in a different way, saying they started to call upon God with the right consciousness. Until that generation, they were coming close to the level of the End of Days (*Acharit haYamim*), of the End of the Correction (Gemar haTikkun), "...for the land shall be filled with the Knowledge of the Lord." (Isaiah 11:9)

All the work that we are doing now—everything we are trying to achieve for the world, to change the world, to guide the people to understand—this Generation of the Flood had almost achieved. It is so easy, with our judgmental eyes, to read the portion of Noach and see the Generation of the Flood as idiots because they caused the destruction of the world. Yet the moment before the Flood, they were higher than we are now. Now, of course, they messed up, and there is something to be learned from there, but we need to understand that these are not terrible people who caused the destruction of the world, they were people who were more elevated spiritually than we are. They were living in the End of Days; they were living almost in the Gemar haTikkun.

The Midrash says that Adam and all the generations that followed him were almost at the level of "An Image of a Straight Man with an erect posture." They were almost like this Straight Man. The real beauty is that as we learn this Study of the Ten Luminous Emanations, we realize that although the process of the Ten Luminous Emanations comes before the story of Genesis (Beresheet), it also happens again and is mirrored in the process of the Creation of Adam and the sin of Adam and that they were all almost perfect beings. However, when they began falling, the Midrash says their faces became like apes. First there was the Straight Upright Man, then came the apes, and then man returned. Before the Generation of Enosh, what we see as humans pales in comparison to what humanity really is because then they were closer to, "a Straight Man with an erect posture." Everything was almost perfect. Humanity was almost at perfection, and therefore each person's body was almost at perfection. After the Generation of Enosh, as they began falling, their connection and the Light of the Creator that shadowed them and made them an Upright Man, left them and they became apes, which is the intermediate level between man and animal.

An interesting revelation of the Midrash is that humanity did not come from apes, but rather we actually stem from Adam and the generations that followed him, which were perfect; they were almost at the End of the Correction. Yet when they began falling, the apes came, and after that some form of man returned. Moses achieved "an erect posture." We are not there yet, but it is important how we view those generations and understand that the process of humanity is to return to this concept of being an Upright Man—correct Lights in the correct Vessels.

Rav Ashlag makes clear here that we live in a world where the correct Lights are in the wrong Vessels. This is not just a spiritual concept, this turns the whole world upside-down. There are a few famous stories in the Talmud where the sages say that this physical world is an upside-down world. Why? The seed of this is that the Lights are not in the right Vessels, and when the Lights are not in the correct Vessels, everything gets turned upside-down and therefore things are not as they should be. This important concept is something we need to discuss over and over again because this is the basis of the work that we do in disseminating the Wisdom of Kabbalah to the world. It is the seed to change the world. It is not only about getting people to transform through the study of Kabbalah, which is an important aspect, there is another whole aspect that we sometimes lose sight of, which is to inspire people to appreciate the Wisdom of Kabbalah, because in our world that is upside-down—wrong Lights, wrong Vessels—people do not have a true perspective of things. This lack of true perspective is the seed of why everything manifests in destruction.

Rav Ashlag, in the Introduction to the Zohar ("Thought of Creation," Sections 66-68), writes:

> You should know that everything has an inner aspect and an exterior one. In the totality of the world, the Israelites—the descendants of Abraham, Isaac, and Jacob—are considered the Interiority of the world, and the 70 nations are considered the Exteriority of the world.

And also among the Israelites there is the Interiority, which are those who fully perform the work with the Creator, and the Exteriority, which are those who are not devoted to the work with the Creator. Similarly, among the [70] Nations of the World, there is the Interiority, which are the Righteous from the Nations, and the Exteriority, which is the vulgar and harmful in them, and so on.

Even among the Israelites who work with the Creator, there is the Interiority, which are those who merit understanding the soul of the Interiority of the Torah and its secrets, and the Exteriority, which are those who deal only with the practicing part of the Torah. And in the same way, every person of the Israelites has Interiority, which is the aspect of Israel in him, which is the secret of the Point in the Heart. And there is also an Exteriority, which is the aspect of the Nations of the World in him, which is the body itself.

And when a person of the Israelites enhances and dignifies the aspect of his Interiority, which is the aspect of the Israelite within him, over his Exteriority, which is the aspect of the Nations of the World in him—that is to say, when he expends most of his effort and his labor to increase and to raise the aspect of Interiority within him for the benefit of his soul, and [expends] little effort, only to the necessary degree, to the existence of the Nations of the World aspect within him, that is, for the bodily needs, as was said: "Make your Torah permanent and your work temporary." (Ethics of the Fathers [Pirkei Avot] 1:15) through his actions in both the Interiority and the Exteriority of the whole world, he causes the Israelites to keep on increasing in their perfection higher and higher, so that the Nations of the World, which represent the Exteriority of the world at large, will recognize and appreciate the value of the Israelites.

When we wake up in the morning, what is our most important concern? Is it the physicality—*how do I feel, how do I look*—or is it *how is my soul*? This is a choice we make with our consciousness. Is our focus of concern for our external part or is it for the most internal of parts? When a person awakens and worries about their most internal part, they make their most internal part the priority; their entire focus gives much less importance and worry to the external part of their essence. And even more so, their consciousness and action affect the rest of the world and make it so that humanity now begins thinking about their internal aspect more than their external aspect. Conversely, if we wake up in the morning or in our lives, and focus equally on both the physical and spiritual or, Heaven forbid, focus more on the physicality—how we are feeling today, how we look today—where all these physical aspects of our life take priority, we not only cause the external aspects of humanity to overrule the internal aspects throughout the world, we also cause the external aspect of the world to become stronger and stronger.

And if, Heaven forbid, the opposite happens—that an individual from Israel emphasizes and gives more importance to the aspect of his Exteriority, which is the aspect of the Nations of the World within him, over the aspect of Israelite within him—then, as is said: "The stranger who is among you" (Deuteronomy 28:43) that is, the Exteriority within you, "shall mount above you higher and higher; and you…" yourself, that is to say, your Interiority, which is the aspect of the Israelite in you, "…shall go down lower and lower."

And thus, through his actions, he causes the Exteriority of the world in general, which is the Nations of the World, to rise up higher and higher, and overcome the Israelites and humiliate them to the ground; and the Israelites, who are the Interiority of the world, [then] go down lower and lower, Heaven forbid.

It is important to keep going back to the words of Rav Ashlag—and I am hoping that most of us have studied the Thought of Creation many times—because what happens is that we get the concept in our mind and then our filth covers up that concept. So even though we remember it, it is not as strong and as pure as it is when we read this straight from Rav Ashlag. When we go back to the actual words, we get the purity, the clarity of the wisdom again. And then over time we will again cloud it up with our filth. This is why it is so important to go back and reread Rav Ashlag's words again and again. My hope is that when we read these words from Rav Ashlag, this gives us the certainty and clarity again about this concept.

> And it should not surprise you that an individual can, through his own actions, cause any rise or decline to the whole world. It is an immutable law that the collective and the individual are equal to each other like two drops of water, and everything that applies to the collective also applies to the individual. [This being said], it is [actually] the individuals who make the collective do what it does. This is because the collective will be realized [as a collective] only after the individuals within [it] have manifested themselves, according to the quantity and quality of the individuals. So surely [it is] the action of the individual, according to its value, [that] causes the whole collective to either rise or decline.

By this, it will be clear to you what we have learned in the Zohar that out of engagement with the Zohar and with the Wisdom of Truth, they shall merit coming out of exile into complete redemption [Tikunei HaZohar, End of the Sixth Tikkun]. Seemingly, [one might ask] what is the connection between studying the Zohar and the redemption of the Israelites from among the nations?

By what has been explained, it is clearly understood that even the Torah has Interiority and Exteriority, just like the world as a whole. Therefore, [it follows that] a person who is engaged with the Torah has also these two aspects. And as he increases his effort in the interior aspect of the Torah and its secrets, then to that same degree he causes the quality of the Interiority of the world, which is the Israelites, to keep on ascending and rising higher above the Exteriority of the world, that is, the Nations of the World.

This demonstrates to you that [both] the redemption and all the virtue of the Israelites depend on the study of the Zohar and the Interiority of the Torah. On the other hand, all the destruction and all the decline of the Israelites has happened because they have neglected the Interiority of the Torah and have degraded its virtue lower and lower and have turned it, Heaven forbid, into something that is not needed at all.

The global reality and the personal reality are exactly the same. Whatever is true externally to the global reality, is true to the person. Clearly, our personal work and consciousness influences the rest of the world. Now we can clearly understand what it says in the Zohar, that through the study of the Zohar and the Wisdom of Kabbalah we will achieve the Final Redemption. What is the connection? The Torah has both the internal aspect and external aspect. The Secrets of Kabbalah, the Zohar, are the internal aspects; the literal stories are the external aspects.

When a person awakens their appreciation and therefore their effort in understanding the secrets, they cause the internal aspects of the world to rule over the external aspects of the world. Conversely, if the person, Heaven forbid, does not gain an appreciation and put effort into it, he causes the Destroyers of the World, those who are out to destroy humanity and the world, to become stronger and rule over the internal aspects of humanity, who are those people who want to make the world better, those people who want to affect the world positively.

Clearly the study of Kabbalah influences the rest of the world and the Redemption, as well as whether the better parts of humanity will rule over the worst parts of humanity, or vice versa. Thus when we discuss having the correct Lights in the correct Vessels, a part of making this happen is getting people to have an appreciation for the true way to look at things. At its essence, it is to awaken the Internal over the External.

The distinction I am making is that part of the work we do is to assist and teach people to use this Wisdom of Kabbalah in their lives, but another part of that is to get them to appreciate the importance of the Internal work, because whether they do an ounce of work or more, the fact that we have changed their consciousness a little bit to now have a greater appreciation for the Internal over the External is what changes the world. Even if they never study one secret of Kabbalah but know that through the Wisdom of Kabbalah there is this amazing essence that is more important than everything else they know—this shift in consciousness shifts the entire world.

Nevertheless until this begins to happen, we have this upside-down world, we have wrong Lights in wrong Vessels, which manifests in our world as people having the wrong focus, Heaven forbid. The process of getting the world back to "a Straight Man with an erect posture," where we are upright, where we are the correct Lights in the correct Vessels, begins with this consciousness. We have to ask ourselves: *What is the focus? What is important?* It is not just the work, the understanding, and the study. It is this shift of consciousness to identify what is important. It is the prioritizing of the internal aspect over the external aspect that creates a shift in the world. This is a very important teaching.

---

4. **Having 248 organs:** Explanation: There are 248 distinctions of Chesed in the Supernal Partzuf, from which 248 body parts are drawn to the Lower Beings, which are laid out in detail (in *Mishnah Ohalot*). This is not the place to expound upon it; it will be explained in its rightful place.

In the Shema Reading there are 248 words corresponding to the 248 parts of the body from the aspect of the Right Column. The 365 sinews come from Left Column. The reason the Shema Reading helps for healing is because these 248 words awaken and perfect all 248 elements of Chasadim. It is important to understand that the perfect body, and therefore the perfect person, has to have all these 248 elements of Chasadim shining to him completely.

Although we are discussing the Supernal Worlds—before the creation of human beings—in paragraph two, the Ari is going to explain the correlation that exists between everything we mention in the Upper Worlds and everything in this world. Here the Ari will go on a bit of a tangent and begin discussing the human soul. We need to always remember that although much of the discussion of the Study of the Ten Luminous Emanations is about the reality that existed before the creation of our physical world, everything we are studying is mirrored in our world as well. Therefore when Rav Ashlag says, "It is a rule," this is true in both the Upper Worlds and the Lower Worlds.

As an aside, the Meor Einayim (Rav Menachem Nachum of Chernobyl, 1730-1797) in the portion of Lech Lecha says that in the process of the creation of our world, before physicality, there was the process of the Tzimtzum, the removal of Light—as we learn in the Study of the Ten Luminous Emanations. He explains: "Just as it is with the goodness of the blessed Creator in general at the time of the creation of the worlds where there first needed to be a restriction from the side of Gevurah and Judgment, so it is in the present and in the particular in each person." In the process of the creation of our world there needed to be the aspect of Judgment, meaning first there is the Creator's Desire to Share endlessly, which is Right Column. Then there is the process of the Tzimtzum, which is the complete removal of Light.

In the Midrash it says that first the Creator thought to create our world with Judgment and then He saw that the world would not survive, so He mixed together Judgment and Mercy and created our world. Yet because the Creator does not make mistakes or change His mind, how do we then understand that the Creator first thought to create with Judgment and then created with a mixture of Right and Left Column energies? Rav Ashlag makes clear that this process by which the world came to be is not about the Creator changing His mind, but rather it is the simple process of cause and effect.

The Maor Einayim says, "Before the Creator wishes to appear to an individual and bestow goodness to him with His great kindness, there needs to first be a restriction and Judgment from the side of Gevurah. This, too, is good for that individual, as through this process he can later receive the goodness, because without the Judgment and restriction that comes before, he could not receive the brilliant Light of the kindness that will come afterward due to the greatness of the brilliance, as is indicated by the general creation of the world."

On a macro level, the Creator, the First Cause, was the Desire to Share (Right Column); to give goodness to all the souls of humanity. Then there had to be a restriction—Judgment (Left Column)—which we call the Tzimtzum. And then the world was created with a mixture of Right and Left, Mercy and Judgment. This is the way the creation of our world occurred.

So it is within every person, all the time. Before the Creator is ready to give us great blessings and abundance; anytime there is going to be a revelation of Mercy, of Right Column, of blessings, there has to first be a stopping of that, a Tzimtzum, a feeling of Judgment. Not only is this the process by which Light has to be revealed in our world, it is also for the good of the person. The only way there can there be an awakening of the Creator to share a blessing is to first experience Judgment. The process always has to be with a Tzimtzum, an awakening of Judgment, an awakening of feeling like everything is stopping, becoming dark, and then there can be the revelation of Light. And as it occurred in the creation of our world before physicality so it occurs all the time with each one of us.

If the blessings the Creator desires to share with us came immediately, without the Judgment and the Restriction of this Light, we would not have the Vessel to receive this blessing, because we would be overwhelmed with this Light. But when we go through the process of going down, the process of the Restriction of the Creator's Light, then we can have a Vessel to receive this Light.

To explain this further, the Me'or Einayim brings the example from the Talmud (Ta'anit 23a) of the famous story of the great soul Choni haMe'agel (Choni, the Circle Maker). During a time when the world needed rain because of a drought, he drew a circle around himself and said to the Creator, "I am not leaving this circle until you bring rain down to this world. Your children have turned their faces toward me as I am like a member of Your household. I take an oath by Your great Name that I will not move from here until you have mercy upon Your children"

Choni was a very connected person, so when he prayed, it was answered right away. And suddenly, not only did it start raining, but there was a storm. Now the storm was not good for the crops, it was not good for many of the reasons for which they needed the rain. Thus Choni said, "God that is not the type of rain that I am asking for." As if God did not know. "I am asking for calm, merciful, blessed rain." And then suddenly, the rain started coming down slowly.

It is a very strange story, right? Why does God first bring a storm? Did God not know that the rain that Choni was asking for should be calm, merciful, blessed rain? The Me'or Einayim asks, "Why did the rain not come down calmly in the beginning?" Obviously the reason it began to rain is because Choni had his connections and was able to bring down this miracle, this opening of blessings to our world. So if the Creator wanted to do Choni a favor, why did the Creator not do it right the first time?

The Me'or Einayim answers, "The reason is as we said earlier, that before any goodness comes to the world there needs to be a Restriction from the side of Gevurah so that people can later receive the goodness. This creates one unification of Chasadim and Gevurot for one intention—only good, as said earlier." The storm rain represents the Judgment, the Tzimtzum, awakening that has to precede any revelation of blessing. And that is why first came the waters of Judgment.

Of course the entire purpose of the rain was only to bring blessings, but it cannot come as just blessings. There has to be an awakening of Mercy, which is what Choni did. He awakened the Desire of a flow of blessings and Light to come down into this world. Then there was a Tzimtzum, there was an awakening of Judgment, which is the storm, and then there can be a revelation of gentle rain—only Mercy. It was not that there was a mistake where God did not hear him correctly and changed His mind, but rather this is the process of our world.

This is an important understanding to remember. If we want Light, we need to be careful about what we are asking for, because there is a process by which blessings can become revealed in our world. If we are asking for great blessings, we need be aware of the process of the revelation of great blessings. There will always be an awakening of a Desire to Share, then a Tzimtzum, and then the blessings. And if a person becomes nervous in the in-between process, they can stop it all, they can cut it off completely.

As an aside, recently I was studying about the 72 Names of God and the Splitting of the Sea. The Israelites were traveling in the desert and they had the sea in front of them and the Egyptians behind them. And until this moment, as they were traveling in the desert, there was an angel of protection from the Creator, there were the clouds that showed them the way and protected them. The first verse of the 72 names says: "The angel of God, who had been traveling ahead of the Israelite army, now moved and followed behind them." (Exodus 14:19) And the reason this happened was to prepare the Israelites for the great miracle of the Splitting of the Sea. But imagine what the Israelites felt? They were standing there in the desert, worried about the Egyptians behind them, but at the same time they felt that they were okay because the angel of God and the clouds were in front of them the whole time, leading them. They felt God was with them. Then all of a sudden, in their moment of greatest need, the angel goes away, the clouds go away. Can you imagine? *Now? Now the angel and clouds are going away?* We know they come back around, but can you imagine if they had a critical mass of doubt, Heaven forbid? Who knows if the angel and clouds would have come back again. Therefore it says: "Thus there was the cloud with the darkness…" (Ibid. 20), meaning that there was darkness of consciousness, because for the great miracle to occur, there had to be that night of darkness before.

We are discussing the same concept here. Our work is to keep the consciousness in that night of darkness when the angel goes away in order for it to come back behind and facilitate the great miracle of the Splitting of the Sea and all the blessings that we need in our lives. This is a tremendously important lesson.

2. **The Lower Man[5] has five kinds of Lights, which are: Nefesh, Ruach, Neshamah, Chayah, and Yechidah.[6] They are five ranks, one above the other,[7] and this is the secret of the five mentions of, "Bless the Lord, my Soul (Nefesh)" (Psalms 103 and 104), as illustrated in Tractate Berachot 10a, since they allude to the five aspects the Soul has.**

The Talmud, in Tractate Berachot 10a, says, "To whom did David say these five instances of 'Bless the Lord, my soul (Barchi nafshi)'? King David said these about none other than the Holy One, Blessed be He, and corresponding to the soul." The Talmud explains that the five times King David says *Barchi nafshi* is discussing the five different qualities of the soul. And Rav Ashlag and the Ari say that although this represents the five different levels of the soul, it is also discussing the five different qualities of the Creator. In other words, the soul and the Creator have the same five qualities. And although the Talmud does not tell us which quality corresponds to which of the five, clearly each one of these five that we are going to speak of represents a different level of the soul.

The Talmud continues: "Just as the Light of the Creator fills the entire world, so too the soul fills the entire body." (Ibid.) This is something I think many of us know but it bears repeating and awakening within each of us. Every part of our body is filled with soul. Just like the Creator fills this entire world, our entire physical body is filled with the Light of our soul. Whenever we damage a part of our body or use it selfishly for negative actions, we are taking the element of the soul that permeates that part of our body and pushing it down into the Klipot; we are giving that Light to the Darkness.

"Just as the Holy One, Blessed be He, sees but is not seen, so too does the soul see, but is not seen." (Ibid.) In both instances, the Talmud is discussing good qualities. The first good quality is that the Creator fills the entire world, and our soul fills our entire body, which makes sense. This is an important characteristic. Yet the second quality, which is that the Creator can see everything but is not seen with our physical eyes and our soul is aware of everything but is not seen with our physical eyes, may not seem as important. Why is seeing but not being seen a quality? Would it not be better for us to be able to see our soul? I am assuming most of us would be up to less selfish actions if we were actually able to physically see our soul.

Imagine being at the level where when you act selfishly with your hand, you actually see the soul being drained from the hand. How we would live our lives if this were the case for us? So why is seeing everything, being aware of everything, but not being physically viewed with our eyes a quality of the soul? The truth is, it is a necessary quality. Part of what gives our soul its strength and part of what really connects us to our soul is to come to that level where we do not need to see in order to know.

In the portion of Lech Lecha, when the Creator promised Abraham that the land of Israel will be his, Abraham asks: "Whereby shall I know that I shall inherit it?" (Genesis 15:8), meaning: "How will I know? Give me proof." The Midrash tells us that because of that desire to see proof, it necessitated the whole going down to Egypt; the whole Exile of Egypt. When a person is on the level where he needs to see, and acts differently when he does see in the physicality, this is a lack and a lesser connection to one's soul. So therefore it is a necessary quality of our soul—just like the Creator—to see everything but not be seen.

The Talmud continues: "Just as the Holy One, Blessed be He, sustains the entire world, so too the soul sustains the entire body." (Tractate Berachot 10a) This leads to the whole understanding that all physical ailments stem from spiritual ailments. When the soul is not fed, is not strengthened through study, through spiritual work, the body will, Heaven forbid, have to be diminished as well.

The Talmud says: "Just as the Holy One, Blessed be He, is pure, so too is the soul pure." (Ibid.) This is an important understanding. No matter what damage we cause or what negative actions we partake in, these do not damage the soul. No matter how low we have fallen, no matter how selfish we have been, no matter how much darkness we have created, we all need to know that the Neshamah is always whole, always pure. There is nothing that we can do to damage our soul. We can put coverings and shells on it, disconnect ourselves from our soul, create a feeling of not feeling our soul; but we cannot damage it. Our soul is always with us while we are in this physical world. Therefore at any given moment, we can completely connect to our soul. We can completely transform because perfection is always with us unimpeded; undamaged purity is with us always. This is an amazing revelation.

There are many stories of people who have transformed themselves instantly. The Talmud tells us: "There is one who acquires his World in one moment." (Tractate Avoda Zara 10b) A person can be terribly negative and in one second transform to become completely connected. Why? Because the pure soul is with us always. Even if our selfish negative actions cover this pure soul, because the pure soul is always with us, we have the ability to connect to it completely. Just as the Creator is pure, so too is our soul pure. This is an important consciousness to always have. We have the Creator's purity within us all the time, and we can connect to the totality of its purity in a second.

"Just as the Holy One, Blessed be He, resides in a chamber within a chamber, so too the soul resides in a chamber within a chamber." (Tractate Berachot 10a) There are many different explanations concerning this concept of the five qualities of the soul. One explanation is that the soul sits in the innermost Chambers and cannot be damaged, and it is always with us, which the Zohar says has positive and negative ramifications. The Zohar says that a person's negative actions are inscribed on their bones. Sometimes when we are in a room, within a room, within a room, and are concealed, for whatever reason, our ego lets us think that the damage that we are doing is not as bad. But no matter how low we go, no matter how concealed we think we are or no matter how concealed our soul is from us, it is still there in the innermost chambers; it is always there. Thus, damage done, that no one knows about, still creates coverings around our soul.

The Talmud concludes: "the one who has these five characteristics should come and praise He Who has these five characteristics" (Ibid.) Since the soul has the same qualities as the Creator, therefore the soul has the ability to come close to the Creator. Therefore King David in Psalms says: "*Barchi nafshi et HaShem* (My soul should bless the Creator)" representing the five qualities that each one of our souls has, by which we have the ability to connect with the Creator.

---

5. **The Lower Man:** There is no entity throughout the Worlds, either in the Upper Worlds or in this World, within which the said Ten Sefirot are not distinguished. They are the well-known Four Phases and their root. This is why it is said that even in the lower man of this world there are five aspects as well.

6. **Nefesh, Ruach, Neshamah, Chayah, and Yechidah:** The Vessels in the Ten Sefirot are called Keter, Chochmah, Binah, Zeir Anpin, and Malchut. The Lights in them are called Yechidah, Chayah, Neshamah, Ruach, and Nefesh (as said in Devarim Raba 2:37). The Light of Yechidah is clothed in the Vessel of Keter, the Light of Chayah is clothed in the Vessel of Chochmah, the Light of Neshamah in the Vessel of Binah, the Light of Ruach in the Vessel of Zeir Anpin, and the Light of Nefesh in the Vessel of Malchut.

The Midrash Rabbah talks about the five levels of soul: Nefesh, Ruach, Neshamah, Chayah, and Yechidah, which is actually the source for the Ari of the five Names that are given to the soul. Yet how many of us have really taken the time to truly ask ourselves the question, why? Why is Yechidah called Yechidah? Why is Chayah called Chayah? Why are these names given to the soul? There is a famous quote from the Ramchal, Rav Moshe Chaim Luzzatto (1707–1746) in the Introduction to the Path of the Just (*Mesilat Yesharim*), where he says that because some things are spoken about all the time, we never really understand them. It is important that all of us think about these Names all the time, as well as asking why? Why is the Name of the Light of Keter called Yechidah? Why is the Name of the Light of Chochmah called

Chayah? The only way we can merit to receive the answers to this is if we are constantly questioning and desiring to know more.

It says in the Midrash Rabbah (Devarim Rabbah 2:37) "Rav Simon said there are five Names given to the soul, and they are: Ruach, Nefesh, Neshamah, Chayah, Yechidah." It is interesting that the Midrash Rabbah first mention Ruach, then Nefesh, Neshamah, Chayah, and Yechidah, when in essence the order from lowest to highest is Nefesh, Ruach, Neshamah, Chayah, and Yechidah. Then the Midrash Rabbah goes on to discuss the different qualities of the soul: "Just as the Creator fills the entire world, so too the soul fills the entire body. Just as the Creator takes upon Himself the difficulty of this world, so too the soul takes on the difficulty of the body. The Creator is singular in this world, so too the soul is singular in the body. Just as the Creator does not sleep, so too the soul does not sleep as well. Just as the Creator is holy in the world, so too the soul is holy in the body. The Creator sees and is not seen, so too the soul sees but is not seen. And therefore the soul can come closer to the Creator, which also sees and is not seen." Thus because of the affinity that both the Creator and the soul share there is the ability of cleaving and bonding between the body and the soul.

Now we will go through each of the names of the soul, in the order that the Midrash says. The word *ruach* is literally translated as "spirit" or "wind." Yet in the Torah, Onkelos—who was the first to translate the Torah to Aramaic—translates the verse "…and man became a living being" (Genesis 2:7) as "and man became a Speaking Spirit (*Ruach Memalela*)." Thus Ruach (Spirit) is the ability to speak, as the ability to speak was given as an addition to humanity as opposed to the Animal Kingdom. The level of Ruach represents the ability to elevate through speech; the ability to use our mouth to create things, to change things.

Onkelos explains that when humanity was created, they were given this ability to have the power of speech—not just speech as unfortunately most of us use it—but speech that has the ability to create change and growth. Therefore, the level of Ruach represents the power of the soul to manifest the ability to create transformation and growth through our mouths. The Zohar says that one of the only powers we really have is with our mouth. Yet, unfortunately, many times we damage our mouth in the way we use it. Nevertheless its ultimate level of *Ruach Memalela* (Speaking Spirit), as Onkelos translates it, represents this ability and power to manifest through speech, which distinguishes us from animals.

Concerning the level of Nefesh, the Torah says, "for the blood is the life (Nefesh)" (Deuteronomy 12:23) meaning that Nefesh, the lowest level of the soul, represents the circulatory system, which is what sustains a person. Even when a person sleeps, the Nefesh remains and sustains the body. Yet the power of *Ruach Memalela* (Speaking Spirit), which is one step higher and is the ability to manifest Light and transformation through speech, leaves for the most part when a person sleeps. Conversely, the Nefesh, the lesser level of a soul that represents the sustainability of the human body with the soul, always remains with a person even when they are sleeping.

Concerning Neshamah, the third level of soul, the Torah says, "…and He blew into his nostrils a breath of life (*nishmat chayim*)…." (Genesis 2:7) What does this mean? It means that the level of Neshamah represents the ability to think, to understand. Therefore, even after man (Adam) had the *Ruach Memalela* (Speaking Spirit), the power of speech, there is an additional level of Neshamah, which is the ability to think about and comprehend spiritual matters.

Concerning the fourth level of soul called Chayah, it says, "He saves his soul from the pit, and his life (*chayah*) from passing under the sword." (Job 33:18) Sometimes this level of Chayah can exist in one part of the body and not in another part. It is what gives the sense of life, excitement, and the renewal of the body that comes from a connection to the Light of the Creator. The word *chayah* literally means "alive."

In Isaiah 40:31, it says: "But they who wait upon the Lord shall renew their strength…." The Mei HaShiloach (Rav Mordechai Yosef Leiner of Izbica, 1801–1854) explains that when people are constantly and consciously connecting themselves to the Creator, always knowing that whatever qualities and abilities they have are only from the Creator, this renews their body all the time. Unfortunately most of us are far from this. To one degree or another we think that these qualities and abilities are ours. However when someone really comes to that point of *ayin* (nothingness), where they know completely that all that they have—the breath of air, the soul that keeps them alive—is only from the Creator, this connection in consciousness to the essence of the Light of the Creator renews their body all the time. And this power of constant renewal and rejuvenation comes from the level of Chayah.

Thus Nefesh is the minimum that sustains the body and is around even when a person is sleeping. Ruach represents the power of speech that separates us from animals. It is the *Ruach Memalela* (Speaking Spirit), as Onkelos explains, which is the ability to create, to do, to reveal Light through speech. Neshamah represents the idea of being able to comprehend spiritual matters. Chayah represents the ability to become rejuvenated. The Talmud says, "The wicked even while alive are considered dead." (Tractate Berachot 18b) A real connection to the level of Chayah is when a person is spiritually alive. Someone who is disconnected from the Light of the Creator, even if they are alive, is considered dead because they are not connected to this level of Chayah, the level of real living. Real living is when there is a constant sustaining power of the Light of the Creator.

The first three levels of the soul—Nefesh (the ability to sustain the body), Ruach (the ability to create through speech), and Neshamah (the ability to spiritually understand)—are more passive levels of the soul. The level of Chayah represents a constant flow, a constant rejuvenation and is therefore called "Alive."

Concerning the level of Yechidah, Psalms 22:21 says, "Save my soul (*nafshi*) from the sword, my soul (*yechidati*) from the hand of the dog." The word *yechidah* literally means "singular." Obviously this highest level of Yechidah is when someone comes to the point where they see nothing but unity. It is the concept of *echad, yachid umeyuchad* (one, singular, and unified), where there is only the Light of the Creator; they see nothing except the Light of the Creator. To see unity in everything is the level of Yechidah. All of us hopefully have some association to each one of these five levels of soul. But obviously at the ultimate level, most of us do not have them because Yechidah is when a person sees no darkness, no negativity—only unity. Yechidah is the level of the End of the Correction, of Bila Hamavet Lanetzach (Death will be Swallowed up Forever; Isaiah 25:8).

The reason each one of us, I hope, at some point have felt at least some parts of these levels of soul is because, as Rav Ashlag makes very clear, even the lowest level of soul—Nefesh—has all these other five levels within it. There is Yechidah of Nefesh, Chayah of Nefesh, Neshamah of Nefesh, Ruach of Nefesh, and Nefesh of Nefesh. So even when a person is on the lowest level he can still glimpse the other five levels. However they cannot have the totality with them to sustain them. This is only achieved when a person completely manifests the level of Chayah or Yechidah. This is the basic understanding of the five levels of soul.

7. **Five ranks, one above the other:** You already know that the distinction among levels is based on their purity and density. Anytime [it says] "above" it refers to a higher degree of purity than the other.

3. As for all the Ten Circular Sefirot, they have all the said aspects, which are Lights and Vessels.[8] The Light is divided into Inner Light and Surrounding Light.[9] The Vessel is divided into Exterior and Interior.[10] Similarly, the Ten Sefirot of Straightness in the form of Man have all those aspects in themselves as well.

8. **Lights and Vessels:** The Lights are Nefesh, Ruach, Neshamah, Chayah, and Yechidah; and the Vessels are Keter, Chochmah, Binah, Zeir Anpin, and Nukvah, as said.

9. **The Light is divided into Inner Light and Surrounding Light:** Spiritual division is caused by a new Difference of Form created there (as said in Volume 1, Chapter 1, Section 12). Anything higher than its neighbor means that it is purer than its neighbor, and anything lower than its neighbor means that it is denser than its neighbor. With the Difference of Form of this density, it separates and leaves its neighbor to become lower than it. And it is known that the Lights are bestowed by every higher [level] to that which is lower than it. For that reason, the Lower must receive the abundance in its highest and purest aspect, while the Upper bestows abundance to it only through its lowest and coarsest aspect. This way the form of the Light that comes from the Upper has affinity with the form of the Vessel in the Lower, for the coarsest and densest part of the Upper is similar to the finest and purest part of the Lower.

It is found that the Lower cannot receive all the Light that belongs to it to receive, except for a very small portion, that is, only as much as the purest Vessel in it can receive. Its other aspects that are not as pure have to remain without the Light associated with them because of their Difference of Form in relation to the Upper that bestows to them.

Here Rav Ashlag teaches us a very important idea. Whenever there is a giver and a receiver, the giver is the more pure element and the receiver is the coarser, lower element. Although the giver desires to give, it can only give its worst and lowest Light. And while the Vessel, the receiver wants to receive, it can only receive in its most pure desire, its most pure Vessel. The giver can only give of its worst, lowest level because there is no Similarity of Form. Therefore whenever Light is shared from the Higher Vessel to a Lower Vessel, from a higher soul to a lower soul, it is always going to be that the lowest of the Lights are being shared from the giver and are received in the highest, purest Vessels of the receiver because this is where they have some Similarity of Form. This is a very interesting spiritual play. For example, you have prepared an amazing feast for someone who comes to your home; food they would love to eat and you desire to give to them. But for whatever reason—medical or something else—you realize they can eat only the most bland food you can provide; not the steak, not the chicken, nor the pasta but a rice cake. Can you imagine the pain experienced in this situation? "More than the calf wants to suckle, the cow wants to give." (Talmud, Tractate Pesachim 112a) The unfortunate reality is that there is such a minute amount of giving and receiving that actually occurs from the Higher Vessel to the Lower Vessel.

The kabbalists say that if we could hear the screaming of our soul because of the pain it experiences from our actions, we would not be able handle the yelling. We really need to appreciate the diminishment and the unfulfilled desires that go into the process of giving and receiving in the Supernal Worlds. The giver wants to give endlessly and the receiver wants to receive endlessly but the giver knows it can only give its coarsest Light and the receiver knows it can only receive in its most pure Vessel. Rav Ashlag explains that this is why there is so much unmanifested Light in our world.

There is an additional element to this—the relationship between teacher and student. The kabbalists say that from what the Ari knew, he only taught a drop in the ocean. And from what the Ari taught, Rav Chaim Vital understood only a drop in the ocean. And from what Rav Chaim Vital understood, he wrote down only a drop in the ocean. And when we learn from the Writings of the Ari from Rav Shmuel Vital, who wrote down from his father Chaim Vital, we understand a drop in the ocean. Even as we study the Writings of the Ari, think about how far removed we are from understanding and knowing; this is the diminishment of the diminishment.

When a person has a relationship with their teacher or someone who is like a teacher to them, they have to understand that the teacher can only really reveal their worst part and the student can only receive in their best part. This can cause a lot of confusion because the teacher on the one hand has to make sure that they do not give everything to the student, and the student from their side has to be receiving only in their purest Vessel. So a great deal of the student's desire, a great deal of their Vessel is going to be unfulfilled. Consequently, the relationship between a real teacher and a real student can be very frustrating. The lesson for us is that if someone wants to have real students or if someone wants to have a real teacher there has to be some frustration that goes along with that relationship, because if they are receiving everything they want and the teacher is giving everything they want then it is not a true giving and receiving. As it is with the Supernal Vessels so too is it with the teacher and the student. There has to be this unfulfilled giving and receiving because the teacher knows they cannot give everything, they can only give a drop. And the student hopefully knows that they can only receive in their purest of Vessels, not in everything they desire.

Therefore we find between real teachers and students—whether it is the Ari and Rav Chaim Vital; the Baal Shem Tov and the Magid of Mezeritch; Rav Ashlag and his teacher; Rav Brandwein and the Rav—that, at least in the beginning, there is a lot of pain involved with the inability of the teacher giving everything they want to their student right away and the inability of the student to receive everything right away. And eventually, as all of these stories showed, one way or another, over time the student was able to manifest everything the teacher wanted to give them.

With the Ari it is a little different. The Ari said because he was not able to completely manifest all he wished to impart that he would incarnate again. We believe he came back as Rav Ashlag. With the Baal Shem Tov and the Magid of Mezeritch there were, of course, challenges in the beginning but he was able to manifest his teachings. With Rav Ashlag and his teacher there was a tremendous amount of frustration. Rav Ashlag lost everything and then later the wellspring opened up. With the Rav and Rav Brandwein, at first there was the great loss the Rav felt when Rav Brandwein left this physical plane, but then the Rav realized that only in this capacity could Rav Brandwein give him everything.

There is an innate difficulty in a true teacher-student relationship. A true relationship comes with friction because the teacher has to give his lowest and the student has to receive in his purest. The unfulfilled Desire to Share of the teacher and the unfulfilled Desire to Receive of the student can cause all kinds of doubts, questions, and frustrations. When we grasp the real spiritual process Rav Ashlag is explaining here, we understand that it has to be this way, and when it happens to us, we accept it. Even with those we teach, we have to understand that this is the way it has to be. We have to be talking to their most pure part, knowing that we have to give them of our lowest understanding and hopefully through a long process we can elevate them. But it cannot be an easy process because a teacher can never give the student everything they want to give and a student can never receive from their teacher everything they want to receive. Only through a long and arduous process can it ever become manifest. This is a very important concept to remember both as students and as teachers.

A distinction is, therefore, made here that the Light that belongs to the Lower is divided into two aspects: the first is the small amount of Light that the Lower receives from the Upper in the Lower's highest Vessel, as said. This Light it receives is called the Internal Light in the Lower. The second is the entire amount of Light that belongs to the remaining parts in the Lower, which they cannot receive due to their Difference of Form from the Upper, as said. This entire amount is considered as remaining in the Upper, not descending into the Lower. It is called Surrounding Light.

Although we have discussed Surrounding Light previously, Rav Ashlag is now expanding on it in a deeper way. The simplest way to explain this is using the relationship between a teacher and a student, the perfect example being the Ari and Rav Chaim Vital. Let us say there are a thousand books worth of wisdom that the Ari wants to give Rav Chaim Vital. But because of the process of his correction, Rav Chaim Vital can only receive a hundred books worth of wisdom and Light from his teacher. Thus only one hundred books worth of wisdom, which is only ten percent, goes into the purest Vessels of Rav Chaim Vital.

Where do the other nine hundred books worth of wisdom go? The Ari holds onto this remaining wisdom, which causes him tremendous pain because it is not the Ari's Light. This Light is wisdom that he is meant to give over to Rav Chaim Vital. But unfortunately right now the Ari knows that the Vessel of Rav Chaim Vital is too Dissimilar in Form to the Light of the Creator, it still has too much of the Desire to Receive for the Self Alone and therefore Rav Chaim Vital cannot receive the remaining nine hundred books worth of wisdom. And the Ari holds onto this Surrounding Light, it does not just float out there in the ether.

However, this causes the Ari pain because he knows that this Light, this wisdom is supposed to go to Rav Chaim Vital but he is not ready to receive it. The hundred books worth of wisdom, one tenth, is called Internal Light, manifested Light within this Vessel. Unfortunately, the Internal Light—the smaller part—is generally the Light that we manifest. The greater Light that our giver wants to give us but cannot because of our Difference of Form is called Surrounding Light, remains in the giver. It does not go down into the Vessel, it stays within the giver and it stays in pain.

"More than the calf wants to suckle, the cow wants to give." There is pain when you want to give and the recipient is not able or ready to receive. Although there is more to this very important concept of Surrounding Light there are three basic points to remember: 1) The Internal Light is always the smaller portion. 2) The Light does not simply float out there, it remains in the giver. 3) The giver is in pain from it.

The positive aspect of this is that the Surrounding Light does not disappear and is still accessible. With the previous example of the Ari, even though the Ari did not give everything over to Rav Chaim Vital, the Ari still drew all that wisdom down. Thus it would be easier for Rav Chaim Vital to attain it, as opposed to this Light never have been sent down from the Endless World to the Ari to give to Rav Chaim Vital at all.

The beauty of a true teacher-student relationship is that even what the student does not receive from the teacher in his lifetime, the teacher prepares it for the student. The Light from the Endless World that he or she is supposed to receive has come down into his teacher. And hopefully the student, through his or her work, is able to open up access and receive even more Light, even more wisdom, which, unfortunately, many times occurs after the death of their teacher. Even if the teacher has left this world, the teacher has prepared this reservoir of wisdom and Light that the student is able to draw from throughout the rest of their life and even throughout the rest of their incarnations.

Very often, concerning the Ari and Rav Chaim Vital, we are told that the Ari was in tremendous pain as he makes it very clear to his student that there is so much more that Rav Chaim Vital is meant to receive from him. The Ari told Rav Chaim Vital: "However when I leave this world, I will come back and give it to you in some shape or form, in a vision, in a different incarnation." We know that the Ari reincarnated in the soul of Rav Ashlag. And Rav Ashlag would not have been able to reveal the rest of the wisdom that the Ari was meant to give Rav Chaim Vital if the Ari had not already drawn this wisdom down from the Endless World. The Ari's work—even what he was not able to impart to Rav Chaim Vital whilst he was with him in this world—was still prepared as a reservoir from which Rav Ashlag was then able to draw and reveal.

So too with Rav Ashlag. His teacher had much more wisdom that he wanted to impart to Rav Ashlag and that Rav Ashlag was not ready to receive—which Rav Ashlag admits was because of his ego, his Desire to Receive for the Self Alone. Yet after the passing of his teacher and a tremendous amount of pain, work, and begging, the wisdom opened up to Rav Ashlag—not from the Endless World but from his teacher's preparation, which is where he drew it from.

This is why when a student goes to their teacher's grave, they are able to access that Surrounding Light, the Light that their teacher had desired to give to them but they were not ready to receive during the teacher's lifetime. After the teacher's passing, when the student is ready, they are able to receive from the reservoir that their teacher had already prepared for them. It is very important to have this awareness.

It is called [Surrounding Light] since it surrounds the Lower, that is, it shines on it from afar even though it is not clothed in it, but it is a far and scant Illumination. This far-away Illumination is capable of purifying the density in the Lower to the point that the forms of all the parts in the Lower will be the same with the form of the Higher. Then the Lower will be able to receive all the Light belonging to it. This is called the entering of the Surroundings; in other words, the Surrounding Lights have entered and are clothed in the Vessels of the Lower that were purified, and they all become the aspect of Inner Light.

What is the purpose of our potential Light shining from afar? This Surrounding Light that the Creator has prepared for us, which gives off a dimmer Light by a shining from afar, is the Light of the Final Correction. Rav Ashlag says—and this is one of the most important understandings in this entire wisdom—this Surrounding Light is what enables us to continuously go from one level to our next level. And as we are learning now about the Surrounding Light, we actually awaken this power and strength within our soul.

He explains that the Surrounding Light that shines from afar has the ability to purify the Desire to Receive for the Self Alone within the Lower Vessel. It has the power to transform. All the reasons why we cannot manifest this Light from the Higher Vessel can be purified by the Surrounding Light. And once this occurs we can receive all of the Light that we need and are meant to receive. This is its singular purpose. This is what is referred to in the writings of the kabbalists as the entering of the Surrounding Light, the manifestation of the Surrounding Light. What does this mean? It means that the Vessel is transformed, elevated, and purified of its Desire to Receive for the Self Alone and now its potential Light is able to manifest within. The Light does not change; the Light is always there.

As we continue the Study the Ten Luminous Emanations we will notice that this concept of the purification of the Lower Vessel to allow a higher Light to come in is the basis for many of the next few chapters of study. This is the process the world is going to go through now. There is going to be this battle between the Surrounding Light that wants to purify the Vessel to allow it to manifest more Light and the Vessel's inability yet to purify itself.

One of the Rav's favorite concepts is called Binding by Striking (*Zivug deHaka'ah*), which illustrates the conflict or battle that rages within us. And this conflict of Binding by Striking is also what created our Worlds. All the Worlds that originate from the World of Adam Kadmon onward came through this process where the Surrounding Light is pushing the Vessel to purify itself so that it can reveal more Light, and the Vessel sometimes battles but then succumbs in a positive way to this purification that allows more and more Light to be manifest. The ultimate purpose of Surrounding Light is to lead us to the Final Correction, where a critical mass of the Vessel is purified, enabling the Light of the Final Correction to manifest.

This is the basis and our spiritual hope of everything because without the Surrounding Light we are stuck. Rav Ashlag continually reminds us throughout this study to push ourselves to delve deeper into this concept because there is a difficulty in connecting to this Surrounding Light. Therefore, the more we understand the Surrounding Light, the greater is our chance of actually connecting to this Light. Most of us connect to what we know, what we can understand, what we feel. The Surrounding Light is none of these; it is not what we know, what we feel, what we connect to.

Rav Ashlag will explain in the next section how we create a Vessel for the Surrounding Light. But first it begins with the understanding of our need for the Surrounding Light, which is something that is beyond our grasp. One of the most important keys in our spiritual work is having this ability to go beyond. As Rav Ashlag says: having Certainty Beyond Logic or Understanding (*Emuna Lemala Min haDa'at*). We did not come to this world to simply reveal Light or be spiritual. Rav Ashlag says that the only hope of our spiritual work accomplishing the purpose for which we came to this world, which is for the process of Purifying our Vessel (*Hizdachechut haMasach*), is by connecting to the Surrounding Light. Yet how do we connect to the Surrounding Light that is beyond? Internal Light is Light that we manifest, wisdom that we understand, connections that we feel. Surrounding Light is an Illumination from afar, and is hard to feel. Something that is difficult to do, something that we do not understand is what enables us to connect to this Surrounding Light.

In the Halel, the section that we sing on Holidays and Rosh Chodesh, we say: "This was the Lord's doing; it is wondrous in our eyes" (Psalms 118:23), meaning that this is coming from the Creator. It is awesome and is beyond our understanding. For us to connect to the Surrounding Light—which as we now know is our only hope of purifying, of correcting, of elevating—our work has to be beyond. Therefore, we have to constantly ask ourselves: *How much of my work, my study, my certainty is beyond?* because even if we are working, teaching, studying, praying, and connecting 24 hours a day within our realm, we are not connecting to the Surrounding Light. And if we are not connecting to the Surrounding Light, we have no hope of purification.

As Rav Ashlag says: "This far-away Illumination is capable of purifying the density in the Lower." Only this Light has the ability to purify. Therefore it is important that we constantly inject this power of beyond into everything we do—in what we study, in the way we do things, in the way we interact, in what we teach. This is our only hope. Lessons that we comprehend, connections that we make, are all a good foundation but it is not the way that we will change, it is not the way that we will elevate, and it is certainly not the purpose for which we came into this world. The purpose for which we came to this world is the Surrounding Light, and we connect to it by constantly making sure that within everything we do there is this element of beyond, this element of: *I do not understand why I am doing it.* We can only elevate if it is something we do not understand.

Consider the story of the Binding of Isaac. One of my favorite sections in the Midrash is as Abraham is walking to perform the Binding of Isaac, the Negative Side comes to him and says; "Tomorrow after you kill your son, the Creator is going to call you a murderer, and He will punish you for that." Abraham replies, "Nevertheless (*af al pi ken*)," meaning "I do not understand it, it makes no sense, and you are 100 percent right; it is beyond." As Abraham is about to cross a very low river, the water rose up to his nose, about to drown him, and he said, "Nevertheless (*af al pi ken*)." Abraham understood that there needed to be a tremendous element beyond his understanding within his work—*why do I have to do this*—otherwise he was not connecting to the Surrounding Light.

This translates practically as follows: even though we often see the logic in our spiritual work, there are times when we are expected to do things that do not make any sense—where we do not see the logical progression from point A to point B. This aspect of beyond needs to be part of our spiritual lives otherwise we are not connecting to the Surrounding Light. This cannot be said enough: If we are not connecting to the Surrounding Light by working beyond then we are not accomplishing what we came to this world to accomplish.

The Kotzker Rebbe (Rav Menachem Mendel of Kotzk, 1787–1859) says that when souls come down to this world, he envisions them as descending down on a ladder. And as the souls come off the ladder, they are born into this world. Some of these souls then jump up to try to grab the ladder as it starts elevating back up to the Heavens. Some jump ten times and they give up, some jump a hundred or a thousand times and then give up. Only a minute few never stop jumping. And it is only those who never stop jumping who accomplish what they come to this world to accomplish.

This is the same concept here. We have to be jumping for something that is beyond us. It is only if we are constantly jumping to a level beyond our grasp that we connect to the Surrounding Light. It is this Surrounding Light that purifies our Vessel, enabling us to manifest the Light for which we came to this world to manifest. If not—if we are not jumping beyond all the time in everything we do—we will have the Internal Light that we are born with and nothing more. The singular purpose for which we came to this world is to connect to the Surrounding Light, and the only way to achieve this is: *he'ara merachok* (an illumination from afar). *I do not understand it, it does not make sense, it is too difficult, it is beyond.* It is in these actions that we connect to and manifest the Surrounding Light.

---

10. The Vessel is divided into Exterior and Interior: In other words, since the Lights were divided into Inner Light and Surrounding Light, as said, two types of receiving are therefore found in the Vessel: a receiving in the inside of the Vessel and a receiving from the outside of the Vessel. The Inner Light is received within the Vessel, whereas the Surrounding Light, which purifies it from its density (as said in the previous paragraph), is considered as being received through the outside of the Vessel, that is, without being clothed in the Vessel.

Many may think that because there is Surrounding Light it shines to us, but this is not so. The Ari makes it very clear that there are two types of Vessels, two distinct ways of receiving. There is an Internal Vessel and an External Vessel. There is a Vessel that can receive the Internal Light, and there is a Vessel that can receive the Surrounding Light. One can have a great Internal Vessel for the Internal Light and almost no Vessel for the Surrounding Light. If we do not have a Vessel for the Surrounding Light, we do not receive it. Just having a Vessel does not mean that the Surrounding Light will shine. This is such an important concept for our spiritual work. There are two completely different ways to feel the Light of the Creator. For most of us, if we feel some Light or feel some connection, it is generally the same. Yet there are two very separate ways of receiving, and they influence in different ways and are felt in different ways.

The division into Exterior and Interior that is said regarding the Vessel is based on the distinction of the purity and density in the Vessel, since only its density is fit to receive the Inner Light, because the main receptacle of the Emanated Being is the Fourth Phase. However, the first Three Phases are incapable of receiving, as they merely cause the Fourth Phase to be revealed. Therefore, every Vessel in itself is distinguished as having Four Phases, where the Light is mainly received in its Fourth Phase,

---

which is why it is called the inside of the Vessel and its interior, where abundance dwells.

The Three Phases that merely cause the revelation of the Fourth Phase in the Vessel, which they themselves are not receptacles, are considered as circling the Fourth Phase from its Exterior. This is likened to a dense wall of a physical vessel that holds four layers encircling each other, where whatever is received in the Vessel is only in its interior, which is the inner layer. The other three layers in the density of the wall merely enable the inner layer to be able to hold the content. In the same way, we can understand here too about the spiritual realm that the main aspect that holds the abundance within it is the Fourth Phase of the Vessel, whereas the first Three Phases are the cause for revealing the Fourth Phase in all its might so it is capable of holding the abundance. But they themselves are not receptacles for the Inner Light.

Rav Ashlag reminds us that we cannot have Light without a Vessel, which is, of course, true of the Internal Light. We cannot manifest Light within ourselves without having a desire for it. What is a Vessel? Desire. The same is true of the Surrounding Light. And we awaken a desire for the Surrounding Light when we awaken a desire for levels that are beyond where we are now.

There are those who are happy where they are with their spiritual work, and then there are those who are, "...the members of the chamber (*bnei heichala*), who yearn to see the Light of Zeir Anpin." (Song by the Ari for the Third Meal of Shabbat) Meaning, who are those who are closest to the Creator? Those who yearn to see the Light of the Creator. This teaches us of the importance of yearning. When we yearn for something, we are awakening a desire for something that is beyond us and not with us now. Many of us have yearnings or desires in the physical realm yet fail to understand that to bring the power of the Surrounding Light into our lives we have to have a spiritual yearning.

All the kabbalists, Rav Shimon bar Yochai, the Ari, Rav Ashlag, Rav Brandwein, explain that the only way a person can grow is through this spiritual yearning because this is what enables the Surrounding Light to shine to us. A true yearning to connect to the Light of the Creator—something that is beyond where we are right now, is an important and necessary element of our spiritual work. Without yearning and awakening within us a constant greater desire for a connection to the Light of the Creator, we do not connect to the Surrounding Light, and we have no hope of growing spiritually. It is through yearning and awakening a strong desire to connect on a stronger, deeper level to the Light of the Creator that we can connect to and draw this Surrounding Light to ourselves and others, which then enables the Light of the Creator to help us grow to our next level.

The Midrash says that one of the greatest qualities of the Patriarchs was this yearning. The Zohar, in describing King David, says: "...my soul thirsts for You (*tzama lecha nafshi*)." (Psalms 63:2) This thirst is what we are supposed to aspire toward, where our spiritual yearning is way beyond our physical desires. For instance, if someone has not eaten for three days, they obviously have a tremendous desire right now to eat. Our spiritual desire has to be even greater than this hunger because our yearning needs to awaken from a place beyond where we are. The stronger our soul yearns for the Light of the Creator, the greater is our connection to the Light of the Creator. This is a very important idea.

They are therefore called the Exterior of the Vessel, since they are outside the aspect that receives the Inner Light. The Third Phase is exterior to the Fourth; the Second Phase is exterior to the Third and the First Phase is the most exterior, encircling them all. Above them all is an Exterior aspect with no density whatsoever, which is the root aspect of all Four Phases of the Vessel. Know that this aspect that is completely pure is the receptacle for the Surrounding Light, for due to its wondrous purity it is capable of receiving the Illumination of the Surrounding Light, even though it is from afar.

Rav Ashlag says that only Keter, the most pure aspect with no Desire to Receive for the Self Alone, is the vessel for the Surrounding Light. We spoke a lot about the importance of this Surrounding Light being our only hope for connection, for growth. Now, Rav Ashlag is telling us that the only way you can receive it, the only Vessel that is the Vessel for the Surrounding Light, is this root, this Keter, which has no Desire to Receive for the Self Alone. This is a scary thought because what this means is that if we want to have hope in our spiritual work, we need to have some element in our lives, some part of our Vessel that is completely pure.

We have to be clear that the only aspect of the Vessel, the only aspect of ourselves that can receive from the Surrounding Light it is not Chochmah, Binah or Zeir Anpin; it is not any elevated aspects of our soul, it is only the seed, the Keter. It bears repeating the words of Rav Ashlag as we think about how we can implement this into our lives: "since due to its wondrous purity it is capable of receiving the Illumination of the Surrounding Light, even though it is from afar." If we want to receive from this Surrounding Light, which clearly is our only hope for spiritual growth, there has to be some part of us that has this *zachut nifla'a* (wondrous purity). We need to look within and see if there is something inside all our garbage that is on this level of the seed, of tremendous purity, that can receive from this Surrounding Light because if not, then we have no hope spiritually; we have no hope to change, to grow, to accomplish what we came to this world to achieve.

Thus the division of the Vessel has been explained, where its Interior means the coarsest part of the Vessel, namely its Fourth Phase, and it is the receiver of the Inner Light; and its Exterior means the purest aspect of the Vessel, namely the root aspect of the Vessel, as explained earlier, and it is the receiver of the Surrounding Light from afar. Do not question that the Fourth Phase should be incapable of receiving due to the Tzimtzum and the Masach, for we are only dealing here with the aspect of the Returning Light that rises from the Fourth Phase (see also Inner Observation).

We know that after the Tzimtzum, no Light can be received by the Fourth Phase, the Malchut. There has to be this whole process of Returning Light, of Light coming down and being sent back—where the Vessel decides: *how much Light can I Receive Only for the Sake of Sharing*, and receives only this amount of Light. Yet even through this entire spiritual process of Returning Light, whatever Light becomes manifest, comes into the Fourth Phase, into Malchut. This is something we discussed at length previously. When the Fourth Phase, Malchut, receives the Light, it only receives it in this roundabout way of the Returning Light.

However the overriding concept that the Ari and Rav Ashlag are revealing to us here is the idea that there has to be a Vessel for the Surrounding Light. Sometimes we think that this Light is surrounding us even a little bit and will shine to us always. No. If there is no Vessel for it, we will not receive Surrounding Light.

Another key point Rav Ashlag makes is the type of Vessel this has to be. Only a tremendously pure Vessel can receive this Surrounding Light. Yet how do we awaken the purest part of our soul, the purest part of our Vessel to receive from this Surrounding Light? I am assuming all of us, at one point or another, become elevated and we feel something spiritually beyond what we have felt before. We have glimpses of things that are beyond us; call them moments of inspiration, moments of great connection. These are moments of the purest part of our soul becoming awakened to connect to that Surrounding Light.

Heaven forbid, if there are those of us who have not had these moments in a long time—we should be concerned. Hopefully every once in a while, at least once a week or once a month, after a tremendous amount of exertion, a tremendous amount of work, we suddenly feel a spark of that Light, something beyond. Now we can put consciousness to it. *What is it? What am I feeling? What am I connecting to during these times when I feel something beyond, some level of elevation?* This is our purest level of our soul, Keter, or that which has *zachut nifla'a*, this tremendous purity and is connecting to the Surrounding Light.

We now have a deeper understanding of the importance of the Surrounding Light and that the only way for spiritual growth is through our connections to the Surrounding Light, and that the only way to connect to the Surrounding Light is through the purest part of our soul. We also now know that these moments of great spiritual elevation, even though short-lived, are the times when we connect to the Surrounding Light.

It is important to understand that we have to hold onto these moments because they are not just fleeting instants of spiritual connection, they are specifically presented to us to give us the ability to change. If we have these awesome moments and we let them go, we lose a tremendous opportunity. The Baal Shem Tov speaks about the fact that whenever we have these moments, we have to do something to ground them immediately because if not, they get lost. There is a famous Midrash that says every day a voice comes out from Mt. Horeb, the mountain on which the Torah was given, and says "Return," meaning "become awakened." And the Baal Shem Tov asks the famous question: "Has anyone ever heard this voice?" Every day, this voice comes out for all of us. The Creator calls out to each one of us every day and awakens us to change. The Baal Shem Tov explains that it is not a physical voice but rather those awakenings we experience from within, and if we merit to, we feel them. But even more important than feeling them is grabbing them and holding on to them; making them manifest, making them stay in our lives. If we connect to the Surrounding Light and then let that connection go, this Light will not be able to push us to the transformation it is meant to do.

The Me'or Einayim, in the portion of Vayetze, quotes, "And Jacob lifted his feet, and he went to the land of the children of the east." (Genesis 29:1) Rashi (Rav Shlomo YItzchaki, 1040–1105) says that after Jacob asked the Creator, "Will you be here with me? Will you protect me?" the Creator tells him, "Yes I promise you I will be with you." Rashi continues, "As soon as he received the good tidings that he was assured of God's protection, his heart lifted up his feet and he walked swiftly." The Me'or Einayim says:

> Before Mashiach comes, before the End of the Correction, the Creator says, 'Lo, I will send the prophet Elijah to you before the coming of the awesome, fearful day of the Lord, and he shall turn the heart of the fathers to the children, and the heart of the children to their fathers' (Malachi 3:23-24). Just as it is true that before Mashiach comes, Elijah the Prophet, will come to this world to awaken all of us to a connection to the Light of the Creator, by which there will be an awakening of consciousness in the world, as it says, 'then the world will be full of knowledge.' (Isaiah 11:9) so too every person at any time can connect to this aspect, to this element of Elijah the Prophet becoming revealed. If you hear some good news, or if you are studying and you suddenly come to an understanding that you did not have before, and from that understanding, from that connection, you become filled with excitement, with life. This is a moment that should not be wasted, but is a moment upon which you can elevate even your lower part, even parts of yourself that need connection.

There has to be this step where Elijah the Prophet comes to awaken the world before the coming of Mashiach. When someone tells you good news, or shares with you a powerful lesson and awakens within you a level of joy and understanding that you did not have before, this person manifests within them a certain level of Elijah the Prophet. Good news, whether great or small, only ever comes to this world through Elijah the Prophet. For instance, a newscaster who tells good news, has some element of Elijah the Prophet within him. When you are teaching or are giving someone good spiritual news, if you are elevating them with new thoughts, an element of Elijah the Prophet is becoming manifest within you.

Only Elijah the Prophet is the one who reveals good news in this world, yet he becomes manifest and clothed in that person telling you the news. This aspect of bringing good news, in spiritual study, is the gift that was created during the Six Days of Creation. When Pinchas, who was Elijah, achieved that level of elevation, through that incident, that moment made him the channel. He became the conduit for good news in the world. This is why so many times when we hear good news we become excited to share with somebody else the good news. Why? Because your soul is feeling a connection to Elijah the Prophet. Even though most people do not see, their soul knows. If you had any understanding of this, you will be able to grab that element of Eliyahu, hold on to it and use it now for your spiritual growth. And you can use it to literally springboard you, to elevate you from one level to the next. And even the person who is receiving this news receives a spark of Elijah the Prophet into him, and he receives also an awakening of consciousness, so he can use that good news to connect to the Creator. Through using this revelation of Elijah the Prophet to you, you can elevate even the lower parts of yourself. And that is why it says, "And Jacob lifted his feet, and he went to the land of the children of the east." (Genesis 29:1) What do the feet represent? The lower part. They represent the darker parts of our soul. Why? Because The Light of Elijah the Prophet that is now being revealed, that comes from the Six Days of Creation, that comes through Pinchas, now purifies his even lower parts.

When the Creator told Jacob this good news, Jacob knew something was happening here. He did not allow himself to be happy by the promise of the Creator to him: "I will be with you and I will protect you." He said: "One second, there is something deeper happening here. This Light of Elijah the Prophet, this Light of good news is coming into my soul, let me use it to grow. Let me use it to elevate my lower parts."

The Me'or Einayim, in the Portion of Vayetze, explains that with the process Jacob went through he received assistance from the soul of Elijah the Prophet, and he grabbed onto it. He did not say, "Oh! This is good news, let me be happy for a moment." He said, "There is something deeper happening here. There is a revelation of the soul of Elijah the Prophet to me, let me grab onto that and use it for my spiritual work." The Me'or Einayim explains that every time we hear good news, we have this same ability to grab onto it and use it in our spiritual work.

Every time there is an awakening of Surrounding Light, every time we get that spiritual awakening, every time we feel inspired, every time there are those moments when we feel a tremendous connection, we need to stop ourselves from just being happy because we had this moment and instead be very conscious of it. Grab onto it and say, "I know this is a connection to the Surrounding Light, and I appreciate that this moment is my hope and I want to grab it and hold onto it. And I want to use it to help me grow, to help me elevate."

If we have these personal moments of the revelation of the Surrounding Light and we just let them go, it is not going to elevate us, it is not going to help us grow. When these moments come, they have a specific purpose. The Baal Shem Tov says that we all experience this during the day. For some people, it is half a second, and we just let it go out of our mind. But every single one of us has these moments. And only if, every time they come in, we appreciate them, know what they are, grab and hold onto them, can we use them for the purpose for which they are meant. They are to give us the strength and the ability to grow and transform.

We need to receive this Light from *he'ara merachok*, this Light beyond us that comes to us now for a second, grab onto it and say, "I know that you are going to help me now. This moment of inspiration, this moment of connection, is going to help me now transform." By being conscious of it, and holding onto it, we can manifest this Surrounding Light that enables us to elevate higher and higher to accomplish what we came to this world to accomplish. This is a tremendously important idea.

4. However, the difference between the Circular and the Straight [Sefirot] is that the Ten Circular Sefirot relate to the Light called Nefesh,[11] and they have Inner Light and Surrounding Light, Inner and Outer. [The Circular] has the aspect of the Ten Sefirot of Vessels, and in each Vessel there is Interior and Exterior, and it also has Ten Sefirot of Lights, each Light containing Inner Light (Ohr Pnimi) and Surrounding Light (Ohr Makif). But the Ten Sefirot of Straightness relate to the Light called Ruach,[12] which is a level above the level of Nefesh, as is known. They too comprise Inner Light and Surrounding Light and contain the Ten Sefirot of Vessels, and in each Vessel there is Interior and Exterior. It is obvious that the Nefesh aspect emanated first, and then the Ruach was emanated.

11. **The Ten Circular Sefirot relate to the Light called Nefesh:** The Light in all the Sefirot that are capable only of receiving Lights but are incapable of bestowing to others is called the Light of Nefesh. It has already been explained that all the Light in the Circles must be received from the Light of the Line (as mentioned in Volume 2, Chapter 1, Section 12). The reason is that the Supernal Light cannot connect with the Vessels except through a Unification (*Zivug*) with the Masach, which raises Returning Light. This Returning Light is what connects the Light with the Vessels, as mentioned (Volume 1, Chapter 2, Section 11).

Therefore, regarding the Vessels that do not have this Masach, the Supernal Light does not connect to them for them to bestow to others from above downward, and they are only fit to receive Light from the previous level, from below upward, only for the sake of their own vitality. This Light is called the Light of Nefesh, as mentioned earlier. Therefore, since there is no Masach in the Circular Vessels, as mentioned, the Supernal Light does not actually connect with them, and they have to receive the Light from the Line. And even this is only to the degree of their own vitality, and not to bestow, as explained. Thus the Light in the Circles is called the Light of Nefesh, as explained.

Here the Ari and Rav Ashlag reveal a very important concept. If a Vessel does not have the ability to give over Light, to share with others, it can only receive the Light of Nefesh. The Vessel can be the purest, most elevated in the world, if it does not have the innate ability to share with others, to give Light to others, the Light it receives can only be restricted to the level of Nefesh. This teaches us that we can never give another person Light that they have not earned.

There is a famous quote from Rav Ashlag, as he speaks to his students: "I would love to be able to do the work for you, but what can I do? Every person has to do his own work." No teacher can ever do the work for the student; the work has to be done by the student. What is the work? The work is the ability to share. We cannot give someone—no matter how much we desire, no matter how much they desire—more Light than they are able to share with someone else.

For instance, someone might want to make all the connections and study everything in the world, but if they have not really manifested the need to share Light with others, their teacher can teach them for the next one thousand years, and they will never get more than the lowest level of Nefesh. Rav Ashlag says this type of person can receive only the amount of Light that can sustain them, keep them alive. Nothing more.

Sometimes we would like our students to come to the understanding of the need to share with others because, for all kinds of reasons, it is good for their spiritual development. But this teaching from Rav Ashlag makes it very stark and very clear. There is nothing a person can do if they do not have the ability to share Light—no years of study, no years of connection, no years of prayer or meditation that can reveal anything above Nefesh, and not only Nefesh but only enough Light of Nefesh to sustain them. Nothing more. Even with all the tools, wisdom, and connection, they will never achieve a level beyond Nefesh of Nefesh. It is a spiritual law. As Rav Ashlag says, "The Light in all the Sefirot that are capable only of receiving Lights but are incapable of bestowing to others is called the Light of Nefesh."

We need to grasp the importance of sharing Light. For instance, helping the homeless is good, it is sharing something physical, but that is still not sharing Light; it is still only at the level of Nefesh of Nefesh. Even if Rav Shimon Bar Yochai came down into this world and spent the next one thousand years teaching, there will still only be Nefesh of Nefesh because any Vessel that does not have the ability to share Light with others cannot receive more than Nefesh of Nefesh.

This should awaken within us the understanding that we can be deluding ourselves by saying, "I'm making this connection, I'm doing all these things." If we want the hope of achieving anything beyond the level of Nefesh of Nefesh, we have to understand that if we are not a vessel that gives Light further to someone else, we can receive no more than the lowest level of Light—Nefesh of Nefesh. Yes, we can make connections; yes, we can use the tools and it will bring a certain amount of Light, because compared to what most people have, Nefesh of Nefesh is a lot of Light. But there is a clear barrier beyond which we will never be able to manifest Light if we do not take upon ourselves the desire, the mission of sharing Light with others.

> 12. **But the Ten Sefirot of Straightness relate to the Light called Ruach:** The Ten Sefirot of Ruach are givers and therefore the Light of Ruach is called Masculine Light, meaning that it bestows. But the Ten Sefirot of Nefesh are called Feminine Light, meaning that it receives and is not able to give. Therefore, the Ten Sefirot of the Light of the Line are called the Ten Sefirot of Ruach, to indicate that they are considered Masculine Light and givers. The reason has already been explained before in the preceding paragraph; look there. Therefore, the Light of Ruach is higher than the level of Nefesh, since it is the giver to the Nefesh.

The terms masculine and feminine are not discussing men and women, it is about the type of Vessel. Just to be clear, a man can be a Female Vessel if he does not bestow and a woman can be considered a Male Vessel if she shares the Light. We are not talking about the physicality of male and female, we are talking about the consciousness of giving and receiving.

When we ask ourselves: *Where am I in my spiritual connection*, for many of us the answer is dependent on what we are feeling—in other words, what we are receiving. The Ari and Rav Ashlag tell us that the only way to gauge where we are in our spiritual connection is how much we are growing our sharing, and how much joy are we experiencing in that sharing.

In the Writings of the Ari (Kitvei ha'Ari)—specifically the Gate of Reincarnations—the Ari discusses elevating from Nefesh to Ruach, from Ruach to Neshamah. We see this beautiful, spiritual process where we gain more understanding, and we receive more Light.

Here, Rav Ashlag is revealing to us an entirely new way of viewing these levels of soul—something I hope did not get missed because it sounds simple. For instance, Nefesh, Ruach, and Neshamah does not connote an elevated soul; someone who has gone from Nefesh to Ruach, from Ruach to Neshamah. Rather they are simply different levels of giving. When the Ari and the Zohar say that a person has to make sure that in a lifetime they elevate from the level of Nefesh to the level of Ruach, and from the level of Ruach to the level of Neshamah, most of us think that this is discussing our spiritual process, that it is an indication of how much more Light, how much more wisdom we have received and taken in.

Here Rav Ashlag is teaching us a very important, almost basic but completely new way to look at this. He says that the only way to elevation is not by attainment of even spiritual Light or wisdom; it is only by sharing. The Ruach is more than Nefesh not because it is a higher type of Light but simply because it has more power of sharing. Neshamah is higher than Ruach not because it has more innate Light but rather because it has more sharing.

When you read the words of Rav Ashlag carefully, he says that this Light is called the Light of Ruach or the Light of Nefesh because of this singular quality. If we have an ability to share then we are on the level of Ruach. No matter how much Light we attained, no matter how connected we are to the Light of the Creator, if we are not more sharing than we were on the level of Ruach, we can have more Light but this does not elevate us to the level of Neshamah, this does not elevate us to the next level of our soul. The only way that we elevate spiritually is by a stronger ability to share. No spiritual attainment, no taking in of Light, of wisdom, will ever elevate us from Nefesh to Ruach, from Ruach to Neshamah. The only way to elevate from one to the other is by attaining more of a sharing capability. This is the difference.

Just to clarify, concerning the three levels of Nefesh, Ruach, and Neshamah that the Zohar says we have to elevate from one to the other, many of us think of this in spiritual terms as how much more Light we need to bring into our lives so as to go on to the next level. The Ari and Rav Ashlag are telling us that this is the completely wrong way to look at it. The question we should be asking ourselves is not, "How do I go from the level I am at now to the next level," but rather, "How much more of a capacity to give can I add to my life so that I can go from one level to the next?" This is the only way. No attainment, no taking in will elevate us from one level of the soul to the next. Only the awakening of a stronger ability and capacity to give is what elevates us from one level to the next level in our spiritual process.

This same concept applies to true love. For most people, love is taking in. For instance, a person says, "I love fish" or "I love meat." This love means they like to take a fish or an animal, kill it, and ingest it. This is our sense of love. Of course this is not love, it is selfishness—the Desire to Receive for the Self Alone. Very often, this translates even into our spiritual matters. We are seeking to have more; more wisdom, more Light, which is completely wrong. Our focus needs to be to desire a greater ability to share. When we look at our spiritual work as simply a way of having a greater ability to give more, this is what elevates us from one level to the next.

These important concepts relate to comprehending the Light in general, as well as to why these new Vessels, called the Line, receive the Light of Ruach as opposed to these beautiful and perfected Circular Vessels from before the Tzimtzum that receive a lower Light called Nefesh.

5. Even while the Ten Sefirot are in the aspect of Circles one within the other,[13] they contain all the aspects of the receiving of abundance that are in the Ten Sefirot of the Straight Line,[14] as follows: in the Circle of Keter—called Arich Anpin after the Correction[15]—there is a hole and a window[16] on the right side of the Circle,[17] and from there the Light of Arich descends to the Circle of Aba,[18] shining to it. There is another window on the left side of the Circle of Arich; the Light emerges to the left side of the Circle of Aba, pierces it so that a window is made in it,[19] from which Light flows to the Circle of Ima within the Circle of Aba, shining to it. Thus when the Light passes through the left of the Circle of Aba it is not for Aba's own sake, as it only passes through there in passing.[20] Rather, the Illumination is mainly for Ima. Thus Arich Anpin shines upon Aba and Ima together, as is the case regarding Their Linear [Sefirot]. And even though They are Circular, one within another, They do have Straight Lines[21]—Right, Left, and Central—via the aspect of these windows in them. And from there, the Light flows into the Ten Circular Sefirot through actual Straight Lines, in all the particular details themselves that are actually in the Ten Sefirot of the Straight Line of Ruach.

One of the reasons Rav Ashlag put the Talmud Eser Sefirot together is because when the Ari was teaching his students it was not in any specific order; it depended on where the students were at. Therefore there was no order to the teachings of the Ari. So Rav Ashlag took from different sections of the Writings of the Ari and wrote his commentary on it. He was very specific and particular about which sections would be in what specific order in the Talmud Eser Sefirot. And what is unique about this section is that there are a lot of advanced concepts spoken about here by the Ari, and obviously there is a reason why they appear here.

Just to recap, in the previous chapters the Ari spoke about the fact that we have two realities now that exist after the Tzimtzum. One is called the Circular Vessels—the pre-Tzimtzum Vessels; the Vessels that do not have any issues with their Desire to Receive for the Self Alone and do not have any sense of being higher or lower. This reality is a copy of what was there before. And then there is also the second reality called the Line, which is the new system of receiving that is set up after the Tzimtzum, where the Light is received only for the Sake of Sharing. Now, the Vessel does not receive anything unless it has this process of Returning Light, where the Vessel says, "How much fulfillment can I Receive only for the Sake of Giving pleasure to the Creator? I will receive that much and no more because I will certainly not receive for myself alone anymore." The Ari explains that in this new reality the Circular Vessels are not the cause of any revelation of Light; they do not bring any new Light but rather only receive their Light from the Vessels of the Line. This is the new law of the Worlds at this point.

What is really beautiful, as you truly start to see the progression of the process of the creation of our world, is that it is always about change. It is always about new realities that progress toward the ultimate perfection, and there is never stability in the sense that one system does not stay forever. The system of the Circles do not stay forever; the system of the Line does not stay forever. There will be many processes in between, and there is also the Second Contraction (Tzimtzum Bet). This is a big picture understanding that our world, and even our spiritual process, is never supposed to be stable, is never supposed to be one system. It is supposed to be this now, and then we change. We are on a different level and so our work is different—there is a different push.

It is so easy to get lulled into a system. This is what the Negative Side wants. The Negative Side wants us to become comfortable in whatever system of comfortability we have developed. Unfortunately, even spiritual people get stuck in this system because it is comfortable, it is what they know, it seems to be working. They can stay in it for five, ten, twenty years. However this is not the way any World after the Tzimtzum, including our world, is ever meant to be. There is always meant to be not just movement, but a complete shift in systems within which we are working.

We have the Circular Vessels, we have the Vessels of the Line, we have the First Contraction (Tzimtzum Alef), we have the Second Contraction (Tzimtzum Bet); these are not small changes that are taking place. These are grand, huge shifts of systems within which the world operates. And our spiritual work needs to mirror this. To whatever degree we are coasting within our comfort zone of spiritual work, there always has to be something that shakes it up. A big shake up; not every day, but every year, every two years, every three years—something. We want there to be a great movement, a great new reality within which we work. And without going into the philosophy of it, this is what really separates Rav Ashlag's revelation of the understanding of the world from most religious or even spiritual systems.

Most spiritual systems, certainly most religions really want to keep everything as close to what was as possible. And although years go by, they are always looking backwards—"let us make sure that we keep in line with what was." Rav Ashlag teaches that the world is progressing in a different way. Based on this Study of the Ten Luminous Emanations, the system of the world is meant to be shifting in great ways. This completely different view of our world is based on the understanding of how this world came to be. And the way this world will come to its Final Correction is through great shifts in the system. This is an important understanding.

The Ari says: "Even while the Ten Sefirot are in the aspect of Circles, one within the other," meaning that they do not have any sense of being higher or lower. Chochmah does not view itself as being any less than Keter. Keter does not view itself as being higher than Chochmah. There is no sense of Difference of Form between these Ten Circles. Even though, of their own essence, these Vessels do not sense a difference between higher and lower, "they contain all the aspects of the receiving of abundance that are in the Ten Sefirot of the Straight Line." Since they are receiving their Light from the Line, from this new way of receiving with Returning Light, they have to be influenced by the way the Line gives Light, by the way the Line manifests Light.

Here we learn a very important and scary lesson concerning the interaction between a giver and a receiver, a teacher and a student. Even if we want to give Light, we want to give wisdom, we want to give teachings to a student, there has to be an awareness that we will also be transferring negative things. We will also be transferring difficulties that this person or student might not possess. But because we are giving them the Light, the wisdom, the information, everything gets transferred with this wisdom; we give them of our essence, which can, Heaven forbid, have negative ramifications. If in what we are giving over there is some distortion, this influences the Vessel receiving it, even if the Vessel does not have the problem to begin with. Therefore, we have a tremendous responsibility as teachers, as friends even, to know that whenever we give over something to someone there is a danger. If we are not strong or pure enough, we are also transferring some non-positive things as we transfer Light, as we transfer wisdom.

This is what is happening here. The Line is giving to the Circles, since it is the giver. And once the Circular Vessels receive their Light from the Line, they have to go through a transformation, they have to be changed to some degree. Rav Ashlag will make clear that it is not to the degree that the Line is different, but nevertheless these Circular Vessels, these old Vessels are influenced by these new Vessels.

How do we understand this difference that is going to occur within the Circular Vessels? The Ari says, "In the Circle of Keter—called Arich Anpin after the Correction." Everything we have learnt until now, and even what we are going to be learning a little further on, is dealing with the reality of the Worlds that exist after Tzimtzum Alef, after the first removal of Light. Later, there is a second process called Tzimtzum Bet, which is called the Correction.

In this new reality, every new spiritual reality has a new name called a Partzuf, which is a bigger construct than a Sefirah. A Sefirah is in this simple world where you have Light going from one Sefirah to the other. After Tzimtzum Bet, each Sefirah is more complicated, and there is a more difficult, longer process for Light to be revealed. Therefore there is more complication in the construct and essence of each one of these Sefirot. Their new name in this new reality is Partzufim. The difference between a Sefirah and a Partzuf is that a Sefirah is in the purer, simpler form. For instance, in the Endless World there are Sefirot, which is Light simply transferred from one to the next. Keter gave to Chochmah, Chochmah gave to Binah, Binah gave to Zeir Anpin, Zeir Anpin to Malchut. After Tzimtzum Bet, the second removal of Light, it gets more complicated.

Now each one of these Sefirot are given a different Name in terms of what Partzuf they are. For instance, the more intricate spiritual construct around Keter is called Arich Anpin. In this new reality, because the Circular Vessels receive their Light from the Line, it cannot be that simple. The Circular Vessels have to start receiving and giving Light in different ways. In the reality of the Line, Chochmah is viewed to be less than Keter, Binah is viewed to be less than Chochmah. There are now more direct lines and distinct boundaries between the Sefirot that did not exist in the Ein Sof, this realm of the Circular Vessels, that must be transferred into the Circular Vessels now that they are receiving their Light from the Line.

Therefore, the Ari says, "in the circle of Keter—called Arich Anpin after the Correction—there is a Hole and a Window on the Right Side of the Circle, and from there the Light of Arich descends to the Circle of Aba, shining to it." From Arich Anpin, from Keter, the Light goes only through an opening on the Right Side of Keter to Chochmah or to Aba. This giving is much more exact in a way that clarifies the boundaries between higher and lower. Yet this is not the true nature of the Circular Vessels. As mentioned previously, in the World of the Circular Vessels there is no real difference between Keter, Chochmah, and Binah. They do not see any differences between them but because they are now receiving the Light from the Line, these new differences have to be migrated over into the Circular Vessels. Therefore, when Keter gives to Chochmah it cannot give simply or purely, it has to only go from its Right Side; meaning from the side that has more affinity and relationship with Chochmah.

The Ari says, "There is another window on the Left Side of the Circle of Arich; the Light emerges to the Left Side of the Circle of Aba, pierces it so that a window is made in it, from which Light flows to Ima's Circle within Aba's circle, shining to it." Chochmah has a new way of giving. The Light that goes from Keter through Chochmah to Binah is not for the purposes of Chochmah; obviously it is for the purpose of Binah. The Ari is telling us that the Light from the Right Column of Keter gives to Chochmah. When it comes time to give Light to Binah, called Ima, the Light goes from the Left Side of Keter through the Left Side of Chochmah, through Aba—not really stopping there, not really being manifest within Chochmah—straight to Ima, to Binah.

To make sure this is clear, there are Ten Circles—one within the other. After Tzimtzum Bet, they now have different Names: Keter is called Arich Anpin, Chochmah is called Aba, Binah is called Ima. When Keter gives Light to Chochmah or to Aba, it gives it from its Right Side. When Keter gives to Binah, it gives Light from its Left Side and it transfers this Light through the Circle of Chochmah, but the Light does not become manifest there; it does not stay there because it is not for the purposes of Chochmah.

The Ari says, "Thus when the Light passes through the Left of the Circle of Aba it is not for Aba's own sake, as it only passes by there in passing. Rather, the Illumination is mainly for Ima." This is very different from the way the Light was received in the previous Worlds. Previously, the Light was first transferred from Keter to Chochmah, from Chochmah to Binah, but now we come to a much more structured reality where the Light comes from Keter and when the Light is meant for Binah, for Ima, it goes through Chochmah because Chochmah is the cause for Binah, but it does not stay there. It only gets transferred through Chochmah to go to Binah.

"Thus Arich Anpin shines upon Aba and Ima together." Meaning Keter shines the Light to Chochmah and Binah at the same time. Whereas previously it was more of a simple transfer from Keter to Chochmah, Chochmah to Binah, now we come into a realm called the Three Column system—Right, Left, and Central—where Chochmah is Right Column and Binah is Left Column. Thus Keter has to give a different type of Light to Chochmah and a different type of Light to Binah, "as is the case regarding their Linear [Sefirot]." This reality is forced upon the Circular Vessels by the fact that they are receiving this Light from the Line and therefore the Light has to be manifest in this way.

"And even though they are Circular, one within another," meaning that in their essence they are fine to receive in the simple way that the Light was received in the Endless World, "they do have straight lines—Right, Left, and Central—by the aspect of these windows in them." In this new Reality, receiving has to be by way of Right Column, Left Column, and Central Column, meaning specific Light to Chochmah, specific Light to Binah, and specific Light to Zeir Anpin. "And from there, the Light flows into the Ten Circular Sefirot through actual Straight Lines," meaning in the exact, limited lines, "in all the particular details themselves that are actually in the Ten Sefirot of the Straight Line of Ruach." In exactly the same way the Light is manifest within the Line.

13. **Even while the Ten Sefirot are in the aspect of Circles one within the other:** Meaning that the five levels—Keter, Chochmah, Binah, Zeir Anpin, and Nukvah—are not drawn directly, meaning one below the other—namely, from the purer to the denser (Volume 2, Chapter 1, Section 5). Rather, the five levels are equal, not one below the other, or one denser than the other.

Yet surely there is the distinction of cause and effect between them, as they emerge from each other and flow from each other. Chochmah emerges from Keter, Binah from Chochmah, Zeir Anpin from Binah and Malchut from Zeir Anpin (as mentioned in Volume 1, Chapter 1, Section 14).

This said distinction between cause and effect is defined by their position within each other. Every cause encircles its effect: Chochmah is encircled by Keter, Binah is encircled by Chochmah and so on, in such a way that "one within the other" means one encircled by the other, as explained. But there is no distinction of above or below whatsoever among them (as mentioned in Volume 1, Chapter 1, Section 19).

There are a few very important lessons Rav Ashlag gives us here. We know that these concepts not only existed in the process of our World coming into existence, but these are realities that exist today. The big difference between the reality of the Line and the reality of the Circles is that within the realm of the Circles there is no pure and less pure, there is no higher and lower, and this of course is the reality of no ego. One of the ways we decide whether we are connected to the World of the Circular Vessels, the World that takes us back to the Ein Sof, or whether we are in the limited World of the Line is whether our world view is one of having higher and lower realms.

Rav Ashlag explains that when the Ari says that the Ten Circular Vessels are one within the other, this means that all five levels view themselves as cause and effect. They are the cause for the other. Chochmah came from Keter, Binah came from Chochmah, Zeir Anpin from Binah and Malchut from Zeir Anpin. For instance, Moses saw himself as the cause of the wisdom coming to the Israelites, and coming to this world. And the fact that he was the cause and they were the effect did not make him any better; there is no sense within Moses that that makes him any better. That was simply the way the system was set up. When we say that the Circles are one within the other it means that although one is the cause for the other, in their essence they view no difference because of that cause. Obviously, the cause creates the effect. Chochmah is the effect caused by Keter and Binah is caused by Chochmah; they are effected one from the other, they are created one from the other. But the fact that one causes the other, gives to the other, does not affect one being higher or the lower.

It says that Moses was the most humble person. The Ramchal (Rav Moshe Chaim Luzzato, 1701–1746) asks, how can that be? He is the one person in the history of the world to be chosen to bring down and reveal the Torah in our world. Clearly, he was a historically unique soul. How is it possible that he achieved this level of the Circular Vessels—not seeing himself higher in any degree? In a Circle even Malchut, the lowest of the lowest Vessels, does not have any sense that Keter is better than it, and Keter, which is the highest and purest of all the Vessels, has no sense of it being higher than Malchut. The Ramchal explains that Moses viewed his work in this world the same as the work of the worms. The Creator put them in our world and they do their job. The animals—cows, horses, donkeys—too have their work in this world.

Moses says, "I have my work in this world. It does not make me any better than someone else. The fact that I was chosen for this work, and the worm was chosen for its work, or the cow was chosen for that work, does not make me better than them." This real consciousness is how Moses achieved the level of true humility. Moses was not blind to who he was, what his purpose was, what he had done and what he needed to do, rather he also had clarity about the fact that it did not make him at all higher than any other species or being in this world. This is the Circular Vessel. Although there is cause and effect, there is the teacher and the student, there is the giver and the receiver, there is no difference in essence that is affected because of that giving and receiving. The giver and the receiver feel no difference one from the other.

This World of the Circles is the world that we are meant to aspire toward. It is where no matter what—we can be Keter, we can be Malchut—it makes no difference. There is no higher and lower. What is the Line? In the World of the Line, Keter gives to Chochmah, and Chochmah gives to Binah—everyone is different, everyone has a distinct type of Light to reveal in this world, which makes them different; this makes them higher or lower than each other.

If we want to go back to the connection to the Ein Sof, for the sake of bringing the Final Correction (Gemar haTikkun), our goal must be to connect to the Circular Vessels. The only way to connect to the Ein Sof is if we truly come to a point where we do not see a pure and less pure, higher and lower. This is the only way. A person can do all the spiritual work in the world, yet if their view of themselves and their friends in this world as being of a higher and lower level in such a the way that it spiritually makes a difference to them, then they cannot achieve a connection to the Ein Sof, they cannot achieve a connection that can bring about the Gemar haTikkun. To be a channel to bring the Gemar haTikkun to our world, we have to be connected to the Circular Vessels, to this consciousness of no higher or lower. This does not mean that one is blind to one's purpose or to one's job, rather we do not view that difference as making us any more or less important, better or worse. This is a very important concept.

14. They contain all the aspects of the receiving of abundance that are in the Ten Sefirot of the Straight Line: The Light receives Impressions from the Vessel with which it is clothed, where even when it leaves and goes into another Vessel it does not change the qualities it had in the previous Vessel. Thus, while the Light was in a Straight Line, it flowed down from one to the other, which means that it gradually thickened according to the sequence of the levels due to the Curtain (Masach) present there, as said (Volume 2, Chapter 1, Section 6). Thus, even after it left and entered the Ten Circular Sefirot that have no Masach, where it of necessity curls, it nevertheless does not change its ways as it flows from level to level.

Explanation: when the Light of the Line reaches the Sefirah of Keter, for example, it curls, meaning it receives the shape of that Vessel, where there is no distinction between up and down. But when the Light extends from the Circle of Keter to the Circle of Chochmah, it does not curl (see Volume 1, Terminology Answers, Number 3) but flows straight down, that is, differentiating between up and down. Due to this it is found that the Circular Sefirah of Chochmah is below the Circle of Keter and is denser than Keter, as their form is not the same.

The same applies when the Light comes from Chochmah to Binah; it flows to it in a linear way. Thus Binah is considered below Chochmah, that is, denser than Chochmah. The same applies to all the Sefirot in such a way that even though the Ten Circular Sefirot have the same form, without a differentiation of up and down on the part of the Vessels, as said, they nevertheless do have a differentiation of up and down, for "they contain all the aspects of the receiving of abundance that are in the Ten Sefirot of the Straight Line."

When the Rav began teaching the Study of the Ten Luminous Emanations classes in Queens 40 years ago, he would often show a picture of an optical illusion that depicted both two faces and a vase in the same image. As we continue in this study, there is a strong underlying understanding that within the Ten Luminous Emanations, and in the study of Kabbalah, our mind has to be able to see two things within one—and this is a concept that repeats itself all the time. Very often, we are naturally inclined to view one thing as we see it, and believe that this is all there is. Yet one of the beauties of the study of Kabbalah is that it truly expands our awareness to see many layers in any one reality. And this is what is happening here. There is this seemingly paradoxical back and forth within the Ari and Rav Ashlag's writings concerning the reality of the Circular Vessels and the Line. Are they influenced, are they not influenced?

In this particular section, Rav Ashlag says that because the Circular Vessels receive their Light from the Line, they are influenced in the way that the Line receives. It is now forced upon the Circular Vessels to receive in this altered, new way. In other words, the Light is influenced by the Vessel within which it is manifest. Of course, we know that the Light does not change but depending on the Vessel that receives It, there are veils put upon this Light. For instance, a purple covering that is placed on top of a light bulb causes the light that shines from the bulb to be purple. The light bulb itself has not changed, it still shines white, but because of the purple covering when you look at it externally, you see purple. Thus the Light has not changed but it has taken on a different shape in some way because of the Vessel within which it has become manifest.

And Rav Ashlag says that once Light is changed by a Vessel, even if that Light will now go into a different Vessel, the change that was influenced upon it by the initial Vessel remains with it always. The essence of the Light does not change but a shell, a covering is put upon it, which makes it look different, and this is what remains.

For example, when the Light of the Line enters the Keter of the Circular Vessels, we say that it becomes a Circle. What does this mean? It now becomes anew. This Light senses a new reality where there is no longer a higher or a lower. When this Light goes from Keter down into Chochmah, it does not still maintain that consciousness of having no higher or lower. It is now manifest in a linear way, where now there is a higher and lower. Once the Light becomes manifest in Chochmah of the Circular Vessels, it still has the Residue of the consciousness of the Line, which means that there is higher and lower in this World—Keter is more important than Chochmah.

There is a paradox existing within the Circular Vessels that now receive the Light from the Line. From the Circular Vessel's perspective, their essence, their true consciousness, there is no such thing as better or worse, higher and lower. But because the consciousness of this new Light comes from the World of the Line and has been altered to perceive a difference between higher and lower, it transposes that reality, this consciousness into the World of the Circles. The Circles are now receiving Light that keeps telling them, "No, there is a difference."

All the Sefirot of the Circles now have this strange consciousness, which is not true in their essence. They are almost forced into this thought process because of the Light that they are receiving. Therefore, to understand what is occurring here and since this concept comes up throughout the study of Kabbalah, we have to develop the ability to perceive two realities in one reality.

A perfect example to illustrate this is the biblical story of Joseph and his brothers. When the brothers came before Joseph because he had taken Benjamin and threatened to keep him as a slave, it is apparent that are two completely separate realities. There is the reality of the brothers, which consists of darkness, pain, suffering, and exile; and Joseph's reality, which is only Light, simplicity, and redemption. It is all one reality, but there exists within this one reality, two completely opposite realities. This idea has a lot of practical ramifications. We must know that we are always living within the realm of exile, the realm of darkness, but that within that same reality there is also the exact opposite. The complete Redemption is always within this reality as well. No matter what our perception, no matter what we are experiencing right now, the opposite of that reality, meaning the opposite of darkness—complete Light, complete redemption—is manifest in this same reality as well.

Thus within these Circular Vessels, there are two realities. There is the consciousness of the Vessel, where there is no higher and lower; everything is simple and alike. And there is the consciousness of Higher and Lower Vessels, higher and lower levels of this Light of the Line that is coming into these Circular Vessels. These two realities now become one. Within one singular reality there are two opposite realities. This is true here, and is true in much of our study. The illustration of Joseph and his brothers is an important tool to keep throughout our studies.

15. **Called Arich Anpin after the Correction:** Explanation: After the Four Worlds—Atzilut, Briyah, Yetzirah, Asiyah—were corrected, each Sefirah became a whole Partzuf complete with a head, middle, and end. They therefore received different Names. The Partzuf made from Keter is called Arich Anpin; the Partzuf made from Chochmah is called Aba;

the Partzuf made from Binah is called Ima; the Partzuf made from the Six Sefirot—Chesed, Gevurah, Tiferet, Netzach, Hod, and Yesod—is called Zeir Anpin; and the Partzuf made from Malchut is called Nukvah. The meaning of these Names will be explained in their proper place, with God's help.

Although further on in our Study of the Ten Luminous Emanations, we will eventually get to the discussion of Tzimtzum Bet, I want to at least touch upon it so we can gain some understanding of this process and the way the world works.

If we take an overview of the process of the creation of our World there are three steps to this process. There is the Endless World. Then there is Adam Kadmon, which is where the Light comes back after the Tzimtzum, and the Vessels of the Line fill the Circular Vessels. And then there is the World of Correction (Olam haTikkun), which includes the Worlds of Atzilut, Briyah, Yetzirah, and Asiyah—Four Worlds that correspond to Chochmah, Binah, Zeir Anpin, and Malchut that came about after the Second Contraction (Tzimtzum Bet), and is the realm within which the Correction can occur.

Although we are going to learn about it later more in depth, it is important to spend a little time understanding Tzimtzum Bet because you cannot understand the Zohar without understanding Tzimtzum Bet. Rav Ashlag, in Zohar Beresheet A, says that when the Torah mentions the Firmament (*Rakia*) that separates the Upper and Lower Waters, it is actually discussing this new reality that comes into effect after the Tzimtzum Bet, and that without the Second Contraction, no Correction could ever occur in our world.

In the Prologue of the Zohar there is a very beautiful section that we will discuss and then continue with Rav Ashlag's explanation. The Zohar in Prologue 17 says, "A Mother (Ima) lends Her clothes to Her daughter and adorns her with Her own adornments. And when does She properly adorn her? When all the males appear before her. As is written 'all you males shall appear before the Master, the Lord' (Exodus 34:23)."

The Zohar explains that, during the process of Creation, the Sefirah of Malchut had to borrow Vessels from the Upper Realm, known as Binah, so as to facilitate the creation of our physical realm. Malchut alone lacked the ability to arouse and draw the Light necessary to construct our physical dimension. Literally this means that the mother gave to of her daughter of her clothing, her Vessels, and she made her pretty. She made her beautiful. And when is this beauty and assistance truly manifest? When all the males come before the Creator, which we know references the three main Holidays.

Rav Ashlag, in the Zohar, Prologue 16, Sulam Commentary, says:

> From the time of the Tzimtzum Alef, Binah had no restriction on Her whatsoever, since the Tzimtzum only applied to the Middle Point alone, which is Malchut that was diminished so as to not receive any Light and was fixed in the secret of Binding by Striking to raise Returning Light. But the upper nine Sefirot were clean of any Tzimtzum and were worthy of receiving the Light of Chochmah. Only in Tzimtzum Bet, so that Malchut can be sweetened with the attribute of Mercy, did Malchut ascend to Aba, and Aba established within her an aspect of Male and Female, by which Malchut acquired the place of Binah.

There is no Tzimtzum in Keter, Chochmah, Binah, and Zeir Anpin. These four first Sefirot can receive all the Light that they received before. It is only Malchut, only the Fourth Phase that cannot receive Light. The first nine Sefirot, Keter through Yesod, do not partake and have no negative influence from the Tzimtzum. They are all able to receive the complete Light of Chochmah. Only in Tzimtzum Bet, so as to sweeten the Judgment of Malchut, does a new Correction occur.

Binah (Ima) says, "I am willing to be damaged to help my daughter." This is the basis of the Correction (Tikkun); this is the basis of everything that we do in this world. This beautiful concept gives us a some understanding of the direction we need to take in our spiritual work. If a person is not willing to say, "I am willing to be broken to help someone else out," they cannot make a correction. Binah, the mother is perfect—there are no problems, no difficulties, no lack of Light. The mother is living the best life possible. However Her daughter, Malchut, cannot receive any Light. Not only that, Malchut has no path toward Correction. So the mother, Ima, Binah, says "I am willing to give up everything to help the process of my daughter (Malchut) to be corrected." She says, "Although everything right now in my life is perfect, I am willing to be completely broken to help my daughter." And this begins the process of Correction. If a person is not willing to be broken to help another person, they cannot assist in the Correction.

There is a lesson from the portion of Vayechi that actually fits in perfectly with this idea. Jacob lived most of his life in pain. He had the pain from running away from his brother. He had the pain with Lavan. Then he had the pain with Joseph. And the question many people ask is, "How can someone who was on such a high level live so much of his life in pain?" The Shem miShmuel (Rav Shmuel of Sochatchov, 1855–1926) explains that each of the Patriarchs took upon themselves a part of the correction of the Sin of Adam. After the Sin of the eating from the Tree of Knowledge of Good and Evil, there were 130 years when Adam separated from Eve. He separated for a proper purpose, to correct himself and do Teshuvah. However, there were negative angels the surrounded Adam and made him sin. Thus these 130 years are the source of a lot of the pain, suffering, and darkness that is in our world.

Jacob took upon himself to correct the 130 years of pain, suffering, and darkness. Jacob knew that he had two options in life. He was a tremendously perfected soul. He could have everything right, perfect, easy, but he said, "I cannot live my life having comfort and joy while I leave this correction for the entire next thousands of years. I cannot let that happen. I am willing to live 130 years in pain and sadness to make the correction for Adam, so that later generations can be in joy."

Jacob did what the Zohar says Binah did at the creation of our world. Binah saw the pain of Malchut and said, "I have two choices. I can live in peace, or I can live in pain. I am going to take upon myself the pain of Malchut to allow a path toward Correction." And Jacob said, "I am not going to let this darkness remain for the next generations to correct." Although Jacob could live his life in peace and have a connection to the Light of the Creator, he took upon himself the darkness of the 130 years of the Sin of Adam so that no one else had to go through that same pain and he could correct it for the rest of the world.

This is the basis for the World of Correction (Olam HaTikkun). Yet none of us are like Jacob or Binah in the initial process of the Correction of our World. If there is not a part of us that is willing to go into pain to assist someone else's correction, we cannot truly be a part of the World of Correction. Many people like to help but from a place of comfort. The seed of the Correction of our World is, "a Mother (Ima) lends Her clothes to Her daughter." Binah said "I am willing to be broken. I am willing for everything to be taken away to help My daughter, to help Malchut." If we want our lives to be a part of this Correction, there has to be an element of us that says, "I am willing to go into pain to help another person." Helping another person when it is easy, from our comfort zone, does something, but it does not really bring us to the Final Correction. To bring us to the Final Correction there has to be an element of Binah taking upon Herself this understanding, "I am going to lose all the Light to help My daughter (Malchut)." It is an amazingly beautiful lesson, but it is also so important for our soul to be part of the process of Tikkun.

I want to now share a section from the Introduction to the Wisdom of Kabbalah, where Rav Ashlag gives a big picture explanation for Tzimtzum Bet. One of Rav Ashlag's teachings is that before you really can go into the details of anything, you have to have a basic picture of it. This is why he recommends that before we begin the Study of the Ten Luminous Emanations, we should study all of the Ari from the Talmud Eser Sefirot and get an understanding of that, and then we can really start understanding Rav Ashlag's commentary. The Introduction to the Wisdom of Kabbalah gives the whole story of the Creation of our world—the Study of the Ten Luminous Emanations—in a very condensed and concise way. Unfortunately, a lot of what Rav Ashlag thought would be for beginners is beyond most beginners. Therefore, it makes more sense to study the Talmud Eser Sefirot in the way we do it.

In the Introduction to the Wisdom of Kabbalah, Sections 57-58, Rav Ashlag discusses the Worlds that existed before the process of Tzimtzum Bet, meaning everything we are currently discussing. He says:

> "The root for the desired correction has not yet manifested, which was the reason for the Tzimtzum. The desired outcome of the restriction that was placed on the Fourth Phase was to correct it to not have any Difference of Form while receiving the Supernal Light."

The entire purpose of the creation of our world is so that we can Receive for the Sake of Receiving. The Thought of Creation was to give endlessly to the Vessel. However currently, where we are in the Study of the Ten Luminous Emanations, the Vessel in this new World of the Line does not receive. Malchut is no longer a Vessel. There is a Barrier (Masach) on top of Malchut that says, "You can never Receive for Yourself Alone." And the Vessel says, "The amount I will take in is how much I can Receive only to Give Pleasure to the Creator." This is the process of Returning Light. The Vessel will not Receive for Itself Alone, it will only Receive for the Sake of Sharing.

This still does not resolve the main problem, which is that the reason the Creator created our world is so that we can Receive in the greatest way for the Self Alone, in the Fourth Phase, the greatest Vessel. Yet there is a Barrier above Malchut, the greatest Vessel, which the Light cannot pass. Thus the greatest Vessel cannot become actualized in this new World of the Line. The Vessels above the Masach can receive Light and go through a process of Returning Light and subsequently receive a certain amount of Light. But the real purpose of Creation, the real cornerstone and reason why this whole process began, is to enable Malchut, the greatest Vessel, to receive Light, which is not achieved in this process.

> "Namely, to create the body of man from that aspect of the Fourth Phase, and by him dealing with the Torah and Precepts for the Sake of Bestowing Pleasure upon his Maker, he transforms the Receiving ability in the Fourth Phase to only be for the Sake of Sharing…"

But the Masach that exists after the Tzimtzum, goes up and blocks any Light from entering Malchut. And if there is no Light that can come into Malchut, there is no way to even begin a process of correction. The ultimate goal is to have a body that has the energy of the greatest Desire to Receive for the Self Alone, capable of beginning a process of correction, of transformation. But after Tzimtzum Alef, after the first removal of Light, there is a law that exists where Keter, Chochmah, Binah, and Zeir Anpin can receive Light but Malchut can receive zero Light. And as long as Malchut can receive no Light, there is no correction occurring to Malchut—nothing is happening.

Tzimtzum Alef, the first removal of Light, leaves us with an enormous problem because the entire purpose of Creation is not even touched. What is the purpose of Creation? The Fourth Phase, the greatest Desire to Receive for the Self Alone. What is the reality after Tzimtzum Alef? The Fourth Phase is completely cut off. No Light can come into the Fourth Phase. If nothing can happen with the Fourth Phase, how can it ever be corrected?

Yes, there is a whole system of Returning Light that can bring Light to Keter, Chochmah, Binah, and Zeir Anpin. That is all wonderful, but this is not the purpose of Creation. The purpose of Creation is to correct below the Masach, to correct Malchut, which now exists below this Barrier that cannot be moved.

Rav Ashlag says that therefore the purpose is to create the body with the energy of this greatest Desire to Receive for the Self Alone, with the Fourth Phase, and then through the spiritual work that each person does, we correct it, we change it, we transform its essence into a Desire to Share.

"…thus aligning the form of Receiving with complete Sharing. Then the Final Correction (Gemar haTikkun) will occur…"

Once we are able to work on the Fourth Phase—greatest Desire to Receive for the Self Alone—and transform it into for the Sake of Sharing, this is the Gemar haTikkun. But as long as we are working as is, the purpose of Creation can never be achieved. We have to be able to work on the greatest level of Desire so as to correct it.

After Tzimtzum Alef, the greatest level of Desire, Malchut, the Fourth Phase is cut off completely. Only the levels of Desire of Keter, Chochmah, Binah and Zeir Anpin are transformed from a Desire to Receive for the Self Alone into a Desire to Receive for the Sake of Sharing. And if we are not touching the greatest Desire, then it will never be corrected, and the purpose of Creation will never be achieved. After Tzimtzum Alef, the Vessel starts receiving Light, and it seems as if things are improving. But the reality is that nothing we have learned about yet, which is the World that exists after the First Contraction, has helped anyone or anything. This is a very important lesson.

So often in our spiritual life, we are doing so much; we are working on ourselves, growing, studying but if we do not touch the core, we do nothing. In the World of Adam Kadmon—the most elevated World—Keter, Chochmah, Binah, and Zeir Anpin are all working on their levels of Desire to be able to transform them into Receiving for the Sake of Sharing. Yet in the big picture, nothing important is happening for the sake of Correction because they are not touching upon the core, which is the greatest Desire.

The kabbalists teach that the Satan, the Negative Side, will allow an individual to be the most spiritual person in the world; allow him or her to do all the connections and all the corrections, except for what they came to this world to do. Most of us live in the World after Tzimtzum Alef, meaning we are correcting the lower levels of Desire—First Phase, Second Phase, Third Phase. We are becoming better people. We are transforming some levels of Desire to Receive into Desire to Receive for the Sake of Sharing. We are doing work and we are growing. But Rav Ashlag makes clear that if we continue to live the way most of us do, which is to make corrections and be spiritual but not touch at the core—the most difficult transformation, the most difficult Desires to transform—we have not even begun to touch the true Correction.

The terrible danger that occurs after Tzimtzum Alef is, unfortunately, the spiritual world within which so many of us live. This is the spiritual world that the Satan wants us to live in. He wants us to be the most amazing correctors of all the Worlds after the First Contraction. "Of all those levels of Desire, please go ahead. Be spiritual, keep studying, keep growing and changing those levels of Desire. Just one thing, do not go to the core; do not change the real difficult stuff; do not change the real ultimate levels of Desire; do not change or touch the Fourth Phase."

Most of us live in the World after Tzimtzum Alef. We are growing, we are making corrections, and we are changing levels of Desire, and we are becoming more spiritual. We might think, I am not doing everything but I am doing a little bit. Rav Ashlag says that we have not even begun to touch anything. Forget about the tree, we have not even touched the seed.

Conversely, after Tzimtzum Bet, which we will soon begin to understand, there will be the ability to create a world where the bodies are made up of the Fourth Phase—the greatest Desire—and we are able to begin their transformation. When we transform the Fourth Phase, the ultimate Desire to Receive for the Self Alone, we are able to receive everything for the Sake of Sharing. We are the greatest Vessel that the Creator desires and are also still able to retain that cleaving with the Creator because we do not Receive for our Selves Alone, we receive for the Sake of Sharing.

> "...because through this, the Fourth Phase will return to be a Vessel of Receiving for the Supernal Light and will also be in complete oneness with the Light, without any Difference of Form at all. However, until this point, the root for this correction has not been revealed because for this matter, man needs to be composed of the aspects above the Fourth Phase as well, so that he may be suitable to perform good deeds of sharing. Had man come from the state of the Partzufim of Adam Kadmon, he would have been completely from the aspect of the empty space because the Fourth Phase—which needs to be the root of the body of man—was completely below the legs of Adam Kadmon, completely empty and void of any Light..."

If, Heaven forbid, we were created in this way, where our entire essence would have been from the Fourth Phase, meaning we would be from the place of complete darkness, our job would be to transform that greatest desire without any tools, without any other parts of ourselves, any inklings of sharing. Can you imagine taking someone who is a hardcore addict to the worst drugs in the world and placing him in the middle of a world of free drugs and you saying to him, "Okay, now stop." It is impossible. This is what would have happened if, in the World of Adam Kadmon, there is a complete separation between Light and darkness, between the first Three Phases and Fourth Phase, the greatest desire. There would be no hope, there would be no way. It would be completely dark and, Heaven forbid, stay in darkness.

> "…since it is found to be in complete opposite form to the Supernal Light, which is why it is considered to be the aspect of separation and death. Had man been created from it, he would not be able to correct his actions at all, for he would have had no sparks of sharing. He would be likened to beasts, which have no aspect of sharing at all, as their entire lives are only for themselves. This is like the wicked people who are engrossed in the lust of receiving for themselves, and even the good they do is only for their own benefit. About them it says that the wicked are called dead even while they are alive, since they are in Difference of Form to the Life of Life."

There are people, even in our world, that seem to be created from this realm of the Fourth Phase before Tzimtzum Bet. Meaning that they have no inkling of Sharing at all because their entire essence is only of the Desire to Receive for the Self Alone. They have only the Fourth Phase.

What an amazing paradox. The most negative people in the world have what we are meant to correct. The work is not in the First (Chochmah), Second (Binah), and Third (Zeir Anpin) Phases. This is not the purpose of Creation. It is the Fourth Phase, the greatest selfishness, Desire to Receive for the Self Alone, that is our focus to work on and transform. When you see someone who is completely self-absorbed in the Desire to Receive for the Self Alone, there is power there because we need that. We need to change the energy that they have. Where is it from? It is not some ethereal selfishness that they possess. They are connecting directly to the source of everything that we need in this world. We need this essence of that greatest Desire so that we can transform it.

Rav Ashlag, in the Prologue of the Zohar, explains that we need these people to exist in our world so that the Righteous People (Tzadikim) can work with this energy and change it. But that is for a different discussion. Here Rav Ashlag is making clear that if humanity would have been created from the Fourth Phase, from Malchut as it existed after the First Contraction, there would be no hope. We would be created with the greatest Desire to Receive for the Self Alone and no other essence imbued within us. If our essence is 100% Desire to Receive for the Self Alone without any sparks of Desire to

Share, we would have no hope. Therefore, man, humanity, could not have been created in that stage.

> "This is the secret of what the sages said: 'In the beginning it arose in thought to create the world with the attribute of Judgment. He saw that the world could not exist, so He brought forth the attribute of Mercy and partnered it with the attribute of Judgment.' (Beresheet Rabbah, end of chapter 12)"

Rav Ashlag and Rav Elimelech of Lizhensk both say that this Midrash sounds like the Creator is making a mistake. Like an architect trying to build a building, and then realizes after he builds the foundation, that they are not strong enough and so he breaks it down and builds another one. Of course, that is not what it means.

> The explanation is that any "before" or "after" said regarding spiritual matters relates to cause and effect. So the first cause of the Worlds, which are the Partzufim of Adam Kadmon that were the first Worlds to be emanated, were emanated with the attribute of Judgment, namely in the aspect of Malchut alone called the attribute of Judgment, which is the Fourth Phase that was diminished and emerged as an empty void and the end of the legs of Adam Kadmon, which is the secret of the point of this world that is found below the legs of Adam Kadmon as an empty void that is vacant of any light. [The Creator] saw that the world could not exist like this, since in this way there would be no way for man, who needs to be created by this Fourth Phase, to be able to do actions of sharing by which the world could be corrected to the appropriate degree. Therefore, He brought forth the attribute of Mercy and partnered it with the attribute of Judgment. The explanation is that the Sefirah of Binah is called the attribute of Mercy and the Sefirah of Malchut is called the attribute of Judgment, since the Tzimtzum occurred on [Malchut]. The Emanator raised the attribute of Judgment, which is the concluding force that was placed upon Malchut, up to Binah, which is the attribute of Mercy, and joined them together, one with the other. Through this conjoining, sparks of Sharing from the Vessel of Binah get included in the Fourth Phase as well, which is the attribute of Judgment. This gives the ability for the body of man, which emerges from the Fourth Phase, to also be composed of the attribute of Sharing, so he can do good deeds for the Sake of Giving Pleasure to his Maker until he transforms his attribute of Receiving to be completely for the Sake

of Sharing. Through this, the world will exist for the Correction that was intended for by the creation of the world.

Sounds like a good story so far. The Creator has a problem. After the first removal of Light, Malchut is completely cut off from darkness. He cannot create humanity from Malchut because if He does that, the Creator creates a completely dark person who only has Desire to Receive for the Self Alone without any inkling of Sharing. We are never going to change. So the Creator has an idea to take this great Desire, this essence of the Desire to Receive for the Self Alone, and push it up to Binah, let it spend some time with Binah to learn the Desire to Share from Binah, and be imbued a little with these sparks of Sharing. And by doing that man, we, can be created from this new Malchut that still has this greatest Desire to Receive for the Self Alone, but because of the time Malchut has spent with Binah, Malchut has been sprinkled with sparks of Sharing.

Now there is hope. We remember that there is something good about sharing because we remember being imbued from those sparks of Sharing from Binah. We can begin a process of transforming. This is the purpose of Tzimtzum Bet.

This is such a fundamental idea. For those of you who do not have clarity, please review this concept again and again, until you do.

There are two realities. After Tzimtzum Alef, the first removal of Light, there is a Barrier (Masach) above Malchut—the greatest Desire to Receive for the Self Alone—from which we all stem. Thus Malchut cannot receive any Light. Man, humanity, the world, cannot be created from this reality because then there would be no hope. There would be only darkness. There would be only Desire to Receive for the Self Alone. Therefore, the Creator took this great Desire to Receive for the Self Alone and elevated it to Binah, and mixed it together with Binah, so that Malchut, when it comes back down, has its own essence—Desire to Receive for the Self Alone—which is now influenced by its Mother with a sprinkling of the Desire to Share.

Then when we are created, although we still are predominantly selfish, we also have that goodness from Binah, which is going to be in the back of our mind telling us: "No, there is a better way. No, you should transform. No, you should grow." Now that you have a Malchut that is a mixture of Judgment and Mercy, Desire to Receive and Desire to Share, humanity can be created from it and have hope of transformation.

This is the Correction that occurs with Tzimtzum Bet. But it is not as simple as that. There is a law (*chok*) that now exists: Wherever Malchut goes, darkness follows. No Light can ever come to where Malchut exists. So when Malchut goes up to Binah, Binah becomes dark. Meaning, not only does Malchut not learn from Binah, Binah is sucked into Malchut's dark hole. This is why it is called Tzimtzum Bet, or the second removal of Light. When Malchut goes up to Binah, the first thing that happens is that now Binah and everything below it has no Light either. This is the first stage.

Then there is a process of what is called the Raising of Female Waters (*Ha'alat Mayin Nukvin*). Whenever we elevate through our spiritual work, whenever we reveal Light, it is for one singular purpose: to bring Malchut back down. And this does two things—first it brings back Light into Binah and second, it also brings Malchut down into our world a little bit more corrected. This is a constant process that continues to this day. Malchut elevates to Binah and gets a little bit of Binah's Light. But Malchut cannot stay like that because Binah is dark and Malchut is not in its place and cannot do its correction. Therefore, there is a process called Raising Mayin Nukvin (Female Waters), where we bring Malchut back down through our spiritual work. And once Malchut is back down, besides Binah now having its Light back, Malchut is also a little better off; it has a little more Desire to Share, a little more hope to transform.

Hopefully the sacrifice Binah goes through is a bit clearer because we understand more of the details. It is not simply difficult and uneasy—Binah loses everything. When Binah accepts Malchut into Her house, She says, "I am willing to lose everything to give my daughter (Malchut) a chance." This is real care, this is real help. This is what Binah consistently does for us. If we want Binah to bring us up so that we can be infused with a little bit of Her essence to make us stronger so that we can achieve our correction, we have to be caring and willing to help other people.

This elevation to Binah is something that occurs during Shabbat and the Holidays. Every time we bring a little bit of pain to ourselves to help another person, Binah says, "I have to bring a little bit of pain to Myself to help the person willing to help another." Therefore, for this cycle of elevation and coming back down to continue for us, for our soul, we have to be willing to bring pain to ourselves for other people.

There is a very important, practical lesson here. And because this is such a fundamental understanding, I hope that we all take the time to really digest this and understand the whole process of Tzimtzum Bet and how it brings us to Correction.

---

16. **A Hole and a Window:** Explanation: You already know that due to the Light of the Ten Sefirot of the Line that is received in the Circles, all the aspects of Straightness are, of necessity, impressed upon the Circles as well (as said in Section 14). Even this aspect within the Line that is called Curtain (Masach), which connects the Supernal Light to the Vessels through its Returning Light, (as said in Volume 2, Chapter 1, Section 11), is impressed on the Circles, albeit without its density. This is because density cannot elevate whatsoever from a low level to one higher than it, for therefore it is called higher since it does not have the same density as the lower. Understand this.

Rav Ashlag presents an interesting dichotomy here. Although the process gets transferred over, the negativity that is really at the core of that process does not get transferred. First, the Vessel of the Line knows at this point that a Desire to Receive for the Self Alone separates it from the Creator. Therefore it says, "I cannot allow myself to Receive for Myself Alone because the Desire to Receive for the Self Alone is negative. It is dark; it is something that, if I allow it to be in my life, will disconnect me from the Light of the Creator. Therefore, I say no to the Desire to Receive for the Self Alone and I am going to only Receive for the Sake of Sharing."

There are three elements to this process. There is the looking inside and realizing that if I act with that Desire to Receive for the Self Alone, it will separate me from the Creator because there is that darkness associated with it. And the awareness of this coarseness, this darkness that is the Desire to Receive for the Self Alone is what precipitates everything that follows. Then there is the decision to not Receive Light into my Desire to Receive for the Self Alone, which is called the Curtain/Barrier (Masach) or the stop. And the third is the decision of how much can I Receive for the Sake of Sharing, which is called the Returning Light.

Rav Ashlag tells us that this system has to be transferred into the Circular Vessel, meaning the Circular Vessels have to not Receive for Themselves Alone, which is their nature as this is the way they were created in the Endless

World. They have to say, "No, we are not going to Receive for Ourselves Alone. We will only Receive what is for the Sake of Sharing."

For instance, when a glass panel is inserted into the middle of a fish tank, the fish will go to the panel and hit their head against it because in the water they cannot see this panel. Over time, the fish will learn not to go near the glass panel. They will train themselves to not go too close to this area in the tank. The fish do not know why they are not going there. They do not think that when the glass is removed, they will be able to swim there. There is no deeper thought process of cause and effect, there is just, *For whatever reason that I do not understand, I cannot go past that glass panel, so I will not go there anymore.*

So too with the Circular Vessels. It is interesting that even though the Circles are more simple than the Line, they are now working in this same fashion. They do not perceive any darkness or negativity from Receiving for the Self Alone because they are the pure Vessels of the Endless World. They are the way the Creator wanted them to be, meaning there is nothing wrong with Receiving for Themselves Alone. The Line, on the other hand, is worried about all of the darkness.

The Circular Vessels, which are viewed as being more pure than the Vessels of the Line, cannot receive that sense of darkness or density (*aviut*). The Circular Vessels do not perceive any darkness, only the good part that results from this entire process of saying, "I am not going to Receive for Myself Alone. I will only Receive whatever I can Receive for the Sake of Sharing, Giving Pleasure." The Circles are much simpler. There is no darkness because they do not see darkness. Thus they use only the positive aspect that comes out of it, and not the darkest part that does not become elevated. However, something else happens in the Circles. There is this system that was created around the darkness that gets transferred into the Circular Vessels. So they now live and work and reveal Light within a system that they do not really understand because it is not part of their perception. It is almost as if they are saying "Well, this is the way and we will receive like this too;" all the while still knowing that there is nothing wrong with Receiving for the Self Alone.

In the Wisdom of Truth, Rav Ashlag writes that to remove our Desire to Receive for the Self Alone, we have to have a true understanding of its darkness. If the Line and the Circles ever meet and try to have a conversation about how bad the Desire to Receive for the Self Alone is, the Circles would not understand what the Line is talking about because they do not see anything wrong with

Receiving for the Self Alone. Yet they still say "We are still going to live within this new realm. We will no longer Receive for the Self Alone. I find this to be a beautiful reality that comes into existence.

Only the beneficial aspect that this Masach manifests in the lower, that is, in the Ten Linear Sefirot, ascends from the Masach of the Straight Line to be impressed upon the Circles. The benefit from this Masach is called a Window (Chalon). Just like a window is set in a room to bring light into the room, so too this Curtain reveals the Returning Light due to its ability to connect the Light with the Emanated Being. This is in such a way that if the Masach is absent from there, the Light would be absent from the Emanated Being, which would remain in darkness, as would happen if a window in a room is blocked. Therefore, when we want to refer to only the benefit from the Masach, excluding its density, we define it as "a window or a hole."

There are sections in the Talmud that speak about certain people whose souls revealed a lot of wisdom and then spiritually fell or left the path. Is it permissible to study their wisdom? Because when they reveal wisdom, it is a part of their essence that is revealed. Many of the sages decided that we are not going to take anything from that person. Yet there were other great sages, like Rav Meir, who were on a higher level and were able to take the Light and throw out the darkness from those teachings and create a Window in all situations. This ability to always only take the Light and never the darkness is what we are discussing here. Nevertheless not everyone is on this level.

This is a very important understanding because if we can use this as a tool in situations where there is darkness and Light, and are able to awaken this power of the Window, meaning we are able to take the Light from it and leave the darkness behind, very often we can gain a tremendous amount of Light. A Window means that we receive benefit from someone else's work or revelation, but not the negativity, darkness, or Judgment.

And it is important that we make this distinction because what is happening here is that since the Circular Vessels do not have the darkness, they also never really own this Light. We learned previously that although the Circular Vessels are elevated Vessels, higher than the Vessels of the Line, the Light that they reveal is still only called Nefesh, the lowest level, and the Light the Line reveals is called Ruach. Why? Because the Vessels of the Line can give Light over and share it with someone else. This teaches us a very important lesson.

It says, "If you toiled and found, believe," (Tractate Megillah 6b) meaning if you work for something, and you earned it, then trust in it. There are different ways to understand this. And one of them is that if we receive wisdom, Light, a spiritual level and did not work hard for it, it will not stay. It will not last. It says that at the time of the Revelation of the Splitting of the Sea, the lowest soul saw greater prophesy than Ezekiel the Prophet. The question of course is, if all these people had such a great revelation, what happened to all that Light? And the answer is: "If you have not toiled and found, do not believe." (Ibid.) If you receive Light, wisdom, revelation but did not work hard to achieve it, do not believe or trust it because it is here now but it is not going to stay. The only way we can hold onto the Light and wisdom is if we worked hard to earn it. "If you toiled and found, believe." If you work hard for something, go through the difficulty and the darkness and you earn it, only then can you be sure that you will be able to hold onto that Light. If you received something in this level of Window (Chalon), where you did not earn it but received the benefit of it, do not trust that it is going to stay with you because it most probably will not. Only Light, revelation, and wisdom that we work hard for, do we merit staying with us.

> **17. On the right side of the Circle:** Meaning that it was also impressed with the values of Right and Left that apply by the Ten Sefirot of Straightness (see Volume 1, Terminology Answers, 23).

Rav Ashlag says the Ari is letting us know that this whole reality of Right and Left that exist in the Line also is transferred over into the Circles. Obviously this does not mean right and left as in physical space.

In Volume 1, Terminology Answers, 23, Rav Ashlag answers the question: What are Right and Left? It is amazing because it is something so different from anything we would naturally think. He says, "A lower level sometimes rises to a stature equal to a higher one when the higher one needs [the lower one] for its own perfection. Then the Lower one is considered as Left while the Upper one is considered as Right."

Rav Ashlag makes it clear that it is so important to understand the words "Right, Left, and Central" used throughout the Zohar and the Writings of the Ari. For instance, right now, we are lower levels working to bring the End of the Correction (Gemar haTikkun)—the completion of the process. Our job is to finish the end, and by finishing the end we become part of the complete whole. We are the Left Side because we are of the lower level that the higher levels need because, as we have learned many times, the End of the Correction can only happen with the lowest of the low, with us.

The Creator, all the Righteous People (Tzadikim), and those who came before us who are perfected, are Right Column. This is why, for instance, when we say *Yamin usmol tifrotzi* ("Right and Left should reveal forward," from Lecha Dodi), it means that the Light from all the previous generations, the Creator, the Shechinah, and all the Tzadikim, and also our Light should shine. We represent the Left because we are the lower level that needs to be elevated to a higher level to complete the process.

With this clear explanation of Rav Ashlag we can understand that whenever we discuss Right and Left we are talking about when a lower spiritual entity is needed by a higher spiritual entity to complete a process. Thus in every spiritual process, whenever a lower level needs to be elevated to a higher level to complete it, it is called Left, and the original is called Right. So too in the process of humanity, the Creator, the Shechinah, and all the Tzadikim are called Right and we are called Left. This is a concept we have to keep in mind throughout our studies.

---

18. **The Light of Arich descends to the Circle of Aba:** In other words, because of the said Window, the distinction of the drawing and descending of the Light was made there, namely that it gradually becomes more coarse, where the lower level is coarser than the previous one. This is: "and from there…Arich descends to the Circle of Aba," meaning that due to the Window, the Light received an aspect of lowering and an aspect of density at the Circles of Aba, namely Chochmah that was lowered in level and is no longer equal to the Circles of Keter as it was before the Light of Straightness was received through the Window. The same applies to Binah below Chochmah.

Rav Ashlag is saying something very clear here. Before the Light came into the Circular Vessels, Keter, Chochmah, Binah, Zeir Anpin, and Malchut were equal. There was no higher and lower. There was no view of one being better than the other. After the Light from the Line comes into the Circular Vessels, because within the realm of the Line there is a hierarchy of one being purer, better than the other, this reality gets transferred over into the Circular Vessels. If you read this initially, it seems to be very confusing. In Section 16, Rav Ashlag previously made it very clear that the coarseness cannot be transferred from the Line to the Circles. This is why it is called a Window (Chalon) where you only receive the benefits and not the negative traits. Now, Rav Ashlag is telling us that there is a coarseness that happens to the Light from Keter to Chochmah, from Chochmah to Binah. There seems to be a contradiction.

The answer is what Rav Ashlag has been reminding us of again and again. When we discuss the fact that coarseness, darkness, negativity, is not transferred from the Line to the Circles, it means that the Vessels are not influenced by the darkness. But the Light that is manifest in the Circular Vessels does have the qualities of the Line, meaning one being higher and one lower. For instance, Chochmah being less than Keter, Binah being less than Chochmah. But this is only as it concerns the Light. The Vessels do not see a difference.

One of the beauties of the Study of the Ten Luminous Emanations and the study of Kabbalah is that in everything there is always a paradox. Let us look now at what is happening. The Vessels of Chochmah and Binah are talking to each other, Chochmah has no sense that it is any better than Binah because it is a Circular Vessel. In the World of the Circles, the reality that existed before the Tzimtzum, everyone is the same. There is no higher or lower. The Light that is going to Chochmah of the Circles is of less quality than the Light that is in the realm of Keter. But even this does not make a difference to the Vessels. They are simple.

When Keter notices that Chochmah has an interesting variety of Light, and is aware that the Light being revealed in Chochmah is of a lower grade, it does not make a difference. They do not know why it is happening and it certainly does not make the Vessel of Chochmah any lower than the Vessel of Keter. They still do not view each other as being any higher or lower than each other. The Vessels of the Circles remain completely alike even though the Light that is manifest in Chochmah is of a coarser, lesser value than the Light of Keter, and so too, throughout the rest of the Circular Vessels.

Thus as it pertains to the Vessels, nothing ever changes. There is always a Window, meaning the transfer of the benefits. The Circular Vessels only feel benefits. However, the Light is influenced because it is the Light that is coming from the Vessels of the Line.

Here we learn, among other things, the importance of simplicity. The difference between the Vessels of the Line and the Circular Vessels is that the Circular Vessels are simple and the Vessels of the Line are judgmental and complicated. The Vessels of the Line see the Light that is coming to Chochmah as of a lesser nature than Keter. Keter says, "This must mean that I am better and that you are worse." Chochmah says, "If the Light that I am receiving is less, this must mean that Keter is better than me." This whole reality of hierarchy and judgment comes into existence in the Line.

In the realm of the Circular Vessels, there is no hierarchy, there is no judgment. Keter says, "You got this Light, I got that Light. It seems this is better Light than that, yet it does not make me any better than you." And from Chochmah's perspective, it sees that the Light it receives is of a lesser quality than the Light Keter receives but it is not complicated about it. It is simple. "I do not know why it happened. This is the way it happened. It does not make me any better. It does not make me any worse."

Our connection to the World before the Tzimtzum, the World before darkness, is simplicity. The reality of the World after the darkness, after the Tzimtzum, is complicated, judgmental—always assessing ourselves as we relate to others. "Why am I getting more, why am I getting less, why is this happening to me," is all the world of darkness. If we want to connect to the realm of the Circular Vessels, the realm before darkness, we have to push all that aside. It is a truly beautiful and important understanding.

---

19. **Pierces it so that a window is made in it:** He teaches us that this window was simultaneously formed in the Sefirot with the descent of Light upon it from the uppermost Circle. In other words, this Light then impresses upon it the matter of the Masach included in it, as said. It is thus considered as if the Light pierces it and makes a window in it.

20. **It only passes by there in passing:** This has already been well explained earlier (Volume 2, Chapter 1, Section 4)

Rav Ashlag says that previously we learned this concept of Light passing through, where every person, every spiritual Vessel has the ability to reveal Light both for themselves but also awaken Light for others. We learn something very important from this.

The Mei HaShiloach, in the portion of Yitro, explains that when the Israelites were chosen to be an Am Segulah, one of the meanings of this is that when a person takes upon themselves the task of becoming a bank of Light for others, it brings them to a completely different level. This is what the Ari and Rav Ashlag are discussing here. A person can either focus on themselves or they can focus on being a bank of Light for others. Selfishly this is not as fulfilling, of course. Even spiritually, one would rather be focused on taking in for themselves, and not this concept of having Light pass through them. However the ultimate purpose of our spiritual work is to become this bank of Light for others. This is what all the great Tzadikim did. For instance, what Rav Shimon bar Yochai did with the Zohar, was that he did not reveal the Light for himself, but he actually created this bank for the rest of the world, forever. He worked all of his life just to create this bank, not for himself at all, only so the rest of us can have this Light.

---

21. They do have Straight Lines: Meaning that the Light descends from one Circle to another by being drawn straight down through Straight Lines, except that this is not considered as actually establishing Lines that descend from the Masach, which have Masculine Light and can bestow to others. Rather, these Lines of the Circles have no power to bestow, since they descend as windows, which are only enough to receive Light for their own need alone, and not to bestow to others. This is the rule—whatever has no aspect of Masach in it has no Masculine Light but only Feminine Light, which is called the Light of Nefesh.

The Ari said that because the Circular Vessels are receiving their Light from the Line, therefore, even within the Circular Vessels there is this new concept of having a Right Column, a Left Column, and a Central Column.

We have to remember that, even though the Circular Vessels are receiving the Light from the Line, and there are these new corrections that seem to be occurring within the Circular Vessels, because if they are receiving the Light from the Line, they have to receive in the way that the Line receives.

The Circular Vessels receive all of this Light only through a Chalon; which means that they do not really transform, they do not do the work, they do not have the process of restriction. They only receive the benefit but none of the spiritual work. And because this type of receiving is only through the level of Windows, meaning without doing the work, the person or the Vessel can receive the Light only for themselves, and not give it over to another person, to another Vessel.

Yet when we look at the Circular Vessels and at the Vessels of the Line, it seems like the whole framework is the same in both Vessels. However there is one big difference. The Line does the work, it has a Desire to Receive, and it restricts, and so on. And although we would think that the Circular Vessels are also going through the whole process of Right, Left, and Central, of having Returning Light, and so on, this is not so. The Circular Vessels receive through the Chalon, they do not do the work. They take the benefit only from the work of the Line. Rav Ashlag says "This is the rule—whatever has no aspect of Masach in it has no Masculine Light but only Feminine Light, which is called the Light of Nefesh." Any Vessel that does not have the Desire to Receive for the Self Alone, and therefore a restriction on it that stops the Light from entering, cannot give further.

In the past we discussed that the only Light we can receive is dependent on our work; the idea of, "according to the labor is the reward." (Pirkei Avot 5:23) And now the Ari and Rav Ashlag are telling us that it is possible to receive Light without a lot of work. We recently learned that at the Splitting of the Sea, the lowest spiritual person saw things that Ezekiel the Prophet saw. One of the dangers of our physical and spiritual world is that we can receive through a Window, whether it is through the work of a teacher or in other ways, such as gifts that are given to us. All of us, to one degree or another, have received Light through this concept of a Window. The danger is, as we find here, that we can look at both realities and say they are about the same. They both have the same Light, they both have the same framework. Yet one worked for it and the other did not.

Very often, we talk about the danger of success. The fact that a person is succeeding in their spiritual work, or succeeding in teaching others, could be very dangerous because it is important to know how you got that Light. *Did it come to me without me doing the work? It may look like I have a tremendous influence but I really only have Feminine Light, which means Light that cannot be shared further. Or did I have the Masach and actually do the work?*

Now, the danger is that we can have both realities. For example, if you look at the Circular Vessels from the outside, these Vessels seem to have the whole framework and way of receiving Light like the Line. The Light is exactly the same in both. The Line does not have more Light than the Circular Vessels. They have the same amount of Light. It also seems like the Circular Vessels receive this Light through the Three Lines (Columns), the work of the Masach, and Returning Light. However, the big difference is one Vessel really did the work, and one Vessel received the Light.

Therefore, the question that we have to always be asking ourselves is not whether we have Light or are being successful to one degree or another, but rather how difficult is our constant work? If our work is not constantly challenging, the fact that we have Light, the fact that we think that we can teach, and help, and so on, does not mean anything. We can have that and still delude ourselves into thinking that we are like the Line and that we have earned the Light, when in reality we may have received the Light through the process of the Window (Chalon). Somehow, we received it. Somehow, we were given it.

The Baal Shem Tov teaches that when a person is at the beginning of their spiritual work, the Creator gifts them unearned Light. The only purpose of this unearned Light is to come to a point where we say "this is what I want, and I am going to spend the rest of my life earning it." Yet so many people get stuck in that first step. They receive the Light without the work, through the Chalon. *I have the Light. Great let me continue the rest of my life sharing this amazing Light that I have. And yes, I will be a little bit spiritual, I will do a little bit of work, but I am just going to build on what I have.*

In reality, what we should say is, "I have nothing. The fact that it seems like that I have some Light, I know it means nothing unless I have worked for it." I cannot repeat this enough, there is a tremendous danger in thinking that, because we have two Vessels with exactly the same Light that they are identical. No. They can be completely different from each other. One can be Nefesh, meaning cannot give over any Light. It can share and look like it is giving Light but it cannot give over any sustained Light. The Line can and the Circle cannot, because the Circular Vessel did not work for it. And having Light is not an indication of having earned it.

Therefore, as we said previously, if you are working hard for the Light, trust that you are going to keep it. Not only will you keep it, anyone you share it with will also be able to keep it. If you are not working hard, and you found

Light, you have Light but do not trust that you will hold on to it or that anyone you share it with will be able to hold on to it. It is Feminine Light, which means Light of Nefesh that cannot be fully shared.

Hopefully this is something that scares all of us because we often think if we have Light, we must be able to share this Light. No. Having Light and being similar to someone else who has Light does not mean anything. The only question is, is our Light Nefesh or is our Light Ruach? Have we earned the Light or is it given to us one way or another through the Window, or like the people at the Splitting of the Sea where they simply saw the vision completely unearned? If it is not earned, Heaven forbid, do not trust that you will hold onto it or that anyone you are trying to share it with will ever be able to hold onto it. This is a tremendously important lesson.

> 6. This Primordial Man[22] (Adam Kadmon) "extends from end to end"[23] (Exodus 26:28); from the Upper end to the Lower end, throughout the entire aforementioned space of Atzilut. All the Worlds are included inside this [Primordial] Man, as I shall explain with the Creator's help. But of the Interior aspect and essence of this Man[24] we have no permission whatsoever to speak or discuss.

There is a lot here we need to understand, and I just want to preface it by reminding all of us to really appreciate the fact that we can say these words. I hope for all of us, that simply being able to recite this one paragraph here and understanding it to some degree, is such an unbelievable revelation and merit because the purpose of the study is not to gain wisdom. As Rav Ashlag makes very clear in the Introduction, as we say these words it is to awaken these Surrounding Lights (Orot Makifim) that will shine to us time after time until they eventually awaken our soul to manifest them.

The gift of this one paragraph that speaks about Adam Kadmon, the totality of Light, means that within it is everything. If any of us was really pure to the extent that we are meant to be, we would see all of reality in this paragraph.

However, most of us are not and therefore we have to spend the rest of our lives being able to connect to this paragraph.

As Rav Ashlag will also explain further on, this is beyond the realm of prophecy. No one really said this before the Ari. And it is not so much in the saying, it is about the fact that through his spiritual work, the Ari was able to purify and elevate himself to where he received this gift of wisdom. And for us to have the merit to have this written down, and be able to repeat it and to connect it in one way or another, is just a tremendous merit that we cannot even truly appreciate. But we have to awaken to this to some degree or another. I hope that we all are as excited about this paragraph as I am. It is one of those things you want to repeat over and over again, and connect with, to whatever degree you can.

---

22. **This Primordial Man:** Do not wonder about the name "man" given here. It is as said (In Midrash Raba, Beresheet 27:1): "Rabbi Yudan said, 'How great is the power of the prophets, for they liken a form to He who formed it, as is said, "And I heard a man's voice in the midst of Ulay…" (Daniel 8:16), "and upon the likeness of the throne was the likeness as the appearance of a man above upon it." (Ezekiel 1:26)" The reason for this will be explained in its place, with God's help.

Initially this does not seem like such a great thing. Anyone of us can talk about the nose of God or the face of God. Nevertheless to say these words is not what Rav Ashlag is discussing. The fact that Daniel said, "I heard a man's voice," (Daniel 8:16) and Ezekiel says, "upon the likeness of the throne was the likeness as the appearance of a man," (Ezekiel 1:26) is not discussing their ability to speak about what they heard and saw but rather it is about the ability to connect with what they heard and saw.

One of the gifts and strengths of the Prophets is that they were able to take Supernal matters, Light that is beyond the realm of most of us—like a helium balloon whose natural tendency is to fly up in the air—and grab the string and hold it down so that anyone could see the balloon. Because of their spiritual elevation and preparation to be conduits for the world, the Prophets had the ability to take the Endless Light and bring it down in a way that people can interact with it. When Daniel repeats his vision and says, "I heard a man's voice," and Ezekiel says, "I saw the appearance of man," what they are actually doing is changing our world. They are making it possible for the rest of us to now connect to some degree to the Creator. And the way they accomplished this was by using forms of speech and comparing the Creator to the appearance of man and the voice of the Creator to the voice of man.

It is important we realize what this Midrash in conveying to us. Rabbi Yudan is saying, "Look at the greatness and strength of the Prophets. They did something that is almost impossible. They were able to take from the Ein Sof, and bring down to this world something that we can touch, that we can connect to. That is the work of the Prophets." Before Daniel and Ezekiel, one could not bring this tremendous revelation to our world. The power and strength of the Prophets was not in their ability to say what they heard and saw, it was in making this reality possible. They took all of this, and in some way through their spiritual perfection, were able to make this Light a little bit more tangible for the rest of us, enabling the rest of us to connect to it. They went up to these tremendous heights and were able to restrict, confine, and manifest a little bit of the Light of the Creator. If they had not done that, we would never have the ability to make a connection to the Light of the Creator.

Rav Ashlag is explaining that when the Ari used the term "Adam Kadmon," he is not simply giving this reality a name. Why did he call it Adam Kadmon? Is it because it sounded good or it is similar. When the Ari says, "This Primordial Man (Adam Kadmon) extends from end to end," it is not because he is giving us the understanding or a name to call Adam Kadmon, he took this realm and is giving us an ability to touch it a little bit, to receive this Light a little bit.

This is one of these paragraphs I hope we all get excited to repeat over and over again, because the purpose of the Ari and Rav Ashlag in revealing this to us is not simply to give us this understanding, but rather it is to give us a taste of Adam Kadmon. Rav Ashlag says the purpose of this study is to "taste and see that the Creator is good." (Psalms 34:9)

How powerful are the Ari and Rav Ashlag that, similar to the prophets, and even beyond prophecy, they were able to take the Endless Light and bring it a little bit closer down to our world so that some of us will be able to taste of it. Whether we understand it or learn something today or not, this is not the purpose of any of the Study of the Ten Luminous Emanations, and certainly not the purpose of this paragraph. How great is the power of the Ari and Rav Ashlag that they are able to bring down this unbelievable Light, and make it tangible for us. By saying these words to us, "taste and see that the Creator is good," (Psalms 34:9) there is a chance now for all of us to taste this Light.

Hopefully this revelation changes our entire perception, if not of all of the Study of Ten Luminous emanations, at least this paragraph. Therefore, the understanding that the purer and more elevated we are, the more this work has done for us, the more this beyond prophecy of the Ari and Rav Ashlag has done for us. This is an unbelievably exciting revelation. I hope we all begin, beyond understanding it, really appreciating the work that the Ari and Rav Ashlag have done, and do what we can to prepare ourselves to be able to taste from this work.

---

23. **Extends from end to end:** Meaning, from the Endless, the purest of all the Worlds, to the Middle Point, the coarsest part in all the Worlds. Thus, the entire existence before us, whether the celestial or terrestrial, are all His branches that developed from Him, hang from Him and clothe Him. He thus connects them all.

Sometimes people make the mistake of thinking that the Worlds are in descending order—there is Adam Kadmon, then there is Atzilut and then Briyah, then there is Yetzirah, then there is Asiyah—when in reality all the Worlds are within Adam Kadmon. Adam Kadmon even includes our physical world. This is an important concept to really appreciate. Adam Kadmon is a different entity. Adam Kadmon is everything from the Endless all the way down to our physical world. It encompasses everything; it touches everything. Everything that comes after—Atzilut, Briyah, Yetzirah, and Asiyah, the Supernal entities, angels, our physical world, and all the people, all the souls that ever came into this world—are all layers and branches of this one Tree called Adam Kadmon. Hopefully this inspires us because when we understand that everything we are and every Light that we connect to means that we are actually connected to the Ein Sof. The lowest soul of this physical world is attached to the Endless World.

Adam Kadmon did not end up somewhere far apart and then there are all the intervening Worlds of Atzilut, Briyah, Yetzirah, and Asiyah, and that we connect to the lowest of the lowest. Everything connects to the Ein Sof. The Talmud says, "There is one who acquires his World in one moment" (Tractate Avoda Zara 10b), meaning a person can elevate in one moment to the highest connection. Why is that? It is because we are always connected to Adam Kadmon. It is tremendously inspiring to know that no matter how low we fall, no matter how low we are, we always have a connection to Adam Kadmon because Adam Kadmon is really the spine of reality.

Everything that happens, everything that becomes manifest are simply layers, coverings, and branches around Adam Kadmon. Nothing that exists is detached from Adam Kadmon. The Ari says that everything, from the highest to the lowest, is encompassed within Adam Kadmon—a concept that if we really understand, is beyond logic. It does not make sense for the greatest Light, Adam Kadmon, to be involved in all the lowest things. For instance, it does not make sense for a king to be dealing with the beggar on the street. There are many gate keepers until you reach the king. However in the spiritual world it is not like that. Everyone and everything is directly connected to the Adam Kadmon. At any given moment we can elevate from one level to the next because we are always connected to Adam Kadmon. We are connected to the highest levels.

---

24. **But of the Interior aspect and essence of this Man:** The Interior is the aspect of the Light of the Endless that is clothed in Him, and His essence is His Upper Three aspect. It has already been explained ("And You Shall Choose Life," Section 27) that we have no permission to speak of any of the Upper Three aspects of any level and Partzuf, even in the World of Asiyah. But we are allowed to deal with the Lower Seven, even the Lower Seven of Adam Kadmon. Look there.

The Ari says, "we do not have permission to talk about it," and Rav Ashlag says, "we do not have permission to talk about the First Three." But what does that mean? We have been talking about and discussing the Ein Sof and the First Three Sefirot of Adam Kadmon. Obviously we talking about it. But what the Ari and Rav Ashlag are talking about is not simply the ability to speak about these things. One of our biggest problems is that we can talk about so many things—even things that are not really part of our essence—and this is the difference.

In the Portion of Terumah, there is a discussion about the building of the Ark of the Covenant, the resting place for the Torah and the Tablets, in the Holy of Holies, the holiest place in the Tabernacle and in the Holy Temple. It says that the Ark was built with gold on the outside, wood in the middle, and gold on the inside. From this, we learn the concept Rabban Gamliel speaks about in the Talmud: "any student whose inside is not like his outside will not enter the study hall" (Tractate Berachot 28a), meaning that if what we show the world and what is really inside are not the same, we cannot study. Yet the sages, who came after Rabban Gamliel disagreed. There are many debates concerning this.

However, before we get into that discussion, let us define what it means to have our external be like our internal. With the Ark of the Covenant, the gold was on the outside as it was in the inside. How many of us are like this, where what we project outside is who we are inside? If we are honest with ourselves, I do not think any of us really are the same outside as we are inside, which is a big problem. We do not need to take it to the level of Rabban Gamliel who said if this is you, do not even study, do not be spiritual. Those people probably could try to be spiritual even if this is true.

We have to understand that it is not about thinking that we will do our spiritual work and will get there one day, and it is another one of those spiritual things I need to do, to make sure my outside and inside are congruent. Most of us think, *It is true that there are all kinds of things I know about myself that I make sure no one else knows, and I make sure that the way I am viewed is much better than who I really am. Yes, it is a problem, and I will work on it.* When this disparity exists, and it does exist, it is unfortunately almost a fatal flaw. And to the degree that it exists, it stops us; we are unable to connect to the Light of the Creator.

The Ark of the Covenant that held the Tablets, which represent immortality, the Tree of Life (Etz haChaim), had to have gold outside and inside. This teaches us that if we are not the same inside as we are outside, if we are not the same outside as we are inside, we cannot connect to the Torah.

Yes, there are people like the sages who said that even if someone whose inside is not projected outside and someone whose outside is different from who he truly is inside, they would let him study so that eventually he would realize this big problem and change. Nevertheless, we all understand that we cannot connect to the Torah, we cannot connect to the essence of the Light of the Creator as long as our inside and outside are different. This is such a scary concept because most of us have our spiritual work, and then we have the other work of making sure everyone sees our external as much better than our internal. We spend so much time making sure that we are viewed in a way that we want to be viewed—which is almost always different from who we truly are.

What the Torah is telling us is that as long as there is a disparity between the inside—who you truly are—and the outside, there is no real connection to the Light of the Creator. Our biggest problem is that we allow ourselves to talk about all kinds of things with which we have no connection. We have no problem speaking about spirituality, spiritual growth, the First Three Sefirot, and the Ein Sof.

The Ari and Rav Ashlag could not understand such a concept because if we are spiritual, and we are talking about the Ein Sof, this means we are connected to it. You cannot be spiritual and think you can talk about things with which you have no connection. In their minds, a person like them would never speak about something they are not truly connected to. Would they talk about a high spiritual level if they were not there? Of course not. But we do it all the time. We talk about all these elevated spiritual concepts that sound good to people, but we ourselves are not there. We can talk about things that we have no connection to. The Ari and Rav Ashlag, for them, they could not understand such a concept.

The Ari and Rav Ashlag were connected to the Endless World. They were connected to the First Three Levels of Adam Kadmon and therefore could talk about this but they could not teach it to us and we cannot study it because it is so far away from where we are.

Rav Ashlag previously said, "Anything we do not comprehend, we cannot give a name" (Origins of Consciousness, Volume 1, Chapter 1, Inner Light, Section 2) because the Wisdom of Kabbalah is often called the Wisdom of Truth. Rav Ashlag says that if you are not a truthful person, if you can tell a small lie, you cannot connect to the Wisdom of Kabbalah. Why? Because it is all based on truth—truth of your level and truth of what you are connected to. Even if someone considers themself a student of Kabbalah, they cannot talk about the Endless World or the First Three Sefirot if they are not there. Of course most of us are not there. Most of us lie. Our external projection is not who we truly are inside. Rav Ashlag says that although, unfortunately, we probably would allow ourselves to talk about these matters even though we have no real spiritual connection to these levels, we should not.

Rav Ashlag will soon explain that what the Ari revealed was to give us some sort of logical progression and understanding so that we can further our study. They are giving us an inkling of what occurred. It has to be very clear that even if we think that we possibly understand the Ein Sof or the First Three Sefirot of Adam Kadmon because we have read about this, we do not. More importantly, is realizing that it is a big problem that we are able to talk about things that we are not connected to. We are like what Rabban Gamliel said. If your filthy inside is not projected outside, and you create this external façade, which is not really a true projection of what is inside, do not study, do not even try to be spiritual.

Yet, as we said, the sages said, "No, try. Do not try because it is okay; try because this gives you a little bit of hope that one day you will get to the point where your inside is like your outside." However, in the Torah, the Creator is telling us that if we want to be a resting place for the Torah, the Etz haChaim (Tree of Life), and for the Light of the Creator, whatever is inside has to be outside. How many of us now understand how crazy it is that we make it okay for our internal truth not to be seen outside and actually spend time and effort creating a false external of a filthy internal? We are not even at the starting point. All of us are here at some level where our external projection is not really who we are inside and we need to know that this is an unbreakable barrier for the Light of the Creator to come in. Therefore, as the Ari and Rav Ashlag say, we do not talk about these concepts of the Ein Sof and the First Three Sefirot of Adam Kadmon because if we are not connected to them, and we are truthful, we are not going to speak about matters we are not connected to.

7. Indeed, at first, Ten Sefirot emerged in a Circular way, one within the other.[25] Then within the Circles the Likeness of a Man extended in a Linear way along all the aforementioned Circles.[26] We do not deal with the Circular aspect at all,[27] just the Linear aspect alone.

25. At first, Ten Sefirot emerged in a Circular way, one within the other: It has already been explained earlier that the Circles were revealed immediately with the Tzimtzum and the removal of the Light. Afterwards, the Straightness was revealed in such a way that the Circles are considered the reason and cause for the Light of the Line. For this reason, they are considered as preceding it (as said in Volume 2, Terminology Answers, Section 42).

26. **Along all the aforementioned Circles:** That is, from the highest end to the lowest end, as said. Look closely at an imagined physical length and you will learn from it its spiritual origin. We understand length according to three distinctions: its upper end, its lower end, and the distance between them. Exactly in this way, you will define spiritual length. At first, you will identify the lowest end of the level, namely its final aspect, which is the coarsest, where nothing is lower in density than it. From knowing the lowest end, you will automatically learn about its highest end, for according to the degree of density in that last aspect is the measure of height of the Returning Light (as said in Inner Observation, Section 86; study it carefully).

Rav Ashlag is teaching us a very important concept. For instance, the Ari made it very clear, the only reason the Ari came into this world was to teach Rav Chaim Vital. But time and again, in The Gate of Reincarnations the Ari tells him that he needs to know that because of the great potential of Light he has to reveal, Rav Chaim Vital also has a tremendous amount of darkness. And specifically, one of Rav Chaim Vital's great corrections was the correction of anger. What we see with Rav Chaim Vital is because his lowest point was very low, therefore his highest point was also very high. The lower, the more coarse, the greater the Desire to Receive for the Self Alone, the greater is the potential for the high point.

It is important to remind ourselves that having a low point is not a bad thing. It is actually a good thing because it is an indicator of how high a person can go within any spiritual reality. Within any spiritual structure, the lowest point is an indicator of the highest point. The lower the lowest point, the higher the higher point.

For example, the density of the Fourth Phase within the Fourth Phase reaches the Stature of Keter of Keter; the density of the Third Phase within the Fourth Phase reaches only the Stature of Keter of Chochmah; the Second Phase within the Fourth Phase reaches only the Stature of Keter of Binah, and so on. Thus, by knowing the lowest end, immediately its highest end is known. After knowing the two ends of the level, the distance between them is automatically known to you as well, since spiritual distance means the Difference of Form between two aspects, as the greater the Difference of Form, the greater the distance between them.

For example, if its lowest end is the First Phase within the Fourth Phase, then its highest end reaches only the Stature of Keter of Zeir Anpin (see Inner Observation mentioned before). Thus, the distance is not so great. But if its lowest end is the Second Phase, then its highest end is the Stature of Keter of Binah. Thus the distance between them consists of two Phases of density—the First Phase and the Second Phase. But if its lowest end has the density of the Third Phase within the Fourth Phase, then its highest end is Keter of Chochmah. Thus the distance here is a length of three Phases, and so on. Understand this well.

There are a number of lessons we learn from here. One is the fact that if a person has very low points, it is actually a good thing because it is an indication that the potential for Light is also very high. Also, we learned previously that sometimes we do not understand how we can be so high one day and so low the next. If we actually see an important Partzuf, then the disparity between the high and low points can actually be big until we achieve Correction. If a person experiences a small incremental change—highs and lows—all this means is that they have a minute amount of desire and therefore a limited amount of Light that they can reveal. Yet if there is a great fluctuation between the high points and low points, it means there is a much greater potential of Light to be revealed.

Rav Chaim Vital is a good example of this. There are times when he completely disregarded the words of the Ari his teacher, and yet we know that the purpose for which he came to this world is to reveal all the teachings of the Ari. There seems to be great fluctuation in Rav Chaim Vital, which is a good thing because when he achieves Correction, it means that he can reveal the greatest Light. Therefore, we learn from the Ari that every single one of us has good and bad, Light and darkness, and the disparity between these two is actually a good thing.

We want to have great highs and potential for great lows because this means that we have within us the potential for great revelation. Of course, if we do not correct this, it is not good. But having these fluctuations, and knowing that this fluctuation actually means that we have great potential to reveal Light, is obviously important, inspiring knowledge to have.

Rav Ashlag is teaching us here that if we want to assess ourself or assess someone else or even a Partzuf, we have to know three things: what are the high points, what are the low points, and the difference between them. This informs us as to how important is this person, how important is this Partzuf. This is a very important concept for the Study of Ten Luminous Emanations as well as in how we assess ourselves and assess others.

---

27. **We do not deal with the Circular aspect at all:** The reason is that the Circles encircle the part of the First Three Sefirot of Straightness (as said in Volume 2, Chapter 1, Section 18). And it is known that from the perspective of their Vessels they are immeasurably superior to the Upper Three of Straightness, as mentioned earlier. And you already know that we are forbidden from talking about and dealing with the Upper Three, and thus have no permission to deal with any aspect of the Circles.

In his Introduction, Rav Ashlag writes that we have to always remember, and make sure everyone knows, that one of the great gifts of the Talmud Eser Sefirot is that we are talking about Lights, and that these Lights we speak about shine to us. And if we are not awakening these Lights—which represent our unmanifested Light, our Surrounding Light—then to really be growing and connecting to the Light of the Creator is almost impossible. Therefore, to whatever degree we understand or do not understand, we have to make sure that the Talmud Eser Sefirot is a constant in our spiritual lives. Otherwise, it is very difficult, if not impossible to be growing in our connection to the Light of the Creator, and manifesting our potential Light.

Rav Ashlag says, "From the perspective of their Vessels they are immeasurably superior to the Upper Three of the Line." It is interesting that there are certain things that are beyond us, and certainly this is way beyond us. There are the First Three Sefirot of the Line that are beyond us, which we do not even discuss, and here Rav Ashlag tells us that the First Three Sefirot of the Circular Vessels are even purer and more elevated than the Upper Three of the Line. The idea of the Circular Vessels is when we have to draw Light that is a miracle or something that is way beyond us. This teaching of Rav Ashlag is really an awakening of being able to draw something from very far away—a miracle that is literally beyond us. The First Three Sefirot of the Line is beyond us, and the Circular Vessels are beyond, beyond us.

It is peculiar that as we are going to discuss some things as we continue, Rav Ashlag will keep explaining to us all the things that we cannot talk about. He will keep talking about them and reminding us that we cannot discuss them. It always makes me happy, that although we cannot fully comprehend them— and it is important that we understand that we do not fully comprehend them—by us making even a limited connection to them we are able to draw miracles, Light, blessings that are beyond us.

I think it is important to clarify that, in the big picture, each one of us has three levels of beyond: there is who we are now, which is probably very limited; then there is our potential, our personal Surrounding Light, which we awaken through this study and it starts shining more and more to us. Our Surrounding Light, our potential, is our first level of beyond. The next level of beyond is the First Three Levels: Keter, Chochmah, and Binah of the Vessels of the Line. Then the third level of beyond, is the Circular Vessels (*Kelim de'igulim*). And every time we say the words, *Kelim de'igulim*, we are connecting to the level beyond, beyond, beyond and to whatever degree, we draw this to us. What an exciting, amazing gift.

.

INNER OBSERVATION (HISTAKLUT PNIMIT)

Circles (Igulim) and Straightness (Yosher). It includes ten chapters.

CHAPTER 1

Chapter 1 explains the Ten Circular Sefirot, comprising six topics:

1. The Circles are the aspect of the Upper Three [Sefirot].
2. Concerning the Sefirot of the Circles, whatever is more Exterior is more important; it is the opposite with the Sefirot of Straightness, where what is more Interior is more important.
3. The Vessels receive in two ways: from their Interior and from their Exterior.
4. The Fourth Phase can only be revealed through the three Phases that precede it and bring about its revelation.
5. The Four Phases resemble four layers laid one upon the other on a Vessel's wall, where the abundance is received by the inner layer.
6. The denser the Masach the higher in Stature it raises Returning Light; and there are five levels.

> **The Circles are the aspect of the Upper Three [Sefirot].**
>
> 1. Of the Ten Circular Sefirot, the Ari spoke very little, and even these few words are seemingly very contradictory. Yet to speak of them at length is impossible, since they are the aspect of the Upper Three Sefirot, of which we are forbidden to study.

The great work of Rav Ashlag—the Inner Light commentary—involves completing the process of gathering together all the Ari's teachings from the Writings of the Ari and explaining them. Now we have Rav Ashlag's next revelation—Inner Observation—where Rav Ashlag builds upon the revelations in the previous section and really explains everything that is either not explained enough or not really explained in the Writings of the Ari.

Why is it that the teachings of the Ari concerning the Circular Vessels seem to be contradictory? This is an important lesson, because our consciousness can only have clarity about levels that we are connected to. And this happens almost all the time. For example, in the portion of Ki Tisa we read "when Moses went out to the tent, that all the people would rise, and each one would stand at the door of his tent and look after Moses, until he had come to the tent." (Exodus 33:8) The commentators explain that the Israelites were not in awe as they watched Moses depart the Tent of Meeting but rather were looking to find all sorts of things wrong with him. Why is that?

We also find throughout the stories of the Tzadikim that their initial introduction to each other was always contradictory—even with their close students, whether it is the Baal Shem Tov with the Maggid of Mezeritch or the Ari with Rav Chaim Vital. This is because we can only accept and understand the level we are on, or maybe slightly above us. When we look at something way above us, we are limited in what we see. For instance, when we see someone holy, do we see Light shining out of them. No. Because if we could see a holy man, if we could truly compute a person's holiness, we would be there. We cannot compute, understand or take in where we are not. Meaning, to some degree we are very limited in our ability to see holiness.

Therefore, it was impossible for the Israelites, those who were not on the level of Moses, or at least similar to the level of Moses, to see him for who he really was. The Israelites saw contradictions and had lack of clarity. They did not understand and judged him because one cannot have clarity about a level beyond them. Therefore, Rav Ashlag says, "The discussion of the

Circular Vessels in the Writings of the Ari seems to be full of contradictions"
because it has to be. As long as we are in the level way below the Circular
Vessels, we can only see contradictions. Of course, the Ari and Rav Ashlag
were connected to the Circular Vessels, but we are not there. Therefore, the
teachings of the Ari concerning specifically the Circular Vessels seem to be
contradictory because that is where we are at.

It says in the Talmud, "Rabba bar Chana said in the name of Rabbi Yochanan:
'What is the meaning of that which is written: "For the priest's lips should
keep knowledge, and they should seek Torah from his mouth; for he is an
angel of the Lord of Hosts" (Malachi 2:7)? The verse teaches: If the teacher
is similar to an angel of the Lord of Hosts, they should seek Torah from his
mouth; but if not, they should not seek Torah from his mouth. (Chagigah 15b)
They ask, 'What does it mean that you can only accept a teacher if he is an
angel?' They explain just like with the angels, one does not ask questions, so
too, when a person accepts upon themselves a teacher, they have to accept
this teacher without judgment." If this person truly is a teacher, meaning
they are someone who is beyond where we are at, this means that we cannot
comprehend them and are going to have questions and contradictions.
If you have someone with whom you have no contradictions or doubts, it
simply means that they are probably not so high. They are probably similar to
you. But if someone is beyond you, someone is truly on a much higher, more
elevated level, there are going to be questions.

Chances are, if most of us met Rav Shimon Bar Yochai, although we would
be excited to see him, we would not understand a word. We would be full of
questions—why is he doing that, why is he saying this, it does not make any
sense—all that. And if you go up higher to Moses, it would be even worse. The
higher the person we meet, the more contradictions and questions there will
be. We can only be at the understanding of someone who is even close to our
level. This is the first very important teaching from Rav Ashlag here.

> Nevertheless, the few words that the Ari wrote require an explanation,
> with an extensive and clear commentary, in such a way that they will
> suffice for the purpose intended by the Ari, that is, as much as is absolutely
> needed to connect the [themes of this] Wisdom.

One of the tremendous beauties of the Wisdom of Kabbalah is that we cannot
begin logical understanding in the middle. We have to have all—as far back

as we can go to the first part of that logical construct. Therefore, to give us clarity about the whole wisdom we have to have some understanding of the beginnings of it. Only by having some comprehension of the beginnings of it can we merit having an understanding of the rest of it; even those parts of it that are closer to us, those parts of it that are easier for us to understand.

Rav Ashlag says that one of the reasons Rav Isaac Luria (the Ari) revealed and spoke about the First Three Sefirot of the Ten Sefirot of the Circular Vessels is because we cannot comprehend the Wisdom of Kabbalah unless we have the whole picture. And to give us the whole picture the Ari had to reveal at least a little bit about the origins of it. There has to be a complete understanding. If a person has only a part of it and not all of it, they do not have a true understanding.

There is a famous section in the Zohar, before the *Safra Detzni'uta* ("The Concealed Book"), that discusses the fact that if a person remains at the level of basic understanding and does not push themselves to delve deeper, they miss almost everything. In this study, the mind and the soul are very much connected. Thus, to the degree that we do not understand the picture, even in our mind—if we are not constantly pushing ourselves to gain the complete picture and delve deeper into it—we cannot possibly be connecting in greater ways with the Light of the Creator. The point being that to the degree we do not have a strong enough desire to deepen our understanding of the Study of the Ten Luminous Emanations, it means that our soul is lacking.

The more connected a person is to the Light of the Creator, the more their desire to deepen their understanding. The less a person is connected to the Light of the Creator, the less they desire to study the Ten Luminous Emanations. This is one of the important ways we can ascertain whether we are growing in our connection to the Light of the Creator or lessening in our connection to the Light of the Creator. There are no two ways about it.

As Rav Ashlag says, the complete picture and the deepening of that picture is the only true understanding. There is no such thing as partial understanding. Of course, most of us, if not all of us, do not have the complete understanding. But the desire to gain that complete understanding and to deepen our understanding and to go toward that revelation is what enables our connection to the totality of the Light of the Creator.

Rav Ashlag teaches that the Light of the Creator cannot really be revealed in parts, there is a totality of revelation that comes with a totality of understanding. This is a big problem for most of us. If we hope to gain a total connection to the Light of the Creator and we still lack a total understanding of the Study of the Ten Luminous Emanations, how do we make that connection? The answer is desire. Because as long as we have a desire to deepen our understanding that then enables us to have that complete connection. But if we do not have an understanding nor the desire for the deepening of that understanding, there cannot be a real revelation of the Light of the Creator. This is a very important understanding.

When the Ari and Rav Ashlag say that we are not permitted to speak about the First Three Sefirot of the Line and the Circular Vessels, the basic idea is, "Whatever we cannot comprehend, whatever is beyond our level we cannot speak about, we cannot truly understand." Rav Shimon Bar Yochai, the Ari, and Rav Ashlag all had a complete understanding of these matters, which means that when we study from the Ari and Rav Ashlag about these levels, even though what they are revealing to us is not even one millionth of their understanding of it, these words are dripping with that understanding.

Rav Ashlag and the Ari had a complete understanding, they had a complete connection to the Circular Vessels and to the First Three Sefirot of the Line, they are telling us that we, most of us, who are not connected to those levels cannot discuss them, cannot really understand them completely. Therefore, they teach us a little bit about it. These few words, these explanations are coming from them, from these souls that do have that connection. So although we are getting a limited amount of understanding concerning the First Three Sefirot of the Line and the Circular Vessels, because this understand is coming to us from the Ari and from Rav Ashlag, it is dripping with that connection. Thus besides whatever we merit to connect to through our own understanding, having the merit to be getting this understanding from Rav Ashlag and from the Ari by and within itself already connects us in a greater degree to that level.

If anyone else in the world wrote down these words, we would be able to gain some understanding of these levels, yet because we have the merit that the Ari and Rav Ashlag revealed them, they are therefore enveloped with this Light even to whatever limited degree that they revealed this understanding. In our study of their words, the Ari and Rav Ashlag really cannot help themselves by imbuing us with greater levels than they explain because this is who they were, and we know that a righteous person's soul and Light is completely revealed in everything they write, in everything they do. This is a beautiful and important understanding.

**Concerning the Sefirot of the Circles,
whatever is more Exterior is more important.**

2. Let us first acquire a general understanding. The Ari splits the entirety of existence into two categories: Circles (Igulim) and Straightness (Yosher). This means that all Partzufim present in the five Worlds—Adam Kadmon, Atzilut, Briyah, Yetzirah, and Asiyah, all the way to this World—each have the aspect of Ten Sefirot of the Circle and Ten Sefirot of Straightness. We see that in the Sefirot of the Circle whatever is most Exterior is most superior and whatever is most Interior is most inferior, since the highest Circle that is closest to the Ein Sof and encircles and surrounds the entire existence is most superior and is called Keter. Within it is the second Circle called Chochmah, which is inferior to Keter, and so on, until the innermost sphere—this World—which is the most inferior of all the Circles, since it is dark, without Light, and full of filth. Thus, the more inward a Circle is the more inferior it is, and the more peripheral a Circle is the more superior it is.

Rav Ashlag speaks about a few important ideas here. One is to understand that although we speak about the fact that the Circular Vessels are levels beyond us, he makes it very clear that there is a distinct connection between our physical world and the Circular Vessels because the one that represents Malchut, our physical world becomes manifested from the innermost Circle. So clearly, there is a connection between our physical world, where we are, who we are, and the Circular Vessels. Of course, the innermost Circle—our world—is the lowest of them, the filthiest of them, the one that has the most darkness. What does it mean that the most external is the most elevated and the most internal is the furthest from the Light of the Creator? Of course, we are not talking about physical circles where you could simply deduce that if it is further out it is closer to the Endless World.

A famous section in the Talmud (Pesachim 50a) speaks about a sage who went up to the Supernal Worlds and saw what happens in that World. When he came back down to this world, they asked him, "What did you see there? What did you see in that world?" He replied, "I saw a world that is upside-down." Meaning that everyone who in this world is elevated is down in that World. And everyone who is down in this world is elevated in that World. This is the reality of the Circular Vessels, meaning that the purer an essence is, the less it can be viewed in our world. The more external something is in the spiritual sense, which means the purer it is, the less Desire to Receive for the Self Alone that it has, the more removed it is from our world. Yet this does not mean that Rav Shimon Bar Yochai cannot exist in our physical world, it simply means that in true essence, he is not of this world, he is external to this world.

Unfortunately most of us are very much internal to this world. We are very much connected to this world. So when we discuss being external or internal, it does not represent physicality or space—where a person physically is—it represents a spiritual connection. It is as Rav Ashlag says, where the outermost Circle, which represents Keter of the Circular Vessels, is the most connected to the Endless World. And the innermost Circle, which is our physical world is the furthest away and therefore, it has the most darkness and the most filth.

Although this is a slightly different idea, it clarifies, and is connected to, what we said earlier. You cannot, from the vantage point of the Internal—from the filth of our world, the Desire to Receive for the Self Alone—connect to or see what is external to our world, meaning the higher and more elevated Light. Therefore, it has to be that our world is an opposite world. Our world being of the most internal, the most distant from the Endless World can only connect to and reveal the lowest of the Lights. Anything that has a great Light revealed in this physical world has to mean that it is greatly diminished from the external. Thus this world is an upside-down world (*olam hafuch*). Whatever is elevated in the internal filthy world has to be less in the external, pure world. Conversely, whatever is connected to the Circular Vessels, which means it is of a purer nature in this world, has to be external to it. Meaning it does not connect to, it is not seen, it is not understood, it is not given the approval that one would expect. Whatever, in its true spiritual essence, is great in this world has to be externalized from our world and can never be seen in the totality of its Light while we are in this physical world.

One can be as Rav Shimon Bar Yochai and Rav Ashlag were, living in this physical world but still being external to it, detached from it. This is why the Tzadikim could create miracles. As long as you are of the innermost world, this world, you cannot be drawing miracles. But to the degree that you live externally from this world is the degree you can draw miracles and blessings into this world. You cannot be in this world and draw blessings to it. You have to be external to it and draw blessings to it.

To the degree we can make ourselves external, separate from the filth of this world, to that degree we can draw blessings, Light, and miracles into this world. Again, this does not represent physical space. We are only talking about spiritual essence. We can be physically in this world and be external to it or we can be, unfortunately, in this world and be completely a part of it. Nevertheless, in the Circular Vessels, which are the purest form of Vessels that have ever existed, being external, unapproved, unseen, is the highest form. And the more seen, the more approved, the more clear—the darker it is, the more it is of this world.

Concerning the Ten Sefirot of Straightness, whatever is more Interior is more important.

3. The Sefirot of Straightness are the opposite. In their case, whatever is more Interior is more praiseworthy. For as the Ten Sefirot of Straightness go, the first and most inner ones are the Ten Sefirot of the World of Adam Kadmon, which is what is referred as the Line that extends from the Ein Sof that flows and reaches close to this World yet does not touch it. External to that are the Ten Sefirot of Straightness of the second World, which is called the World of Atzilut, which envelope it. The quality of this World is lower than that of Adam Kadmon.

External to the World of Atzilut are the Ten Sefirot of Straightness of the World of Briyah that envelope it, which are inferior to Atzilut, and so on down to the Ten Sefirot of Straightness of the World of Asiyah, which is the most inferior of all, and which envelopes the outer side of all the Worlds. Thus, among the Sefirot of Straightness we find that that which is more Exterior than the other is inferior to it, while that which is more Interior than the other is superior to it. This is opposite to the Ten Sefirot of the Circles, as said. Indeed, a great and deep matter lies in this opposition between the Sefirot of the Circles and the Sefirot of Straightness, and we need to understand it well.

Rav Ashlag raises the question: "Why in the Circular Vessels, is the most external the most elevated and the most internal of the lowest spiritual degree, and in the Linear Vessels, the most internal is the most elevated and the most external is of the lowest spiritual quality?" The Ari makes it very clear that the most external of those Vessels, which represents the Keter of the Circular Vessels, is the purest, most elevated, most connected to the Endless World. And the deeper, more internal we go into the Circles, the lower we go spiritually until we come to the Innermost Circle, which represents our physical world, at the lowest of all the Worlds. Conversely, when we discuss the Linear Vessels, we begin with the Innermost World called Adam Kadmon, which enclothes all the lesser Worlds. There, what is most internal is the highest and what is most external is the lowest.

What Rav Ashlag says here always excites me: "Indeed, a great and deep matter lies in this opposition between the Sefirot of the Circles and the Sefirot of Straightness, and we need to understand it well." Before we go to the answer, I just want to awaken again, this understanding that when Rav Ashlag is revealing these secrets, he is not just revealing information, he is actually revealing Light. And as we study it, we also partake of and reveal this deep and great Light. And it is not coincidental, that one of the beautiful things that you begin to notice as you deepen your study is how many secrets there are in each word.

Rav Ashlag wrote a letter explaining his relationship with his teacher. And those of us who have had the opportunity to read this letter, realize that there is so much to learn, on one hand, as well as tremendous depth. One of Rav Ashlag's students, Rav Yosef Weinstock, who was also a friend of the Rav, has a whole, in-depth, lengthy explanation of the secrets that Rav Ashlag put in his letter. So too here as we learn in the Inner Observation. If we had any real insight into what Rav Ashlag was actually doing when he says these words, we would be amazed.

Rav Ashlag uses the word "gadol" (great or big), referring to the great secret in this section. It says in Derech HaMelech ("The Way of the King") by Rabbi Kalonymus Kalmish Shapiro, (1889–1943) about how interesting it is that we call the Shabbat before Pesach, Shabbat HaGadol (the Great Shabbat). And although he has a whole explanation about it, there is just one point I would like to mention because it relates to what Rav Ashlag is discussing here.

He says:

> "When the kabbalists who preceded the Ari would speak about the Sefirah of Chesed (Kindness), they would say Gedulah (Greatness). The word Chesed, relates to someone receiving goodness. If you give someone something that he needs—if he is hungry and you give him food—you are doing a Chesed, you are doing goodness to

him. If you take someone who is stuffed, who is not hungry at all, and you give him food that is not Chesed. Therefore, we see that the term Chesed has to be dependent on the need of the receiver. The kabbalists before the time of the Ari, did not talk about the Worlds below the World of Atzilut, and because in the World of Atzilut where there is only unity there is no separation between giver and receiver, you cannot talk about a receiver because there was only unity, there is no giver and receiver. And therefore all the kabbalists before the Ari, used the word Gedulah, which represents Greatness, which is related to Right Column in the revelation of great Light. So when you say Gedulah, what they meant is that there is a great opening of Light, but no receiving yet because they were talking only in the World of Atzilut. And therefore, the Light could have been even greater, too great for the Vessel to receive it."

Chesed is when you give something to someone who needs it and enjoys the receiving of it. Giving goodness to someone who does not want it is not Chesed, it is actually the opposite. Someone who gives something to someone does not necessarily mean that they are doing a Chesed. It is the receiving of that gift by someone who needs it and desires it and enjoys it that makes your action Chesed. As the Esh Kodesh states, "Chesed is dependent on the receiver." If you give a homeless person who has not eaten in three days a hamburger, now you have done a Chesed because the person receiving it has a desire and enjoys the receiving. So, when you use the term Chesed, it represents a receiver who is receiving and enjoying.

We know that the World of Separation begins in the Worlds of Briyah, Yetzirah, and Asiyah—the lower Three Worlds and that in Adam Kadmon and Atzilut, which is the First World, there is unification. Because the world was only ready for these kabbalists to speak about and reveal the Light of the Upper World of Atzilut and bring it down to our world, in their studies and revelation of Light they could not refer to the Sefirah as Chesed (Kindness) only as Gedulah. Chesed appears in the Worlds of Briyah, Yetzirah, and Asiyah, meaning the Worlds within which there are receivers who lack and givers who give.

The kabbalists, preceding the time of the Ari, spoke only within the realm of the World of Atzilut, they could only refer to it as *Gedulah* because *Gedulah* represents a great flowing of Light from the Creator but no receiving of it by the Vessel. Therefore, because the Light was not yet coming into a Vessel that desires it, and then receives it, it would have been too great for the

Vessel to receive it. Now we understand the greatness of the soul of the Ari. What the Ari did was not simply explain what occurs after the World of Atzilut in the Worlds of Briyah, Yetzirah, and Asiyah, in our world, but with his explanation he actually forced, caused, that Light to trickle down into our world; he caused the Light to start being revealed in the Lower Worlds. His study and revelation made it so that the Light began to flow down into the Worlds of Briyah, Yetzirah, and Asiyah, where there exists Vessels that are separate and can receive, and thus he began calling the Sefirah, Chesed.

When you understand that there is a reason the kabbalists before the Ari refer to Chesed as *Gedulah*, and what the Ari was doing when he began referring to it as Chesed, it is such an amazing thing. Throughout the Zohar, Rav Shimon asks the students, "Which one of you are ready to do battle?" What the Ari did when he was forcing this Light to trickle down into the Worlds of Briyah, Yetzirah, and Asiyah, he was doing battle with the Negative Side. Every time he said the word Chesed, there was tremendous opposition from the negative angels, from the darkness of our world because in saying the word Chesed, he was forcing the Light down into the Worlds of Briyah, Yetzirah, and Asiyah. This had never happened previously, and there was tremendous opposition that might have manifested in all kinds of ways. It might have manifested in sickness or in arguments, and so on. Rav Shimon, in the Zohar, refers to the work that he did then, and the work the kabbalists do, as "those who work the field and cut off the thorns," (Zohar Naso, Idra Rabba 1) because they clean the world for us.

That is what we have to do when we learn from the Study of the Ten Luminous Emanations. We have to know that we are not simply studying information. Those of us who are ready, are actually doing battle every time we say the word Chesed; we are actually forcing a flow of Light down into the Worlds of Briyah, Yetzirah, and Asiyah. And obviously on the higher levels, the levels that Rav Shimon, the Ari, and Rav Ashlag work on, this was a very dangerous task they took upon themselves.

Throughout the ages, there was the danger of revealing the Light of Kabbalah. It was not that it was too holy for people to hear, the kabbalist knew that when you are truly studying Kabbalah, when you are truly revealing these secrets, what you are actually doing is forcing a flow of Light into these places, into these Worlds. When we speak about the World of Asiyah and the Light that is revealed in that World, we are forcing that flow down and it is dangerous work. Bli ayin hara, Rav Shimon, the Ari, and Rav Ashlag cleared a path for us so it is easier. They were and are doing battle. This is the true study of

Kabbalah. The real study of Kabbalah is not simply to study these things but to understand them as a way to force this Light down into our world.

When Rav Ashlag says, "it is a great and deep concept," he does not just mean this is a deep concept, he means there is great and deep Light that we are revealing to the world as we study this answer. And obviously to the degree that this is our consciousness, to that degree we are able to be conduits of this revelation. This is an amazing and important understanding that Rav Ashlag says we have to understand very well.

Two ways the Vessel receives: a) from its Interior; b) from its Exterior.

4. You already know the matter of the Middle Point in the Ein Sof, where the Tzimtzum took place, where the Light was distanced from around that Point and an empty space was formed (see Volume 1, Chapter 1, Section 14). It was explained there that the reason it is called the Middle Point is to indicate that it does not receive through its inside and Interior, but only through its Exterior from around it. This way it receives the Light without limit or measure, since that which receives from its Exterior does not make a limitation on the Light, study there well. Thus, we have two categories of receiving in the Vessels—one is that which receives from its Exterior and the second is that which receives from its Interior. Surely, we are not speaking about space or area, where one can imagine Exterior and Interior. We therefore need to understand well what kind of Interior and Exterior we are dealing with here.

The Vessel of the Endless World does not receive the way we receive. We spoke at length that most of us are aware of one way of receiving, which is taking inside—whether it is physical things, food, respect, or approval. Unfortunately, all of our receiving is a Vessel that takes inside. And as Rav Ashlag explains, the type of Vessel that takes inside is a very limited and limiting Vessel. The Vessel of the Ein Sof is a different type of receiving. It does not receive internally but rather externally.

There is a higher level of receiving that we all have to work toward, which is receiving externally. We know all the great spiritual leaders got to the point where they were able to see someone else's joy as their own. To experience someone else's fulfillment as our own, being able to take pleasure in another's receiving, is an element of external receiving. Meaning any pleasure, any receiving that we take that is not coming to us, is an element of receiving through our external.

Therefore, the sages say that only a person who can partake of someone else's pleasure as their own and can partake of someone else's pain as their own, will merit to see the Redemption. Only a person who comes to the point where they feel, not just has empathy, but really comes to the point where they feel another's pain as their own and feels another's pleasure as their own will merit to see the Redemption because it is the development of these external Vessels. It is the external Vessel's ways of receiving pleasure by not taking inside that can prepare us for the ultimate Light of the Ein Sof, that can prepare us for the ultimate Light of the Redemption.

Therefore, an important question we have to constantly be asking ourselves is: *Is my external Vessel growing? Is my sense of pleasure from another's pleasure growing? Is my sense of pain for another's pain growing?* And if we are honest with ourselves, I think for many of us the answer will be "No," which unfortunately means that we are not developing our external Vessels, as Rav Ashlag calls them. And if we are not developing our external Vessels, then Heaven forbid, we are not preparing ourselves to receive the Light of the Final Correction, because the Light of the Ein Sof, the Light of the Final Correction, is external Vessel Light. When we understand the importance of growing our external Vessels, and of asking ourselves constantly: Are my external Vessels growing, and the answer is "Yes," can we be preparing ourselves for the Gemar haTikkun, for the Light of the Redemption.

> **The First Three Phases merely bring about the revelation of the Fourth Phase, but they themselves cannot receive. This is likened to the four layers of a Vessel's wall.**
>
> 5. As you already know, the concept of the spiritual Vessel is the aspect of Desire in the Emanated to receive abundance from the Ein Sof. (see Volume 1, Terminology Answers, number 25) You also already know that this Desire has Four Phases, one below the other. In other words, this Vessel, namely the said Desire to Receive, is not established in the Emanated to be suitable for its function until it has gradually gone through Four Phases. The First Phase is a very weak Desire, the Second Phase is greater than the First Phase, and so on until the Fourth Phase, which is

the maximum Desire according to the degree required to establish the completion of the Vessel.

The reason has been explained earlier (Volume 1, Chapter 1, Section 14) that since this Desire to Receive is in polar opposite form to the aspect of the Desire to Share included in the Light of Ein Sof, it therefore cannot be revealed all at once but only very slowly.

Something hit me strongly as I was reading through this section. And the beauty of being able to learn from Rav Ashlag is that as he explains the spiritual framework, every once in a while, he will throw in a spiritual rule. We have also by now come to realize that whatever Rav Ashlag is revealing to us is only a tiny fraction of what he knew. And obviously, what we understand from what he is telling us is only a fraction of what he had meant to tell us. Whenever we study from Rav Ashlag, we are clearly never getting the entire picture. We are getting a little of what he realized he could explain and of that, we can understand a little from his explanation. Therefore, it is a big mistake to ever study anything, and certainly from the Study of the Ten Luminous Emanations, and think that we have grasped all of it. We only grasp a small part of it. It is important to have this clarity because the problem with the study is that often it is so clear, so logical that this logic tells us: "Oh, I understand it." Yet we have to always know that whatever we understand is a tiny fraction of the totality.

The Ramchal (Rav Chaim Luzzatto, 1707–1746) would always say that the ultimate purpose of wisdom is to know that we do not know. For instance, if there are three blind people all feeling a table from different angles, even though it is a table, each of them will have a different experience. One person can touch the corner and realize this is something sharp, another one can touch the top of the table and think this is something that you can put things on; and one of them could touch the leg of the table and think this is a stick that you cannot do much with. Thus even when we come to a level of understanding of the Study of the Ten Luminous Emanations, it is a tiny fraction of the totality of things.

The reason I bring this up is because we have studied from Rav Ashlag as well as the Rav, my father, who has many tapes on the Four Phases the Vessel has to go through to become a Vessel. In this section of Rav Ashlag, it is very logical. You read through it, you understand it, you understand why there has to be Four Phases.

Rav Ashlag tells us, yes it is true, there is a logic to it, but there is also an added reason why the Vessel has to go through Phases: "since this Desire to Receive is in polar opposite form to the aspect of the Desire to share included in the Light of the Endless, it therefore cannot be revealed all at once but only very slowly." The point Rav Ashlag makes is that there had to be a process, separate from the logical understanding that it had to be a Four Phase process. When you are going from such a Desire to Share, which is the Light of the Creator, to a Desire to Receive, it cannot happen in one Phase. Even if the logic would work, where the Creator could have created a Desire to Receive in one Phase, it still could not have happened because when we go through change, it is a process. This is an important spiritual understanding.

When things happen quickly, it means this person is living in the World of Desire to Receive for the Self Alone—the World that is opposite from the Light of the Creator. If someone is going through a spiritual transformation, there has to be a process. We have to respect this process. We have to honor this process or else we are stuck without change.

Rav Ashlag says that it is impossible to go from the Light of the Creator to the Vessel and conversely from the Vessel of Desire to Receive for the Self Alone, complete separation from the Light of the Creator, into the Light without a process. Logic is one thing, but if we want transformation, if we want change there has to be a process. Whether it is a four-step process or a five-step process, we can talk about logic another time. But there cannot be change, growth, connection to the Light the Creator without a process.

We have to remember Rav Ashlag's words, "it therefore cannot be revealed all at once but only very slowly. It starts from the Desire to Share included in the root, which is called Keter; then to the denser." It cannot happen quickly, it is a process. For it to be real it has to take time. And this is a bigger discussion than just here in the Study of the Ten Luminous Emanations, it is certainly true in the Kabbalah Centres, and in trying to accomplish any revelation of Light. Rav Ashlag makes clear that if it is a true process that is going to bring about any lasting Light, it is a slow process, it cannot happen quickly. If it happens quickly, if there is no process, there is no growth, there is no long-term Light revealed.

It starts from the Desire to Share included in the root, which is called Keter; then to the denser, meaning that which is a little different than it, which is the First Phase; then to the even denser one called the Second Phase, and so on, until the Fourth Phase, whose form is totally opposite to the Light. Only [the Fourth Phase] is uniquely suitable to serve as a Vessel in the emanated, unlike the former Three Phases, wherein the Desire to Receive is not revealed to the desired degree to be the aspect of a Vessel of Receiving. Therefore, only the Fourth Phase is considered the main Vessel of Receiving of the Emanated, which is called the inner and Interior aspect of the Emanated Being due to this. However, the Third Phase of the Desire is considered to be outside the Fourth Phase, the Second Phase outside the Third, the First Phase outside the second, and the Keter part outside them all.

This resembles a wall in a physical vessel made of four layers one on top of the other. The abundance received in that vessel can surely be found in the fourth, innermost layer alone, while the outer three layers around it are there only to strengthen the fourth, innermost layer alone. You can conclude here too that the Light is received only in the Fourth Phase, while the preceding three Phases are exterior to it and only appear there since the Fourth Phase cannot be revealed without an evolution, as explained earlier.

> **Interiority and density are the same;**
> **Exteriority and purity are the same.**

6. Thus, the Interiority and Exteriority distinguished in every Vessel have been well explained to you. Since there has to be Four Phases in every Vessel, as known, therefore the last one is called the inner part and Interior of that Vessel, for it is the main receiving aspect found in the Vessel. The Phases that precede it to reveal the last Phase are considered the Exterior of the Vessel. The farther a level is from the last Phase, the more External it is considered. You also know that the First Phase is purer than the Second, while the Fourth Phase is the coarsest of them all. Thus, Interiority and density are one and the same, and the reason the Fourth Phase is considered as the part that receives abundance is simply because it is the densest. And Exteriority and purity are one and the same, since

its Desire is weak and pure and closer to the aspect of the Emanator. Therefore, it is the most peripheral, namely, the farthest from being the receiving aspect, which is the inside and Interior.

Distance or closeness to the Emanator is measured based on the [level of] receiving in the Emanated.

7. This is [the meaning of] what the Ari wrote concerning the Circular Sefirot that whatever is more External is more superior and is closer to the Emanator, since the root aspect called Keter is the purest of all and is therefore closest to the form of the Ein Sof than the rest, which is called "closer to the Emanator." This is also called "most Exterior," meaning that it is very distant from the inner and Interior aspect, namely the receiving aspect, as mentioned earlier. Next comes the First Phase, which is more inward than Keter, namely, closer to the Receiving aspect than it. The Second Phase is further inward than it, namely, it is closer to the Fourth Phase, which is the receiving aspect, and so on until the Fourth Phase, which is the true internal aspect, which means that abundance is received within it, and therefore its form is furthest from the Emanator than the rest, as mentioned.

Among the Ten Sefirot of Straightness, height depends on the Returning Light that rises from the density of the Masach. The denser it is, the greater the Returning Light.

8. However, among the Sefirot of Straightness there is the concept of Returning Light that rises from the unification of the Masach with the Supernal Light (see Volume 2, Terminology Answers, 43)

Rav Ashlag explains that in the realm of Line, there is a new concept called Returning Light (Ohr Chozer). In the World before the Tzimtzum the Vessel desired to Receive for the Sake of Receiving. Meaning, the Creator says, "I want to give you a lot." The Vessel says, "Oh great! I want to receive a lot for myself." Now in the Realm of the Line, the Vessel says, "I cannot Receive for Myself Alone. I have to ascertain how much I can Receive Only for the Sake of Sharing."

Using the example of food, if a person somehow wants to diminish his enjoyment of food, he can say, *If I eat grass I can have that not for myself alone. But if I eat a steak, there is too much temptation to enjoy it, so I will not have a steak. If I want to eat for no selfish pleasure, what can I limit myself to eating, and only eat it for the sake of giving my body strength, for example, but not for the sake of my Desire to Receive for the Self Alone? So I will eat grass, so I will take pills that have nutrients. I can do all kinds of things that will not tempt me to enjoy them. But when it comes to steak, or a cake then I will not have it. Why? Because I know that I am not strong enough yet to be eating that, and not partaking pleasure for myself.*

This is the concept of Ohr Chozer. Every Vessel has to decide on its own how much it can take in only for the Sake of Sharing, and anything more than that it will not take in. With the concept of Ohr Chozer, the Vessel says "How much can I take in only for the Sake of Giving it Forward?

The size of this Returning Light is measured by the degree of density in the Masach that interacts with the Supernal Light. We find that the densest Masach, namely the Fourth Phase, reveals a complete Stature of Ten Sefirot up to Keter.

If, however, the amount of density in the Masach is one Phase smaller and has only the Third Phase, it then reveals only Ten Sefirot that each have the Stature of Chochmah without Keter. If it only has the density of the Second Phase, it then reveals Ten Sefirot that each have only the Stature of Binah, without Keter and Chochmah. If the Masach has only the density of the First Phase, it reveals Ten Sefirot that each have but the Stature of Zeir Anpin. And if the Masach is pure, not having even the density of the First Phase, it reveals no Stature but the aspect of Malchut alone. The reason for this will be explained in Volume 3, with God's help.

When the desire is the strongest and combined with this greatest desire is also the certainty that we will only be Receiving it for the Sake of Sharing, then we can have the strongest desire, and, of course, have the biggest Returning Light, meaning the greatest giving out of our desire. This is what we will call the World of Adam Kadmon, the first World that existed after the removal of Light.

For example, how much money can you have that you would not get self-involved? A person could ask, "If I give you $1, can you make sure you give it to someone else?" And the answer could be, "Yes, $1, you can have. But if you give me a million dollars, I am sure I will be sharing say $600K of it, but a few $100K I will be using for myself." That is the decision the Vessel is making.

The Vessel in Adam Kadmon, the First World that existed after the removal of Light, says, "I am sure that I can take in a tremendous amount of Light and only be thinking of sharing it with other people, having no thought of taking it in for myself. Otherwise I will not receive this Light." Then the Vessel in the World of Atzilut gets a little bit weaker and says, "I am not as strong as the World of Adam Kadmon, I can only receive this much and still be sure that I will be Receiving it only for the Sake of Sharing." This is the Third Phase, the third level Desire not the Fourth Phase—the ultimate level of desire.

If, in the World of Adam Kadmon, the Vessel says, "I can receive everything, and be certain that I am only Receiving it for the Sake of Giving it out to others and not Receiving Pleasure for Myself," it receives all Ten Sefirot because its Returning Light has all Ten Sefirot. It is important to realize that the Returning Light is what makes the Vessel hold onto the Light because from the Creator's side, the Creator gives all the Light all the time.

Thus in the World of Adam Kadmon, the Vessel says, "I can receive everything and be sure that I will only be thinking to share it." In the next World, the World of Atzilut, the Vessel says, "I cannot receive all that Light; I have to receive a little bit less. Only by receiving less can I be sure that my consciousness will be to Receive it only for the Sake of Sharing." Therefore, the Vessel in the World of Atzilut receives less Light, meaning it only receives up to Chochmah and it does not receive the Light of Keter.

Then the Vessel in the World of Briyah, says, "I feel that I can only receive a diminished amount of Light that can I be sure I will Receive for the Sake of Sharing. I cannot Receive the Light of Keter, nor the Light of Chochmah, because if I receive that Light, it will overwhelm my spiritual nature of only Desire to Share with the Desire to Receive. Therefore, do not give me that Light."

And if the Vessel decides that it can only have Returning Light and therefore the Curtain (Masach), of the First Phase, the first degree of Desire, we say that it only reveals the Light of Zeir Anpin and Malchut, meaning Chesed,

Gevurah, Tiferet, Netzach, Hod, Yesod, and Malchut. It does not receive and reveal the Light of Keter, nor Chochmah, nor Binah, because it has decided that it can only handle a diminished Light for the Sake of Sharing. And if the Vessel only has the lowest level, then it only reveals the level of Malchut.

Even though Rav Ashlag says, "The reason for this will be explained in Volume 3, with God's help," the reality is it is going to take us quite a while to get to Volume 3, so I want to spend a little bit of time, and Rav Ashlag will as well, to discuss this new reality. The real change in the understanding of the Supernal Worlds and the Wisdom Kabbalah is the concept of Returning Light that the Ari revealed to the world, and it is only Rav Ashlag who completed the understanding of what that means. This revelation is unique to any of the writings and revelations of other kabbalists who existed before the Ari.

And just to clarify again, it is in this World of the Line that the Vessel knows that it will not, cannot Receive for Itself Alone. It cannot receive in the old paradigm, the old way of receiving, meaning, "You want to give me, I will take it and enjoy it." Now there is a new concept that begins with the Masach, meaning, "I will not and cannot Receive for Myself Alone; I will not and cannot receive any Light, any pleasure that will fill me selfishly." Light cannot be Received for the Self Alone. And from this Masach stems the Returning Light, which is the real internal consciousness decision of the Vessel: "How much can I receive and still maintain a Desire to Share on all of that totality of Light? A drop above that I cannot receive because there is a Masach that tells me I cannot receive selfishly, I cannot Receive for Myself Alone." This now is the calculation that the Vessel keeps experiencing.

What happens is, as the Worlds are created, the Vessel becomes weaker spiritually, and it is true to itself. It says, "I realize now, that now I can only Receive a lower amount of Light for the Sake of Sharing." And when we use the terms: "It does not have Keter, it does not have Chochmah, it does not have Binah," all this means is just a diminishment of the Light that it can receive. When the Vessel decides how much Light it can receive, it is called a new Vessel because this is a new paradigm of Receiving called Returning Light. And whatever the decision is, whatever the truth of that consciousness is, is how much Light this Vessel, this new reality will have.

We now comprehend both the Masach and Ohr Chozer, and understand this new paradigm of Receiving only Light that is received through this consciousness of, "How much I can Receive for the Sake of Sharing" that is manifested in the Vessel. The Light of the Creator gives all the Ten Sefirot, gives the totality of the Light all the time, but the Vessel limits the amount of Light that it will receive by how much it can manifest only for the Sake of Sharing.

With this, Rav Ashlag explains the question that we began previously, which is: "Why in this World of the Line, which is the basis of the World within which we live, we say that whatever is more internal, meaning has more Desire to Receive, is more elevated?" He says that because now in this new reality of Returning Light, the only way to Receive, the only way to connect to the Light of the Creator is by having a great desire that can be overcome. Having less of a desire, which is Keter, does not reveal Light anymore. There is a new paradigm, there is a new way of revealing Light in this reality. We have to have a duality. We have to have a great desire and a great power to overcome that desire.

Whereas in the World of the Circles, the previous World, simply being pure was enough. The purer, the less Desire to Receive for the Self Alone the Vessel had, the closer it was to the Creator. Now it is not true anymore. Now in the World of Line, we have to have two things: we have to have the Desire and we have to have the Masach and Ohr Chozer—the ability to overcome that Desire for the Self Alone. Only together can we be close to the Light of the Creator, can we have the Light of the Creator in our life.

Therefore, we say that this World of Line, the first World, the World of Adam Kadmon, is the most internal World because it is the World with the greatest Desire to Receive for the Self Alone. And it also has the greatest ability to overcome that desire and only Receive the Light for the Sake of Sharing. Whereas, in the World of Circles, being pure was important, in the World of the Line, being filthy is important.

And if you take a step back and look at it, there is a whole revolution that occurred in the process of humanity. Our world is a world where you have to be low and able to overcome it. If you are simply good, if you are simply pure with no Desire to Receive for the Self Alone, you will not be able to accomplish great things in this World. This is the beauty of this change that occurred in the World of the Line.

This revelation gives us a view about ourselves and the world within which we live. In our world, it is important to be low with the ability to overcome it; this is what reveals Light in our world. We do not live in a pure World where our connection to the Light of the Creator is dependent on its purity. Rather we live in a World where the more selfishness a person has, the lower a person is, the more Light they can actually reveal in this world. Besides being a powerful understanding, hopefully this gives us a completely different view about the way this world is meant to work.

CHAPTER 2

Chapter 2 explains the five main distinctions between the Five Worlds—Adam Kadmon, Atzilut, Briyah, Yetzirah, and Asiyah. It contains six topics:

1. The Five Worlds called Adam Kadmon, Atzilut, Briyah, Yetzirah and Asiyah are categorized by the Four Phases of density in the Masach.
2. The upper bestows upon the lower only with its coarsest part, and the lower receives from the upper only with its purest part.
3. The reason for the disappearance of the Light from the Three Phases preceding the Fourth, when only the Fourth Phase contracted.
4. An explanation about Binding by Striking (*Zivug deHaka'ah*).
5. What is the Returning Light that rises upward through Binding by Striking.
6. The Returning Light that rises from Binding by Striking becomes a Vessel of Receiving for the Supernal Light instead of the Fourth Phase.

In his Introduction to the Talmud Eser Sefirot, Rav Ashlag writes that the main purpose of this study is not so much the wisdom that it gives us but the fact that the study itself—the saying of these words—awakens our Surrounding Light for each one of us. It is impossible for any person to really consider themselves a student of Kabbalah unless we are constantly studying the Talmud Eser Sefirot. A perfect metaphor to explain what the Study of the Ten Luminous Emanations does is an American product called Drano. When a toilet gets clogged, you pour Drano into the toilet bowl and you flush it. This product has the power to flush out and unclog the pipes. The Study of the Ten Luminous Emanations is just that.

Unfortunately, throughout our lives, we clog our brain with thoughts of Desire to Receive for the Self Alone, all kinds of negative thoughts. What the Study of the Ten Luminous Emanations does, if we take the time to think about it, is really unclogs the thought process in our mind. Thus to be able to grow, to have a real connection to the Light of the Creator is impossible unless we at least once or three times a week, take in these concepts and allow them to flow through our brain. As they flow through our brain, what they are actually doing is cleaning our brain passages of all the garbage and clog that we have put in it throughout our lives, with our negative thoughts.

I would like to reawaken everyone to the importance of the Study of the Ten Luminous Emanations; not so much because it gives us practical lessons but because of its power. As Rav Ashlag says, the first power that it gives us is the ability to awaken our Surrounding Light, thereby enabling us to manifest it. The second power it gives us is that it cleans our mind. It is important, not simply to hear these concepts but to allow them to go into our mind because as we study them, these concepts clean our mind. Without this study, it is almost impossible to be able to have a clean, clear mind.

The main distinction between the Five Worlds—Adam Kadmon, Atzilut, Briyah, Yetzirah and Asiyah—is based on the density of their Masach. The one in Adam Kadmon is the Fourth Phase.

9. Know that regarding the Five Worlds—Adam Kadmon, Atzilut, Briyah, Yetzirah and Asiyah—of Straightness, the main distinction between these Worlds lies in the degree of density found in the Masach of their Vessels. The Masach in the Vessels of the World of Adam Kadmon is very dense, namely the density of the Fourth Phase, of which there is no greater density throughout the Worlds. Therefore, its Ten Sefirot are complete, meaning that each one of them has the Stature of Keter that is close to the Ein Sof. It is the first and most important World of them all, and it traverses from one end to the other, from the Ein Sof to this World. It is therefore considered as situated in the Interior of all the Worlds, for you already know that Interiority and density are the same, and since the Masach in the Vessels of this Adam Kadmon is the Fourth Phase, that is, the densest of them all, it is therefore the innermost of them all.

The World of Atzilut is from the Masach of the Third Phase and is therefore Exterior to Adam Kadmon, which is the Fourth Phase.

10. The Masach in the Vessels of the World of Atzilut is not as dense as the Masach in the World of Adam Kadmon, since the density of the Masach of Atzilut is just the Third Phase. Therefore, the Stature of every one of the Ten Sefirot of Straightness of Atzilut goes no further than Chochmah. They lack Keter and are therefore considered inferior in comparison to

the Ten Sefirot of the Stature of Keter in the World of Adam Kadmon. They are considered external in comparison to the Ten Sefirot in Adam Kadmon, since the density of the Third Phase is exterior to the density of the Fourth Phase, and purity and exterior are the same, as said. Thus the World of Atzilut becomes a clothing, which means an outer layer that envelopes the World of Adam Kadmon that is more internal.

The Masach of Briyah is of the Second Phase and is therefore Exterior to Atzilut.

11. The Masach in the Vessels of the Ten Sefirot of the World of Briyah is even purer than in the World of Atzilut and has only the density of the Second Phase. Thus the Stature of these Ten Sefirot is no greater than the Stature of Binah. The World of Briyah is thus considered more external than the World of Atzilut, which has the Third Phase density, and is therefore more internal than the World of Briyah, since it has only the density of the Second Phase. Therefore, the World of Briyah is considered external and a clothing over the World of Atzilut.

The Masach of Yetzirah is of the First Phase and is thus Exterior to the World of Briyah.

12. The Masach in the World of Yetzirah has but the density of the very weak First Phase, and thus the Stature of the Ten Sefirot in the World of Yetzirah is short and reaches but the Stature of Zeir Anpin, lacking the Upper Three Sefirot—Keter, Chochmah, and Binah. The World of Yetzirah is therefore more external to the World of Briyah, since [Briyah] has the density of the Second Phase that is more internal than the First Phase density in the World of Yetzirah, as said. Therefore the World of Yetzirah is considered external and a clothing over the World of Briyah.

The Masach of Asiyah is only from the root of density and is therefore exterior to them all.

13. The Masach in the Ten Sefirot of Straightness of the World of Asiyah is completely pure and has no density at all. Therefore, the unification with the Supernal Light, which raises Returning Light, does not apply to it. And since they have no Returning Light, they do not have any Supernal

Light because the Supernal Light cannot be encased in the Partzuf without Returning Light. Therefore, these Ten Sefirot have but the Stature of Malchut and are missing the first Nine Sefirot, which are: Keter, Chochmah, Binah, and Zeir Anpin (that includes the six Sefirot: Chesed, Gevurah, Tiferet, Netzach, Hod, and Yesod).

And since their Masach is purer than in all previous Worlds, they are consequently considered the outermost, for you already know that purity and exteriority mean the same, as said. Thus the World of Yetzirah, in whose Vessels there is at least the Masach of the First Phase, is considered an inner World in relation to the World of Asiyah. And the World of Asiyah—being the purest of them all—is considered external and a clothing to the World of Yetzirah and to all the Worlds.

There is an inverse proportion between the bestowal of Light and the Light being clothed.

14. One can say that logic would dictate that the most superior Light would be clothed in the purest Vessels, since the pure Vessel's form is closest to the Light, as we know, so how can we state here that the denser one has a higher Stature? However, we need to know that the matter of the Light being clothed in the Vessels is an issue unto itself and the bestowal of the Supernal Light to the Partzuf is an issue unto itself, and they are far apart. Not only that, but there is a completely inverted proportion between them because this is the rule: the higher does not bestow upon the lower except through its densest part, and the lower does not receive from the Supernal Light except through its purest part. You need to understand this very well, since it is an important key in [this] wisdom.

Rav Ashlag says there are certain concepts that we need to understand so clearly, as if they are placed in a box and we can simply reach and draw them out whenever we want. Here Rav Ashlag is saying that the Supernal, the Giver, always gives from His lowest part. The receiver, the Vessel, always receives in his purest, highest part. Meaning, that although we say the Desire to Receive for the Self Alone is what reveals Light, it can never partake of that Light. It can cause Light to be revealed but it can never manifest Light. The manifestation of Light has to be in pure Vessels.

Rav Ashlag explains in the Light of Wisdom that in our world it is necessary to have very selfish people and have very righteous people, because the selfish people awaken the desire and the righteous people manifest the Light. If we did not have tremendously selfish people in the world, the righteous people would not be able to manifest the Light that they manifest. For instance, Rav Ashlag says that you might need maybe 10,000 selfish people to be able to assist the one righteous person to manifest Light. With their selfishness, what the selfish, negative people are doing is awakening more and more Light. But, of course, they will never be able to manifest it in their lives if their lives are based on the Desire to Receive for the Self Alone, and therefore a righteous person will manifest that Light.

This interesting concept has obvious ramifications in our life. The Zohar has a lengthy discussion about the fact that there is nothing in this world that does not have a purpose. Sometimes, you look at people whose entire life is based on the Desire to Receive for the Self Alone and we might think that their life is almost not worthy, or even question why they are in this world. Here Rav Ashlag is saying that both in the Supernal Worlds and in our world we have to have both. We have to have the great desire and we have to have the great Vessel, and they are opposite. The righteous people and the selfish people need each other to make this world survive. Most importantly, the righteous person needs the selfish people to manifest Light. The Light that is manifested by the righteous will be diminished if there are less selfish people in the world.

Rav Ashlag will go a little bit deeper into this but for now it is important to understand this reality where the drawer of the Light is almost never the revealer of the Light. We also have these concepts amongst ourselves, where very often there are people who can reveal Light and there are people who can manifest that Light.

The Tzimtzum took place in the Fourth Phase alone.

15. In order to understand this we need additional understanding regarding the Tzimtzum and the Line. As you know, the Tzimtzum took place only in the Fourth Phase called Malchut of Ein Sof or the Middle Point. The reason is simple: the meaning of the Tzimtzum is the prevention from Desiring to Receive, namely that [the Vessel] prevents itself from receiving abundance from the Light of Ein Sof. Therefore, the Tzimtzum applies

---

only to the Vessel of Receiving, and since there is no other Vessel of Receiving except the Fourth Phase, the Tzimtzum applies only to the Fourth Phase.

It has already been explained earlier that the Three Phases preceding the Fourth Phase are not considered Vessels of Receiving but only causes. Through their development, they reveal this Vessel of Receiving called the Fourth Phase. Therefore, the Tzimtzum does not apply to them at all but only to the Middle Point alone, which is the Fourth Phase, as explained.

All the Light withdrew, since there was no other Vessel of Receiving except the Fourth Phase.

16. Therefore, since it diminished its Fourth Phase Desire, the Light departed from the preceding Three Phases as well because there are no other Vessels of Receiving there to hold the Light within them. And even the Lights associated with the previous Three Phases are obligated to be received in the Fourth Phase because they have no Vessel of Receiving in their own aspect, as explained. Therefore, once it withdrew itself from receiving with its Fourth Phase, all the Light immediately disappeared.

Only the first Three Phases were present in the Light of the Line.

17. After the Light departed due to the Tzimtzum, it [the Vessel] returned to draw Light from the Endless in the aspect of a Line, which means a small amount of Light that has only the first Three Phases of the Desire to Receive, where there is no Fourth Phase, as explained earlier (Volume 1, Chapter 2, Section 2). According to this explanation, that there is no Receiving Vessel whatsoever in the first Three Phases of the Desire, we should ask here how it is possible for the Light to be received without a Vessel of Receiving, since there is not yet an aspect of Receiving in these Three Phases, and the Fourth Phase, which is the only Vessel of Receiving for the Partzuf, does not appear here in the aspect of the Line.

The explanation of Binding by Striking (*Zivug deHaka'ah*).

18. The idea is that since the Tzimtzum is mainly only on the part of the Emanated Being and not at all on the part of the Emanator, the Supernal

Light does not care at all about that Tzimtzum done by the Middle Point. Because of this it is considered as if the Supernal Light descends to the Fourth Phase as well, but the Fourth Phase obstructs it on its way so that it does not shine within it, due to the Tzimtzum that lies upon the Fourth Phase before the coming of this Light.

This issue is called in the books "Binding by Striking," since this is likened to two objects, where one wants to pass through and break the wall and boundary created by the other, while the other stands up with all its might against it, preventing it from invading its boundary. Thus, each one strikes against the other's boundary.

It is also likened to two hard objects. It is the nature of liquid to allow something else to enter and mix with it. A soft object also allows another substance to enter it to some extent and press its outer shell. This is not the case with two hard objects, as one does not let the other push it from its boundary, even a little. Thus, hard objects that encounter each other strike each other as the encounter itself causes striking.

As in the past, Rav Ashlag makes very clear, the Light of the Creator never changes, the Light always shines in the same way, to the same place. The Tzimtzum, the Removal of Light, occurs when the Vessel says, "I will not experience that Light." The Light does not go anywhere, the Light does not disappear, the Creator does not change, the Light of the Creator does not change. The Vessel makes a difference by deciding how it will begin to experience the Light of the Creator. Thus the Tzimtzum, this the Removal of Light, was only the Vessel's decision; only the Vessels' created illusion. Again, the Light of the Creator makes no change, the Light the Creator continues shining.

And usually, "binding" and "striking" are mutually exclusive words. We do not hit and hug; we either hit or hug. They are not done at the same time. But here, as the kabbalists teach, there is a Unification (Zivug), a coming together that is brought about by striking. Here, the Creator's Desire to Share and the Vessel's Desire not to Receive for the Self Alone are hitting each other. There is this spiritual battle between the Light's nature, which is to flow and fill everything, and the Vessel's renewed nature of: "I am not going to Receive anything selfishly for Myself Alone."

When you realize what this means, Binding by Striking has many ramifications. Unlike liquids or soft objects that come together, the Light of the Creator, which is the nature of Sharing, and the Vessel's new nature of restricting the nature of a Desire to Receive for the Self Alone, make it so that there is a spiritual colliding that occurs at this moment. This process that the Ari and Rav Ashlag are revealing here, and that the kabbalists revealed previously, is not something that occurred once but is continual and occurring all the time.

This concept of Binding by Striking helps us understand that for there to be spiritual growth, there has to be friction because only in the place of friction is Light revealed. In the place of comfort or lack of friction there can be no Light revealed. After the Tzimtzum, in the new reality, for Light to be revealed there has to be friction. There has to be one force pushing against another force. Without Binding by Striking, without the hitting, there is no Unification (Zivug), there is no revelation of Light.

With this you can understand the concept of the extension of the Supernal Light from the Ein Sof, whose way is to fill even the Fourth Phase, namely, how it was in the Endless. Therefore, the Light descends truly to enter the Fourth Phase, but the force of Tzimtzum over the Fourth Phase prevents it and does not let it descend into it. This encounter between the Supernal Light and the force of Tzimtzum is therefore understood by the name Binding by Striking, meaning that each one interrupts and obstructs the way and rule of the other, for it is the rule of the Light of Ein Sof to fill the Fourth Phase, and it is the rule of the Fourth Phase to reject the Supernal Light rather than receive it, as explained.

The explanation of Returning Light.

19. By the force of the said encounter and striking that occurs in the Fourth Phase, a new Light is born and emerges. This is similar to sunlight that encounters the surface of a mirror, namely glass that is coated with paint on the other side, where the rays of the sun cannot pass through the mirror due to the coat of paint on its other side, and because of this, the rays of the sun bounce back and beget bright Light there.

In the same way, when the Supernal Light encounters the force of Tzimtzum in the Fourth Phase, which is called Masach, it is considered that this Masach returns it back to its Source. However, this is not a matter of concealment. On the contrary, the return of the Supernal Light from the Fourth Phase upward is considered a new and unique Light that rises up upon the Supernal Light, encasing it, and containing It within itself. Because of this, it is considered like a Vessel that receives the Supernal Light.

This is a very strange new reality; it is almost like there is a change in the nature of Light because the Light's nature is "there is a Vessel, I am going to fill it completely." And when the Vessel says, "No. You cannot fill me anymore," the Light does not disappear, instead it turns into a new form of Light, just like in the mirror. The light that comes down onto the mirror is light and when it is reflected off of the mirror it becomes a different light.

Rav Ashlag explains that when the Vessel decides that it can no longer Receive for Itself Alone even though the Creator would still like to give to the Vessel, the Vessels says, "Okay, what can we do here? I cannot receive the Light. You want to share Light with me. I have an idea, why don't I change myself to a degree that I no longer receive selfishly. I am going to come to the point where I am able to purify my desire so much so as to only be Receiving for the Sake of Giving Pleasure to You, the Creator." And the Vessel asks itself, "How pure am I, meaning, how much can I Receive in truth, only for the Sake of Sharing, meaning Giving Pleasure to the Creator in giving me Light?"

This is the new reality the Vessel lives within, which means that every time Light is meant to come down into the Vessel, the Vessel stops and says, "One second, where am I at spiritually, where am I at in my level of purity? How much pleasure, Light, can I receive and not enjoy selfishly at all but only enjoy because it gives the Creator pleasure for me to receive this Light? And whatever amount that is, is how much I will take in."

We have to be clear, this is not a game the Vessel plays. To illustrate this concept, let us use the example Rav Ashlag gave of visiting someone who has prepared a steak for us to eat. Now in this context, we can have one of two desires: we can be very hungry and because of this, have a vessel of desiring to eat. And we take the steak that is prepared for us into our vessel of Desire to Receive for the Self Alone, which can no longer exist after the Tzimtzum because this way of receiving can no longer exist. What can exist is if we make it so that we no longer have any desire to eat when we visit our friend, even though he is so adamant in his Desire to Share with us. "What can I eat in his house that will not give me any pleasure; where my eating can be purely for the sake of giving him pleasure?" Now, if we are really hungry, no matter how pure we think we are, a steak will probably touch our selfish hunger. So, we come up with a different idea to just have a salad because we do not really enjoy eating salads but we know that eating something will give him pleasure. This is the decision the Vessel is making now.

But if you are an extremely evolved spiritual person, you can be very hungry and even have the steak that you really enjoy but take no selfish enjoyment out of it. Most of us are not there. Most of us are on a very low level, where if we are honest with ourselves, could visit someone while feeling hungry, and eat very few things, maybe even things we do not even like, for the Sake of Giving Pleasure to our host. But to be able to take in pleasure and not have it touch our selfish enjoyment, is almost impossible.

Incidentally, this explains what Rav Ashlag spoke about earlier concerning the different Worlds. For instance, he said that the greater desire exists in the World of Adam Kadmon, and it becomes diminished up until our World of Asiyah. Being able to disassociate our receiving from our selfishness is the level of a righteous person. And most of us, as we said, are on a very low level, meaning we can only Receive very little for the Sake of purely Giving Pleasure. This is the indication of how connected we are, of how much we have grown.

Ultimately, a person is meant to come to a place where they can receive endless pleasure and have no selfish receiving but only Receiving for the Sake of Giving Pleasure. This is a new decision of the Vessel. This fight within the Vessel of: "How much can I partake, how much can I receive and still be pure in my Desire that I am only Receiving this for the Sake of Giving the giver Pleasure" is the Binding by Striking (Zivug deHaka'ah). The Vessel initially says, "I do not think I can do anything." Then the Light says, "One second, I really have to give you something. Is there any level of yourself that has become purified where you can Receive only for the Sake of Giving to Me, the Giver, Pleasure?" Then the Vessel finds it. The Vessel finds how much of itself has been purified so that it can Receive only for the Sake of Giving Pleasure. And to that degree it now receives Light. This battle between the Light of the Creator wanting to give to the Vessel endlessly, and the Vessel finding how much it can Receive only for the Sake of Giving the Creator Pleasure, and deciding "a salad not a steak, nothing more," is called Binding by Striking (*Zivug deHaka'ah*). This *Ohr Chadash uMeyuchad* (a new and unique Light), as Rav Ashlag calls it, is the Returning Light.

The reason the Rav always stressed this is because this reality of Binding by Striking is the basis of the beginning of the World within which we live. This Returning Light is the only way Light can become manifest in this new reality and is the way we can receive Light. This is a very important understanding.

The Returning Light became the Vessel of Receiving instead of the Fourth Phase.

20. Know that the Head aspect of any Partzuf has no other Vessels of Receiving besides the said Returning Light, as shall be explained in its place. The entire receiving ability in this Returning Light is due to it emerging and being born from the aspect of the striking that takes place in the Fourth Phase, as said, and since it is a result of the Fourth Phase, it became an aspect of receiving like it. This concept will be explained in its entirety in Volume Three, where it belongs.

Here Rav Ashlag says something really important, which too often gets overlooked. Rav Ashlag makes a distinction between the Receiving that occurs in the Head (*Rosh*), in the beginning of any Spiritual Form (*Partzuf*), and the Receiving that occurs in the Body (*Toch*) or the real essence of any Spiritual Form. Although he does not explain the details, I just want to touch upon it because it is an important understanding that will carry us throughout comprehending of the Study of the Ten Luminous Emanations.

For instance, we can be purer in our thoughts than in our actions, like the person who goes to his friend's house to eat, is hungry and makes a calculation in his mind about how much he can eat and still maintain purity of consciousness, purity of desire—this is the Binding by Striking (Zivug deHaka'ah). However, this is easier in thought than in action because sometimes in our head, we are pure. We can think, *I can probably not eat a steak because that tastes too good, but chicken I can still eat only for the Sake of Giving Pleasure to my friend.* But then when we are eating, we start experiencing the pleasure. Thus, trying to manifest that initial thought that was in the Head becomes more difficult. There is a clear distinction, even in our own lives, between things we think we can accomplish in our head, and what happens once it begins to become manifest.

Therefore Rav Ashlag says that in the Head, the First Stage, the only Light revealed will be through the Returning Light, through this Binding by Striking. Things become more complicated in the body once this Light becomes manifest, which Rav Ashlag states that we are not going into the details of this now. However it is important to understand that it is easier to be pure in our minds and not always in actions. For instance, a pure thought of what we think we can accomplish can involve the ego once it starts manifesting. Rav Ashlag makes the distinction that there are, in fact, different realities. We can be pure in what we think we will be able to accomplish in our head, and then when we begin acting to manifest it, things begin to change. The Head (Rosh) represents the unmanifested thought, and the Body represents the manifesting of that thought. And often, things change between thought and manifestation. It becomes a bit more complicated because things that we think we can do in thought are not necessarily the way we manifest them. Sometimes, we often have more power to restrict in thought than power to restrict once the action actually begins. This is an important distinction.

There is a scientific concept called, "Attentional Collapse." What scientists have found is that people often enjoy things once they are doing them more than what they thought they would. The reason they give is because before you do something, you can compare it to other things. So you can diminish the amount of pleasure you think you will get out of it. But once you actually start doing it, you are already starting to feel the pleasure. Your attention is focused on what you are doing. You do not have the time to start comparing it to other things you might enjoy more, so you actually start enjoying it more while you are doing it than you thought you would in thinking about that enjoyment prior.

This also speaks to the idea of what Rav Ashlag is saying. There are two steps to this process: the Head, which means what we think we will be able to restrict, and then there is the Body, there is the manifestation, where things in the Body become more complicated. But the reality is that the work of the Fourth Phase, the Vessel, the ability to manifest through this concept of Returning Light, can only really achieve its purpose once the thought turns into action, once the receiving is actually taking place.

Thus there are two sets of Vessels: there are Vessels of the Head, which we compare to thought, and there are Vessels of Body. Everything we have been discussing until now has been the Restriction or the Returning Light that is done by the Vessels of the Head, of the thought. But really Light is only evident once it is manifest, and it is only manifest within the Body, which is a second set of Vessels and the only real Vessels, as Rav Ashlag is saying. These are the real Vessels because Vessels in thought are not real Vessels. Thinking we will be able to restrict a certain amount of our pleasure is one thing, but when it starts manifesting, that is the real test.

Now we are coming to a new and deeper understanding of the Four Phases. As often happens with Rav Ashlag, he will first give a basic explanation and then in almost all of the wisdom of Rav Ashlag there are layers, upon layers, upon layers concerning the same topic. Previously in our study, Rav Ashlag gave a lengthy explanation of the Four Phases. And as Rav Ashlag makes clear, for those of us who have not reviewed it recently, it is important to review his initial revelations concerning the Four Phases, to really understand what he is going to reveal now. What we are about to study from Rav Ashlag, besides the beauty of this wisdom, is a deeper understanding of the actual coming about of the Four Phases, which is very important for any true understanding of Kabbalah.

The Returning Light is the Receiving Vessel in the Line.

21. Now you can understand the question we raised earlier; how is it possible for the Supernal Light to extend only into the Three Phases when they still have no Vessel of Receiving in these Three Phases? See there (Section 17). From what we explained, you will properly understand that the aspect of receiving for that Light stems even now from the Fourth Phase alone; except that it is a Receiving Vessel in the form of the Returning Light rising from the Binding by Striking in the Fourth Phase. This Returning Light is the Vessel of Receiving that is found in the Line drawn from the Ein Sof into the space, and it is exactly like the Fourth Phase itself, which is the aspect of Receiving in the Endless. It is in such a way that now after the Tzimtzum, which lacks the Fourth Phase, the Returning Light formed by the Masach in it comes in its stead—and understand this well.

The Vessels of the Ten Sefirot of the Head (Rosh) are but roots for Vessels.

22. It has been thoroughly explained that, even though there are Four Phases in the Desire to Receive, not all Phases are considered Vessels of Receiving, but only the Fourth Phase alone. It has also been explained

that the Vessel of Receiving of this Line that flows from the Ein Sof into the space after the Tzimtzum is the aspect of the Returning Light that rises from the Masach that is in the Fourth Phase, for since it is born from the Fourth Phase, it becomes capable of being a Vessel of Receiving due to it. It will be explained in its place that this Returning Light is not completely ready for its function to receive, until it extends from the Masach down as well. In this way, the Masach further spreads to Four levels, until the Fourth Phase. And these are the real Vessels of the said Line.

This is not the case with the first Four Phases that emerged from the force of Binding by Striking from the Masach upward to the root, as mentioned earlier, for they are considered merely the roots of the Vessels, since the force of the Masach is not able to ascend with this Returning Light higher than its place. Therefore, nothing exists there except the aspect of Light without any density of the Masach, and thus these are not real Vessels but only the root for Vessels. But afterwards, when this Returning Light extends below the place of the Masach, it carries with it the density of the Masach as well. Then it becomes the aspect of real Vessels. But this is not the place to discuss it at length.

CHAPTER 3

Chapter 3 explains the essence and matter in the Vessels, and contains two subjects:

1. The three fundamental distinctions in the Vessels:

    (a) The essence of the material in them.

    (b) The force of Tzimtzum in them.

    (c) The Masach in them.

2. There are two categories in the essence of the material within the Vessels:

    (a) Malchut of the Upper becomes the first material of the Lower.

    (b) The Light that flows to that first material is considered as the actual aspect of the Lower.

An extensive explanation of the Four Phases of Desire.

23. Now the gateway has been open to understand the question we raised before about the order of the Sefirot of Straightness, in which the denser is higher and superior, which is contrary to logic.

Hopefully, we remember the one question previously posed by Rav Ashlag: "How can it be that in the Linear Vessels, in this new reality that exists after the Tzimtzum, that whatever is more coarse, whatever has more Desire to Receive, is considered to be better or at least revealing more Light?" One would think that the purer the Vessel is, as exists in the Worlds of Circles, and the purer one is, the more Light they should be able to reveal.

What is a righteous person? It is a person with no desire. It is a person who has purified their Desire to Receive for the Self Alone completely. This does not seem to be the case in the Linear Vessels. In Linear Vessels, in this new reality that exists after the Tzimtzum, the greater the desire, the greater the coarseness, the more Light is revealed. How can this be? "It makes sense, I understand," Rav Ashlag says, "It makes logical, spiritual sense that in the

Circular Vessels, the purer the Vessel is, the more Light it will manifest, the more Light it will reveal. But how can we understand that in the Vessels of the Line—in the Vessels and Light that manifest after the Tzimtzum—the more coarse the Vessel is, the more Desire to Receive for the Self Alone it has, the more Light it will reveal. This does not seem to follow spiritual logic."

Logic would dictate that the purest Vessel encases the highest and superior Light, and the coarse Vessel encases the lowest and inferior Light; look there. But from what we explained, you can understand this. Yet first we need to expand our understanding regarding the Four Phases of Desire, which are the Vessels of the Ten Sefirot called Chochmah, Binah, Zeir Anpin, and Malchut, and their root that is called Keter. (Zeir Anpin alone includes six Sefirot—Chesed, Gevurah, Tiferet, Netzach, Hod, and Yesod.) They require an extensive explanation.

Rav Ashlag is saying that we cannot go any further in our comprehension of the Kabbalah and our understanding of the Study of the Ten Luminous Emanations unless we gain this deeper understanding of the Four Phases. We truly need to appreciate Rav Ashlag because he was so exact in his revelation; he revealed what he knew one could understand at each exact point in their studies. And although there was more that he wanted to discuss concerning the Four Phases, he said, "You will not be ready for it and therefore, I will not reveal it yet. You will have to go through a whole learning process from the first revelation of the Four Phases up until Volume 2, Chapter 3, in the Inner Observation." Now he says, "If you have learned everything until now, you are ready for this next level of revelation concerning the Four Phases." Rav Ashlag was exact and precise not to reveal everything but only what the student would be able to comprehend at any given point in the study. Then assuming the student has gone through a real process of study, and is now ready for another layer, another level of revelation, he will then reveal it. This is what is happening now.

Three categories: (a) the material of the Vessel, (b) the force of Tzimtzum in the Vessel, and (c) the Masach in it.

24. There are three fundamental categories in these Vessels. The first is the essence of the Vessel's material. The second is the force of Tzimtzum

in it, meaning the withdrawing from the great Desire to Receive through its own choice and will, and not because of the control of the higher upon it. The third is the aspect of the Curtain (Masach) in it, meaning the withdrawing from the ultimate Desire to Receive due to the control of the higher over it, which is an unconscious and imposed withdrawal. We will explain them one by one.

Here it gets technical but it is very beautiful and necessary. In any Vessel there are three important elements that we have to be aware of. The first is the essence of the Vessel. Every person also has a core, an essence of who they are. Very often we confuse aspects of a person with their essence. Yet these are not to be confused, and certainly not in the comprehension of the Vessel. There has to be a clarity about what one's essence is, what the Vessel's essence is.

The second element of any Vessel is how much of the removal of the Light it wants through its own volition, by its own choice. This is the force of Tzimtzum in it. However, after the Tzimtzum, in the World of the Line, where the Light becomes manifest in a much narrower way, there is no longer a choice. The Vessel cannot Receive for Itself Alone. This is what is called the Masach. This is the third element.

The difference between the Tzimtzum and the Masach is that the Tzimtzum is a choice, and the Masach is a rule. Rav Ashlag says, "Whatever is a desire in the Upper Worlds becomes an unbreakable rule in the Lower Worlds." Therefore, we have to make a distinction between the Tzimtzum, which is when the Vessel on its own volition decided that it wanted not to Receive for Itself Alone anymore, and the Masach, which is when the rule that Light cannot be Received for the Self Alone comes into effect. And it is important to understand that if, Heaven Forbid, as happens, one tries to Receive for the Self Alone, negativity will come with it, darkness will come with it.

Rav Ashlag says first there is the essence of the Vessel, then there is the second element, which is the Tzimtzum, which is the degree to which the Vessel said, "I no longer want to Receive for Myself Alone because I want to achieve the same level and cleaving (Dvekut) with the Light of the Creator." The third element is this new reality where it can no longer Receive for Itself Alone, even if it wanted to, because now there is a rule that is called the Masach, a barrier that prevents Light from ever coming into a Vessel for Itself Alone.

What is interesting is that when you look at the three elements Rav Ashlag has just parsed within a Vessel there is actually a paradox: Leaving that first element of the Vessel's essence aside, the other two elements are almost contradictory because there is the Vessel's Tzimtzum and the Vessel's Masach. For instance, let us say a person's essence is that he enjoys food, yet because he wants to go on a diet, he decides to restrict his food intake because his goal is to lose weight. Most of us can relate to this restriction. Then there is the third element that is called the Masach, which is where the Vessel also realizes that it no longer has a choice to restrict and not to Receive for the Self Alone. This is why, very often in life, people are confused. There are these two realities existing within every Vessel: the thought that "I need to restrict but it is in my control," which is called the Tzimtzum. And the third element that is called the Masach, where the reality is, "I do not have control anymore. I cannot Receive for Myself Alone." This dichotomy between these two elements often causes problems for people.

However, regardless of that, Rav Ashlag makes clear that every Vessel has three elements: there is the Vessel's basic essence—whatever Light it desires, whatever Light it wants to receive. There is the Tzimtzum—it knows that to achieve cleaving (Dvekut), a connection to the Light of the Creator, it has to restrict its Desire to Receive for the Self Alone. And the third element is its understanding that it no longer has free will to Receive for the Self Alone—there is this Masach reality, a barrier that says no Vessel can Receive for Itself Alone. These are the three basic elements of any Vessel that Rav Ashlag will explain in depth.

The Four Phases of the Desire to Receive are the material of the Vessel.

25. You already know that the material of every Vessel is the four levels of the Desire to Receive, one below the other, where the higher is the cause and reason for the emergence of that which is below it. The root is the cause of the revelation of the Desire at the degree of the First Phase. The First Phase is the cause of the revelation of the Desire of the Second Phase. The Second Phase is the cause of the revelation of the Desire of the Third Phase. The Third Phase is the cause of the revelation of the Desire of the Fourth Phase. The subject of this evolution and why it has to be in the way of cause and effect has already been well explained in Volume 1, Inner Light, Section 14. (Study the rest of it carefully, since I do not want to

---

repeat that lengthy explanation for no reason. Go back and study what was brought there since I build on them as I continue with the explanation I add here).

Two distinctions in every phase—what it has from its superior and what it has from its own essence.

26. Indeed, we must be precise [and say] that there are two distinctions in each of the Four Phases. The first is the amount of material that reached it from its cause, and the second is the amount of material in its own essence that is affected by the Light that enters it. And it is known that the aspect of Desire found in a level is called the Malchut of that level. Even where no trace of Vessel is apparent, namely in the Ein Sof, we still call the Desire present there by the term Malchut of Ein Sof, as is known regarding the secret of "He and His Name are One," where "Name" is a term for the Sefirah of Malchut and "His Name (*Shemo*; 346)" has the same numerical value as "Desire (*ratzon*; 346)."

So everyone of the Four Phases and every creation has two aspects to it. There is the essence of that Vessel, and then there is the way that Vessel is affected and changed by the Light that it receives. Clearly, the Malchut of Ein Sof is a different reality than the Malchut that is in the Worlds that come afterwards because a true Vessel, a true desire does not really exist in the Ein Sof.

It is important to realize that throughout the study, Rav Ashlag is not simply teaching us about the way the Worlds came about, he is also giving us basic information about words and concepts that we use throughout. For instance, every time Rav Ashlag says the word Malchut in his Sulam commentary in the Zohar, what he is clearly referring to is Desire, is Vessel, not simply the concept of Malchut. Here Rav Ashlag is explaining two distinct aspects to us: one is the understanding that every spiritual entity has two parts to it. There is the part of the Vessel, the part of the entity that has its own nature; and then there is how it becomes affected and changed by the Light that it receives. What this means is that every time Light comes into a Vessel, the Vessel needs to change.

But, unfortunately, what happens with many people is that even when new Light comes in, it does not change their essence. And this is a problem. There is a danger if new Light is awakened and the Vessel does not change. If new Light is awakened and the Vessel does not change but remains in whatever essence it was created with, Heaven forbid, this causes a tremendous amount of damage.

Rav Ashlag speaks about this danger in And You Shall Choose Life, quoting the Talmud, which says: "To those who use [the Torah] to the right it is a drug of life, and to those who use it to the left it is a drug of death." (Tractate Shabbat 88b) This means that spiritual work and the revelation of new Light can actually damage a Vessel, if the new Light that is coming into the Vessel is not affecting change on the Vessel.

Rav Ashlag also tells us that whenever we discuss desire or manifestation, this is always referred to by the name Malchut of any level, Malchut of any degree.

Malchut of Keter descended and became the aspect of the material in the Sefirah of Chochmah.

27. We will now explain the two distinct categories in each of the Four Phases. The root of the Phase, which is the category of the bestowal of the Light of the Endless upon it, is called the Keter of that Phase.

I want to really clarify the difference between a previous understanding of the term Keter and the deeper understanding that Rav Ashlag is revealing now. Many of us may think that Keter is the first Sefirah, the first level of Light in any Vessel. Keter is not simply the first Sefirah of any Vessel, it is not simply the First Stage where Light is revealed to any Vessel, rather Keter actually is a connection to the flowing of the Light of the Endless World into that Vessel.

Rav Ashlag specifically says, "It represents the flow of the Light of the Endless World into that Vessel. That is what is called the Keter of that Level." Whether it is Keter of Chochmah, or Keter of Zeir Anpin, or Keter of Malchut, or Keter of the individual, or Keter of the World, wherever the term "Keter" is used, it is connecting us to, and revealing, that this is where the Light of the Endless World begins to flow into that Vessel, into that individual. So, for instance, in the human body Keter is the head. That does not simply mean that the head is where the Light that we manifest starts coming, but that the head of the individual, both physically and spiritually, is where the flow of the Light of the Endless World begins coming to that person. The concept of Keter is not simply the first Sefirah of any Vessel or the First Stage of any Vessel, but more importantly, it is where the Light of the Endless World begins flowing into that Vessel.

And it is known that in the Supernal Light there is nothing but the aspect of the Desire to Share and do goodness for others, meaning to the entire reality that exists in the Worlds He created. But there is no Desire to Receive whatsoever in Him, Heaven forbid. This has been explained well and at length in the Inner Observation of Volume 1. See there.

The one thing we know about the Supernal Light, the Light of the Endless World, is that it has no desire except to give, to cause Light, sustenance, fulfillment to be received by something outside, external of Itself. *Lezulato*, a word the Rav always mentioned, really encompasses both the entire Wisdom of Kabbalah and also all the revelations of Rav Ashlag. The one thing that we know about the Light of the Endless World is *lezulato*; that the singular desire of the Light is to be able to flow and to give to something external of Itself. And clearly the way we connect to the Light of the Endless World is with *lezulato*, by thinking and doing things for those outside of ourselves, without any Desire to Receive in return.

The Malchut of Keter is the cause for the First Phase, since that which is a Desire in the upper becomes a compulsion and obligation for the one lower than it.

Now we have a beautiful understanding of the term Malchut of Keter. What is Keter? Keter represents the desire of the Endless World to flow down into our World. The Malchut of Keter is that desire. Now it is not just any real desire, it is a pure Desire to Share. When we talk about Malchut of Keter we are discussing the desire of the Ein Sof to give to our world and to give to all of us.

One of Rav Ashlag's spiritual rules is that whatever is a desire in the Supernal Worlds always affects change in the Lower Worlds. Meaning, just like in the Malchut of Keter there is a Desire to Share, in Chochmah, which is the next level, there has to be a Desire to Receive that Light. It is not a choice that Chochmah makes. As long as there is a desire, a Malchut in Keter to flow Light into the Lower Worlds—Chochmah, which is the next emanation, it has to receive that Light. There is no real Desire to Receive, there is no thought of wanting to receive, there is just this spiritual effect. If the desire of the Supernal Keter is to give Light into the Lower Worlds, a Chochmah is created. There is no real awakening of thought of desire, there is simply a Vessel that says, "If Keter wants to give, I will receive it."

Therefore, the Desire to do good and share, which is Malchut of Keter, becomes the aspect of the Desire to Receive in the First Phase called Chochmah. With this it is considered that Malchut of Keter itself descended, became vested, and turned into the Desire to Receive of the First Phase, namely, into its actual material. This is because the Desire within the First Phase is the material in that Phase, and the Supernal Light called Chayah is clothed in that material. It is, therefore, considered that Malchut of Keter became the material of the Sefirah called Chochmah. This is the first distinction we need to make in the material of the First Phase.

Here we learn that the cause for the Desire to Receive in Chochmah is the Malchut of Keter. Meaning the desire of the Ein Sof, represented by its seed, at least in Keter, caused that there has to be an awakening of Desire to Receive in the Vessel, which is called Keter of Chochmah. Thus the essence of the First Phase, which is called Chochmah is a manifestation of a desire of Keter. Therefore, Chochmah is created as a Vessel to receive this Light. So what is the essence of the First Phase, what is the essence of Chochmah? It is the Desire to Receive the Light that Keter wants to give. And this Light is called the Light of Chayah, which is now the second aspect of Chochmah.

As Rav Ashlag said earlier, there are two aspects to any Vessel. There is the essence of that Vessel and then there is the Light that comes in that changes the Vessel. Therefore, within the First Phase, which is called Chochmah, there is the essence of Chochmah, which is its Desire to Receive because Keter wants to share, and a second aspect, which is the Light of Chayah that comes into it that fulfills that desire. Chochmah is now going to change because of this new Light of Chayah that has come in. We need to always keep in mind this dual essence of any Phase, specifically now that we are discussing Chochmah. First is the essence of the Vessel, its Desire to Receive that was caused by Keter's Desire to Share. Second, once the Light of Chayah comes into that Vessel, it is going to cause a change to that Vessel.

This is truly a beautiful revelation. Most of us think the Four Phases and how they emerge from each other as there is Keter and then there is Chochmah, and they are their own thing, that is maybe caused by the previous Phase. Yet the beauty of what Rav Ashlag is revealing now is that Keter and Chochmah are one, they are intertwined. In the Spiritual Worlds, this evolution makes it so that all levels, all Sefirot are actually intertwined, they are actually one.

The actual Vessel of Chochmah emerged after the revelation of the Light of Chochmah.

28. The second distinction is [as follows]. After the Supernal Light called Chayah spread into Malchut of Keter, which is the said material of Chochmah, Malchut of Keter then received the aspect of the real material of the First Phase.

In the Portion of Bo, the kabbalists speak about the fact that one of the most important understandings the Israelites received is the malleability of nature and time. Unfortunately, because of the way we are born into this physical world, we accept the physical reality of time and space as being something that cannot be changed. It all exists. Even those of us who have been studying Kabbalah think that time is time, and space is space. And even though Rav Ashlag makes clear that these are not realities, it is hard to break our natural instincts that are fortified by years of experiencing time as time and space as space.

In the Portion of Bo, the Creator gives the Israelites the understanding that time and space are not stable nor real. The first Precept that was given to the Israelites in Egypt is the Blessing of the New Moon, or the ability to bring in the new month. The kabbalists explain that the secret of this Precept is that the Creator gave us the control of time. Humanity, as a whole, needs to come to the point where we control time; whether a month has 28 days, 29 days, or 30 days, all this becomes literally controlled by a person.

And this has many implications. Rav Ashlag explains that there are two ways that Mashiach, the end of pain suffering and death, can come. There is the concept of "in its time (*be'itah*)" (Isaiah 60:22) or "I will hasten it (*achishena*)." (ibid.) What does this mean? It means that although the Mashiach has to come in a few hundred years, if we control time, we can make that moment in time elapse so that Mashiach can come today.

The ability to control time is given on Shabbat Bo. And when we begin to see—which is really is part of the purpose of the Study of The Ten Luminous Emanations—that time and space are malleable, then we can begin to comprehend both the Study of the Ten Luminous Emanations but more importantly, also how we can control time and space.

What Rav Ashlag is revealing here is that in the physical world when you create something, there is you and there is the thing you create. This is not so in the Spiritual World. When you create something in the spiritual World, the Creator and the Creation are one. Therefore the essence of the First Phase, called Chochmah, is really just an evolution of the Malchut of Keter—an evolution of the Desire to Share of the previous Phase, called Keter, called the Ein Sof. And we do not even view a new reality, a new essence, of the First Phase until the Light starts coming into this newly created Vessel.

Prior to that, although there exists the Desire to Receive of Chochmah, it is still ambiguous. Is this a Malchut of Keter? Is this the Keter of Chochmah? Those two Phases overlap and are connected. It is only when the Light of Chayah becomes manifest into that Desire to Receive, called the First Phase or Chochmah, that we actually say that it is changed now and becomes a First Phase or Chochmah.

In other words, even though Malchut of Keter, which is the Desire to Share that is included in the Supernal Light, became the aspect of the Desire to Receive and the primal material of the First Phase, as said, this merely sufficed as the root aspect for the First Phase, namely, just for the Desire to Receive to draw the Supernal Light into it, which can be called the primal material for the Sefirah of Chochmah as it is still in the aspect of the Emanator and Keter.

When does it emerge from being the aspect of the Emanator and Keter to the aspect of Emanated and Chochmah, which is called the First Phase? This happens only after the said Desire to Receive draws into it the Light of Chayah that is associated with it. It then emerges from the category of Emanator and is called Emanated or Chochmah. Understand this well and you will not miss the mark. Thus, we have explained the two distinctions in the material of the Vessel called Chochmah. The first is called Malchut of the upper, namely before it draws its Light. The second is called the Vessel of Chochmah itself, namely Malchut of Chochmah, since the Vessel is always called by the term Malchut.

Malchut of Chochmah became the first material of Binah. As its Light emerged, so did the Vessel of Binah itself.

29. You can similarly understand as well about the material of the Second Phase called Binah. Its cause is the Desire included in the First Phase called Chochmah, namely just the Malchut of Chochmah, as the Desire within a level is always called the Vessel or Malchut of that level, as mentioned earlier. This Malchut of Chochmah entered and became the primal material in the Sefirah of Binah so that Binah would draw the Light associated with it. This is the first distinction in the material of the Second Phase called Binah. Afterwards, when it drew the Light associated with it, which is called Neshamah, its material left the aspect of being Malchut of Chochmah, which is the First Phase, and assumed its own shape, namely the actual Second Phase called Binah.

Malchut of Binah became the first material of Zeir Anpin. With the emergence of its Light, the Vessel of Zeir Anpin itself was revealed.

30. In this very way you will also understand the material of the Third Phase called Zeir Anpin, as Malchut of Binah is its cause and it was [Malchut of Binah] who became the aspect of the primal material for Zeir Anpin, the Third Phase, namely so that it could draw the Light associated with it called Ruach. The second distinction is after it drew and received its own Light, its material left the aspect of Malchut of Binah and became the aspect of Malchut of Zeir Anpin, as said.

> **Malchut of Zeir Anpin is the first material of Malchut.**
> **With the emergence of its Light, the Vessel of Malchut itself was revealed.**

31. Likewise are the two distinctions in the material of the Fourth Phase: Malchut of Zeir Anpin is its cause that was vested and became the primal material of the Fourth Phase called Malchut, until it managed to receive the Light of Nefesh associated with it. Then Malchut of Zeir Anpin left from being the aspect of Zeir Anpin and became the Fourth Phase, namely the aspect of Malchut of Malchut.

> **The said Vessels of Receiving are only for the purpose of drawing down.**

32. Understand that even though we explained and defined the receiving aspect for each and every Phase on its own, this refers only to the purpose of drawing down the Light, wherein each Phase draws down to itself the Light related to it. But a real Vessel that can justly be called the Vessel of Receiving of the emanated is specifically the Fourth Phase, and not the three preceding Phases, as explained before.

CHAPTER 4

Chapter 4 expounds on an exact explanation of the four levels of density based on the Four Phases mentioned by the sages (Tractate Pesachim 25b):

1. The First Phase is "unable and does not intend."
2. The Second Phase is "able but does not intend."
3. The Third Phase is "unable but intends."
4. The Fourth Phase is "able and intends."

Explanation of the Four Phases of Desire, based on the Four Phases of "able and intends."

33. To be able to give a precise and lengthy explanation, I shall explain it to you using the words of the sages. "It was stated: [regarding forbidden] pleasure that comes to a person against his will, Abaye said it is permissible and Rava said it is prohibited. If he is able and he intends, or if he is unable and he intends, everyone agrees that it is prohibited. If he is unable and he does not intend, everyone agrees that it is permitted. The disagreement is where he is able and he does not intend." (Pesachim 25b) Rashi explains that "able" means that he is able to withdraw, and "intends" means that he intended to approach to derive enjoyment, such as a forbidden scent. Look there.

The First Phase is "unable and does not intend."

34. Thus, you find in their discourse Four Phases of deriving enjoyment. The First Phase is when one is "unable" to withdraw and "does not intend" to approach and enjoy. Everyone agrees that receiving pleasure from something prohibited in this way is permissible, since it is not considered receiving and desire when one has neither counsel nor choice to not receive. Nor does one have any yearning to approach something prohibited in order to enjoy it.

The Second Phase is "able but does not intend."

35. The Second Phase is when one is "able" to withdraw yet "he does not intend" to approach and enjoy. When deriving forbidden enjoyment in such a way, there is disagreement between Abaye and Rava. Abaye argued that even though he is "able," meaning that he has a way to distance himself from it and not to take pleasure in the forbidden [scent], he is nevertheless allowed to approach and enjoy it since he "does not intend." In other words, because he has no craving in his heart to approach the forbidden [scent], it is therefore not considered as receiving, even though he approaches and enjoys the forbidden [scent]. Rava argues that since he is "able" to avoid approaching and benefiting from the forbidden [scent], he is therefore not allowed to approach and benefit, regardless if he has no craving to approach the forbidden [scent] and benefit.

The Third Phase is "unable but intends."

36. The Third Phase is "unable but intends," meaning that he is "unable" to withdraw and distance himself from the prohibited [scent] so as not to enjoy it, but he "intends," since he has craving to enjoy the forbidden [scent]. Everyone agrees that receiving enjoyment from something forbidden in this way is prohibited, since even though he is unable and has no option of withdrawing from the forbidden [scent] and not take pleasure, nevertheless, since he has a craving in his heart to enjoy and approach it, this craving is considered as receiving enjoyment from something that we are not allowed to enjoy, and thus he is a sinner. There are those that say that even in this case Abaye argues that it is permissible. Look there.

The Fourth Phase is "able and intends."

37. The Fourth Phase is "able and intends," meaning that he is "able" to withdraw and distance himself from the forbidden [scent] so as to not enjoy it, and he also "intends," as he also has craving to approach and enjoy the forbidden [scent]. Here everyone agrees it is prohibited, since it is receiving forbidden pleasure in the most shameless way, because he desires to enjoy and he is also able to withdraw but does not. Therefore, this is the maximal Desire to Receive in its final stage, which is forbidden according to all.

And even those who consider it permissible in the Third Phase, following Abaye, admit that in this case it is forbidden. Look there in the Gemara.

38. We thus found in the discourse of the sages the precise wording to define each of the Four Phases of the Desire to Receive in a way that will accurately hit the target without missing the desired goal. They have given us four levels, one below the other, concerning the sin of forbidden pleasure, which depends on the Desire to Receive of the sinner. In the First Three levels—"unable and does not intend," "able but does not intend," and "unable but intends"—the prohibition to enjoy is not agreed upon by everyone, but only in the case of the Fourth Phase alone, as explained.

39. We see that the sages put two things together, which are the "ability" to withdraw and not receive pleasure, and the "craving" and temptation of the heart to desire that enjoyment. The combination of these two leads to the Four Phases. We shall now take these words and apply them to our subject in the Upper Worlds, which are the roots for all kinds of Desires that appear in reality. And from the Lower we can learn about the Upper.

**When the Desire to Receive was revealed in Malchut of Keter,
it left Keter and became the First Phase.**

40. Two distinctions are apparent in the First Phase called both Chochmah and Chayah (as mentioned previously in Section 27). The first distinction is its primal material, which as you already know is considered the Malchut of its superior (see Section 23), namely Malchut of Keter, which received the form of the Desire to Receive. With this new form, the Malchut of Keter received a new name—the First Phase. And you already know that when a spiritual entity acquires a new form it is separated as its own autonomous entity. So too regarding Malchut of Keter, which is the Desire to Share present in the Emanator, when the Desire to emanate emerged in it, so to speak, surely it does not need a tool to manifest it, Heaven forbid, but Its Desire was manifested instantly, meaning that it acquired the form of the Desire to Receive, which is the primal material of the Emanated, as mentioned, and this is called the First Phase.

**The exiting of Malchut of Keter to become the First Phase is likened to
lighting a candle from a candle, where the first does not diminish.**

41. Remember now that there is no disappearance [or lack] in spirituality
and what was said, that Malchut of Keter received the form of the First
Phase does not mean that Malchut of Keter is gone or is lacking from
Keter, Heaven forbid. Rather, Malchut of Keter remains with its original
quality without any change. This resembles a candle lighting another
candle while the original candle does not diminish. This Malchut of Keter
that received the First Phase does not lack Keter at all due to this. It is
only that a new aspect has been added, meaning that Malchut of Keter
remained in its place with all its perfection and excellence as before, yet a
new aspect was further added to Malchut of Keter, which is the aspect of
Malchut that received the First Phase and became the primal material in
the Sefirah of Chochmah. Remember this going forward and you will not
get confused.

**After the first material received the Light,
the actual Vessel of Chochmah was revealed.**

42. The second distinction is the material of that Vessel after it receives its
Light, since then the Vessel is complete and is called Chochmah. In other
words, before it receives its Light, it is named after its aspect alone, namely
the First Phase, and is not yet the aspect of the Vessel of Chochmah, but
only Malchut of Keter. This can be likened to a fetus in its mother's womb,
which is not called by name before it is born and has received the Light and
vitality belonging to it.

The same [is true] with the primal material. Before receiving its Light it
does not bear the name Chochmah but is still included in Malchut of Keter.
But afterwards, when the material has drawn its Light called Chayah, the
Vessel acquires its designated name, namely Chochmah (study Section
27 carefully). These two distinctions exist in each and every Sefirah. They
are the Vessel before it receives the Light, when it is still considered by the
name of the upper, and the Vessel after receiving the Light because then it
is considered its own aspect.

**From the side of the first material, Chochmah is considered "unable";
from the side of its being full of Light, it is considered "not intending."**

43. Now you understand that the First Phase—Chochmah—is considered "unable and not intending," because from the side of its primal material, which is Malchut of Keter that received the new form of the First Phase before the Sefirah of Chochmah acquired a name for itself, as was said, the emergence of this Desire to Receive is surely considered as "unable" toward the Sefirah of Chochmah itself. And also from the side of Malchut of Keter, it is considered "unable" since it is unable to emanate Chochmah without Chochmah having the aspect of Desire to Receive, as receiving abundance without the Desire to Receive is coercion and a burden, which is the opposite of the intention of the Emanator to benefit and bestow pleasure, as is well known.

It is also considered "not intending," which means that it has no draw and Desire to Receive the Light. As you already know, Desire is not complete before a craving and attraction to the Light is revealed in it (as said in Volume 1, Chapter 1, Section 14). It was also well clarified there that the yearning becomes apparent only when there is no Light or abundance in the Vessel because then it is possible for it to yearn for the Light, as this cannot be revealed while the Vessel is filled with its own Light, study there well. Therefore, since the said Vessel of Chochmah is filled with its own Light, it does not yet have a yearning for the abundance, and therefore Chochmah is considered as "not intending," which means it has no attraction or yearning toward the abundance, as explained.

**The strengthening of Desire in Binah is considered as "able";
from the side of it receiving this from the first material,
it is considered as "not intending."**

44. The Second Phase, Binah, is considered "able but not intending." Its primal material (see Section 29) is the Malchut of the upper, namely Malchut of Chochmah that received within itself the new form of the Second Phase by the awakening it made (as explained well in Volume 1, Chapter 1, Section 14). Thus, this strengthening of Desire pertains to the category of "able," which means it was capable of not awakening this strengthening of Desire.

It is also in the category of "not intending" since it is Malchut of Chochmah and is full of its own Light, for which reason no yearning is revealed in it. And understand that any additional revelation of Desire in the Second Phase beyond the First is only of the category of "able," meaning the increasing of Desire it awakened, which comes from the power of the emanated itself (see in Volume 1, Chapter, 1, Section 14).

The Light of Chochmah is sufficient; it did not have to intensify and draw Chasadim.

45. Do not argue that Malchut of Keter that became the first distinction in the Sefirah of Chochmah also had the possibility to reject this new aspect of the Desire to Receive, so why then is the First Phase considered "unable"? However, there is a big difference in this case, since Malchut of Keter was unable to emanate the Emanated Being without it having the Desire to Receive, as said earlier. This is not the case with Malchut of Chochmah, which is the aspect of the emanated itself. It could have been content with its Desire to Receive without awakening the Desire to Share, which is the Second Phase, and drawing the Light of Chasadim since the Light of Chayah is entirely sufficient for the Emanated Being and it needs no addition whatsoever.

Zeir Anpin is considered as "unable" because it lacked the Light of Chochmah.

46. The Third Phase, Zeir Anpin, is considered "unable but intending." It is "unable" because after the Second Phase awakened and drew the Light of Chasadim, this created an aspect of obstruction on the Light of Chochmah in the emanated; for the aspect of the Desire to Share is the opposite of the First Phase, which is the Desire to Receive, as that is where the Light of Chochmah is. And since the Light of Chochmah is the main vitality of the Partzuf, for which reason this Light is called Chayah (Life-Force) as said, therefore Malchut of Binah went back and drew the Illumination of the Light of Chochmah into its Light of Chasadim. And when Malchut of Binah drew it and created this new form, it emerged from being the Second Phase and became the Third Phase (as said in Section 30), which is called Zeir Anpin.

Zeir Anpin is considered as "intending" since it yearns for Chochmah.

47. In this drawing down, which is the Third Phase, we should distinguish two things: the first is that it is "unable," which means it had no other choice since there was no Light of Chayah in the Emanated. The second is that it was "intending" because there is yearning here for the Illumination of Chochmah it drew down, since it drew it when it was empty of it—as the Second Phase was covering the Light of Chochmah, as said, containing only the Light of Chasadim without Chochmah. For this reason, its Malchut that drew the Illumination of Chochmah did so in a state of yearning, which is called "intending," as said. Therefore, the aspect of Zeir Anpin is called "unable but intending," as explained.

Malchut is considered as "able" for it could have been content with the Chochmah that is in Zeir Anpin, and as "intending" since it was yearning.

48. The Fourth Phase, which is Malchut, is considered "able and intending." "Able" since the Illumination of Chochmah is already present in Zeir Anpin, namely the Third Phase, as said, and the Malchut of Zeir Anpin does not have to do this new awakening of drawing the Light of Chochmah to a greater degree than in the Third Phase. And it is "intending" since it did this awakening for the Light of Chochmah out of craving, that is, when it did not possess the Light of Chochmah. It is then that the craving is revealed, as said.

The difference between the Light of Chochmah and the Illumination of Chochmah.

49. Do not ask here: If in the Third Phase there is the Illumination of Chochmah, as mentioned earlier, for which reason the Fourth Phase is considered "able," how then does the craving for the Light of Chochmah emerge in the Fourth Phase? However, understand well that there is a great difference between the Illumination of Chochmah and the Light of Chochmah. The Illumination of Chochmah means that the essence of the level is the Light of Chasadim but it receives an Illumination from the Light of Chochmah. This is not the case with the Light of Chochmah, where the entire essence of the Light is all Chochmah and not Chasadim at all.

As for the vitality of the level, even an Illumination of Chochmah is sufficient, as it is in the Third Phase, Zeir Anpin, and therefore Malchut of Zeir Anpin did not have to strengthen its Desire to draw down the Light of Chochmah. Rather, it had a craving for the essence of the Light of Chochmah that is far superior to the aspect of the Illumination of Chochmah that is in the Third Phase, because in relation to the said Light of Chochmah it is considered as empty of this Light. Thus it is possible that craving would emerge following this, as explained.

The Fourth Phase alone is considered a Vessel of Receiving since it is of the category of "able and intending."

50. Thus, it has been explained that not all Desires are considered Vessels of Receiving, but only the Fourth Phase alone, since a Desire is only regarded as an aspect of receiving when two conditions are fulfilled: "able" and "intending," that is, it is not forced to receive and the craving to receive is revealed in it. This excludes the Third Phase, for even though the craving to receive is there, namely it is "intending," nevertheless since it is obligated to receive, for it is its necessary vitality as said, it is not considered a Vessel of Receiving. This also excludes the Second Phase, which, even though it is not obligated to receive, nevertheless since there is no craving there, it is not regarded as a Vessel of Receiving. Needless to say about the First Phase, which has neither the one nor the other since it has to receive its Light, which is its vitality, and it has no craving, so surely it is a totally weak Desire.

CHAPTER 5

Chapter 5 explains the Tzimtzum and the Masach. It contains four subjects:

1. The Tzimtzum was uniform on all sides.

2. Since any drawing of Light happens in the Fourth Phase, a resisting force is needed so the Light will not flow into the Fourth Phase as well. This force is called a Masach.

3. Two aspects in Malchut:

    (a) Where She is contracted by Her own choice so as not to receive Light within Her. This applies to the Circles.

    (b) And where She is contracted due to the resisting force over Her, namely the Masach. This applies to the Sefirot of Straightness.

4. The Supernal Light is in a state of complete stillness and does not cease from shining even for a moment. Whenever the Emanated yearns, it draws the Light to itself.

The difference between Tzimtzum and Masach.

51. After we thoroughly know the four levels of the Desire to Receive, one below the other, to their exact degrees, let us now explain the Tzimtzum, the Masach, and the difference between them. The Tzimtzum was well expounded upon in Volume 1 and also in the Inner Light in this Volume, so we will not repeat it. What we mainly need for our purpose is the uniformity that was there (see Volume 1, Inner Light, Chapter 1, Section 18). Study there carefully.

The Four Phases received the issue of cause and effect during the Tzimtzum.

52. It was explained there that since the Light of the Endless was completely uniform, it had to contract itself uniformly from all the Phases, meaning that all Four Phases that were contracted are equal and in the same rank, without any distinction in regard to purity and density that make the four

levels one lower than the other, till the Fourth Phase, which is the densest and the lowest of them all. Rather, they are uniform. All that was added by the Tzimtzum to make it distinct from the Ein Sof is merely the matter of the Four Phases, from the aspect of them being caused and evolved from each other by way of cause and effect; the First Phase being a cause and a reason for revealing the Second Phase; the Second Phase a cause for the Third Phase; the Third Phase a cause for the Fourth Phase; yet they are equal in terms of purity and rank, as discussed.

The cause and effect in the Four Phases did not exist in the Ein Sof.

53. This issue of cause and effect, which nevertheless divides them into Four Phases, was not apparent in the Ein Sof before the Tzimtzum, since there even the aspect of the Vessel as a whole is not apparent but it is all Light, as said in Volume 1. Rather, after the Light of Ein Sof departed from those Phases, only then did these Phases become apparent and the matter revealed. Now we can distinguish [between] the Light in itself, namely what was in them before the Tzimtzum, and the Four Phases in themselves that remained empty of Light, since after the Tzimtzum it became apparent that the Phases are not one with the Light of Ein Sof, as it seemed before the Tzimtzum. This resembles a candle that cannot be recognized when it is part of a torch, but when it is separated from the torch it is well recognized to all, understand this well.

54. This seemingly raises the question that since the Tzimtzum occurred mainly in the Fourth Phase alone, it thus became apparent that this phase is not worthy of receiving the Light. Only the First Three Phases, which did not have the Tzimtzum upon them, are found worthy of receiving it. If so, what emerges from this is a distinction of rank and importance between them, namely that the Fourth Phase is lower than the first Three Phases.

The Tzimtzum did not happen due to the lowliness of the Fourth Phase, but as an adornment alone.

55. However, the idea is that the Tzimtzum of the Light from the Fourth Phase did not happen due to its lowliness, Heaven forbid. After all, we are still dealing with Malchut of the Endless, where the Fourth Phase was the

aspect of the Endless Light Itself. How then can we even think that the Tzimtzum happened due to the lowliness of the Fourth Phase? Rather, the Tzimtzum took place just for the sake of adornment, as this Malchut longed for a state of cleaving in a possibly higher level, to completely cleave to the Emanator, which is about having greater Similarity of Form with the Emanator (as said in Volume 1, Chapter 1, Section 18. Study it carefully). Therefore, the Fourth Phase did not fall from its high status even after the Tzimtzum.

The drawing down of the Line was first in the Fourth Phase; therefore a resisting force over the Fourth Phase was needed so the Light would not enter it.

56. We shall now explain about the Masach that was formed over the Fourth Phase, which is Malchut. Malchut of Ein Sof was vested in the World of Tzimtzum, as is known that every level begins with the Malchut of its upper that becomes the aspect of its primal material (see Section 27). So when this contracted Malchut returned to draw the Supernal Light to only the Three Phases, of necessity, this drawing took place using the yearning in its Fourth Phase, because the first Three Phases are not at all a Vessel of Receiving and [a force of] drawing. Therefore, it inevitably drew the Supernal Light to all Four Phases at first, even to its own Fourth Phase, but so that the Light would not reach the Fourth Phase it had to add a new force to withhold the Light from flowing into the Fourth Phase.

The resisting force that was added to the Fourth Phase is called a Masach.

57. This new force it added is called the Masach, where this Masach is the root cause for the drawing of the Light of the Line to the Three Phases. This is because the Contraction it made, withdrawing its Desire from receiving in the Fourth Phase, was sufficient only for removing the Supernal Light from it alone. But afterwards, it drew the Light anew, so it had to awaken its Fourth Phase again to further draw this new flow. Hereby, had it not formed a new force against the extension of the Light, the Light would have again reached the Fourth Phase. Thus the main reason for the drawing of the Light of the Line upon the Three Phases is due to the force of the Masach, which it newly formed against the Light.

Understand well these two aspects, namely the Tzimtzum and the Masach, for these are the foundations for all that follows in this wisdom.

The Tzimtzum took place by its own intent.
The Masach forcefully rejects the Light without its intent.

58. Understand the difference between the Tzimtzum that Malchut of Ein Sof enacted, which is the aspect of the withdrawal of the greatest Desire to Receive from its own desire and choice for the sake of greater Similarity of Form to the Emanator, and the Masach, which is the aspect of the force that prevents the Light from reaching the Fourth Phase with compulsion and coercion.

59. The reason is that even though both the Tzimtzum and the Masach were formed by Malchut of Ein Sof, as mentioned earlier, you already know that when a spiritual entity acquires a new form in addition to its own form, due to this it is considered as two spiritual entities and two aspects distant from each other according to the degree of the Difference of Form that exists between these two forms. This is so because just as material entities are separated from each other by the axe and are removed from each other through place and space, so do spiritual entities separate from each other through newness of form and move apart according to the degree of the difference between one form and the other, whether lesser or greater.

The Masach is an offspring of the contracted Malchut.
Whatever is a Desire in the Upper becomes a rule for the Lower.

60. For this reason, after the said Malchut created a drawing down of the Light of the Line to the Three Phases, this drawing down is considered a new form added to the form of the Tzimtzum. It is in a way where now there are two aspects to that Malchut: The first is the contracted Malchut, which is the first form made by Malchut of Ein Sof, as it acquired the new form called "contracted Malchut." Afterwards, when this Malchut caused the flowing of the Light to the Three Phases, a new form was created and emerged called a Masach against the Light, so it would not appear in it in the Fourth Phase. And it is known that any Desire in the higher becomes

dominant over the branch growing from it. And since the Masach is a branch and outcome of the contracted Malchut, therefore even though Malchut contracted itself knowingly of its own will and without any coercion from that which is higher than it, nevertheless the outcome caused by it, namely the Masach, already has the Tzimtzum completely dominant over it, as the Masach is a second level to the World of Tzimtzum, as mentioned earlier.

The difference between the Circles and Straightness is the Masach that was newly created in the Ten Sefirot of Straightness.

61. From the explanation above, we understand that there are two aspects in Malchut: the first is the contracted Malchut, and the second is Malchut that has a Masach. Know that this is the entire difference between the Circular Sefirot and the Sefirot of Straightness, which are called Line. Malchut of the Ten Circular Sefirot is the aspect of the contracted Malchut, where there is no Masach, as said. And the Malchut in the Ten Sefirot of Straightness is fixed with the said Masach, as shall be discussed.

The reason the Light strikes and wants to enter the Fourth Phase is that the emanated drew it this way.

62. Now you shall clearly understand the matter of the Returning Light that rises due to the Binding by Striking from the encounter of the Supernal Light with the Masach that is on the Fourth Phase, which we started explaining earlier (see Section 18). You will also understand what we said there that the Supernal Light does not regard the Tzimtzum made by the Emanated Being, and it descends to spread into the Fourth Phase as well; study it well. The reason is that the Emanated Being itself inevitably draws it like this originally because, as has already been explained (in Volume 1, Chapter 2, Inner Light, Section 2), the Supernal Light is always in a state of absolute rest and does not cease from shining upon the Lower Beings even for a moment, as it does not fall subject to change or newness, Heaven forbid. All the said situations of the extension of the Supernal Light refer to the drawing down from the side of the Emanated Being, which receives from the Supernal Light in accordance with the preparation of the Desire to Receive, namely, its craving, as explained earlier (see Section 50).

**When the Emanated Being draws down we call it
"the extension of the Supernal Light."**

63. The same moment the Emanated Being yearns to receive from the Supernal Light, it immediately pulls the Supernal Light to itself. Just like a candle being lit from another candle does not diminish the original candle, so too when the Emanated Being draws the Supernal Light to itself, the Supernal Light loses nothing due to the part that the Emanated drew to it. It also does not spread, nor is it affected by the pull of the Emanated, but just to appease the ear we call the drawing of the Emanated "the extension of the Supernal Light." Remember this in every place, because we always phrase it as the spreading of the Supernal Light, but it really refers to the drawing of the Emanated itself through its own yearning alone.

**The part of the Light that should have entered the Fourth Phase
but was pushed back became Returning Light.**

64. Therefore, after the Tzimtzum, when the Malchut of Ein Sof drew the Supernal Light back, the Supernal Light flowed into the Fourth Phase as well since it drew it through the craving of its Fourth Phase, as said. But because of the Masach it made to prevent the Light from flowing into the Fourth Phase, that part of the Light turned back. This fulfills its original desire for the Light to only reach the Three Phases.

But that part of the Light that the Masach returned to its source, namely the part meant for the Fourth Phase, did not disappear from it. Rather, it becomes a great Light that encases the Three Phases of the Supernal Light, from the place of the Masach up to the Source. This Returning Light functions as a Vessel of Receiving for the Three Phases of the Supernal Light, instead of the Fourth Phase, as said (Section 21, study there well).

CHAPTER 6

Chapter 6 explains why the Masach of the Fourth Phase raises Returning Light up to Keter, [the Masach of] the Third Phase up to Chochmah, and so on. The reason is that the measure of the height of Returning Light accords with the extent of the Light that could have entered into the Fourth Phase had the Masach not pushed it back. Chapter 6 also explains that the Ten Sefirot of Direct Light are from above downward, namely that the purest among them is most praiseworthy, and the Ten Sefirot of Returning Light are from below upward, namely that the coarsest among them is most praiseworthy.

Returning Light is divided into Sefirot as it envelopes the Sefirot of Direct Light.

65. From this explanation you will understand well the extent of height and size of this Returning Light. It is neither more nor less than the amount of Light that the Masach pushed back, that is, the part that was meant to flow into the Fourth Phase had the Masach not pushed it backward. It ascended up and enveloped the Phases of the Supernal Light, which are: the Third Phase called Zeir Anpin, the Second Phase called Binah, the First Phase called Chochmah, and also the Source called Keter. For this reason, the Fourth Phase is considered as if it itself divided into those Four Phases, which its Returning Light enveloped, and became Four Phases arranged one above the other in the Vessel of the Fourth Phase itself, since the Light that belonged to it ascended and enveloped these Four Phases. Thus, the Fourth Phase is considered a root to them and is called the Keter of this Returning Light.

The Ten Sefirot of Direct Light are from above downward; the Ten Sefirot of Returning Light are from below upward.

66. We find now that there are two kinds of Ten Sefirot in the Emanated Being: the Ten Sefirot from above downward and the Ten Sefirot from below upwards. There are Ten Sefirot in the Supernal Light, which are: the root, which is called the Keter of the Supernal Light, and the Four Phases

that extend from Keter. The First Phase is called Chochmah; the Second Phase, Binah; the Third Phase, Zeir Anpin (comprising the six Sefirot Chesed, Gevurah, Tiferet, Netzach, Hod, and Yesod), and the Fourth Phase is Malchut. Their order is from above downward, meaning from pure to dense, where the purer is superior. The purest, the root, is called Keter. After it, meaning the one a bit denser than Keter is called Chochmah, and so on until the densest of all, which is Malchut—the most inferior.

From below upward means that the coarsest is the most important.

67. There is yet another set of Ten Sefirot in the Emanated Being that are in an inverse proportion to the Ten Sefirot of the Supernal Light mentioned earlier. They are the Ten Sefirot in the Returning Light that rises from the Masach over the said Fourth Phase, which envelope the Ten Sefirot of the Supernal Light. They are arranged in an upward sequence, that is, from the dense to the pure, where the densest is first in rank and the purest is the lowest. This is in opposite order to the Ten Sefirot of the Supernal Light.

Malchut of Direct Light is Keter of Returning Light.

68. This is in such a manner that the densest, which is the Fourth Phase, is the most important of them all, for it is the source of all these Ten Sefirot of Returning Light, since this entire Returning Light is nothing but the portion of Light belonging to it alone that the Masach pushed back. For this reason the Fourth Phase is considered the aspect of Keter, which means root, as is known.

Malchut of Returning Light is in the Keter of Direct Light.

69. The Third Phase, which is not as dense as the Fourth, is considered the Sefirah of Chochmah of Returning Light, meaning second to Keter in level. The Second Phase, which is purer than the Third Phase, is considered the third level from Keter, namely Binah. The First Phase, still purer than the Second Phase, is considered the Fourth Level from Keter, namely the Sefirah of Zeir Anpin that comprises the Six Sefirot—Chesed, Gevurah, Tiferet, Netzach, Hod, and Yesod. The aspect of Keter of Direct Light,

which is the purest of all, is considered only as Malchut in relation to the Returning Light, that is, the most inferior of them all in rank, because whatever is denser is more superior and whatever is purer is more inferior, since the levels flow from dense to pure—and remember this well.

Malchut comprises all Ten Sefirot of Returning Light.

70. The Fourth Phase itself, by means of its Returning Light that spreads to the Ten Sefirot, is itself divided into Ten Sefirot, meaning into Four Phases and Keter, since the Fourth Phase itself is the Keter of Returning Light, namely the root as said, and the nine Sefirot of Returning Light that flow and rise from it are its branches. And as we know, all branches are included and present in the root, which is why there are five distinct Phases in the Fourth Phase itself, which are Keter and the Four Phases from below upward.

The purification of the Masach divides the Fourth Phase into Five Phases.

71. This will explain what we brought before (in Section 8) where the size of the Returning Light is measured by the density of the Masach. The densest Masach, the Masach of the Fourth Phase, reveals a complete Stature up to Keter; the Masach of the Third Phase, only up to Chochmah; the Masach of the Second Phase, only up to Binah; and the Masach of the First Phase, only up to Zeir Anpin. And the Masach that does not even have the density of the First Phase, which resembles the root, reveals no Stature of Light but only the aspect of Malchut—study that section. By this explanation you will understand the subject of the purification that applies to the Masach on the Five mentioned Phases, which is the matter of the division of the Fourth Phase itself into the Five Phases mentioned here, where it is the way of the Masach to ascend and be purified in these divided levels of density that are found in the Fourth Phase, for the reason we will shortly explain.

Rav Ashlag explains that now, in this new World, there is no difference between the Masach and the Vessel. I have to say that when I initially began learning the Talmud Eser Sefirot, this was one of those concepts that was a little difficult to understand because we refer to this barrier, meaning this consciousness that says, "I can only receive however much I can Receive only for the Sake of Sharing," as the totality of the Vessel now. The reality is, that besides this being part of the Vessel, the rest of the Vessel concerns, "how much do I actually Receive for the Sake of Sharing." This thought process of calculating and realizing the actual manifestation of the receiving is a second reality. In the study, Rav Ashlag always refers to the new Vessel as being mainly the Masach, this barrier, because there is no way to receive anymore after the Tzimtzum unless a Vessel has a Masach.

For instance, the Circular Vessels, which also exist after the Tzimtzum, cannot receive any Light because they do not have a Masach, this new structure that is able to make the delineation of how much can be Received Only for the Sake of Sharing. The Circular Vessels cannot draw any Light on their own. They can only receive what the Line awakens and reveals. After the Tzimtzum, there is a new way of receiving. Only a Vessel that has a Masach can receive Light. This is where the concept of Surrounding Light comes from. In this new reality where the Vessel only receives the amount of Light that it can Receive for the Sake of Sharing, there is a tremendous amount of Light that is not manifested in the Vessel, which is what becomes the Surrounding Light.

This Surrounding Light plays a very important role in the continuation of the manifestation of the Vessel because now there are two opposing forces. There is the Vessel that says, "I can only receive 80% of the Light and still have the consciousness that I am only Receiving to give the Creator pleasure because I know He wants to give me Light. The other 20% of the Light would be selfishly received, and therefore, I am not taking that 20%." It is this 20% of the Light that becomes the Surrounding Light. And this Surrounding Light has one desire in life, to manifest within the Vessel. Therefore, it does not like the Masach, the barrier that is now telling the Light, "You cannot come in." We know that all Light has consciousness, and the consciousness of this Surrounding Light is, "No, I have to find a way to manifest within this Vessel." There is a conflict between these two realities: The Vessel with the Masach and this Surrounding Light, which is the unmanifested Light that says, "I have to find a way into that Vessel. I have to find a way to manifest Light."

In this new reality there are now really five new Vessels, but for our purposes, let us say four new Vessels. After the Tzimtzum, the first reality is called a Masach of the Fourth Phase, a Vessel that because of its purity is able to say, "I can receive 90% of the Light that was received in the Ein Sof, and 10%, which is still a tremendous amount of Light, I cannot receive." The Ari says and Rav Ashlag explains that this Light is viewed as almost filling the entire Ten Sefirot. Meaning, the amount of Light that it is able to draw, was enough to almost completely refill the Light that was revealed in the Ein Sof.

Since each one of the Phases represents a level of desire, the Fourth Phase has the greatest desire. Three has less than Four but more than Two. Two has less than Three and more than One, and the First Phase, which is called Chochmah, has the least amount of desire besides Keter of course, and therefore is able to reveal the least amount of Light.

It is important to remember this because as we go further into the Study of the Ten Luminous Emanations, we will begin noticing how each one of these Phases corresponds to one of the Spiritual Worlds. The first reality, the first World, that came out after the Tzimtzum is the Masach of the Fourth Phase, meaning a Vessel that because it ascertains its purity, decides it can receive almost all of the Light that was received in the Ein Sof for the Sake of Sharing. And this begins the first battle between the Surrounding Light and this Masach, this barrier.

CHAPTER 7

Chapter 7 explains the matter of the Purification of the Curtain (Hizdachechut haMasach) and expounds upon the emergence of the Five Statures —Keter, Chochmah, Binah, Zeir Anpin, and Malchut—one below the other, due to the Purification of the Curtain (Masach).

The preventing force in the Masach and the degree of density in Malchut are equal.

72. To understand the said Purification of the Masach, we need to preface it with two things. The first is that the preventing force in the Masach is equivalent to the degree of density, which is the yearning that is in the Fourth Phase, like two pans on the scale. The reason is simple. If there is great yearning to receive, a person needs much effort to withdraw himself from receiving. If there is little yearning, there is no need for much effort to withdraw himself from receiving. Thus, the preventing force in the Masach is equivalent to the density in the Fourth Phase—whether more or less.

Here Rav Ashlag explains this process of Purification of the Vessel (*Hizdachechut haMasach*). And it is really amazing because when you look in the Writings of the Ari, there is no real discussion of the Purification of the Vessel. This battle that is really at the core of the process of the creation of our world is almost not spoken about in the Writings of the Ari. This is one of these moments, and there are many of them, where we should awaken great appreciation for both the Ari and Rav Ashlag.

Among the students of Rav Ashlag there was always an understanding that at least once a year they have to make a Seudat Mitzvah, a meal to thank the Creator for, first of all, sending the soul of Rav Ashlag down into this world and also allowing him to reveal these secrets, because there is no way that a person, except someone like the soul of Rav Ashlag—even if they were to study the Writings of the Ari for a million years—who would ever come to understand and to reveal the concept of the Purification of the Vessel. This is something that only Rav Ashlag had the merit and the ability to reveal.

Rav Ashlag explains something interesting. He says that the Masach, the Vessel and this 20% of Light that is left out have exactly the same force, the same amount of energy, the same amount of power, because for the Masach to be able to push out that Light it has to have as much energy, as much power as that left out Light. Rav Ashlag says, "the preventing force in the Masach is equivalent to the degree of density."

For instance, someone who is really working on his Desire to Receive for the Self Alone—wanting to make sure he receives nothing for his own sake—is offered a steak. He has to really ask himself, *Where am I at? How hungry am I? How great is my Desire? How great is my spiritual strength? What from this offer can I eat and keep the consciousness of only for the Sake of Sharing?* If he has a steak, that will just overwhelm his Desire to Receive for the Self Alone, and he will start feeling that enjoyment in his level of Desire to Receive for the Self Alone. So, instead, he wants to settle for a glass of water and a cookie.

However, this example is not perfect because what actually happens is that the friend is literally forcing him to eat the steak. He wants to force-feed him. So the person who is trying to push the food back has to be as strong as the person who is trying to feed him. If the giver is stronger, then even though the other person does not want to eat the steak, he will be forced to eat it. And if the receiver is stronger, he will clearly be able to push the food away. Rav Ashlag says that the Masach, the barrier, that is pushing back on that Light has to be as strong as the power of that Light; they are exactly fifty-fifty in their strength, they are exactly equal in their strength.

It is the way of the Surrounding Light to purify the Masach.

73. The second preface is that regarding the Surrounding Light that has not entered the emanated, its nature is to purify the density in the Fourth Phase slowly and gradually in the order of the Four Phases until it purifies all its density entirely. First it purifies it from the Fourth to the Third Phase, then to the Second, and then to the First. Eventually it becomes completely pure without any density due to it.

> **It is because it wants to enter, and the Masach prevents it.**
>
> 74. The reason is as follows: Surrounding Light refers to the Supernal Light that cannot be vested within the Emanated Being due to the Masach that prevents it from expanding more than its Stature. So it remains outside the Partzuf and surrounds it, meaning that it shines on it from afar. But since the Surrounding Light wants to shine inside the Partzuf as well, as was its way in the Ein Sof where it shone to the Fourth Phase as well, therefore it strikes the Masach and purifies it, that is, it nullifies its density and resistance so that it can enter.

We really have to think deeply about this because it is something I struggled with when I began studying the Study of the Ten Luminous Emanations with the Rav. Rav Ashlag is telling us that the nature of the Surrounding Light is to purify the Vessel. Why? Because it wants to shine as it shined in the Endless World.

But the logical question is, what is the Purification of the Vessel? It means the diminishing of the Vessel's desire. The Desire to Receive causes the Masach, the barrier. The first Vessel that emerged after the Tzimtzum has a great Desire to Receive for the Self Alone and it is able to receive 80% of the Light and still have the consciousness of, "I am only Receiving for the Sake of Sharing." Then comes the Surrounding Light and pushes against this Vessel and says, "You have to remove some of your Desire to Receive because once you purify your Desire to Receive then I will be able to manifest within you."

Yet what actually happens, which is the process that Rav Ashlag explains, is that the Vessel begins with a Masach of the Fourth Phase, a Desire to Receive of the Fourth Phase, meaning the greatest level, and it is able to receive almost the complete Light for the Sake of Sharing. Then the Surrounding Light comes and purifies it, and says, "No, remove some of your Desire to Receive." And it drops down into what is called the Third Phase, a Third Level of desire.

If you compare those two realities, before the Vessel was having four and now the Vessel has only three out of the five, so which is better for the Light that wants to come in? One would think that the Light would be happier when there is more Light being revealed, more Light being manifest. However what is actually happening is that the Light is forcing the Vessel to change, and with the change there is less of a desire; there is less Light manifested in the Third Phase.

This process is very important to understand, because this process of the Purification of the Vessel brings about our Worlds. It goes from five to four, to three, to two, to one, to almost zero. Yet, how does that help if the desire of the Surrounding Light is to have more Light revealed, more of the Light manifest? How does it help it that in this new World of the Third Phase there is now less Light revealed into the Vessel?

The answer is relatively simple, and I remember studying this very important understanding with the Rav many years ago. We know the concept of "there is no disappearance in spirituality, in Light." So what happens is that after the Vessel of the Masach of the Fourth Phase, the Vessel of the Fourth Level of Desire, has manifested a certain amount of Light, the Surrounding Light knows that the only way to reveal more Light is by having a new Vessel. And it is true that this new Vessel will manifest less Light than the previous one, but quantitatively there will be some more Light revealed.

Let us illustrate with by using five foods—water, cookies, salad, steak, and truffles. Someone who is spiritual but also has a hearty appetite, sees the food and says, "I can eat four out of the five and still have a Desire to Receive Only for the Sake of Sharing." When he finishes eating, I say, "What about the truffles?" He replies, "I cannot eat that and only have it for the Sake of Sharing." I say, "Okay, so you have done all you can, let me bring someone else." This new person I bring has less of an appetite than the first guy, and he is also less spiritual. So he can only drink the water, the cookies, and the salad; he cannot have the steak like the guy before. But there is still more Light revealed now—it is with a different person, it is in a different World but more Light is revealed. This is what is going to happen throughout this process. The Vessel is going to get weaker and weaker and weaker, and smaller and smaller and smaller, but still at each step there will be more Light revealed, less Light than in the previous Phase but more Light in totality.

Rav Ashlag has a beautiful explanation about this process in the Zohar. He states that the purpose of the creation of our Worlds, and the need for so many Worlds and so many people in the Worlds, is that Mashiach can only come when many, many new souls come into this world because everyone is revealing a tiny amount of Light. And we need a lot of people revealing tiny amounts of Light until the totality of the Endless Light is re-revealed in our world. I believe this a very important stage in preparing ourselves to understand the rest of the Inner Observation, the rest of the manifesting of the Light.

First the Masach prevails, and then the Light prevails.

75. At first the Masach prevails and pushes it back, and afterwards the Light prevails and purifies the Masach, though it nullifies nothing but that aspect of density upon which the Binding by Striking took place. If the Binding by Striking occurred in the Fourth Phase, it would cancel the density of the Fourth Phase that prevents the Light from entering the Stature, and it would leave the density of the Third Phase, which it has no business with. If the Binding by Striking was on the density of the Third Phase, it would only nullify the density of the Third Phase and leave the density of the Second Phase, and so it goes on (as said in Volume 4, Inner Light, Chapter 1).

**The Fourth Phase does not disappear, even though
it was purified into its Third Phase.**

76. As you already know, the newness of form developing in a spiritual entity does not indicate that the previous form is absent, since there is no lack at all in spirituality. Rather, there is an additional form. Accordingly, you will understand that this Fourth Phase, which was purified into its Third Phase, is considered that it emerged from this Emanated Being into the category of a new Emanated Being that is added to the first Emanated Being. The Fourth Phase [of this new Emanated Being] is not the Fourth Phase of the Fourth Phase but the Third Phase of the Fourth Phase. However, no change was affected in the first Emanated Being due to this purification.

**Immediately as it was purified into the Third Phase,
the Supernal Light interacted with it for it does not cease to shine.**

77. It has been explained before that the Supernal Light does not cease from shining upon the Lower Beings even for a moment. Its extending into the Emanated Being depends only upon the preparation of its Vessel, namely according to the level of the Desire to Receive in the Emanated.

Whenever the Emanated Being awakens with yearning for the Supernal Light, it immediately attains it, according to the amount of its Desire, as said earlier (see Section 63); study it carefully. Therefore, after the Fourth Phase has purified into its Third Phase and has emerged as a new Emanated Being into itself, it drew to itself the Supernal Light. Then a new set of Ten Sefirot of Supernal Light from above downward emerged in it, as well as a new set of Ten Sefirot of Returning Light from below upward, in the same exact way as the extension of the first Emanated Being. However, there is a big difference between them in Stature, as the new Emanated Being lacks the Stature of Keter and has only the Stature of Chochmah.

The reason the Third Phase lacks Keter.

78. The reason for the absence of the Stature of Keter in this second Emanated Being is because it does not have the density of the Fourth Phase of the Fourth Phase, which in the frame of Returning Light is the Keter of the Fourth Phase. Therefore, the Masach pushed back the Supernal Light only from the aspect of Chochmah and below, meaning the exact amount that was supposed to enter the Third Phase of the Fourth Phase. This is not the case with the Keter aspect of the Fourth Phase that had no extension even if the Masach did not prevent it, since the Vessel that drew the Supernal Light drew no more than Chochmah and below, from the very beginning. For this reason, the Masach did not push back the Light of Keter, but only the Light of Chochmah and below. Therefore, the Light of Keter is absent from this Returning Light.

And since there is no Light of Keter of Returning Light there, the Light of Keter of the Supernal Light is absent there as well, for there is no Light that can enter the Emanated Being without Returning Light to encase it, which is the aspect of its Vessel of Receiving, as said (see Section 21). Therefore, it has only the Stature of Chochmah.

Every drawing down is done by the Fourth Phase, which is why it needs a Masach so that the Light does not spread to the Fourth Phase.

79. This is the rule: Every drawing of Light has to take place only in the Fourth Phase of the Emanated, even though the intention is not to draw

Light into it. The reason is that the density that is above the Fourth Phase is not fit to draw, as said (see Section 56). Even the First Phase in the Fourth Phase is more fit to draw than the actual Third Phase that is above, namely purer than, the whole Fourth Phase. Thus, if the entire aspect of density in the Fourth Phase is finished, then there is no longer anything there to draw Light from the Endless, and the Light ceases there completely.

Since the drawing needs to be done by the Fourth Phase, which still needs to protect itself so no Light would extend into it due to the Tzimtzum formed over the Fourth Phase, it therefore set the Masach itself to safeguard this. So when the Light extends and reaches the Fourth Phase, the Masach awakens and returns that portion of it back to its root. And that part that was returned does not disappear but rather becomes the aspect of the Returning Light, which means that the Vessel of Receiving for the Supernal Light comes from it.

With regard to drawing the Light, the Fourth Phase and the Masach are as one.

80. This way, the Fourth Phase and the Masach over it are as one in relation to drawing Light from the Ein Sof, since the resistance of the Masach rests over the density of the Fourth Phase. Therefore, most of the time, we only mention the Masach alone regarding the drawing of Light, even though it surely refers to both, as explained. We too, in order to be brief, will refer to the drawing of Light from the Ein Sof only based on the Masach, and also the developing of the levels from each other we will refer to as "the purification of the density," even though it refers to the resistance in the Masach. And remember that what is meant is the degree of the density in the Fourth Phase that creates the four levels of resistance in the Masach.

The emergence of the level of Chochmah from the Third Phase.

81. The emergence of the level of Chochmah from the level of Keter was well explained earlier, where the first Ten Sefirot to emerge after the Tzimtzum did so through the encounter of the Supernal Light with the Masach that comprises the full density in the Fourth Phase, as said (see Section 64). It thus raised Returning Light with a complete Stature all the way to the root called Keter. After that level was complete with a Head,

Middle, and End, part of the density was purified from the Masach, that is, from the Fourth to the Third Phase, as said (see Section 74). And since the Masach acquired a change of form, it is considered to have gone out of the level of Keter, as said. And through the encounter of the Light of the Endless with the Masach, which was purified into the Third Phase, a second set of Ten Sefirot emerged, whose Stature reaches up to Chochmah alone, lacking Keter, as said (see Section 78, study it carefully).

The emergence of the level of Binah from the Second Phase.

82. After the level of Chochmah was completed with a Head, Middle and End, the Surrounding Light returned and purified yet another part of the degree of density of the Masach, that is, from the Third Phase of the Fourth Phase into the Second Phase of the Fourth Phase. This new Masach of the Second Phase of the Fourth Phase is considered to have gone out of the level of Chochmah for the same reason mentioned by the level of Keter (see Section 76). From the encounter of the Supernal Light with this new Masach of the Second Phase, Ten new Sefirot emerged with the Stature of Binah alone, lacking Keter and Chochmah.

The reason for the absence of Chochmah in the Masach of the Second Phase.

83. The reason for the lack of Chochmah in this new level is the same reason mentioned in regard to the lack of Keter (see Sections 75 and 76), study it carefully because since this Fourth Phase has but the density of the Second Phase, which is considered Binah of the Fourth Phase, this drawing that it caused was originally only from Binah and below. Therefore, even if the Masach would not have prevented the Supernal Light, it would still not have extended to the Fourth Phase itself, but only from Binah down. We find now that the Masach did not push back the Keter and Chochmah that are fit for the Fourth Phase, and therefore Keter and Chochmah are not found in this Returning Light. And since the Returning Light is not there, neither is the Supernal Light of Keter and Chochmah, for they have no aspect of a Vessel for Receiving.

The emergence of the level of Zeir Anpin from the Masach of the First Phase.

84. After this new level of the Stature of Binah was completed with Head, Middle, and End, the Surrounding Light returned and purified another portion of the degree of density in the Masach, namely from the Second Phase to the First Phase, and it too is considered as emerging out of the level of Binah. And from the encounter of the Supernal Light with the Masach of the First Phase of the Fourth Phase, Ten new Sefirot emerged with the Stature of Zeir Anpin. And here the First Three Sefirot—Keter, Chochmah, and Binah—are missing for the reason mentioned earlier.

The emergence of the level of Malchut.

85. After the level of Zeir Anpin was completed with Head, Middle, and End, the last portion of the density of the Fourth Phase was purified as well. It is also considered that this completely purified Masach emerged out of the level of Zeir Anpin, and it is called the level of Malchut in which no new Light appeared. Rather, it receives an Illumination from Zeir Anpin, since it is no longer fit to draw, as said. Therefore, it only has the Light of Nefesh. The rest of this matter will be explained in Volume 3, God willing.

Rav Ashlag says that the Binding by Striking (*Zivug deHaka'ah*) is really one of the most basic understandings of how the Worlds came to be. He explains that when the Light first returns after the Tzimtzum, it first comes and wants to enter into Malchut as it did in the Ein Sof. And then there is a Masach, a barrier that says, "You cannot come in." And although a lot of the Light came back again to manifest in that Vessel, a lot more remained outside and is called the Surrounding Light. As mentioned previously, Rav Ashlag says that the job of the Surrounding Light is to purify the Masach, and purify the desire of Malchut to make it desire less.

Therefore, after the Binding by Striking, the first Light that comes down into the Vessel is returned back as Returning Light, then the Surrounding Light, which is not manifest in the Vessel, purifies the desire—makes the desire more spiritual it seems—and makes it go down from a level Four desire to a level Three. Yet we know that the greater the desire in Malchut, in the Vessel, the more Light is revealed, so what good does it do the Surrounding Light if the Masach, if the desire is now less? How does diminishing the desire of the Vessel make more Light manifest? One would think that a lessening of desire is not what the Surrounding Light wants. What does it want? It wants more Light manifest.

The answer is that the Surrounding Light's job is not that in any one given World all the Light will be revealed; this is no longer possible after the Tzimtzum. Rather it understands that the more Vessels, the more Worlds that will come about, the more Light will eventually be revealed. Rav Ashlag always uses the term—a penny plus a penny plus a penny over time will create a lot—and the same is true here. When you go down, when there is the Purification of the Vessel, when there is a diminishment of desire where the Surrounding Light makes desire go from a level Four desire to a level Three desire, less Light will be revealed than in the previous World where our Fourth level of desire was manifest, but there is more Light in the big picture.

Now you have two worlds: one of level Four desire and one of level Three desire, yet in totality there is more Light revealed. Then the Surrounding Light that is not yet manifest is going to purify the level Three desire, and there will be a new World based upon a lower level of desire, which is called the Second Phase. Yes, it will reveal less Light than in the previous World, but in totality there is now more Light revealed. There are three Worlds, each with diminishing Light but in totality more Light is revealed. When the Surrounding Light purifies the Second Phase to the First Phase, takes it from level Two desire to level One, and so on. This is the purpose and job of the Surrounding Light. It is to make it so that there is always a diminishment of desire; that the desire becomes purer and over time, there is more and more Light revealed. And this process continues until the totality of Light is revealed.

When we do the spiritual work, we expect to see the result. Meaning, we would like to think that if we are working for ten years, we would be able to see that the world is getting closer toward the End of the Correction (Gemar HaTikkun), because in the physical world, when one builds a house, obviously in the first week there is less to show of the work. Yet, after six months the walls will be erected, so one can see the results of their work. And hopefully after a year, the house is built. In the physical world, when you are working toward something, and you are manifesting something, there is always more and more and more for you to see. Therefore, we assume that after a year, two years, three years we would be able to see the results of our work. And if we do not see the results of our work, we get discouraged.

We can get discouraged because we have been doing this for a number of years and do not see how everything that we have done has brought us to the Gemar haTikkun. However, based on this very important understanding, we learn two tremendously important lessons. One, that if you are doing the spiritual work, you are actually going to see less and less manifestation. For instance, in the process from the World of the Fourth Phase, called the World of Adam Kadmon to the World of Atzilut, which one has more Light revealed in it? The World of Adam Kadmon. The progressive World, the next World, called the World of Atzilut has less Light revealed in it. And the next World that comes down is the World of Briyah, and World of Briyah has less Light than the World of Atzilut.

Thus, the process of the Worlds coming about seems very discouraging. There is always less Light. There is less Light in the World of Atzilut from the World of Adam Kadmon, there is less Light in the World of Briyah than in the World of Atzilut, there is less Light in the World of Yetzirah from the World of Briyah, there is less Light in the World of Asiyah than in the World of Yetzirah. In our World there is less Light than ever before.

Is this a process of Correction? It seems to be counterintuitive. If anything, the more we go on, the more Light should be revealed in the World. Why is it the other way around? And the answer is that the spiritual work that we are doing is not going to manifest in this World. Any Light that we have revealed is an addition to the totality of revelation that has occurred, and it does not stay in our world.

The kabbalists use the example of a Temple that is being built in the Upper Worlds, and every positive action that we do builds a part of that Temple. And when that work is completed by humanity, then this Temple will come down and be revealed in our World. What does it mean? They are not simply referring to a physical structure, of course, but are discussing the perfection of humanity.

We have to understand that when we perfect something it does not stay in our world so that, at the end of the year, we can add up our great accomplishments and say, "Oh, wow. Look at all I have done." If we have accomplished something, it is immediately taken away from us and put into the store, into that Temple that is being built for the world.

The Arvei Nachal (Rav David Shlomo Eibeschutz, 1755–1813) teaches that if you can still remember the good that you have done, it is not in the Upper

Worlds, it is still caught down in this world. If you have forgotten about the work that you have done, it is in the Upper Worlds. Meaning that we should not expect that at the end of a year or even at the end of five years, to look back and take an accounting of all our great spiritual accomplishments. If we can account for all our great spiritual accomplishments, we have not accomplished anything. The way the system works is that when we have finished a manifestation it is removed from us. It is taken away and put into that store of perfection that the world is coming closer and closer toward.

We learn from this concept that as we do more, we see less. We have to maintain the understanding that anything that we have done that has been really good, that has been perfect, has been taken away. This Light has been taken away and it goes onto that bank of perfection that brings us closer to the critical mass. Every progressive step is going to be manifested in our world, even in the spiritual worlds, as less and less.

However, every small perfection gets added to the total critical mass, and then when that is complete it will be manifested in our world. It is a very important concept that bears repeating because I want to make sure it is clear as this is essential both in our Study of the Ten Luminous Emanations and in our own spiritual work. The way the Worlds are going to manifest is from more Light to less Light to less Light to less Light to less Light to less Light. Every next step is less Light than the step before. However, the way this will bring us to perfection is that all of this Light in the descending levels of revelation are added all together. This means that as we view the work, as we view our manifestation, we will always see diminishing Light being revealed, and at the same time to know that this Light goes back to the total goal of humanity.

If we think we are seeing the totality of our manifestation of our spiritual work in this world, it means that we are not manifesting. If we look back at a year and do not see all that Light, there is a very good chance that this Light was so perfect that it was taken and added to the critical mass. If we can make an accounting of all our great accomplishments, this means that it has not gone to the bank of critical mass; it is still maintained or caught in my small ego prison. This how the Worlds come about.

The reason the Surrounding Light is pushing the Worlds to become smaller, pushing the Worlds to have less desire is because then it can create a new World where new Light will be revealed. Yes, less Light than in the previous World, but at least some more Light, and eventually all this Light will add up and manifest the Gemar haTikkun. This is a very important understanding, both in the study of the processes of the Light being manifested in our World, but also in our own spiritual work and how we view our accomplishments, our manifestations.

CHAPTER 8

Chapter 8 explains three things:

1. Why in regard to the drawing down of Lights, the denser is greater, but in regard to their entering inside the Vessels, the purer is superior.
2. The reason for the inverse relationship between the Vessels and the Lights, where with the Vessels the higher ones grow first and with the Lights the lower ones enter first.
3. Why the circles are considered the Light of Nefesh.

The measure of the Light that is drawn depends on the density of the Masach.

86a. It has been well explained how the entire degree of the Supernal Light bestowing to the Emanated Being depends on the degree of density of the Masach, where the greatest density, which is the Fourth Phase, is bestowed with the Stature of Keter, while the lesser one is only bestowed with the Stature of Chochmah, and so on until the purest Masach, upon which the Supernal Light gives nothing since it has no density, as explained.

The measure of the Light that enters depends on the purity of the Vessel.

86b. However, all this is said from the point of view of the sharing and the extending of the Supernal Light into the Emanated, because whatever bestows only does so to the densest part, since the denser the Masach, the more the Supernal Light extends to it (see Section 62). But from the point of view of the order of the Emanated receiving the Supernal Light this is not so. Rather, the more important Light is received in the purer Vessel and the lesser one is received in a dense Vessel.

In the Vessels, the higher appear first, and in the Lights, the lower appear first.

87a. This is as we said earlier (see Section 14) that whatever bestows does so to the densest part, but whatever receives does so in its purest part. To clarify these matters, I will explain to you the order of the Lights entering

303

into the Emanated after the Correction, for then it receives the Light gradually, according to the succession of the levels. It first attains the Light of Nefesh, then the Light of Ruach, and so on, until the Light of Yechidah. In regard to the Vessels, it is the opposite: it first attains Keter, then Chochmah, and so on.

When the Light of Nefesh is attained, it is clothed in the Vessel of Keter.

87b. This is the order: First the Emanated comes out as the aspect of ten Vessels—Keter, Chochmah, Binah, Zeir Anpin (that comprises Chesed, Gevurah, Tiferet, Netzach, Hod, and Yesod), and Malchut. This means that the Higher Vessels come first. Then, when the Nefesh is bestowed onto it, it is considered that this Nefesh comes to it in the Vessel of Keter, which is the purest Vessel. The reason it still does not have the Light of Ruach is that the Masach in Keter has no more density, not even that of the First Phase, and the aspect of the Light of Ruach is only bestowed through the encounter of the Supernal Light with the Masach of the First Phase. And since the Masach is in the Vessel of Keter, which means that the Masach is pure without any density, it has only the Light of Nefesh that relates to Malchut.

When the Light of Ruach is attained, the Light of Nefesh descends to Chochmah and Ruach is clothed in the Vessel of Keter.

88. When it acquires the density of the First Phase, then through the encounter of the Supernal Light with this Masach of the First Phase the Light of Ruach is bestowed to it. The place of this Masach is in the Vessel of Chochmah, which is the First Phase. However, even though it is the Masach of the Vessel of Chochmah that drew the Light of Ruach into the Partzuf, as said, the Light of Ruach nevertheless enters the Vessel of Keter, and the Light of Nefesh it had in Keter before descends to Chochmah. And the reason is according to what we said, that in the order of the receiving of the Lights, the most important Light enters the purest Vessel and the one inferior to it enters the denser one, which is opposite to the sequence of bestowing. Therefore, the Ruach, which is superior to the Nefesh, ascends and enters Keter, and the Nefesh descends and enters Chochmah.

**When the Neshamah is attained, it is clothed in the Vessel of Keter,
Ruach descends to Chochmah and Nefesh to Binah.**

89. Afterwards, when its Masach acquires the density of the Second Phase, which is considered that the Masach is in the Vessel of Binah, then through the encounter of the Supernal Light with this Masach the Light of Neshamah is bestowed upon it, which is much more important than the Lights of Ruach and Nefesh. Here too, it receives the Light of Neshamah in the purest part, namely the Vessel of Keter, as the Light of Nefesh that is the most inferior, which is in the Vessel of Chochmah, descends to the Vessel of Binah where the Masach of the Second Phase is located, which is currently the densest Vessel of all. The Light of Ruach descends from Keter to the Vessel of Chochmah, and the Light of Neshamah, the most superior, enters the Vessel of Keter, the purest of all.

**When the Light of Chayah is attained it is clothed in Keter,
Neshamah descends to Chochmah, Ruach to Binah, and Nefesh to Zeir Anpin.**

90. When its Masach acquires the density of the Third Phase, it is considered that the Masach is now in the Vessel of Zeir Anpin, which is the Third Phase. Then, through the meeting of the Supernal Light with the Masach of the Third Phase the Light of Chayah is bestowed to it, which is even more superior to the Light of Neshamah, and for this it must be received in a purer Vessel. Consequently, the Light of Nefesh, the most inferior of all, descends from the Vessel of Binah to what is now the densest Vessel of all, namely Zeir Anpin, where the Masach of the Third Phase resides. The Light of Ruach, which is in Chochmah, now descends to Binah, the Light of Neshamah in Keter descends to Chochmah, and the Light of Chayah that is the most superior enters the Vessel of Keter.

**When Yechidah is attained, it is clothed in Keter, Chayah descends to
Chochmah, Neshamah to Binah, Ruach to Zeir Anpin, and Nefesh to Malchut.**

91. Afterwards, when the Masach acquires the density of the Fourth Phase, it is considered that the Masach is now in the Vessel of Malchut, the Fourth Phase. Then, through the encounter of the Supernal Light with this Masach of the Fourth Phase, the Light of Yechidah is bestowed

upon it, which is the most superior of them all, and for which reason it receives it in its purest part, which is the Vessel of Keter. It now follows that the Light of Nefesh that is the most inferior, descends from Zeir Anpin to the Vessel of Malchut within which is the Masach of the Fourth Phase, which is the densest. The Light of Ruach descends from Binah to the Vessel of Zeir Anpin, the Light of Neshamah descends from Chochmah to the Vessel of Binah, the Light of Chayah descends from Keter to the Vessel of Chochmah, and the Light of Yechidah that now comes, is clothed in Keter. Now each Light of Nefesh, Ruach, Neshamah, Chayah, and Yechidah reached the Vessel truly associated with it.

The difference between the bestowing of the Light and the sequence of the Light being clothed.

92. You thus see the big difference between the sequence of the bestowing of the Supernal Light to the Partzuf and the sequence of the entering of the Light in the Vessels. The one bestowing requires the densest part, as the Light of Yechidah is bestowed to the Partzuf only when a Masach with the Vessel of the Fourth Phase specifically, is present there, as explained. Before this, when this density was not there but only a weaker density, namely that of the Third Phase, it was not possible for this superior Light called Yechidah to be bestowed upon the Partzuf. But even so, when this most superior Light is drawn into the Partzuf, it does not enter inside the Vessel of the Fourth Phase, but inside the purest one, namely the Vessel of Keter.

Any Light that comes to the Partzuf is not received except in the Vessel of Keter.

93. The same applies to the Light of Chayah, where it is bestowed only to the Masach in the Vessel of Zeir Anpin, namely the Third Phase, and nevertheless when it is clothed by the Emanated it is not clothed in the Vessel of Zeir Anpin but only the purest Vessel, namely the Vessel of Keter, as explained. Similarly, the aspect of the Light of Neshamah is bestowed only to the Masach of the density of the Second Phase in the Vessel of Binah, though when it enters, it only enters the Vessel of Keter. And so the Light of Ruach is bestowed only to the Masach of the First Phase in the Vessel of Chochmah, yet when it enters it does not enter the

Vessel of Chochmah but rather the purer Vessel, namely the Vessel of Keter, as said. Thus, each and every Light that comes to the Partzuf only comes to it at first in the Vessel of Keter, as we said that the receiver receives only with its purest Vessel even though the abundance arrived to it through the densest Vessel—and understand this well.

The Circles do not receive the Supernal Light since they have no density.

94. From what we have explained, you will also understand why the Circles receive no abundance from the Supernal Light. Rather, they have to receive all their Lights from the Light of the Line, even though the Circular Vessels precede the Vessels of Straightness of the Line. The reason is simple: they have no density at all, as all their Four Phases are equally even (see Volume 1, Inner Light, Section 19). For this reason, only the Vessels of Straightness in the Line, which possess the Masach and the density, are given abundance from the Supernal Light, and the Circles receive from them.

**Any level that receives from another,
yet in itself has no aspect of giving, is called Nefesh.**

95. This is why the Light of the Circles is called the Light of Nefesh, for this is the rule: any level that is not given abundance from the Supernal Light but receives its Illumination from another level, its Light is called the Light of Nefesh or Female Light. And since the Circles are not given abundance from the Supernal Light but they receive their Illumination from the Line, they are considered Female Light or the Light of Nefesh. Even regarding the Vessels of Straightness, it has been explained (see Section 85) that if the entire density in the Masach is purified, then there is no more bestowing from the Supernal Light, and there is nothing there but an Illumination from the level preceding it, for which reason it is called the Light of Nefesh. Understand this well.

CHAPTER 9

Chapter 9 explains why each and every Sefirah is comprised of Ten individual Sefirot, each of which is too comprised of Ten individual Sefirot, and so they go and spread, *ad infinitum.*

**The division of the Sefirot into individual subdivisions
and further subdivisions, ad infinitum.**

96. It is a wondrous law in the Supernal Worlds that in any Sefirah we choose to examine, we find Ten individual Sefirot. When we further consider any one Sefirah of those individual Ten Sefirot we further distinguish Ten Sefirot, which are the subdivision of the subdivision of that original Sefirah. And so if we take one Sefirah of those Sefirot that are further subdivided, we again find in it Ten Sefirot, which are the subparts of the subdivision of the previous individual ones, and so on, *ad infinitum.*

**Any Light that passes through the grades leaves its root in each
and every grade it passes through.**

97. You will understand the reason for this based on what we explained, that there is no disappearance in spirituality (see Volume 2, Inner Light, Chapter 1, Section 4). What is explained there is that it is impossible to find any kind of Light in the lower that is not included in all that is above it, up to the Ein Sof. The reason is that even a very small Illumination that appears in the lowliest grade in the Worlds has to emerge from the Ein Sof and pass through all the Worlds and grades preceding that low grade until it emerges there.

It cannot be that this Illumination is removed, as it progresses through the grades, from the First grade due to it entering the Second, or removed from the Second when it enters the Third, and so on, until it enters the last Grade that receives it, like the way of a material object that passes from place to place. This cannot be among spiritual entities, to which lack or exchange do not apply. Rather, of necessity, every Illumination that goes through any grade, even if it is only by passing through, has nevertheless already acquired a place there.

Any Light that has appeared once in any grade never moves away from there.

98. The process of it entering and moving into the following grade does not, due to this, diminish at all from the Light it left, which acquired a place in the grade it passed through. Rather, this resembles lighting a candle from a candle, where the first is not diminished. So too here, when the Light is transferred from the First level and descends to the Second, the entire Light is found fully present in both the First and the Second. In the same way, when the Light reaches the Third level, the Light does not leave the Second but is found in its entirety both in the Second and in the Third.

In the same way, when it passes through all the grades preceding the last one, which is the true recipient, namely the grade for which the Light descended from the Ein Sof, it is fixed in all of them. All this transpires because no lack applies to spirituality, and any Light that ever shone upon a spiritual phase does not ever move from it, even a little bit.

When the Light of Chochmah passes to its place through Keter, it leaves its root in Keter.

99. From what we explained you will understand well the matter of the Ten Sefirot being comprised of each other, *ad infinitum*. For example, when the first two Sefirot, Keter and Chochmah, appear, the Light of Chochmah must emerge from the Endless, as said, and thus the Light of Chochmah has to pass through the Sefirah of Keter before it reaches the Sefirah of Chochmah. So, since the Light of Chochmah has shone once in the Sefirah of Keter, namely when it passed there, it is impossible for it to ever disappear from there, as said. It is thus stipulated that even after the Light of Chochmah reached the Sefirah of Chochmah, this Light of Chochmah remained fully in Keter as well. Thus, the Sefirah of Keter has two Lights now, the Light of Keter and the Light of Chochmah.

When the Light of Binah passes through Keter and Chochmah,
it leaves its root in them, and so it goes on in this manner.

100. The same applies to the Light of Binah. Since it has to pass through the preceding two Sefirot before reaching the Sefirah of Binah, by necessity the Light of Binah acquired a place both in Keter and Chochmah, as said. So now there are three Lights in Keter: the Light of Keter, the Light of Chochmah, and the Light of Binah; there are two Lights in Chochmah: the Light of Chochmah and the Light of Binah; and there is one Light in the Sefirah of Binah: its own Light. It goes on in this way until, when the Light of Malchut emerges, there are all Ten Sefirot in Keter, as all the nine lower Lights necessarily passed through Keter and thus acquired their place there, as said. There are nine Sefirot in Chochmah, as all eight Sefirot below it necessarily passed through it and remained there, as said. In the same way, there are eight Sefirot in Binah, seven in Chesed, six in Gevurah, and so on, until Malchut that only has its own Light, since there is no Sefirah below it to pass through.

There is no Direct Light in the Vessel of Malchut, only Returning Light.

101. As for the issue of the mentioned Light of Malchut, both its own Light and the Light that is included from Her in the first nine Sefirot is but Returning Light. For you already know that from the Tzimtzum on, a Masach was formed in the Sefirah of Malchut, so the Endless Light is not received there. Rather, a unification is made there by the encounter of the Endless Light with the Masach. Then a new Light emerges and rises from the Masach in Malchut, which is called Returning Light, and shines up to the Sefirah of Keter above. It thus clothes all Ten Sefirot from below upward. Only in this way is [Malchut] included in each of the first nine Sefirot (as said earlier in Section 19).

Malchut is considered as the Keter of the Ten Sefirot of Returning Light.

102a. Since the Sefirah of Malchut is the source for this new Light, and each source is considered as Keter, therefore Malchut is considered as the Sefirah of Keter of this new Light. The preceding Sefirah, Yesod, is considered Chochmah of the new Light; and the one in front of that, Hod, is considered Binah. Eventually, the top Keter is now considered Malchut in respect to what it receives from the said new Light.

The Ten Sefirot of Direct Light are from above downward.

102b. It has been explained that we need to distinguish in every level of Ten Sefirot, as having two directions of Ten Sefirot: One is the direction of the Ten Sefirot that are drawn from the Endless from above downward, from Keter to Malchut, and they are called the Ten Sefirot of Direct Light, since they go straight down, level after level, that is, from the purer Vessel to the denser, and from there to one denser still down to Malchut, the densest of them all.

The Ten Sefirot of Returning Light are from below upward.

103. There is also a second direction of the Ten Sefirot there that spread upward from the Sefirah of Malchut to the Sefirah of Keter, where Malchut becomes the source for this new Light. They are called the Ten Sefirot of Returning Light. They are so called since they are bestowed and go in an opposite direction to the levels' sequence, that is, it does not flow from the purer to the denser Vessel wherein the final recipient is the densest; but on the contrary, they flow from the densest Vessel to not so dense, until eventually the final recipient is the purest. It is therefore called as shining from below upwards.

All the Sefirot of Returning Light that enter the nine Sefirot of Direct Light, pass through Malchut.

104. We explained earlier about the inclusion of the Sefirot regarding the sequence of the Ten Sefirot of Direct Light that it is because there is no disappearance in spirituality, and every Illumination that passes anywhere remains there in its entirety, even after it moves into another place, for which reason it is considered that with the emergence of the Ten Sefirot of Direct Light, all Ten Sefirot are present in Keter, nine in Chochmah, eight in Binah, and so on. (as said in Section 99; study it carefully). For the same reason, the same applies to the Ten Sefirot of Returning Light. Since in this case the Sefirah of Malchut becomes a source for this Returning Light, we consider that every aspect of Returning Light that reaches the

Sefirot above it must pass through the place of Malchut, since it is Malchut that emits that Light by means of its Masach that unites with the Endless Light that meets with that Masach.

When the Returning Light of Yesod passes through Malchut,
it leaves its root in Malchut, and so on.

105. For this reason, when the Sefirah of Yesod receives its Returning Light from Malchut, it must be that the Light it receives was received before by Malchut through the Unification with the Light of the Endless, and it passed through Malchut and went to the Sefirah of Yesod. Thus, the Light of Yesod is found both in Malchut and in Yesod. It is in the same way regarding the Returning Light that Hod receives, for surely as it passed, it acquired its place both in Malchut and Yesod. So now there are three Lights in Malchut, two in Yesod, and one in Hod. Likewise, is the last aspect of Returning Light that Keter received, for then the Ten Lights of the Ten Sefirot of Returning Light are already present in Malchut, in Yesod are nine Lights, and in Hod are eight Lights, and so on, in the same way that was explained regarding the Ten Sefirot of Direct Light.

Through the Returning Light being included by way of passing,
Ten Sefirot were fixed in each and every Sefirah.
In Keter there are nine Sefirot of Direct Light and one of Returning Light.

106. Therefore the outcome is that we have Ten Sefirot in every one of the said Ten Sefirot, namely, combined with Returning Light. In other words, the Light of Malchut received in each and every Sefirah brings the number to Ten Sefirot. In Keter there are nine Sefirot of Direct Light: Keter, Chochmah, Binah, Chesed, Gevurah, Tiferet, Netzach, Hod, and Yesod, and one Sefirah of Returning Light, which is Malchut, since Keter is the last to receive Returning Light, as said. It therefore has but one Light of Returning Light.

In Chochmah there are eight Sefirot of Direct Light and two of Returning Light.
In Binah there are seven of Direct Light and three of Returning Light.

107. Chochmah has eight Sefirot of Direct Light, which are: Chochmah, Binah, Chesed, Gevurah, Tiferet, Netzach, Hod, and Yesod, and two Sefirot

of Returning Light, one is its own portion that it received from the Returning Light of Malchut, which is Yesod of Returning Light, and the other is the portion of Keter that passed through it and never moved from there, which is Malchut of Returning Light, as said. Binah has seven Lights of Direct Light, which are: Binah, Chesed, Gevurah, Tiferet, Netzach, Hod, and Yesod, and three Sefirot of Returning Light: Hod, Yesod, and Malchut. Hod from itself, Yesod from the portion of Chochmah that passed through it, and Malchut from the portion of Keter that passed through it, that is, from Binah up, as said.

> **In Chesed are six of Direct Light and four of Returning Light.**
> **In Gevurah are five of Direct Light and five of Returning Light.**
> **In Tiferet are four of Direct Light and six of Returning Light.**

108. Chesed has six Sefirot of Direct Light, which are: Chesed, Gevurah, Tiferet, Netzach, Hod, and Yesod, and four Sefirot of Returning Light, which are those from Chesed up; namely, its own portion, which is Netzach, and the portions of Binah, Chochmah, and Keter, which are Hod, Yesod, and Malchut that passed through it and were set there, as said. In the same way, Gevurah has five Sefirot of Direct Light, which are: Gevurah, Tiferet, Netzach, Hod, and Yesod, and five Sefirot of Returning Light from Gevurah up, namely, the four portions of Keter, Chochmah, Binah, and Chesed, which are Netzach, Hod, Yesod, and Malchut that passed through it, plus its own portion that is Tiferet of Returning Light. Tiferet has four Sefirot of Direct Light, which are from Tiferet down, and six Sefirot of Returning Light from Tiferet up, namely the five portions of Keter Chochmah, Binah, Chesed, and Gevurah, which are Tiferet, Netzach, Hod, Yesod, and Malchut that passed through it, plus its own portion that is Gevurah of Returning Light.

> **In Netzach are three of Direct Light and seven of Returning Light.**
> **In Hod are two of Direct Light and eight of Returning Light.**
> **In Yesod are one of Direct Light and nine of Returning Light.**
> **Malchut contains Ten Sefirot of Returning Light.**

109. Netzach has three Sefirot of Direct Light, which are from Netzach down, which are Netzach, Hod, and Yesod of Direct Light, and seven Sefirot of Returning Light that are from Netzach up, which are the six

portions of Keter, Chochmah, Binah, Chesed, Gevurah, and Tiferet that passed through it, which are Gevurah, Tiferet, Netzach, Hod, Yesod, and Malchut, as well as its own portion, Chesed of Returning Light. Hod has two Sefirot of Direct Light, Hod, and Yesod, and eight of Returning Light from Hod up, which are the seven portions of Keter, Chochmah, Binah, Chesed, Gevurah, Tiferet, and Netzach that passed through it, which are Chesed, Gevurah, Tiferet, Netzach, Hod, Yesod, and Malchut of Returning Light, plus its own portion that is the Binah of Returning Light. Yesod has one Sefirah of Direct Light and nine Sefirot of Returning Light from Yesod up. These are the eight portions of Keter, Chochmah, Binah, Chesed, Gevurah, Tiferet, Netzach, and Hod that passed through it, which are Binah, Chesed, Gevurah, Tiferet, Netzach, Hod, Yesod, and Malchut of Returning Light, plus its own portion, which is Chochmah of Returning Light.

Malchut, with her Returning Light, completes each and every Sefirah into Ten Sefirot.

110. It has been well explained that in every aspect of revelation of the Ten Sefirot, wherever they may be, they need to comprise each other as soon as the Ten Sefirot of Direct Light emerge. Still none has Ten Sefirot until the Light of Malchut is included in them, namely the Ten Sefirot of Returning Light, because it has no other Light, as said. So this Light of Malchut completes the count to Ten Sefirot in whatever is missing, in each of the Ten Sefirot, until there are Ten Sefirot in each of them.

The same applies to the subdivision of the subdivision. When you take Keter of the Ten Sefirot of Keter, it too necessarily has nine Sefirot of Direct Light and one of Returning Light.

111. Take for example, now the general Sefirah of Keter of the general Ten Sefirot, which itself already comprises Ten individual Sefirot, as said. This means that after the Light of Malchut was revealed there, we can immediately infer that the first Sefirah of the general Keter, now called Keter of Keter, or sub-Keter, of necessity comprises the nine Sefirot of Direct Light that are present in it below, which are Chochmah, Binah, Chesed, Gevurah, Tiferet, Netzach, Hod, and Yesod of Direct Light in Keter.

**Keter of Keter is the aspect of itself,
whereas the nine lower Sefirot are but passing Lights.**

112. Even though only their Keter is the aspect of itself, its other nine sub-Sefirot are considered passing Lights only, that is, lower Lights that acquired their place there in passing from the Ein Sof to the Sefirot below Keter. Nevertheless, since they are present in Keter, it must be that the higher Sefirah, which is their sub-Keter, now includes in itself the nine sub-Sefirot found in it below it, for since these nine Sefirot are below it, of necessity they have passed through it. Once they did, they necessarily acquired a place in it, as there is no lack in spirituality, exactly as discussed in relation to the general Ten Sefirot. This way, this sub-Keter in itself comprises Ten sub-Sefirot, which are the nine Sefirot of Direct Light: Keter, Chochmah, Binah, Chesed, Gevurah, Netzach, Hod, and Yesod, and one of Returning Light, which is the Light of Malchut, the same as with Keter of the Ten general Sefirot.

**Similarly, Chochmah of Keter necessarily has eight Sefirot of Direct Light
and two of Returning Light.**

113. In exactly the same way, when you consider the individual Chochmah of the Ten sub-Sefirot of general Keter, which is called Chochmah of Keter, it surely now has Ten sub-Sefirot in the same way we explained in relation to the said sub-Keter. For all eight sub-Sefirot of general Keter of Direct Light that are below it, of necessity, passed through sub-Chochmah from above downward. Once they passed through it, they necessarily acquired a place in it. This, together with two Sefirot of Returning Light from the Light of sub-Malchut that also passed through that sub-Chochmah on its way up, which are its own Returning Light portion and the portion of Returning Light that pertains to sub-Keter. Thus there are Ten sub-Sefirot even in the individual Chochmah of general Keter, the same way there are in the general Chochmah of the general Ten Sefirot.

**Similarly, Binah of Keter has seven Sefirot of Direct Light and
three of Returning Light.**

114. In exactly the same way, when you consider the individual Binah of the Ten sub-Sefirot of general Keter, which is called Binah of Keter, you

will surely find that it has now Ten sub-Sefirot, as was discussed by the sub-Chochmah. All six sub-Sefirot: Chesed, Gevurah, Tiferet, Netzach, Hod, and Yesod of the general Keter of Direct Light that are below it, of necessity, passed downward through the sub-Binah and acquired their place within it. Now they are, together with Binah itself, seven Sefirot of Direct Light. Similarly, the three sub-Sefirot of Returning Light passed through that Binah from the individual Malchut of the general Keter upward. These include Binah's own portion of Returning Light, the Returning Light portion of the individual Chochmah, and the Returning Light portion of individual Keter. Thus there are ten sub-Sefirot in the individual Binah of the Ten Sefirot of general Keter, exactly as with the general Binah of the general Ten Sefirot.

Similarly, Chesed of Keter has six Sefirot of Direct Light and four of Returning Light, and so on.

115. In exactly the same way, you find Ten sub Sefirot within the individual Chesed of the Ten individual Sefirot of general Keter, which are six of Direct Light from above downward: Chesed, Gevurah, Tiferet, Netzach, Hod, and Yesod, and the four of Returning Light from Chesed up to Keter. In exactly the same way, you find Ten sub-Sefirot within Gevurah, and so on down to the individual Malchut of those Ten Sefirot, which is called Malchut of Keter.

116. You should not raise the question that the Ten individual Sefirot of general Keter only have, from the Returning Light rising from general Malchut, the Nefesh part alone, namely the last portion of Returning Light that is the least of all Ten Sefirot of Returning Light as said (see Section 112), so how can we say that this small part of Returning Light expands itself now into Ten new Sefirot of Returning Light to complete each individual Sefirah with all the sub-Sefirot it lacks to be Ten Sefirot?

The Nefesh of Returning Light within the general Keter, of necessity, divides to clothe the Ten individual Sefirot in Keter.

117. However, the answer is that eventually it must be that the individual Nefesh part of the Returning Light that ascended from Malchut to general

Keter, of necessity, clothed there all nine individual Sefirot present in the general Keter. Otherwise, the nine Sefirot of Direct Light would not have clicked and shone in the general Partzuf, as is known that it is not possible for the Direct Light to connect with the Partzuf except through the Vessel of Receiving aspect of Returning Light, as said. And since this Light of Nefesh clothed the nine individual Sefirot within Keter, it is found of necessity that as it passed from below upward it completed the number of the sub-Sefirot to be Ten in each of those individual Sefirot. To Chochmah it gave the two Lights it lacked: one Light to clothe it, and a second Light on its way to clothe Keter. To Binah it gave three and to Chesed four, as explained before.

The same applies to the Ten sub-Sefirot of each of the individual Sefirot within the general Chochmah. The Keter within it has nine Sefirot of Direct Light and one of Returning Light.

118. The same explanation regarding the Ten sub Sefirot in the Ten individual Sefirot of general Keter applies to the Ten sub-Sefirot within each of the Ten individual Sefirot of the general Sefirah of Chochmah. In the Keter of the Ten individual Sefirot of the general Chochmah, called Keter of Chochmah, you will surely find Ten sub-Sefirot, which are its own particular Light, and eight individual Sefirot: Binah, Chesed, Gevurah, Tiferet, Netzach, Hod, and Yesod that passed through it from above downward. This adds up to nine. Add one Returning Light coming up from the individual Malchut of the general Chochmah, and thus you have Ten sub-Sefirot within the Keter of the general Chochmah.

The sub-Chochmah of the individual Chochmah has eight Sefirot of Direct Light and two of Returning Light.

119. In the same way, the sub-Chochmah of the Ten individual Sefirot of the general Chochmah, called Chochmah of Chochmah, has eight of Direct Light from above downward and two of Returning Light from below upward. Similarly, the sub-Binah of the Ten individual Sefirot of the general Chochmah has seven of Direct Light from above downward and three of Returning Light from below upward. The same way with Chesed, the same way with Gevurah, and so on, until the sub-Malchut of the Ten Sefirot of the general Chochmah, which is called Malchut

of Chochmah. It too has Ten sub-Sefirot of Returning Light since, of necessity, it clothes all Ten individual Sefirot of the general Chochmah and sends them its Illuminations, as said, so we find that, of necessity, they all passed through it and acquired their place within in, as said.

120. In exactly the same way, we distinguish Ten sub-Sefirot in the individual Binah. The same applies to sub-Chesed, sub-Gevurah, all the way to sub-Malchut. There is no need to expound this further. Instead, let us further discuss about one sub-Sefirah to show how it in itself is considered, under the same requirement, Ten Sefirot in itself, which are now Ten sub-Sefirot of a sub-Sefirah of an individual Sefirah.

121. When we want to distinguish a sub-Binah, which is for example, one of the Ten sub-Sefirot in the individual Chochmah of the Ten Sefirot of general Chochmah, which is called Binah of Chochmah of Chochmah, you will find within it alone Ten Sefirot in the same way mentioned before: seven of Direct Light that passed through it from above downward and three of Returning Light that passed through it from below upward.

122. And so you can subdivide and distinguish like this endlessly. If you take any Sefirah, even after the thousandth subdivision, that Sefirah is always taken out of a Ten-Sefirot sequence. Of necessity, some of those Sefirot passed through that Sefirah from below upward. This way, those Ten Sefirot, of necessity, acquired an eternal place in that Sefirah, as said. Thus, you necessarily have all Ten Sefirot in that Sefirah. Understand this well!

123. However, understand that even when you subdivide one set of Ten into another set of Ten, and the second set of Ten into the third, and so on, do not imagine that all Sefirot remain the same. Rather, they go and change greatly as they divide, and one is not equal to another. The reason is that all the Lights of Direct Light always come, not in their place, in the process of the subdivision in all the Sefirot, except Keter. In Chochmah there are just eight Sefirot of Direct Light, namely from Chochmah down, and two of Returning Light, which are Yesod and Malchut. If so, the eight Lights of Direct Light come in the Vessels that are more pure, as said, namely from Keter to Hod, and the two of Returning Light in Yesod and

Malchut. Thus, the Light of Chochmah comes in the Vessel of Keter, the Light of Binah in the Vessel of Chochmah, and so on down until the Light of Yesod in the Vessel of Hod. Thus, the Lights of Direct Light all come not in their place, but only the Returning Light comes always in its place. The Returning Light of Yesod comes in the Vessel of Yesod, and the Returning Light of Malchut in the Vessel of Malchut.

124. In this way, Binah that has only seven Lights of Direct Light are received in the purer Vessels, as mentioned earlier that every recipient receives with its purer part, namely from Keter to Netzach. We find that the Light of Binah is in the Vessel of Keter, the Light of Chesed in Chochmah, until the Light of Yesod in the Vessel of Netzach. Only the three Lights of Returning Lights arrive in their proper place: Hod, Yesod, and Malchut in the Vessels of Hod, Yesod, and Malchut.

125. According to what was explained, there is a great difference between the individual Binah of Keter, the individual Binah of Chochmah, and the individual Binah of Binah, and so on, because only in Binah of Keter is the Light of Binah in its Vessel. This is not the case with Binah of Chochmah, where the Light of Chesed is in the Vessel of Binah, and in Binah of Binah there is only the Light of Gevurah in the Vessel of Binah, and so on with all of them. Thus, no one is like the other.

126. Even in the Lights of Returning Light, which do not switch their place as mentioned, changes can nevertheless be detected in the dividing process. This is because an Illumination of Direct Light extends to the Returning Light wherever it may be. Therefore, if we take Yesod of Chochmah for example, an Illumination of Direct Light from Hod of Chochmah extends to it. But as for Yesod of Binah, an Illumination extends to it from Netzach of Binah, since there is no Direct Light in Hod of Binah, as said.

127. The one exception is when you specifically divide only the same general and sub-Sefirah, meaning if you take, for example, the general Sefirah of Binah and divide it from Ten into Ten. For example, if you subdivide the sub-Binah of the Ten individual Sefirot of the Ten Sefirot of the general Binah, which is called the Binah of Binah of Binah, then they will all be equal to each other without any difference. All of them will contain seven

Sefirot of Direct Light: Keter, Chochmah, Binah, Chesed, Gevurah, Tiferet, and Netzach, and three of Returning Light in the Lower Vessels: Hod, Yesod, and Malchut, even if you divide it for the thousandth time. And the same applies to the other Sefirot.

CHAPTER 10

Chapter 10 explains the subject of Binding by Striking (*Zivug deHaka'ah*) that includes two forces: the force that pulls and the force that rejects. They act simultaneously, one by the density and the other by the rigidity of the Masach, respectively.

An extended explanation of the meaning of the phrase Binding by Striking.

128. This subject of Binding by Striking requires an extensive explanation, for there is seemingly an implication of both positive and negative together. One is binding and the other is striking, which means rejection, separation, and great hatred. How then can there be a Unification by Striking, which means a love of hate, or a cleaving of separation, or attraction of rejection? This is seemingly very confusing.

129. Indeed it is true that they are two opposites in one force, yet this control is made of two unique matters, namely two forces: the pulling force and the repelling force. The pulling force lies in the density of the Vessel and the repelling force lies in the Vessel's Masach. They were embedded within each other so both have simultaneous influence in two places.

130. In order for me to clarify well so as to make this acceptable without raising any confusion or perplexity, I shall discuss it a little further. Let me use an allegory, drawing on the physical reality that we can see and grasp. When, for example, you see a man or a stone falling to the ground from a high place, it is evident that the man is pulled down with great force and speed. Yet when he reaches and touches the earth, the earth hits him and bounces him back up a little.

131. There are two opinions regarding this. One is that planet Earth extends a great gravitational pull on anything placed in the air of the skies, unless it has something solid to protect it. Therefore, when a man is, for example, detached from a rooftop to the air, immediately the gravitational force of Earth has power over him. This explains the fall down to the

ground at great speed. However, there is a doubt here, since according to this the Earth should have hugged him with great love without him being able to move even for an instance. Yet we see the opposite. The moment he touches it, it immediately pushes him back quickly and he retreats back up a little.

132. Corresponding to this is another opinion that there is a type of repelling force above from the planet's atmosphere that acts on whatever is in the air and repels it toward the ground, and Earth too, has just the repelling force and nothing of the pulling force. Therefore, when a man is pushed from a rooftop into the air, the repelling force immediately applies on him and pushes him down to Earth. So when he touches the earth, it repels him back up again.

133. However, if we compare the branch to its root in the Supernal Realms, where in the majority of the matters they are aligned with each other, we find that both opinions are incorrect. We can say even here that each sphere has the pulling force and the repelling force interwoven into each other. That is, it has the force of density, which is the pulling force, to draw within it all that is outside it. And it has, opposite to it, the force of resistance that repels any external body from penetrating into it. Thus, any pulling is surely activated by the force of the central point in its interior, as this is where its pulling force lies, for the central point is denser than the rest of the sphere. And therefore, it pulls to itself all that is found in the surrounding space under its dominion and force.

134. Nevertheless, it does not pull anything to the point of absorbing it, as would have been stipulated by its pulling force alone. Rather, as soon as the pulled object touches its outer shell, the repelling force that lies in its shell, which is the resistance, is immediately awakened and pushes it back up.

135. Thus, the object it pulled to itself came to be received, not by its pull but in a different way, for it stops midway due to the force of resistance that rejects it and stops it in its way, as explained. So Binding and Striking work together here, as the Binding is what attracts and the resistance is what repels, and this way it accepts the object to it, yet does not swallow it

alive into its belly. This way you can say that the mainstay of the Vessel of Receiving is its repelling force that accepts the object and holds it properly. Were it not for the repelling force, the object would have been swallowed and gone down alive into the abyss.

136. See also that pulling and repelling are evenly balanced in strength, like two drops of water. Had the pulling force been a little stronger than the repelling force, the object would have had no possibility of moving upon it, for it would have been glued to it as iron to a magnet. And had the repelling force been somewhat stronger, the whole universe could have danced upon it unable to touch it. Thus they are even.

137. In this manner, you will understand well about Binding by Striking that applies on High. Even though Unification and Striking are opposites, they nevertheless partner together in simultaneous control, though in two places: density and resistance, as said. Remember this throughout this wisdom.

TABLES OF
QUESTIONS AND ANSWERS

TERMINOLOGY QUESTIONS

1. What is Adam Kadmon?
2. What is Returning Light?
3. What is Direct Light?
4. What is Surrounding Light?
5. What is Inner Light?
6. What is Length?
7. What is Binah?
8. What is Unattached?
9. What is Boundary?
10. What is Roof?
11. What is Body?
12. What is Wheel?
13. What are the Upper Three Sefirot?
14. What is Physicality?
15. What is Way of Passing?
16. What is Illumination from Afar?
17. What is Purification of the Masach?
18. What is Complete Distancing?
19. What is Bowing the Head?
20. What is the Inclusion of the Sefirot
21. What is Connecting?
22. What is One within the Other?
23. What is Binding by Striking?
24. What is Zeir Anpin?
25. What are the Lower Seven Sefirot?
26. What is Material?
27. What is Chayah?
28. What is Exteriority?
29. What is Chochmah?

30. What is Window?

31. What is Yechidah?

32. What is "Going Outside Of"?

33. What is Descent?

34. What is Straight?

35. What is Keter?

36. What is Slowly and Gradually?

37. What does "Connects" mean?

38. What are the Waters of Light?

39. What is Malchut?

40. What is "From Above Downward'?

41. What is "From below Upward'?

42. What is Circling?

43. What is Masach?

44. What is Surrounding?

45. What is Nullified?

46. What is Drawn?

47. What is Nefesh?

48. What is Nefesh, Ruach, Neshamah, Chayah, and Yechidah?

49. What is Neshamah?

50. What is Encircling?

51. What is Ending?

52. What is meant by "Close"?

53. What is Density?

54. What is meant by "Passing Through"?

55. What is Higher and Lower?

56. What is Essence?

57. What is Interiority?

58. What are Interior and Exterior?

59. What is Channel?

60. What is Line?

61. What is an Erect Posture?

62. What is Ration?

63. What is Ground?

64. What is Head?

65. What is Ruach?

66. What is Spirituality?

67. What is Far?

68. What is the Beginning of the Extension?

69. What is Immediately?

70. What is the Objective of All?

SUBJECT QUESTIONS

71. What is the source of the Circular Vessels?

72. What are the Impressions that remained in the Circles after the Tzimtzum?

73. Why are the Circles one within the other?

74. Why is there no aspect of "one within the other" in the Endless?

75. What is the root for all Lights?

76. What is the root for all Vessels?

77. What is the source of Returning Light?

78. Why do Lights precede Vessels?

79. Why does Binah not precede Chochmah?

80. From where is the Source of the ruling power in the Worlds?

81. Where does the Masach come from?

82. How many causes preceded the Masach?

83. What is the source of Direct Light?

84. From where do the Circles receive Light?

85. How do the Circles receive Light from each other?

86. Why do the Circles have to receive from the Sefirot of Straightness?

87. What are the windows in the roof and at the bottom of every Circle?

88. What caused the Circles to be one below the other?

89. Why do the Circles need to be connected by the Line?

90. What is the difference between the Sefirot of Straightness and the Circular Sefirot?

91. Why is the force of Tzimtzum insufficient so that a Masach is needed as well?

92. What are the Direct Lights?

93. What is the difference between a Straight Illumination and a Curling Illumination?

94. In what way are the Circles better than the Sefirot of Straightness?

95. In what way are the Sefirot of Straightness better than the Circles?

96. Why is it that in the Circles whatever is Exterior is better?

97. Why is it that in the Vessels of Straightness whatever is Interior is better?

98. Why is the World of Asiyah external to all the Worlds?

99. What caused the emergence of the Masach?

100. When was the Masach made?

101. Why does the quality of the Masach depend on the density of the Fourth Phase?

102. What are the Vessels of Receiving in the Light of the Line?

103. What are the two kinds of Ten Sefirot in every Emanated Being?

104. Why is Returning Light considered a Vessel of Receiving?

105. How is the size of the Returning Light determined?

106. Why is Malchut considered Keter of Returning Light?

107. Why do the Masach and the density apply as one?

108. Why are density and Returning Light interdependent?

109. By what means is the Masach purified?

110. Why are the Circular Sefirot considered as Nefesh?

111. Why are the Sefirot of Straightness considered as Ruach?

112. What is the advantage of the Upper Three Sefirot of Straightness?

113. How are the Sefirot of Straightness positioned within the Circles?

114. Why are the Circles situated in the Upper Three Sefirot of Straightness?

115. What is the distance between any two Circles?

116. Why don't the Circles circle the Lower Seven Sefirot of Straightness?

117. Why is it forbidden to study the Upper Three Sefirot of any level?

118. Is it forbidden to study all Ten sub-Sefirot within the Upper Three Sefirot?

119. Why do we not study about the Circular Sefirot?

120. How are the Ten Sefirot divided into the Five Aspects of Desire?

121. What is exactly meant by "ten, not nine; ten, not eleven"?

122. Why is the Desire to Receive not revealed all at once?

123. Why is density considered Interior?

124. Why is the Interior specifically considered a Vessel of Receiving?

125. How is the size of the Worlds, great or small, measured?

126. Why was the Light gone from the Upper Three Sefirot as well during the Tzimtzum?

127. What are the three distinctions in the Vessels?

128. What are the two distinctions in Spiritual Matter?

129. Until what point is the Emanated Being considered as still belonging to the higher?

130. When does the Emanated Being become its own domain?

131. What is meant by "unable"?

132. What is meant by "does not intend"?

133. Why is the First Phase considered "unable and does not intend"?

134. Why is the Second Phase considered "able but does not intend"?

135. Why is the Third Phase considered "unable but intends"?

136. Why is the Fourth Phase considered "able and intends"?

137. Why, of all Phases of Desires, is the Fourth Phase alone fit to be a Vessel of Receiving?

138. Why does every change of form that occurs in the density of the Fourth Phase emerge as a new Emanated Being?

139. Why does the Supernal Light never cease from shining on the Emanated Beings, even for a moment?

140. What is the difference between the aspect of bestowing abundance and the aspect of receiving in the Vessels?

141. Why does a giver give upon the densest, but the receiver receives with the purest?

142. How is newness of form understood in the spreading of Supernal Light?

143. How does an Emanated Being come out of the aspect of the Supernal Light?

144. What is the difference between the names of the Four Phases and the names of Keter, Chochmah, Binah, Zeir Anpin, and Nukvah?

145. What is the order of the entering of Lights in the Emanated Being after the Correction?

146. What is the order of the growth of the Vessels in any Partzuf after the Correction?

147. What is the primal material of every Emanated Being?

148. What are the two Crowns in every level?

149. Why is the Light not absent from one place when moving to another?

150. In what way does any higher being include all that are below it?

151. In what way does any lower being include all that is above it?

152. What is the key to finding the distinctions among the Sefirot that comprise each other?

153. What are the aspects of Direct Light and the aspects of Returning Light present in Keter?

154. What are the aspects of Direct Light and the aspects of Returning Light present in Chochmah?

155. What are the aspects of Direct Light and the aspects of Returning Light present in Binah?

156. What are the aspects of Direct Light and the aspects of Returning Light present in Chesed?

157. What are the aspects of Direct Light and the aspects of Returning Light present in Gevurah?

158. What are the aspects of Direct Light and the aspects of Returning Light present in Tiferet?

159. What are the aspects of Direct Light and the aspects of Returning Light present in Netzach?

160. What are the aspects of Direct Light and the aspects of Returning Light present in Hod?

161. What are the aspects of Direct Light and the aspects of Returning Light present in Yesod?

162. What are the aspects of Direct Light and the aspects of Returning Light present in Malchut?

163. What are the aspects of Direct Light and the aspects of Returning Light present in Keter of Keter?

164. What are the aspects of Direct Light and the aspects of Returning Light present in Chochmah of Keter?

165. What are the aspects of Direct Light and the aspects of Returning Light present in Binah of Keter?

166. What are the aspects of Direct Light and the aspects of Returning Light present in Chesed of Keter of Keter?

167. What are the aspects of Direct Light and the aspects of Returning Light present in Gevurah of Chochmah of Netzach?

168. What are the aspects of Direct Light and the aspects of Returning Light present in Tiferet of Binah of Hod?

169. What are the aspects of Direct Light and the aspects of Returning Light present in Netzach of Yesod of Keter?

170. What are the aspects of Direct Light and the aspects of Returning Light present in Hod of Tiferet of Malchut?

171. How are the Lights of Direct Light and Returning Light encased in the Vessels?

172. What is the sequence of cause and effect from the Endless to Malchut of Adam Kadmon?

TERMINOLOGY ANSWERS

1. **Adam Kadmon** (Volume 2, Chapter 1, Inner Light, Section 22)
   It is the first World to receive from the Endless. It is also called a Line that is immediately drawn after the Tzimtzum, from the Endless until close to this World. The name Adam (Human) relates only to the Sefirot of Straightness in the first World, which is the Light of Ruach, which means the Light of Sharing. It does not relate to its Circular Sefirot that have only the Light of Nefesh, which means a Light of Receiving for Themselves without being able to share with others. And it is the root for the human aspect in this World.

2. **Returning Light** (Volume 2, Inner Observation, Section 79)
   It is the Light that is not received in the Fourth Phase. Meaning, it is the Light meant to fill the Fourth Phase but is not received by it due to the Masach that obstructs it and pushes it back. This action is called Binding by Striking (see Inner Observation, Section 22). All the Vessels of Receiving in the Partzufim from the Tzimtzum onward are drawn from this Returning Light, which serves for them instead of the Fourth Phase in the Endless.

3. **Direct Light** (Volume 2, Inner Observation, Section 94)
   It is the Supernal Light that is drawn from the Endless and bestowed upon the Partzufim after the Tzimtzum onward. It is so called to indicate that it is not bestowed on the Circular Vessels, nor any other grade that has none of the density of the Fourth Phase, but only on the Sefirot of Straightness alone. This accords with the rule that a giver only gives to the densest, which is the density of the Fourth Phase.

4. **Surrounding Light** (Volume 2, Chapter 1, Inner Light, Section 13)
   It is the Light intended to be clothed in the level but is obstructed due to a boundary there. Within this name there are two implications. The first is that it is an Illumination from afar, and the second is that it is a guaranteed Illumination, which means that eventually it is destined to enter there, since the Light surrounds it around and gives it no place to escape from it until it is ready to receive it completely.

5. **Inner Light** (Volume 2, Chapter 1, Inner Light, Section 13)
   It is the Light clothed in the Vessel.

6. **Length** (Volume 2, Chapter 2, Inner Light, Section 26)
   The distance between the two extremities in the level, in other words from the purest part to the densest part, is called length, for this also applies to physical length that alludes to the space between something's upper end and lower end.

7. **Binah** (Volume 2, Chapter 1, Inner Light, Section 20)
    The contemplation of the ways of cause and effect to find out all the outcomes that result and emerge from something is called Binah.

8. **Unattached** (Volume 2, Chapter 1, Inner Light, Section 9)
    The Similarity of Form between two spiritual entities is Cleaving (*Dvekut*), while the Difference of Form between them makes them unattached to each other.

9. **Boundary** (Volume 2, Inner Observation, Section 79)
    The Masach that is in any level calculates and makes a boundary on the level, in the Stature of the Returning Light that the Masach raises (see Number 2, Returning Light) by the extent of its density. The Masach of the Third Phase limits the Stature of the level from attaining the Light of Keter, and the Masach of the Second Phase limits it also from the Light of Chochmah, and so on.

10. **Roof** (Volume 2, Chapter 2, Inner Light, Section 1)
    It is the Keter in any level, as well as in the Sefirot and the Worlds.

11. **Body** (Volume 2, Chapter 2, Inner Light, Section 3)
    The true Vessels of Receiving in any level, which spread below the Masach by the power of the Returning Light in it, are called the Body of the level, since they follow the Lights. This does not include the Lights that spread down for Binding by Striking over the Masach, as they precede the Vessels.

12. **Wheel** (Volume 2, Chapter 1, Inner Light, Section 8)
    The Circular Sefirot are called Wheels, since the Lights curl in them. In other words, we cannot recognize in them purity and density.

13. **Upper Three Sefirot** (Volume 2, Chapter 1, Inner Light, Section 18)
    These are the Lights that preceded the Vessels, which are clothed by Returning Light that rises toward them up from the Masach, namely the Upper Three Sefirot: Keter, Chochmah, and Binah; or the head of the Partzuf.

14. **Physicality**
    All that can be grasped or sensed by the five senses or that occupies space and time is called physical.

15. **Way of Passing** (Volume 2, Chapter 1, Inner Light, Section 26)
    The Lights that flow from the Endless to the Lower Sefirot, of necessity, pass through the Upper Sefirot, and since the Spiritual Entity does not disappear from one place when it passes to another place, but it stays both in the first place and in the second place, we therefore distinguish two kinds of Lights in every Sefirah: the Lights

that are their own and the Lights that remained in them "by Way of Passing."

16. **Illumination from Afar** (Volume 2, Chapter 1, Inner Light, Section 13)
The Illumination that applies in the Partzuf when the Partzuf has no Vessel to receive that Light is called "Illumination from Afar." The implication is that there is a great distance and difference between the Light and the Vessels of the Partzuf that are associated with that Light, for which reason the Vessels are not fit to receive and clothe that Light but instead receive from it an Illumination from Afar.

17. **Purification of the Masach** (Volume 2, Inner Observation, Section 74)
This is the purification of the density in the Fourth Phase. The Stature of the Returning Light that the Masach raises and that encases the Direct Light depends on the extent of density in the Fourth Phase (see Number 2, Returning Light), which refers to the amount of yearning in it. Therefore, after a grade is filled with its own Light it drew, the Surrounding Light intensifies and purifies the Masach to the extent of the amount of yearning. This is considered that it was purified from its density. This is also called the "Purification of the Masach."

18. **Complete Distancing** (Volume 2, Chapter 1, Section 8 of the Ari)
When the Difference of Form is so great to the point it becomes opposite of form from end to end, it is called "Complete Distancing."

19. **Bowing the Head** (Volume 2, Chapter 2, Inner Light, Section 3)
When the Lights of the Lower Seven are used in the Head called the Upper Three, since the Lights of the Upper Three that are meant for the Head are not there, this is called "Bowing the Head." This means that the Head is lowered to be on the same level as the Lower Seven that are called Body.

20. **Inclusion of the Sefirot** (Volume 2, Inner Observation, Section 97)
The Sefirot include each other by "Way of Passing" (see Number 15, Way of Passing). The Ten Sefirot of Direct Light that flow down from Keter to Malchut cannot appear in a grade except by them being clothed in the Ten Sefirot of Returning Light that flow and ascend from Malchut to Keter. Therefore, each of these Sefirot has two Sefirot in itself: one of Direct Light and one of Returning Light, as well as eight extra Sefirot that are included in it by way of passing, where some passed through it from above downward and some passed through it from below upward.

21. **Connecting** (Volume 2, Chapter 1, Inner Light, Section 11)
The encasing of the Ten Sefirot of the grade's Head with the Ten Sefirot of Returning Light that rise from Malchut is called "Connecting." The reason is that it is considered here that Lights

precede the Vessels, since no density rises even a little with this Returning Light higher than its place, which is Malchut, and therefore the Ten Sefirot of Returning Light are not considered Complete Vessels fit to clothe the essence in them. This is why this encasing is only called "Connecting," that is, the Direct Light connects and rests on the Partzuf by means of these Ten Sefirot of Returning Light, even though it is not really clothed in them. The clothing of the Direct Light within the Vessels is only said when the Returning Light spreads below the Masach, where the density of the Malchut of the Head can extend, descend, and clothe the Ten Sefirot of Direct Light entering it.

22. **One Within the Other** (Volume 2, Chapter 2, Inner Light, Section 13)
This means one causing the other. Any Outer Circle is understood to be the cause and reason for the Inner Circle within it that is an effect and outcome of the Outer, in such a way that "One Within the Other" indicates a relationship of cause and effect, that is, reason and consequence, between them.

23. **Binding by Striking** (Volume 2, Inner Observation, Section 18)
The action of the Masach that prevents and hides the Light from the Fourth Phase, rejecting the Light belonging to it back to its root, is called Binding by Striking. The implication of this name indicates that this action carries within it two opposites: on the one hand it "strikes" the Light, which means it rejects and hides it from shining. On the other hand, it "binds" with the Light, which means it causes it to greatly increase and expand, for the degree of Light that is hidden and rejected from the Fourth Phase turns into a great, revealed Light that encases the Direct Light, which is called Returning Light, and without which the Light of the Endless cannot possibly be clothed in the Partzuf.

24. **Zeir Anpin** (Volume 3, Chapter 1, Inner Light, Section 27)
Zeir Anpin means "Small Face," for the Light of Chochmah is called the "Light of the Face," in the secret of the verse, "A man's wisdom lights up his face." (Ecclesiastes 8:1) This is why the general Partzuf of Keter in the World of Atzilut is called Arich Anpin (Long Face), which means a large face, since it contains the essence of the Light of Chochmah. Therefore, the Third Phase, whose essence is merely the Light of Chasadim that flows from Binah, yet contains an Illumination from Chochmah but not the essence of the Light of Chochmah, is called a Small Face or Zeir Anpin, as its facial Light is reduced and diminished compared to the First Phase.

25. **Lower Seven Sefirot** (Volume 2 Chapter 1, Inner Light, Section 18)
The Ten Sefirot that flow from the Masach downward are called "Body" or "Lower Seven Sefirot" (see Number 11, Body). When a Partzuf is

sometimes considered as only Ten Sefirot, its First Three Sefirot are Keter, Chochmah, and Binah in the Head of the Partzuf, and the Lower Seven Sefirot are Chesed, Gevurah, Tiferet, Netzach, Hod, Yesod, and Malchut in the Body of the Partzuf.

26. **Material** (Volume 2, Inner Observation, Section 40)
The density of the Partzuf from the Fourth Phase of Desire (see Number 53, Density) is called the "material" of the Partzuf. This name is borrowed from the physical, graspable material that has three dimensions: length, width, and depth; and six directions: up, down, east, west, north, and south.

27. **Chayah** (Volume 2, Chapter 2, Inner Light, Section 6)
This is the Light of Chochmah (Wisdom), based on the verse, "Wisdom gives life to those who have it." (Ecclesiastes 7:12)

28. **Exteriority** (Volume 2, Inner Observation, Section 6)
The purest part of any Vessel is considered its "Exterior." It is considered a Vessel to the Surrounding Light that shines on it from afar.

29. **Chochmah (Wisdom)** (Volume 2, Chapter 1, Inner Light, Sections 20-21)
Knowing the end results of all the details that exist in reality is called wisdom.

30. **Window** (Volume 2, Chapter 2, Inner Light, Section 16)
The force derived from the density of the Masach that is distinguished in the Ten Sefirot of the Head of a level or in the Ten Sefirot of the Circles that acts upon them together with the Returning Light that rises to them from the Masach is called a "Window." Meaning, the Returning Light rejected by the Fourth Phase due to its density becomes a Vessel of Receiving for the Supernal Light instead of the Fourth Phase that served as a Vessel of Receiving in the Endless. The reason is that the Returning Light truly includes within it the density of the Fourth Phase, since it [is the Fourth Phase that] drew it to itself from the Endless (see Inner Observation, Section 79)

Yet this density is only apparent in the Vessels of the Body since they spread below the Masach, meaning below the Fourth Phase of the Ten Sefirot of the Head. The density of the Fourth Phase therefore governs them, and thus they are considered Complete Vessels for the Supernal Light to be clothed in them. This is not the case with the Ten Sefirot of the Head, which are of necessity above their Fourth Phase. It is just that the Returning Light rises up to them, and the density of the Fourth Phase within the Masach cannot be included in and rise with the Returning Light above its place to the nine Sefirot above it. Therefore, this Returning Light does not become Complete Vessels there, but only the aspect of roots for the Vessels alone.

For that reason the encasing of the nine Sefirot with the Returning Light is only called Connecting (see Number 21, Connecting). Nevertheless, in relation to the nine Sefirot of the Head, this Returning Light is also considered "a force of density," since it nevertheless became a connecting force to attach them to the Emanated Being. This force is called a Window, since when the Returning Light and Direct Light enter to shine on the pure Circular Vessels where no trace of density is apparent, the force of density in the Returning Light is much more inferior than them and thus lowers and lessens the sides of the Circular Vessels as it enters them.

This resembles a crack and a hole in the room, which is a defect and flaw in the wall of the room, yet it is an entry way for the light of the sun. Here too, the defect and flaw that happens to the sides of the Circular Vessels by the density in the Returning Light is not considered as a flaw at all in them, but as a Window, for without it they would have no Light, since they receive Light only through the Line by means of its Masach.

31. **Yechidah** (Volume 2, Chapter 2, Inner Light, Section 6)
The Light encased in the Sefirah of Keter is called Yechidah.

32. **Going Outside Of** (Volume 2, Inner Observation, Section 59)
A change of form attained by a spiritual entity is called "Going Outside Of" it, since the change of form that takes place in part of the Partzuf is considered to mean that this part went outside the Partzuf. This resembles a candle lighting another candle yet not being diminished, since there is no disappearance in spirituality. It thus is found that when the part begins to change its form, simultaneously with the change, it begins to leave the Partzuf and go outside of it to become its own entity, in such a way that the change of form and the going outside are one and the same.

33. **Descent** (Volume 2, Chapter 1, Inner Light, Section 27)
Thickening means descent, namely, going down from a grade. Purification means ascent, rising by means of Similarity of Form to the Endless. It is the rule that whatever is purer is higher and whatever is denser is lower.

34. **Straight** (Volume 2, Chapter 1, Inner Light, Section 5)
When the Supernal Light descends to the Vessels that have the density of the Fourth Phase, which means craving, as the Fourth Phase draws it by its craving, it is considered as if the Light descends in a

straight way, that is, in exact accordance with the degree of density and craving. This resembles a heavy object that falls to the ground from above. It falls down in a completely straight line and at a great speed due to the gravitational pull of the Earth on it. This is not so with a light object that falls to the ground, where there is no room for the gravitational pull over it so it slowly curls in the air until it rests on the ground.

The same applies here. Vessels without density, such as Circular Vessels, are considered as if the Light arriving there by the power of the Sefirot of Straightness curls, since they possess no density, namely yearning, with which they can draw to themselves by a drawing force. This is not the case with the Vessels of Straightness where there is density that draws the Light with great force, thus the Light descends fast and with exact straightness, resembling a straight line.

35. **Keter** (Volume 2, Chapter 1, Inner Light, Sections 20-21)
    The induction of the root over the grade is called Keter (Crown), which comes from the word maktir, which means encircling, since it is the purest part of the grade. For that reason it circles the whole Partzuf from above.

36. **Slowly and Gradually** (Volume 2, Chapter 1, Inner Light, Section 6)
    The drawing down of Lights in order of the grades by way of cause and effect is called "Slowly and Gradually."

37. **Connects** (Volume 2, Chapter 1, Inner Light, Section 12)
    Malchut of the higher becomes the Keter for the lower. It is thus found that Malchut "connects" every higher with its lower. This means that a Similarity of Form has been achieved between them and a "connection" was formed among all the grades, from the World of Adam Kadmon to the end of Asiyah. This concept applies to the Vessels of Straightness that are called Line but not to the Circular Vessels. Any connection of the Circles with each other is facilitated by the Line.

38. **Waters of Light** (Volume 2, Chapter 1, Inner Light, Section 4)
    The Light that descends from its grade is called "Water" or the "Waters of Light."

39. **Malchut** (Volume 2, Chapter 1, Inner Light, Sections 20-21)
    The last phase is called Malchut, so named because from it comes the quality of leadership with force and complete control, as in "the fear of the government (Malchut)." (Avot 3:2)

40. **From Above Downward** (Volume 2, Inner Observation, Section 102)
The Light that flows into the Vessels in order, from purer to denser, is considered "From Above Downward." This Light is called Direct Light.

41. **From Below Upward** (Volume 2, Inner Observation, Section 103)
The Light that flows in order, from dense to purer to purest, is considered "From Below Upward." This Light is called Returning Light.

42. **Circling** (Volume 2, Chapter 2, Inner Light, Section 13)
That which causes the revelation of a grade is considered as circling it. Circling (*mesabev*, מסבב) comes from cause and effect (*mesovav*, מסובב). "Cause" means reason, and "effect" means that it follows and comes out of that reason and cause.

43. **Masach** (Volume 3, Chapter 1, Inner Light, Section 14)
The force of Tzimtzum is awakened in the Emanated Being against the Supernal Light to stop it on its way from descending to the Fourth Phase. This means that as soon as it reaches and touches the Fourth Phase, this force is immediately awakened, and it strikes it and pushes it back. This force is called the "Masach." You need to distinguish the difference between the Masach aspect in the Emanated Being and the Tzimtzum aspect in it, for these are two completely separate matters. The force of Tzimtzum over the Fourth Phase is directed against the Vessel in the Emanated, which is the yearning to receive. This means that due to the Desire for a Similarity of Form with the Emanator, it stops itself from receiving when it craves to receive, since its yearning, called the Fourth Phase is a Supernal Force that the Emanated can neither annul nor somewhat reduce. Yet it can stop itself from wanting to receive, even though it yearns to very much.

This obstructing force always rests over the Fourth Phase in the Emanated, except when it draws a new Light. It then must annul the obstructing force, namely the Tzimtzum in it, and the yearning for the Supernal Light becomes revealed in it. With this it is able to draw the Light to itself. Here starts the action of the Masach in the Emanated, since any yearning fully draws the Supernal Light as it was in the Endless, since it is a Supernal Power that the lower has no control over to reduce, as said. Therefore, the Light descends to fill the Fourth Phase.

However, at the very moment the Light touches the Fourth Phase, the Masach immediately awakens, strikes the Light and turns it back, as said. Thus, it is found that it only receives the Light of Three Phases while the Fourth Phase does not receive it. Thus you see that the action of the Masach only applies when the Light enters, after the force of Tzimtzum was momentarily annulled in order to draw new Light, as said. However, this action of Tzimtzum to restrain itself from drawing Light is constant. Thus, Tzimtzum and Masach are two completely separate aspects. Know that the Masach is an outcome of the Tzimtzum.

44. **Surrounding** (Volume 2, Chapter 1, Inner Light, Section 13)
See answer Number 4, Surrounding Light.

45. **Nullified** (Volume 2, Chapter 1, Inner Light, Section 10)
When two spiritual entities are completely Similar in Form without any difference, they again become one, and the smaller is cancelled out by the larger.

46. **Drawn** (Volume 2, Chapter 1, Inner Light, Section 18)
The descent of Light by means of density, which means by the power yearning in the Emanated , is called "drawn" or "drawing down."

47. **Nefesh** (Volume 2, Inner Observation, Section 95)
A Light that does not enter the Partzuf by means of being bestowed by the Light of the Endless, but is received from the higher grade near it, is called the Light of Nefesh or Female Light.

48. **Nefesh, Ruach, Neshamah, Chayah, and Yechidah** (Volume 2, Inner Observation, Section 87)
The Vessels in the Ten Sefirot are called Keter, Chochmah, Binah, Zeir Anpin, and Nukvah. The Lights in the Ten Sefirot are called Nefesh, Ruach, Neshamah, Chayah, and Yechidah. The reason they are named in an upward sequence, Nefesh, Ruach, Neshamah, Chayah, Yechidah, rather than a downward one, is that this is the order of the entrance of the Lights into the Partzuf. Nefesh comes first, then Ruach, and so on. It is the opposite with the Vessels, where Keter appears first, then Chochmah, and so on, down to Malchut at the end.

49. **Neshamah** (Volume 2, Chapter 2, Inner Light, Section 6)
The Light clothed in the Vessel of Binah is called Neshamah. It is named after breathing (neshimah), since Neshamah is the source of Zeir Anpin, the Light of Ruach, which inhales its Life-force from it by way of ascent and descent, in the secret of the verse, "and the creatures ran and returned," (Ezekiel 1:14) and from the wording of the verse, "and breathed into his nostrils the breath of life." (Genesis 2:7) Understand this.

50. **Encircling** (Volume 2, Chapter 2, Inner Light, Section 13)
Whatever causes a grade to be revealed is called "encircling" that grade.

51. **Ending** (Volume 2, Chapter 1, Inner Light, Section 29)
The Fourth Phase is called "conclusion or ending," since it stops the Supernal Light from spreading into it and thus concludes the grade.

52. **Close** (Volume 2, Chapter 1, Section 3 in the Ari)
A closeness of form to another is called close to another.

53. **Density** (Volume 2, Inner Observation, Section 5)
The full-fledged Desire to Receive with great yearning is called much "density," while little yearning is called little "density." It is the part of the Vessel that draws abundance for the entire Partzuf and is therefore called the Interior of the vessel.

54. **Passing Through** (Volume 2, Chapter 1, Inner Light, Section 26)
The Illumination of a lower grade must pass through that which is higher than it. Meaning, since the lower is an effect and comes out of the higher, it is considered as if it were "passing through" the higher. Once it passes through the higher, it is fixed there and is called a passing Light, never to move from there. Only a branch aspect comes out of it and reaches its place, namely the lower grade. This resembles a candle lighting another candle yet not being diminished. This way you will understand the transposition of Lights from one level to another, for the Light is not absent from the first position by reaching the second, as is the way of material objects, but as explained.

55. **Higher and Lower** (Volume 2, Inner Observation, Section 86b)
We have to make two main distinctions in any Partzuf. They are its Vessel for drawing abundance and its Vessel for Receiving the abundance. They diametrically oppose each other, since the extent of abundance depends on the extent of density in the drawing Vessel. The greatest Light in the Partzuf, called Yechidah, requires the densest drawing vessel, which is the Fourth Phase of the Fourth Phase. The Vessel of Receiving is the opposite; the greatest Light called Yechidah is only clothed in the purest Vessel.

For this reason, when we make a distinction among the Vessels of drawing abundance, we do so by the names Internal and External. The more Internal the Vessel, the denser it is and the greater the Stature it draws, as said. The more External it is, the purer it is and the smaller the Stature it draws. When we distinguish among the Vessels for Receiving Lights in the Partzuf, we call them higher and lower. Whatever is higher is purer and clothes the greater Stature, and whatever is lower is denser and clothes the smaller Stature.

56. **Essence** (Volume 3, Chapter 1, Inner Light, Section 2)
The Light of Chochmah is called "essence," since it is the essence and Life-force of the Emanated Being.

57. **Interiority** (Volume 2, Inner Observation, Section 86b)
The density aspect of the Partzuf is called its "Interior," since this is the place of drawing abundance.

58. **Interior and Exterior**
See Answer 55, Higher and Lower.

59. **Channel** (Volume 2, Chapter 1, Inner Light, Section 2)
The Vessels of Straightness are called "Channels," since they draw and limit the Light with their boundaries, like a channel that limits the water passing through it.

60. **Line** (Volume 2, Chapter 1, Inner Light, Section 2)
The Ten Sefirot of the Vessels of Straightness are called Channel from the perspective of their Vessels, and Line from the perspective of the Light in them. Only the Ten Sefirot of the World of Adam Kadmon are called one Line, unlike the Ten Sefirot of the World of Atzilut that have Three Lines.

61. **Erect Posture** (Volume 2, Chapter 2, Inner Light, Section 3)
When the Lights of the Head are clothed in the Vessels of the Head, the Partzuf is considered to have an "erect posture."

62. **Ration** (Volume 2, Chapter 1, Inner Light, Section 16)
The Returning Light creates a "ration" of the Supernal Light to the extent of its own measure, since the Light does not reside on the Emanated Being without the encasing of Returning Light.

63. **Ground** (Volume 2, Chapter 2, Inner Light, Section 1)
Malchut of any grade or World is called the "ground" of that World or grade.

64. **Head** (Volume 2, Inner Observation, Sections 20-22)
Nine Sefirot of Supernal Light that extend to a Binding by Striking over the Masach in Malchut to raise Returning Light are called the Head of the grade, since these Lights precede the Masach and the Returning Light, and the density of the Masach cannot ascend to them (see answer 21).

65. **Ruach** (Volume 2, Chapter 2, Inner Light, Section 12)
The Light clothed in the Vessel of Zeir Anpin is called Ruach, since its way is to rise to Binah to draw abundance and descend to give it to Malchut, similar to a Wind (Ruach) that comes and goes (see Answer 49, Neshamah)

66. **Spirituality**
The word "spirituality" [or metaphysical] brought in books of Kabbalah means that it is divested of all physical occurrences, such as space, time, and shape, and so on. Sometimes it indicates just the aspect of the Supernal Light in the Vessel, even though a Vessel is also spiritual in all conditions.

67. **Far** (Volume 2, Chapter 1, Inner Light, Section 13)
The change of form in the greatest degree.

68. **The Beginning of the Extension** (Volume 2, Chapter 1, Inner Light, Section 7)
The source of any flow of Light is called "the Beginning of the Extension" or Keter.

69. **Immediately** (Volume 2, Chapter 1, Inner Light, Section 6)
A Light descending without gradually evolving through the Four Phases, since it has no more than one of them, is considered as descending "immediately." If it descends through the sequence of Phases, this is called "slowly and gradually."

70. **The Objective of All** (Volume 2, Chapter 1, Inner Light, Section 7)
The last Phase of all the levels, namely the Fourth Phase of the Fourth Phase, is called the "objective of them all," since it is the densest, called end, and since all the levels came to correct only it.

SUBJECT ANSWERS

71. The Endless is the source for the Circular Vessels, since these Vessels were included in the Endless though not apparent there, in the secret of, "He and His Name are One." (Volume 2, Inner Observation, Section 52)

72. After the Tzimtzum, when the Endless Light retreated from all Four Phases, as is known, an Impression was nevertheless left in every single Phase, resembling the Endless Light it had before the Tzimtzum. (Volume 2, Chapter 2, Inner Light, Section 17)

73. It indicates that there is no other distinction there except for the distinction of cause and effect alone. (see Answer 22, One Within the Other; Volume 2, Inner Observation, Section 53)

74. It is because in the Endless there was no recognition of a Vessel at all. (Volume 2, Inner Observation, Section 53)

75. The Endless is the root of all the Lights in the Worlds. (Volume 2, Chapter 1, Inner Light, Section 26)

76. The Circles are the roots of all the Vessels in the Worlds. (Volume 2, Chapter 1, Inner Light, Section 17)

77. The Fourth Phase called Malchut is the source for Returning Light. (Volume 2, Inner Observation, Section 66)

78. At first the Lights emerged in Three Phases, one below the other. These Three Phases are not yet called Vessels until the Fourth Phase is revealed, where only it alone is considered a Vessel. Thus, the Vessels are an outcome of the Lights. (Volume 2, Inner Observation, Section 5)

79. In the order of the emanation of the Worlds from above downward, perfection is always found to precede and cause the revelation of imperfection, for this is how the grades evolve one from the other, where a lower grade is inferior to the higher, until this World emerges, which is the most corrupt. (Volume 2, Chapter 1, Inner Light 20)

80. The Masach is the original source for the ruling power over the Worlds. (Volume 2, Chapter 1, Inner Light, Section 2)

81. The Masach is a product of Tzimtzum Alef. (Volume 2, Chapter 1, Inner Light, Section 2)

82. Two causes preceded the Masach. They are the Tzimtzum and the arrival of the Light, since the Masach is revealed only when the Supernal Light reaches and touches the Fourth Phase. (see Answer 43, Masach)

83. The Circles are the source for the Vessels of Straightness, since the Malchut of the Circles drew the Light of the line, and from it the Masach was formed. (Volume 2, Inner Observation, Section 56)

84. They receive it from the Vessels of Straightness. They themselves cannot draw from the Endless since they possess no Masach or density. (Volume 2, Chapter 1, Inner Light, Section 12)

85. They receive it via the force of the Masach that is impressed upon them without the Masach bringing with it its density. The said Impression of the Masach is called the Windows of the Circles. (Volume 2, Chapter 2, Inner Light, Section 16)

86. The reason is that the Circles have no kind of Masach. (Volume 2, Chapter 1, Inner Light, Section 12)

87. See Answer 85 above.

88. The Light of the Line that the Circles received caused a recognition of grades being one below the other, where Windows were made from the Impression of the Masach, and all the grades of the Line emerged also in the Circles. (Volume 2, Chapter 2, Inner Light, Section 18)

89. The reason is that the Circular Vessels are on the same level as the Head of any Sefirah of the Vessels of Straightness that are above the Masach. They are therefore considered to be located at the Head of the Sefirah and do not extend below the Head of the Sefirot of Straightness at all. The Vessels below the Head are already below the Masach of the Malchut of the Head and density influences them, and they are therefore below the Circles, since lower means denser, and the Circles have no Masach or density. Therefore, the Body of any Sefirah is vacant of the Circles.

   This way the Ten Sefirot of Keter of the Circles all clothe the Ten Sefirot of the Head of Keter of Straightness, while the Ten Sefirot of the Body of Keter are Circle free. Similarly, the Ten Sefirot of Chochmah of the Circles clothe the Ten Sefirot of the Head of Chochmah of Straightness, and so on. Thus, the Body of Straightness interrupts between any two Circular Sefirot, and there is no connection among the Circular Sefirot. They therefore need the Line to connect them. (Volume 2, chapter 1, Inner Light, Section 25)

90. The entire difference between them lies solely in the Masach that is present in the Straightness but not the Circles. (Volume 2, Chapter 1, Inner Light, Section 2)

91. 91. See Answer 43, Masach.

92. They are the aspect of the Light of Ruach. (Volume 2, Chapter 2, Inner Light, Section 30)

93. See Answer 34, Straight.

94. From the aspect of Vessels, the Circles are better than the Straightness, since the Circular Vessels have neither Masach nor density, while the Vessels of Straightness have both. Moreover, the Circular Vessels precede the Straight ones. (Volume 2, Chapter 1, Inner Light, Section 2)

95. From the aspect of Lights, the Straightness is better than the Circles, since the Sefirot of Straightness draw the Supernal Light and give it to the Circles, and the Lights of Straightness are called the Light of Ruach, while the Lights of the Circle are called the Light of Nefesh. (Volume 2, Chapter 2, Inner Light, Section 30)

96. The reason is that External means pure, and whatever is purer is found to be more Similar in Form to the Endless and is considered more praiseworthy. (Volume 2, Inner Observation, Section 7)

97. Inner means denser, meaning that there is more yearning there, and thus the Light it draws is greater and the Returning Light that is pushed back has greater Stature. (Volume 2, Inner Observation, Section 5)

98. The reason is that its Fourth Phase does not have the density fit for drawing the Supernal Light. From that standpoint it is considered the purest of the Worlds. (see Answer 55, Higher and Lower; Volume 2, Inner Observation, Section 13)

99. The Supernal Light that reached and touched the Fourth Phase to spread within it, caused the force of the Masach to immediately appear, stopping the Light and pushing it back. (Volume 2, Inner Observation, Section 18)

100. When the Supernal Light reached and touched the Fourth Phase to spread within it, the force of Tzimtzum, which is the Masach, was roused to stop it and push it back. (Volume 2, Inner Observation, Section 56)

101. The reason is the Returning Light that the Masach raises is nothing but the amount of Light that wanted to spread into the extent of density within the Fourth Phase, which means the extent of its yearning and pulling the Supernal Light. If the density is very great, namely, the Fourth Phase of the Fourth Phase, the Light that wanted to spread in the Fourth Phase is very great. If the density is little, that is, just the First Phase of the Fourth Phase, the amount of Light that wanted to spread in the Fourth Phase is very small. Thus the Stature of the

Returning Light in the Masach and the degree of density in the Fourth Phase are one and the same. (Volume 2, Inner Observation, Section 60)

102. Even though the Light of the Line has only Three Phases, its Vessels of Receiving are nevertheless only due to the Fourth Phase, though the Fourth Phase itself does not receive Light. (Volume 2, Inner Observation, Section 16)

103. There are two directions of Ten Sefirot in each grade. The first direction is from above downward, starting with Keter and ending with Malchut, and these are called the Ten Sefirot of Direct Light. The second direction is from below upward, starting with Malchut and ending with Keter, and these are called the Ten Sefirot of Returning Light. (Volume 2, Inner Observation, Section 104)

104. The reason is that this entire Light belongs particularly to the Fourth Phase and would have been fit to be clothed in it had the Masach not pushed it back. It therefore became a receiving agent instead of the Fourth Phase. (Volume 2, Inner Observation, Section 21)

105. It is estimated by the amount of Light fit to have entered the Fourth Phase had not the Masach pushed it back. (Volume 2, Inner Observation, Section 60)

106. The reason is that the Returning Light is no more than Light fit for the Fourth Phase, Malchut. But since Malchut did not receive this Light within it, this Light became an encasing and receiving agent for all nine Sefirot above it. Thus Malchut is a source for all Ten Sefirot of Returning Light and is thus considered the Keter of Returning Light (Volume 2, Inner Observation, Section 102)

107. See Answer 101, above.

108. See Answer 101, above.

109. The density in the Masach means the amount of its yearning. For that reason, through the attaining and clothing of the Inner Light in the Partzuf, the Surrounding Light increases and purifies the density in the Masach. (Volume 2, Inner Observation, Section 74)

110. Since the Circles have no Masach or density, they have no tool to draw the Supernal Light. Rather, they receive their Lights through the Vessels of Straightness. Therefore their Lights are called the Light of Nefesh, meaning that this Light has no aspect of sharing except for their own need alone. (Volume 2, Inner Observation, Section 95)

111. Since the Vessels of Straightness have a Masach and density, they are fit to draw the Supernal Light and bestow upon others. A Light that has

the aspect of sharing is called the Light of Ruach or Masculine Light. (Volume 2, Chapter 2, Inner Light, Section 30)

112. The Upper Three are clear of the Masach's density, since the Masach and Malchut are the last aspect within them and no density ever rises to them, since density cannot rise beyond its place even a little. Know that the Upper Three Sefirot—Keter, Chochmah, and Binah—mean the Head of the level (see Answer 13, Upper Three Sefirot) that has Ten Complete Sefirot. (Volume 2, Chapter 1, Inner Light, Section 18)

113. Each Sefirah is considered as having a Head, called the Upper Three, and a Body, called the Lower Seven (see Answer 64, Head). The Sefirah of Keter has an Upper Three and Lower Seven, and also Chochmah has an Upper Three and Lower Seven, as does Binah, and so on. All Ten Sefirot of the Circles—Upper Three and Lower Seven—are situated only in the place of the Head and Upper Three of Straightness. The Ten Circular Sefirot of the Sefirah of Keter encircle only the Upper Three Sefirot of Keter of Straightness, while the Lower Seven Sefirot of Keter of Straightness are free of Circles (see Answer 89 above). All Ten Circular Sefirot of Chochmah also encircle only the Upper Three Sefirot of Chochmah of Straightness while the Lower Seven of Chochmah of Straightness are free of Circles. This applies to them all. (Volume 2, Chapter 1, Inner Light, Section 18)

114. The reason is that both have nothing of the density of the Masach. (see Answer 89 above; Volume 2, Chapter 1, Inner Light, Section 18)

115. The measure of the Lower Seven Sefirot of a Sefirah of Straightness, which interrupt between each circle. The Lower Seven of Keter of Straightness interrupt between the Ten Sefirot of the Circle of Keter and the Circle of Chochmah, and the Lower Seven of Chochmah of Straightness interrupt between the Ten Sefirot of the Circle of Chochmah and the Circle of Binah, and so on. (see Answer 89 above; Volume 2, Chapter 1, Inner Light, Section 18)

116. See Answer 89 above.

117. The reason is that Lights precede Vessels (see Answer 13,), and the Returning Light that rises from below upward and encases them is not considered as real vessels, but only roots for vessels. And we have no comprehension about Light without a Vessel (see answer 21).

118. Even in the Upper Three of a grade there is within them a distinction of Upper Three and Lower Seven, and we are permitted to deal with the lower seven of the Upper Three (Volume 2, Chapter 2, Inner Light 5).

119. It is because they are considered the aspect of Upper Three, since all Ten Circular Sefirot are situated in the Upper Three of Straightness. (see Answer 13, Upper Three Sefirot)

120. The root of the Four Phases is called Keter. The First Phase is called Chochmah; the Second, Binah; the Third is called Tiferet or Zeir Anpin that includes within it six Sefirot: Chesed, Gevurah, Tiferet, Netzach, Hod, and Yesod, and the Fourth Phase is called Malchut.

121. It teaches us that even though the Fourth Phase, Malchut, receives nothing from the Supernal Light after the Tzimtzum, it is considered as having the same value as the other Sefirot by virtue of its Returning Light. Thus they are "ten, not nine." And "ten, not eleven" further teaches us that we should not think that there is also a type of receiving agent for the Supernal Light in the Fourth Phase, thus making Malchut considered as two Sefirot: Malchut of Direct Light and Malchut of Returning Light, making the number of the Sefirot eleven. He therefore warns us, "ten, not eleven," since Malchut does not receive even an iota of Direct Light.

122. The reason is that it is opposite from the root. The root's form is only of Sharing and that of the Fourth Phase is only Receiving. Two opposites cannot emerge from each other by means of cause and effect, except by a very slow evolution of grade. The root is only the cause for the first phase that is closest to it, the first phase is to the second, and the second to the third. After the third phase, the fourth phase can be revealed. (Volume 2, Inner Observation, Section 5)

123. The reason is that the density is the drawing Vessel, and the aspect of the main Vessel of Receiving is via the Returning Light rising from it. Thus, the Vessel's density is considered its Interior, while the part in it that is less dense is considered more External, and the part in it that is completely pure the most Exterior. (see Answer 55, Higher and Lower; Volume 2, Inner Observation, Section 5)

124. It resembles the thickness of a Vessel's wall that is conditioned by and made of four layers enclosing each other, where abundance touches only its Interior, that is, the Vessel's inner layer. (Volume 2, Inner Observation, Section 5)

125. It is measured by the Returning Light the Masach raises in that particular grade or World. (Volume 2, Inner Observation, Section 65)

126. The reason is that the Vessel of Receiving of all Four Phases is only the Fourth Phase alone, while the other Three Phases have no aspect of drawing and receiving. Therefore, since the Fourth Phase contracted itself so as not to receive, the First Three Phases remained without

Vessels of Receiving and their Lights were also gone. (Volume 2, Inner Observation, Section 16).

127. The first is the Vessel's essence material, that is, the degree of its density. The second is the force of Tzimtzum resting over the Fourth Phase of its density. The third is its Masach (see Answer 43, Masach). In the first distinction alone we should differentiate between two parts: the first is its primal material, which is considered the Malchut of the previous grade that is considered to be its cause and Emanator. This is considered mainly before the Light reached the Emanated grade. The second is the essence of the Emanated grade's material. This is after all the Light meant for the Emanated grade reached it. (Volume 2, Inner Observation, Sections 24 and 27)

128. The first is what is considered the Malchut of the higher, the second is what is considered the material of the Emanated grade itself. (see Answer 127)

129. As long as the Emanated grade has not received the Light meant for it, it is considered as the Malchut of the grade above it. (see Answer 127)

130. When the Emanated grade has attained its Light, it is considered that it is no longer in the category of the Malchut of the higher, called Emanator, but is now in its own domain. (see Answer 127)

131. Necessary receiving is called "unable." This specifically fits the Light of Chochmah, or the Illumination of Chochmah, which is considered the essence and Life-force of the Partzuf, where the Partzuf is "unable to separate from it." This resembles a man who has to preserve his life and existence. (Volume 2, Inner Observation, Section 46)

132. Yearning is called "intends," since when someone yearns very much to receive something we say, "he sets his heart on obtaining it," for yearning is felt in the heart and so is intention. This applies only when someone lacks Light, but when he does have it, this is named, "does not intend." (Volume 2, Inner Observation, Section 43)

133. Because only the Light of Chochmah is designated for the First Phase, which is the Life-force and essence of the Partzuf, and therefore Chochmah is considered "unable" since it has no choice but to receive its Life-force and essence, and mandatory receiving is not receiving. It is also considered as having no apparent yearning for the Light of Chochmah, since yearning only appears when it does not have the Light and yearns to attain it, not when it is full of that Light. (Volume 2, Inner Observation, Section 43)

134. The reason is that the Second Phase is the augmentation of the Desire to Share that thus draws the Light of Chasadim. It does not have to

enact this augmentation and is "able" to refrain from it altogether. It is therefore called "able." Indeed it is also considered "does not intend" since this yearning is only after the Light of Chochmah, not the Light of Chasadim, for the Desire for the Light of Chasadim is not considered as density, since the Tzimtzum only took place on the Light of Chochmah, not the Light of Chasadim. Therefore, the yearning for the Light of Chasadim is not considered intention. (Volume 2, Inner Observation, Section 43)

135. The Third Phase is the drawing of the Illumination of Chochmah into the Light of Chasadim that Binah drew. This drawing is called "unable," since the Illumination of Chochmah is a mandatory receiving for the Partzuf. It is called "intends," since this drawing took place when it was lacking the Illumination of Chochmah, and thus there was yearning there.

136. Since the Illumination of Chochmah was already present in the Third Phase, it did not have to make a new awakening after the actual Light of Chochmah. The Illumination of Chochmah itself was sufficient for its Life-force. Thus this drawing is considered as "able," since it could have done without it. It is considered "intends," since it lacked the actual Light of Chochmah it drew and had great yearning while drawing it.

137. A Vessel is incomplete until it has the craving to receive. This is revealed under two conditions: "able and intending." (see Answer 136 above)

138. It is a law that the Supernal Light never ceases to shine upon the Emanated Beings even for a moment. Rather, wherever a drawing Vessel properly appears there, the Supernal Light immediately shines. Therefore, after the drawing aspect of the Fourth Phase of the Fourth Phase was filled, and a new form of a drawing Vessel was produced with the density of the Third Phase of the Fourth Phase, it too, was immediately filled with the Supernal Light. Afterwards, when it further emanated and brought forth a new form with the density of the Second Phase of the Fourth, this too, was immediately filled with the Supernal Light, and it is so always.

139. The reason is that the Supernal Light is always in a state of total rest, without any newness of form, since newness in spirituality is considered movement. All newness of forms that apply to the Extension of the Supernal Light are only due to the drawing force that emerges in the Emanated (see Volume 1, Answer 64). And even this extension of the Supernal Light is like lighting a candle with another candle while the first one does not diminish at all. This is done in such

a way that only that part of the extension of the Supernal Light that reached the point of being received by the Emanated is the one to receive a newness of form, relative to the shared ratio between the Vessel and the Light clothed in it. Yet the Supernal Light itself lacks nothing and nothing is renewed in it due to the extension reaching the Emanated.

140. The difference is from one end to the other, since for the sharing of the Supernal Light, the Partzuf must have great density, to the utmost extent in existence, for then it draws the greatest and most complete Light. Its opposite, from one end to the other, is the aspect of the Supernal Light being clothed in the Vessels, since the greatest and most complete Light is clothed only in the purest Vessel that can possibly exist.

    Therefore, we must always distinguish between these two mentioned matters in every Partzuf. The Sharing aspect that is measured by the great density is distinguished by the names: "Inner and Outer." The aspect of Receiving and being clothed in the Vessels is distinguished by the names: "Upper and Lower." This way, the greatest Partzuf in the entire existence has to be the most Inner, that is, the densest of all Partzufim throughout existence. At the same time, it has to be the highest of all the Partzufim throughout existence, which means it is the purest of them all, since there are two separate Vessels: one for drawing the Light and the other for receiving it. (see Answer 55 above and Answer 141 below)

141. The Supernal Light is only attached to the Partzuf to the extent of the Returning Light rising from the Masach in the Partzuf. Its size depends on the degree of density in the Fourth Phase (see Answers 101 and 2 above). The giver, therefore, needs the greatest aspect of density in the lower, unlike the receiver that needs the purest Vessel for the Light to be clothed in, namely so that there will be Similarity of Form between Light and Vessel, as the Difference of Form between them distances the Light from the Vessels. (see answers 16 and 140 above)

142. See Answer 139 above.

143. The Supernal Light, of necessity, has the Desire to Share. This Desire is considered the last aspect included in the Supernal Light. This part—the said Desire to Share aspect—transforms to become the Light-drawing aspect of the First Phase. This Light-drawing aspect is certainly a newness of form within that Desire to Share, and it is therefore considered to have been parted to itself, emerging from the category of the Desire to Share and becoming the First Phase of the Desire to Receive. In other words, it went out of the category of

Emanator to the category of Emanated, for the Difference of Form separates and distances spiritual entities from each other, as we know. However, the separation of the "part" mentioned here does not diminish the "all" in any way. Rather, this is like lighting a candle from another candle while the original does not diminish at all. Understand this well.

144. When we distinguish only the material part in the Vessels, we categorize them as the Four Phases. When we also want to include the Impressions in each and every Vessel, we categorize them by the names Keter, Chochmah, Binah, Zeir Anpin, and Nukvah.

145. First the smaller ones enter, then the larger ones—starting with Nefesh, then Ruach, and so on, up to Yechidah. (see Answer 48 above)

146. First the more important Vessels develop, then the small ones, starting with Keter, then Chochmah, and so on, to the Vessel of Malchut that comes last.

147. The Malchut of the higher that becomes the Keter for the lower. In other words, the Desire to Share of the higher is considered as having become the primal material of the lower. (see Answer 143 above)

148. The root of the Four Phases is called the Keter of the Ten Sefirot of Direct Light in the grade. The Malchut of the grade is considered the Keter of the Ten Sefirot of Returning Light in the grade.

149. If it were subject to exchange or replacement, it would not have been eternal. And this is simple.

150. It is through the Ten Sefirot of Direct Light, since every Light flows only from the Endless, and thus the lower has to pass through all the higher ones above it, in the order of cause and effect, until it reaches the lowest effect for which it was designated. And since the Light does not disappear from one place when It moves to a second place, all the Lights that pass through the higher are thus fixed there.

151. It is through the Ten Sefirot of Returning Light, to which Malchut is considered a root and Keter (see Answer 148 above). All the parts of Returning Light that encase everything above it pass through it from below upward. Thus each lower is considered as including all the parts of Returning Light belonging to the Sefirot above it.

152. The inclusion of the Sefirot in each other until each one includes Ten, and those Ten have Ten, and so on, ad infinitum, is through the two directions of the Ten Sefirot of Direct Light and the Ten Sefirot of Returning Light present in every grade (see Answer 20 above). You need to obtain the key to easily find the changes made in the sequences of

the Ten sub-Sefirot that appear in the Sefirah by means of inclusion and not of its own essence. Therefore, remember and know three things that you can always use. For example, if you want to know the Ten Sefirot included in Binah, the first thing to know is that there are two Sefirot in its essence, which are the Binah of Direct Light and Hod of Returning Light. The second is to count the Sefirot below it down to Yesod, as these are its Direct Light, namely: Chesed, Gevurah, Tiferet, Netzach, Hod, and Yesod that pass downward through it. The third is to count the Sefirot above it up to Keter, which are two: Yesod and Malchut, and then you will know its Sefirot of Returning Light that pass through it upward. Now calculate its own two Sefirot, plus six of Direct Light and two of Returning Light, thus they are ten. Calculate this way with every Sefirah and you will know, with a brief glance, all the aspects included in it.

153. Nine of Direct Light from Keter to Yesod, and one of Returning Light, namely just Malchut.

154. Eight of Direct Light from Chochmah to Yesod, which enter the purer Vessels, that is, the Light of Chochmah in the Vessel of Keter, and so on, and two of Returning Light, Yesod and Malchut, which enter the Vessels of Yesod and Malchut.

155. Seven of Direct Light from Binah down. Here too, the Light of Binah is in the Vessel of Keter, and so on, down to the Light of Yesod in the Vessel of Netzach. And three of Returning Light: Hod, Yesod, and Malchut in the Vessels of Hod, Yesod, and Malchut.

156. Six of Direct Light from Chesed to Yesod, and four of Returning Light from Netzach to Malchut. The Returning Light of Netzach is in the Vessel of Netzach, and so on.

157. Five of Direct Light from Gevurah to Yesod and five of Returning Light from Tiferet to Malchut. They are clothed in the aforementioned way, where the Direct Light are in the purer Vessels and each of the Returning Lights are in their appropriate Vessel.

158. Four of Direct Light from Tiferet to Yesod and six of Returning Light from Gevurah to Malchut.

159. Three of Direct Light from Netzach to Yesod and seven of Returning Light from Chesed to Malchut.

160. Two of Direct Light from Hod to Yesod and eight of Returning Light from Binah to Malchut.

161. One of Direct Light, Yesod, and nine of Returning Light from Chochmah to Malchut.

162. Just the Ten Sefirot of Returning Light without any Direct Light.

163. Nine of Direct Light from Keter to Yesod and one of Returning Light, namely Malchut.

164. Eight of Direct Light from Chochmah to Yesod and two of Returning Light: Yesod and Malchut.

165. Seven of Direct Light from Binah to Yesod and three of Returning Light from Hod to Malchut.

166. Six of Direct Light from Chesed to Yesod and four of Returning Light from Netzach to Malchut.

167. First we need to understand the Ten individual Sefirot included in general Netzach, which are: three of Direct Light, where the Light of Netzach is clothed in the Vessel of Keter of general Netzach, the Light of Hod in the Vessel of Chochmah of general Netzach, and the Light of Yesod in the Vessel of Binah. Now take the individual Chochmah of general Netzach. It too, of necessity, includes Ten Sefirot by means of the eight Sefirot of Direct Light that pass through it from above downward, and even those that only have Returning Light, because once the Sefirot are included the Sefirot of Direct Light always shine into the Sefirot that have Returning Light.

However, the eight Sefirot of Direct Light that passed from Chochmah down, are not the aspect of the Light of Chochmah but rather the Light of Hod, since it is the Light of Hod that is clothed in the Vessel of Chochmah of Netzach, as mentioned. It is in such a way that now there are, in the Ten Sefirot of Chochmah of Netzach, only the passing Lights of Direct Light from Chochmah of Hod down, as Chochmah of Hod is in the Vessel of that Keter, Binah of Hod in Chochmah, Chesed of Hod in Binah, Gevurah of Hod in Chesed and Tiferet of Hod in Gevurah. And we know that in Gevurah of Chochmah of Netzach there is Direct Light from the aspect of the Light of Tiferet of Hod.

Let us now take this Gevurah of Chochmah of Netzach, which of necessity is also composed of Ten sub-Sefirot of the Direct Light that passes through it from above downward and the Returning Light that passes through it from below upward. It contains five Sefirot of Direct Light from Gevurah down, though this is not the Light of Gevurah at all but rather it is the five lower aspects of the Light of Tiferet of Hod that are clothed in the purer Vessels. Thus, the Light of Gevurah of Tiferet of Hod is clothed in the Vessel of Keter of Gevurah of Chochmah of Netzach, the Light of Tiferet of Tiferet of Hod is clothed in the Vessel of Chochmah of Gevurah of Chochmah of Netzach, the Light of Netzach of Tiferet of Hod in the Vessel of Binah of Gevurah of Chochmah of Netzach, the Light of Hod of Tiferet of Hod is clothed in the Vessel of Chesed of Gevurah of Chochmah of Netzach, and the Light of Yesod of Tiferet of Hod is clothed in the Vessel of Gevurah of Gevurah of Chochmah of Netzach. As well as five Sefirot of Returning Light that are clothed in accordance with the Vessels, as they always do.

168. When you first take Binah of Hod, it has only Returning Light without any Direct Light, yet the Direct Light of the nearby grade shines in it, which is the Light of Yesod. This Binah also includes the Lights passing through it, which are the seven of Direct Light from Binah down. And since the Light within it is only the Light of Yesod of Direct Light, as said, its Direct Light starts from Binah of Yesod and down. So the Light of Binah of Yesod is clothed in the Vessel of Keter, and so on, and the Light of Hod of Yesod [is clothed] in the Vessel of Tiferet of Binah of general Hod. Afterwards, when you take sub-Tiferet of the said Binah of Hod, which itself comprises Ten Sefirot, it has four of Direct Light from Tiferet down, which are clothed in the Higher Vessels. Namely, the aspect of Tiferet of Yesod of Yesod in the Vessel of Keter, the aspect of Netzach of Yesod of Yesod in the Vessel of Chochmah, the aspect of Hod of Yesod of Yesod in the Vessel of Binah, and the aspect of Yesod of Yesod of Yesod in the Vessel of Chesed. As well as six aspects of Returning Light that pass through it from below upward, which are from Gevurah to Malchut, which are clothed in accordance with the Vessels, as they always are.

169. First let us take Yesod of Keter. Among its Ten Sefirot there is only the Light of Yesod in the Vessel of Keter, and the rest are Returning Light. When you take Netzach of Yesod of Keter, there is only Returning Light there, though the Light of Yesod of Direct Light that is in Keter shines there. So Netzach of Yesod of Keter is considered Direct Light of Yesod, and when it gets composed of Ten Sefirot, it has three Lights—Netzach, Hod, and Yesod—of Direct Light from it down to Yesod, which pass downward from the aspect of Yesod of Direct Light. They are clothed as follows: Netzach of Yesod in the Vessel of Keter; Hod of Yesod in the Vessel of Chochmah; Yesod of Yesod in the Vessel of Binah; and the seven Sefirot of Returning Light—Chesed, Gevurah, Tiferet, Netzach, Hod, Yesod, and Malchut—in the corresponding Vessels, as said.

170. There is only Returning Light there, since all that flows from Malchut has only Returning Light.

171. This is the rule: The more valuable Lights are clothed in the purer Vessels, while the lesser ones are clothed in the lesser Vessels. This way, in the Sefirah of Keter, Malchut of Returning Light is clothed in

Malchut of Keter. In the Sefirah of Chochmah, the eight Sefirot of Direct Light: Chochmah, Binah, Chesed, Gevurah, Tiferet, Netzach, Hod, and Yesod are clothed in the Vessels of Keter, Chochmah, Binah, Chesed, Gevurah, Tiferet, Netzach, and Hod, while Yesod and Malchut of Returning Light are clothed in Yesod and Malchut there. In the Sefirah of Binah, the seven Sefirot of Direct Light: Binah, Chesed, Gevurah, Tiferet, Netzach, Hod and Yesod are clothed in the Vessels of Keter, Chochmah, Binah, Chesed, Gevurah, Tiferet, and Netzach; while Hod, Yesod, and Malchut of Returning Light are clothed in Hod, Yesod, and Malchut there; and so on.

172. There are Ten Causes here, and they are as follows:
First Cause: The Cause of all Causes is the Endless. It is the cause for the Four Phases in such a way that enables them to be apparent after the contraction of Light. But in the Endless Itself no Vessel is apparent, for it is all Light. You can only learn about the higher from the lower, namely, the World of Tzimtzum.
Second Cause: The first Three Phases that are caused by each other are considered a cause for producing the possibility for the yearning for further Similarity of Form in the Fourth Phase, which is called Malchut of the Endless.
Third Cause: Malchut of the Endless is the cause of the Keter of the World of Tzimtzum, since the aspect of yearning for further Similarity of Form acquired by Malchut of the Endless is considered a change of form in Malchut of the Endless. It thus separated itself from Malchut of the Endless and emerged as a name unto itself outside of that Malchut. This is called the Keter of the World of Tzimtzum. (read Answer 32, Going Outside Of, carefully)
Fourth Cause: This Keter is the cause for the first Tzimtzum since it spread anew till its Fourth Phase (see Answer 38, Waters of Light). Then it contracted that Desire to Receive and the Light was gone.
Fifth Cause: The departure of Light that took place after the Tzimtzum is the cause of the revelation of the Vessels of the Ten Circular Sefirot. (see Answer 72 above)
Sixth Cause: The Vessel of Malchut of the Circles, namely their Fourth Phase, is the cause of the drawing of the Supernal Light from the Endless anew. (see Answers 83 and 138 above)
Seventh Cause: The Supernal Light that was drawn anew is the cause for the emergence of the force of the Masach in the Vessel of Malchut. (see Answer 43; Masach)
Eighth Cause: The Masach is the cause of the Ten Sefirot of Returning Light that rise from it up to the Keter of Direct Light. They are called the Head of Adam Kadmon. (see Answer 101 above)
Ninth Cause: The Returning Light rising from the Masach is the cause

for the revelation of the Vessels of Straightness, that is, it gives the force of expansion to the Fourth Phase to expand within itself to Ten Sefirot, until Malchut of Malchut.

Tenth Cause: The said Fourth Phase that was given the force of expansion by the Returning Light is the cause of the Ten Sefirot of the Vessels of Adam Kadmon called the Body of Adam Kadmon until its Malchut. (see Answer 11, Body)

RAV ISAAC LURIA

Born in Jerusalem in 1543, Rav Isaac Luria is known as the most influential kabbalist in history. Before the Ari's birth, his father was visited by Elijah the Prophet who announced, "Through him shall be revealed the teaching of the Kabbalah to the world." A brilliant scholar even as a child, by the age of eight he was recognized as a prodigy who outshone the greatest minds, and became known as the Ari, the "Holy Lion."

Shortly after the Ari's eighth birthday, his father passed away, he and his mother moved to Cairo, Egypt, to live with a wealthy uncle for 13 years. In Cairo, the Ari was placed under the tutelage of Rav Bezalel Ashkenazi. The Ari was married at 15, and at 17, he discovered the Zohar, obtaining his own copy. It was not unusual for the Ari to meditate upon one verse of the Zohar for many months, until the hidden meaning was revealed to him. The years the Ari spent in Egypt were dedicated to the process of purifying his consciousness, overcoming the aspect of physicality in his life.

The levels of spiritual enlightenment and understanding he attained led him to Safed, Israel, in 1570. It was in Safed that he completed his life process by sharing the secrets of Kabbalah with his most cherished student Rav Chaim Vital, who arrived in Safed in February, 1571. The Ari told Rav Chaim that the only reason he had come to this world was to teach him, and in turn us, the secrets of Kabbalah. The moment his task was completed, the Ari left this physical world at the young age of 38 on July 15, 1572 (5 Av 5332).

Unlike other kabbalists who have written commentaries throughout the ages, the Ari did not write down any of his teachings. It is reported that he once said, "I can hardly open my mouth to speak without feeling as though the sea had burst its dams and overflowed. How then shall I express what my soul has received, and how can I put it down in a book?" The task of scribing all of the Ari's teachings remained for Rav Chaim Vital and his son Rav Shmuel Vital.

The Ari's greatest legacy are his kabbalistic compositions. He left behind a spiritual system, Lurianic Kabbalah, a road map and guide for body and soul that will relieve people of all chaos, fear, pain, and suffering—that when fully understood, will enable humanity to take control over its individual and collective destiny. Lurianic Kabbalah has made a dramatic impact on the world, and the wisdom disseminated by the Kabbalah Centre is firmly rooted in Lurianic Kabbalah.

The main works of the Kitvei Ha'Ari ("Writings of the Ari") are the *Etz Chaim* ("Tree of Life"), *Pri Etz Chaim* ("Fruit of the Tree of Life"), and the *Shemoneh She'arim* ("Eight Gates") including *Sha'ar HaGilgulim* ("Gate of Reincarnations").

RAV YEHUDA ASHLAG

Rav Yehuda Ashlag was born in Warsaw, Poland, in 1884. From early childhood, he showed astonishing ability, originality, and commitment in the study of the Talmud, the Zohar, and other sacred works.

While in his 30s, Rav Ashlag made the acquaintance of a Warsaw merchant whose identity has never been revealed. Unbeknownst to anyone, this merchant was a great kabbalist who became Rav Ashlag's teacher—until, as Rav Ashlag expressed: "My arrogance caused a separation between us," and his teacher disappeared. Some months later, Rav Ashlag reunited with his teacher and, after much pleading, convinced him to reveal an important kabbalistic secret. The next day, the teacher died. His name, as well as the details of the secret he disclosed to Rav Ashlag, have since remained hidden.

Following the death of his teacher, Rav Ashlag lived most of his life in what is now Israel. There he began the fundamental transformation of Kabbalah from secret wisdom to a readily available body of teachings, the purpose of which is to revolutionize the world. Drawing on the Zohar, Rav Ashlag even designated the exact year—1995—that would mark the turning point in building a mass movement toward Kabbalah and spiritual transformation.

Rav Ashlag wrote and published two great works: *Talmud Eser Sefirot* ("Study of the Ten Luminous Emanations) and his *Sulam* Commentary on the Zohar. This phenomenal work, earned him the name Ba'al HaSulam (Master of the Ladder), and took ten years to complete, from 1943 to 1953. The *Sulam* comprises a translation of the Zohar from Aramaic to Hebrew, as well as a detailed commentary and interpretation.

In addition to his writings, Rav Ashlag founded the Kabbalah Centre in 1922 in Israel. There he was the teacher and spiritual master of Rav Yehuda Brandwein, to whom leadership of the Kabbalah Centre was handed when Rav Ashlag left this world in 1956. Rav Brandwein, in turn, designated Rav Berg to lead the Kabbalah Centre when he left this world in 1969

Rav Ashlag was the first kabbalist to bring the Zohar and the wisdom of Kabbalah to all the people of the world. The Kabbalah Centre continues Rav Ashlag's work of guiding humanity every day on the path toward personal and global transformation.

RAV MICHAEL BERG

Rav Michael Berg is co-director of the Kabbalah Centre International and a distinguished kabbalistic scholar and teacher. He was born into a kabbalistic tradition as the son of the Rav and Karen Berg, the founders of The Kabbalah Centre. Raised within a lineage that dates back more than 100 years, Rav Michael Berg steeped himself in the wisdom of the Zohar from a young age. He became adept at combing through ancient materials and distilling complex information into elegant thought and language. He was the first person to translate the entire 23-volume Zohar and commentary from ancient Aramaic into English, beginning this monumental task when he was only 18 years old and completing it ten years later. He also completed the translation of the Tikunei HaZohar ("Corrections of the Zohar") Volume III from Aramaic into Modern Hebrew. Under his supervision, the Kabbalah Centre has increased the distribution of Zohars to millions of people in need across the globe.

His compendium of works includes the translation and editing of some of Rav Ashlag's fundamental texts: The Wisdom of Truth, And You Shall Choose Life, On World Peace, and The Thought of Creation. Rav Ashlag is the founder of Yeshivat Kol Yehuda, the forerunner of The Kabbalah Centre, and the author of the Sulam ("The Ladder") and Talmud Eser Sefirot ("Ten Luminous Emanations,") both central texts in the study of Kabbalah.

Rav Michael Berg penned the first book under the Kabbalah Centre Publishing imprint: The Secret, in addition to, Becoming Like God, Secrets of the Zohar, and Secrets of the Bible. His book The Way (Wiley) became a national bestseller.

Born in Israel, he studied at The Rabbinical Seminary of America in New York City, and at Yeshiva Shaar HaTorah, following which he earned his rabbinical ordination.

Along with his wife, Monica, he co-hosts the Spiritually Hungry podcast, exploring life's big questions offering spiritual guidance in contemporary terms. He also directs Kabbalah.com, the Kabbalah Centre's online learning platform, which provides kabbalistic wisdom through written and video content in multiple languages.

His teachings bring new insights to this ancient wisdom, reaching thousands weekly on Kabbalah.com. He resides in New York with his wife Monica and their four children, David, Joshua, Miriam, and Abigail.

www.ingramcontent.com/pod-product-compliance
Lightning Source LLC
Chambersburg PA
CBHW040845100426

42812CB00014B/2608